THE DRAMATIC WORKS

OF

MOLIÈRE

RENDERED INTO ENGLISH

BY HENRI VAN LAUN

A NEW EDITION

WITH A PREFATORY MEMOIR, INTRODUCTORY NOTICES, AND NOTES

ILLUSTRATED WITH

NINETEEN ENGRAVINGS ON STEEL

FROM PAINTINGS AND DESIGNS BY HORACE VERNET, DESENNE, JOHANNOT, AND HERSENT

COMPLETE IN THREE VOLUMES

VOLUME I.

NEW YORK
A. W. LOVERING, PUBLISHER.

TO

H. A. TAINE,

THE WELL-KNOWN FRENCH AUTHOR AND LITERARY CRITIC,

THIS TRANSLATION

OF

THE DRAMATIC WORKS OF MOLIÈRE

IS AFFECTIONATELY INSCRIBED.

GENERAL INDEX

TO THE

THREE VOLUMES.

GENERAL INDEX.

TABLE OF CONTENTS.

VOLUME FIRST.

LIST OF ILLUSTRATIONS.

VOLUME FIRST.

PREFACE.

I THINK it will be generally admitted that Molière is the greatest comic poet France has produced, and that he is equal, if not superior, to any writer of character-comedies on the ancient or modern stage. His plays may be divided into six classes or groups: *First*, the small dramatic poems or pastorals, such as *Psyché*, *les Amants magnifiques*, *la Princesse d'Élide*, *les Facheux*, *Mélicerte*, *la Pastorale comique*, and *Amphitryon*, which he wrote for court festivals, by order of Louis XIV.; *Second*, his farces, written to suit the taste of the less refined, such as *les Fourberies de Scapin*, *le Bourgeois-gentilhomme*, *la Comtesse d'Escarbagnas*, *Monsieur de Pourceaugnac*, *le Médecin malgré lui*, *George Dandin*, *le Sicilien*, *l'Amour Médecin*, *le Mariage forcé*, *Sganarelle*, and *les Précieuses Ridicules*,—and yet, notwithstanding their absurdity, attracting the higher classes by their witty descriptions of grotesque characters; *Third*, his comedies —*l'Étourdi*, *l'École des Maris*, *l'Ecole dés femmes*, *l' Avare*, *Don Garcie de Navarre*, *le Dépit amoureux*, and *le Malade imaginaire*,—in each of which the principal object seems to have been to bring into prominence one particular vice or folly, with all its necessary consequences; *Fourth*, those splendidly conceived plays, *Don Juan*, *les Femmes savantes*, *Tartuffe*, and *le Misanthrope*, which pourtray humanity in all its aspects; *Fifth*, those critical short pieces, *la Critique de l'École des femmes* and *l'Impromptu de Versailles*, in which, with masterly acumen, he defends his own plays and attacks his adversaries; and *Sixth*, those early attempts of his comic muse *le Médecin volant* and *la Jalousie du Barbouillé*, which gave ample promise of what he afterwards became.

It is always difficult to state when a playwright has taken from any other author, for the saying, "*Je prends mon bien partout ou je le trouve*," has covered, and still covers, a multitude of literary sins. Moreover, Molière possessed a power of absorption and assimilation which enabled him so to vivify the materials he borrowed that they became new creations of incomparable value. In this sense, to take an idea or a mere thought from another author can hardly be called an imitation; and though Molière, in his first two or three plays, translated several scenes from Italian authors, he has scarcely ever done so in his latter pieces. To mention which of his comedies I consider, or rather which are generally thought, the best, would be difficult, where everything is so eminent; for in all his plays characters will be found which demonstrate his thorough knowledge of human nature, and display his genius. To discover these little peculiarities in which the specific difference of character consists; to distinguish between what men do from custom or fashion, and what they perform through their own natural idiosyncracy; to select, unite, and draw these peculiarities to a dramatic point, demands real genius, and that of the highest order.

Generally Molière's satire is directed against hypocrites, against quacks, against the affectation of learning amongst ladies, and against snobbishness. If I were to enumerate, however, all the characters our author has created, I should arrive at the sum total of all human passions, all human feelings, all human vices, and at every type of the different classes of society. In *l'Avare* sordid avarice is represented by *Harpagon*, and want of order and lavish prodigality by his son *Cléante;* in *le Festin de Pierre* the type of shameless vice is *Don Juan*, *Donna Elvira* displays resignation amidst love disgracefully betrayed, *Mathurine* primitive and uncultivated coquetry, and *Mons. Dimanche* the greed of a tradesman who wishes to make money. *Tartuffe*, in the comedy of that name, represents hypocrisy and downright wickedness. *M. Jourdain*, a tradesman who has made money and who imitates a nobleman, is, in *le Bourgeois-gentilhomme*, no bad specimen of self-sufficient vanity, folly, and ignorance; whilst *Dorante*, in the same play, is a well-copied example of the fashionable swindler of that period. In *le Misanthrope*, *Alceste* pourtrays great susceptibility of tenderness and honour, *Célimène*, wit without any feeling, and *Philinte*, quiet common sense, amiability, intelligence, instruction, knowledge of the world, and a spirit of refined criticism. This is also displayed by *Chrysalde* in *l'École des Femmes*, by *Béralde*, in *le Malade imaginaire*, and by *Ariste* in *l'École des Maris;* whilst *Sganerelle* in the latter play is an example of foolish and coarse jealousy. *George Dandin*, in the comedy of that name, is a model of weakness of character and irresolution. *Angélique*, an impudent and heartless woman, and her father, *Monsieur de Sotenville*, the coarse, proud, country squire of that age. *Argan*, in *le Malade imaginare*, represents egotism and pusillanimity; *Vadius and Trissotin*, in *les Femmes savantes*, pedantic foolishness and self-conceit; *Agnès*, in *l'École des Femmes*, cunning as well as ingenuity; and *Aglaure*, in *Psyché*, feminine jealousy. Finally, *Nicole*, *Dorine*, *Martine*, *Marotte*, *Toinette*, and *Lisette* personify the homely servant-girls, who, possessing plain, downright common sense, point out the affectation and ridiculous pretensions of their companions and superiors; whilst *Claudine*, in *George Dandin*, *Nérine*, in *Mons. de Pourceaugnac*, and *Frosine*, in the *Avare*, represent the intriguant in petticoats,—a female *Mascarille*.

In how far it is true that many of Molière's characters were copied from persons well known at the time his plays were represented, there is now no certain means of judging; but I think it extremely unlikely that he should have brought on the stage and ridiculed persons of the highest rank, as it is said he has done; though it is very probable that a general likeness existed between the character produced and the person whom it was thought he imitated. In the Introductory Notice to each play of this translation, due attention will be paid to any such inuendos, and to the degree of credence which they deserve.

The style of Molière is the style suitable for comedy, and therefore extremely difficult, if not impossible, to render into any other language. Perhaps of no writer are so many phrases quoted in French conversation; not seldom by people who have never read him, and who only, parrot-like, repeat what they have heard. Several of his expressions have become proverbial, or are used as wise saws to be uttered with solemn face and bated breath.

Another not less remarkable faculty of Molière is that the language his personages employ is precisely suited to them. It varies according to their age, character, rank, and profession, whilst the very sentence becomes long or short, stilted or tripping, pedantic or elastic, finical or natural, coarse or over-refined, according as an old or young man, a marquis or a citizen, a scholar or a dunce, has to speak. It can be said of Molière, more than of any other author we know, that he always employs the right word in the right place. Hence different commentators have tried to show that he was a kind of Admirable Crichton, and that he knew and understood everything. Mons. Castil-Blaze wrote a book to prove that Molière was a perfect musician; MM. Truinet and Paringault, barristers, printed one to convince the world he was a most able and learned lawyer; Mons. M. Raynaud, that he must have studied medicine most thoroughly in order to be able to imitate so accurately the medical jargon of his time. And still a number of books might have been written to prove that he knew perfectly many more things. Even his peasants speak correctly the dialect of the province or county Molière gives them as the land of their birth; all his creations bear proofs of his genius in an incisiveness of expression and clearness of thought which no other writer has equalled.

Molière has written some of his comedies in prose, others in verse,—and in verse that has none of the stiffness of the ordinary French rhyme, but which becomes in his hands a delightful medium for sparkling sallies, bitter sarcasms, well sustained and sprightly conversations. He has also managed blank verse with wonderful precision,—a rare gift among French authors. The whole of *le Sicilien*, the love scenes of the *Avare*, the monologues of *Georges Dandin*, and certain scenes of *le Festin de Pierre*, are written in this metre.

Molière's plays have been translated into every language of Europe, and some of them even into the classical tongues; they have found admirers wherever intellectual beings are congregated; they have been carefully conned and studied by literary men of every age and clime; and Goethe himself read some of these comedies every year.

I have attempted to give a new translation of all Molière's plays. After mature consideration the idea has been abandoned of reproducing, either in rhyme or blank verse, those which in the original are in poetry. The experiments which have been made to represent some of these in metre have not greatly charmed me; and as they were tried by men of talent, and as I do not pretend to possess greater gifts than my predecessors, I have come to the conclusion that an imitation of Molière's style in any metre is next to an impossibility, but that a faithful and literal translation in prose, even if it cannot preserve the fire of the original, may still render the ideas, and represent to the English reader as clear a perception of Molière's characters as can be obtained in a foreign tongue.

I have however endeavoured not to be satisfied with a mere verbal version, but to preserve and convey the genuine spirit, as far as is consistent with the difference of the two languages. In the Introductory Notices a compact, critical judgment of the merits or demerits of each play is also given. But in order to place ourselves on a right standpoint for judging them, we must not forget that Molière wrote his plays to be represented on the stage, and not to be read in the study only; that therefore we must recall, on reading him, the change of voice, the step, the smile, the gesture, the twinkle of the eye or movement of the head in the actor. Thus we are never tired of perusing him; he never cloys; we can remember all his good sayings, quote them, study him again and again, and every time discover fresh beauties.

A remarkable characteristic of Molière is that he does not exaggerate; his fools are never over-witty, his buffoons too grotesque, his men of wit too anxious to display their smartness, and his fine gentlemen too fond of immodest and ribald talk. His satire is always kept within bounds, his repartees are never out of place, his plots are but seldom intricate, and the moral of his plays is not obtruded, but follows as a natural consequence of the whole. He rarely rises to those lofty realms of poetry where Shakespeare so often soars, for he wrote, not idealistic but character-comedies; which is, perhaps, the reason that some of his would-be admirers consider him rather common-place. His claim to distinction is based only on strong common sense, good manners, sound morality, real wit, true humor, a great facile, and accurate command of language, and a photographic delineation of nature. It cannot be denied that there is little action in his plays, but there is a great deal of natural conversation: his personages show that he was a most attentive observer of men, even at court, where a certain varnish of over-refinement conceals nearly all individual features. He always makes vice appear in its most ridiculous aspect, in order to let his audience laugh at and despise it; his aim is to correct the follies of the age by exposing them to ridicule. Shakespeare, on the contrary, has no lack of incidents; he roves through camp, and court, and grove, through solitary forests and populous cities; he sketches in broad outlines rather than with minute strokes; he defines classes rather than individuals, and instead of pourtraying petty vanities and human foibles prefers to deal with deep and tumultuous passions, to such an extent that some of his comedies are highly dramatic. But both poets are great, and perhaps unsurpassed in their own way, and both have many similar passages. Whenever these occur I have taken notice of them. As specimens, let me refer to Mascarille's soliloquy in the *Blunderer* (iii. 1), and Launcelot Gobbo's speech in the *Merchant of Venice* (ii. 2); in the same play Mascarille refusing money, and Autolycus in the *Winter's Tale*, (iv. 3) doing the same; the speech of Gros-René in *Sganarelle* (i. 7), and the scene between Sir Valentine and Speed (ii. 1) in the *Two Gentlemen of Verona*. Monsieur Jourdain, in *The Citizen who apes the Nobleman* (*le Bourgeois-gentilhomme*), when putting on his hat at the entreaty of Dorante, says "*J'aime mieux être civil qu' importun;* Master Slender, upon entering the house before Mrs. Page, says, in the *Merry Wives of Windsor*, (i. 1), "I'll rather be unmannerly than troublesome;" Sosia, in *Amphitryon* (i. 2), sings, in order to show that he is not afraid when Mercury appears; Nick Bottom, in *A Midsummer Night's Dream* (iii. 1) says, "I will sing, that they shall hear I am not afraid." The description of the horse in *the Bores* (*les Fâcheux*) is also worthy of being compared with that spoken by the Dauphin in *Henry V.* (iii. 6), and with the "round-hoof'd, short-jointed" horse in *Venus and Adonis.*

Molière's plays have been already several times translated into English. I shall give a short history of each of these translations, observing however, beforehand, that though many faults may be found in them, I have no inclination to cavil at anything that my predecessors may have badly done or wholly omitted. And I here once and for all state that I have never scrupled to adopt any expression, turn of thought, or even page, of any or every translation of my predecessors, whenever I found I could not improve upon it.

The oldest of these English translations is by Mr.

John Ozell, appeared in six volumes, was published in London, and printed for Bernard Lintott, at the *Cross-Keys*, between the *Two Temple Gates*, in *Fleet Street*, MDCCXIV. It is full of racy and sometimes even witty expressions. Unfortunately where Molière slightly hints at something indelicate, Ozell employs the broadest language possible. Moreover, he very often paraphrases or imitates, and on the whole translates rather too freely. This work is dedicated to the Earl of Dorset, in words which are rather a genealogical history of the Sackville family than an introduction to Molière.

The second translation is called, "Select Comedies of M. de Molière, French and English, in eight volumes, with a frontispiece to each Comedy; to which is prefix'd a curious print of the author, with his life in *French* and *English*. Hic meret æra liber Sociis; hic et mare transit et longum noto scriptori prorogat ævum. *Horat.* London, printed for John Watts, at the Printing-Office in *Wild-Court* near *Lincoln's-Inn Fields*, MDCCXXXII." This translation is less racy, but far more literal than the former. One of the translators, in the Preface to *The Self-deceived Husband* (see page 172), oddly enough dedicated to Miss Wolstenholme, dates from Enfield, Jan. 1st, 1731-2, and signs himself "H. B.," probably Henry Baker; the other, in the Preface to *Tartuffe*, dedicated to Mr. Wyndham, dates from the Academy in *Soho-Square*, *London*, *July* 25, 1732, and subscribes himself, "*Your most obliged and obedient humble servant*, Martin Clare;" who appears to fame unknown. Some of the pictures in this edition have been drawn by Hogarth, of which the one before *Sganarelle ou le Cocu imaginaire* is the best. Of the thirty-one plays then known to have been written by Molière, only seventeen are translated; each of them is dedicated to a separate person, and the whole to the Queen, in the following words:—

TO THE QUEEN.

MADAM,—When MAJESTY vouchsafes to patronize the *wise* and the *learned*, and a QUEEN recommends KNOWLEDGE and VERTUE to her people, what blessings may we not promise ourselves in such happy circumstances? That this is the great intention and business of your MAJESTY'S Life, witness the reception, which the labours of a *Clark*, a *Newton*, a *Locke*, and a *Wollaston* have met with from your MAJESTY, and the immortal honours you have paid their names. Whatever therefore can any ways conduce to those glorious ends, need not question your royal approbation and favour; and upon this presumption MOLIERE casts himself at your MAJESTY'S feet for protection.

This merry philosopher, MADAM, hath taken as much pains to laugh ignorance and immorality out of the world, as the other great sages did to reason 'em out; and as the generality of mankind can stand an argument better than a jest, and bear to be told how good they ought to be, with less concern than to be shown how ridiculous they are, his success, we conceive, has not been much inferior.

Your MAJESTY need not be informed how much the manners and conduct of a people are dependent on their diversions; and you are therefore convinced how necessary it is (since diversions are necessary) to give 'em such as may serve to polish and reform 'em. With this view, MADAM, was the following translation undertaken. By a perusal of these scenes, every reader will plainly perceive that obscenities and immoralities are no ways necessary to make a diverting comedy; they'll learn to distinguish betwixt honest satire and scurrilous invective; betwixt decent repartee and tasteless ribaldry; in short, between vicious satisfactions and rational pleasures. And if these plays should come to be read by the generality of people (as your Majesty's approbation will unquestionably make 'em), they'll by degrees get a more just and refined taste in their diversions, be better acquainted, and grow more in love with the true excellencies of dramatick writings. By this means our poets will be encouraged to aim at those excellencies, and blush to find themselves so much outdone in manners and vertue by their neighbours. Nay, there's no reason can possibly be given, MADAM, why these very pieces should not most of 'em be brought upon the *English* stage. For, tho' our translation of 'em, as it now stands, may be thought too literal and close for that purpose, yet the dramatick writers might, with very little pains, so model and adapt them to our theatre and age, as to procure 'em all the success could be wished; and we may venture to affirm, that 'twould turn more to their own account, and the satisfaction of their audiences, than anything they are able to produce themselves. This, too, they ought to be the more earnest to attempt, as the most probable means of drawing down a larger share of royal influence on the stage, which has been too justly forfeited by the licentious practice of modern playwrights.

We might here, MADAM, take occasion to particularize our author's perfections and excellencies, but those your MAJESTY wants no information of. All we shall therefore observe to your MAJESTY is, that wherever learning, wit, and politeness flourish, MOLIERE has always had an extraordinary reputation; and his plays, which are translated into so many languages, and acted in so many nations, will gain him admiration as long as the stage shall endure. But what will contribute more than all to his glory and happiness, will be the patronage of a BRITISH PRINCESS, and the applause of a BRITISH audience.

We dare not think, MADAM, of offering anything in this address that might look like panegyrick, lest the world should condemn us for meddling with a task above our talents, and saying too little—Your MAJESTY, for presuming to say anything at all. There are many vertues and perfections, so very peculiar in your MAJESTY'S character, and so rarely found amongst the politicks of princes, that they require a masterly and deliberate hand to do 'em justice—Such a zeal for religion moderated by reason—such a benevolent study for composing all factions and dissensions—such a laudable ambition, which aims at power only in order to benefit mankind, and yet such a glorious contempt, even of empire itself, when inconsistent with those Principles whose Truth, you were satisfy'd of. These are such elevated and shining vertues, as even the vicious themselves must have a secret veneration for—But as your MAJESTY'S great pleasure is privately to merit applause, not publickly to receive it; for fear we should interrupt you in that noble delight, we'll beg leave to subscribe Our Selves,—May it please your MAJESTY, your MAJESTY'S most obedient and most devoted humble servants,

THE TRANSLATORS.

The third translation is "The works of Molière, French and English, in ten volumes, a new edition, London, printed for John Watts, MDCCXXXIX." This translation appears to be precisely the same as the former one, a few words slightly altered; the motto from Horace on the title-page is the same; and the plays not found in the "Select Comedies" are here translated. The pictures are identical with those of the translation mentioned above, with the exception of those in front of the fourteen comedies added, which have engravings, and very good ones too, drawn by the celebrated Boucher. According to Lowndes, this translation was executed by Henry Baker and the Rev. Mr. Miller. The work is dedicated to the Prince and Princess of Wales, and the dedication of the former translation to the Queen does duty here, somewhat abridged. The chief difference is, that whilst, in the former, the virtues of the Queen are all specified and catalogued in the paragraph beginning, "We dare not think," under the headings "zeal for religion," "benevolent study," "laudable ambition," and "glorious contempt," they are only mentioned in the present preface in a lump as "many vertues and perfections;" but, to make up for it, the Prince and Princess of Wales are praised for their "unparallel'd union of hearts and affections."

The dedication begins thus:—

To their Royal Highnesses the
PRINCE and PRINCESS OF WALES.

May it please your Royal Highnesses,—The refined taste your Royal Highnesses are both so celebrated for in the *Belles Lettres,* and the peculiar countenance you have shewn to theatrical performances, have embolden'd the editors and translators of the following work to lay it at your feet.

Molière has been translated into most of the languages, and patroniz'd by most of the Princes in *Europe:* But if we have been capable of doing him as much justice in our version, as we have been prudent enough to do him in the choice of patrons, he'll be more happy in speaking *English* than all the rest.

The rest of the dedication is taken from that to the queen, beginning from "Your Majesty (your Royal Highnesses) need not be informed" until "with the true excellencies of Dramatick Writings." The ending varies, and we give it here below:—

By this means our poets will be encourag'd to aim at those excellencies, and be assisted in producing entertainments more agreeable to nature, good sense, and your Royal Highnesses taste.

We dare not think of offering anything in this address that might look like panegyrick ; there are many vertues and perfections so singular in your Royal Highnesses characters, that they require a masterly and deliberate hand to do 'em justice. Give us leave, SIR and MADAM, only to hint at one, which is that unparallel'd union of hearts and affections so rarely found in the palaces of princes, and which shines so conspicuously in your Royal Highnesses that we durst not presume so much as to separate your very names, or make our address to either singly.

That your Royal Highnesses may long enjoy that mutual bliss is the universal prayer of mankind, and of none more than of your Royal Highnesses' most obedient and most devoted humble servants,

THE TRANSLATORS.

Another similar edition of our author was published by the same firm in MDCCXLVIII.

Two editions of the same translation of Molière's works were also published by D. Browne and A. Millar in MDCCXLVIII. and in MDCCLV.

The next Molière, an elegant Scottish reprint of the English part of the above edition in ten volumes, was published in Glasgow in five volumes, "printed by Robert Urie, and sold by John Gilmour, Bookseller in the Saltmarcat, MDCCLI."

An edition of our author, according to Lowndes, was also published in Berwick-on-Tweed, 1770, 6 vols., but I have not been able to get hold of a copy of this translation. In the *British Museum* there is however a translation of five plays by Molière, published in one volume, and printed at Berwick for R. Taylor, 1771.

Seven comedies of Molière, most spiritedly translated from the fourth and fifth volumes of the "Comic Theatre, being a free translation of all the best French Comedies by Samuel Foote, Esq., and others, London: printed by Dryden Leach, for J. Coote, in Paternoster Row; G. Kearsly, in Ludgate Street; and S. Crowder & Co., in Paternoster Row, MDCCLXII." The proprietors state, however, to the public, "One Comedy in each volume of this work will be translated by Mr. Foote, his other avocations not permitting him to undertake more; and the rest by two other gentlemen, who, it is presumed, will acquit themselves in such a manner as to merit the approbation of the public."

It appears that of the above "Comic Theatre" an edition was prepared for Ireland. At least I have seen a volume with a separate printed title page; "printed for J. Coote, and sold by R. Bell, in Stephen Street, Dublin. MDCCLXV."

Of single translated comedies of Molière no notice has been taken, in order not to increase these already too long bibliographical remarks.

Generally the proper names used by Molière have not been Italianized or rendered into an English form in this translation, for wherever the scene of his play is laid, his characters, manners, and customs are always thoroughly French, and should therefore as much as possible remain so.

English dramatic authors have borrowed, and then

adapted or imitated from Molière. Dryden, Vanbrugh, Flecknoe, Fielding, Bickerstaffe, Murphy, Miller, Ravenscroft, Shadwell, Mrs. Centlivre, Mrs. Aphra Behn, Crowne, Lacy, Wycherley, Colman, Garrick, Swiney, Sheridan, Otway, Foote, Cibber, and several other less known dramatic authors, are among the borrowers; and though not rarely showing great talent in their adaptation, yet as a general rule they have always been careful to leave nothing to the imagination, and to emphasize the slightest *mot* of our author in the broadest language possible. Too often they have verified the saying of one of the admirers of our poet, "*Là où Molière glisse, ses traducteurs appuyent et s'enfoncent.*"

Several farces which have never been printed have been attributed to Molière. Two of these, *le Médecin volant* and *la Jealousie du Barbouillé*, have of late been added to the complete edition of his works. They give indications of what our author promised to become, and will be found in the last volume of this edition, for the first time rendered into English.

Nearly all known editions of Molière have been consulted by me whilst engaged upon this translation; but in any cases of doubt I always referred to the literal reprints of the original editions published in 1666 and 1682, and only lately republished in eight volumes by Mons. A. Lemerre, of Paris; as distinguished for their accuracy and good and pithy notes as for their typographical excellence.

In the *Prefatory Memoir* I have admitted no hypothetical or fanciful assertions, but have only stated what is really known of him.

My best thanks are due to Mons. Eugène Despois, the learned editor of the new edition of Molière, now in course of publication by Messrs. Hachette, for valuable advice and elucidations kindly given.

I have likewise to express my great obligations to Mons. Guillard, the archiviste of the *Comédie Française*, for willing and kind assistance rendered with regard to the correct costumes of the times of Louis XIV.

Last, but not least, I have to thank the superintendents and employés of the reading-room in the British Museum, for many kind suggestions, which have often shortened my labours, and for their untiring willingness to aid me, whenever required.

H. VAN LAUN.

PREFATORY MEMOIR.

JEAN BAPTISTE POQUELIN, afterwards Molière, was born at Paris, January 15th, 1622. His father, Jean Poquelin, was a well-to-do upholsterer in the Rue St. Honoré, who in 1631 attained to the height of his ambition in becoming one of the "tapissiers ordinaires," and later one of the "valets de chambre tapissiers" to the king. It was a post which Jean Poquelin's brother had held before; and he coveted nothing better for his son than that he should pursue the path thus clearly mapped out for him. But the boy did not take kindly to the upholsterer's shop; and his maternal grandfather, Louis de Cressé, is said to have secretly encouraged him in his rebellion. His mother died when he was ten years old, and the father lost no time in providing the house with a new mistress. Tradition states that it was partly due to the ungenial influence of the stepmother that Louis de Cressé took every opportunity of carrying off his grandson to the hôtel de Bourgogne, where the king's tragedians gave their bombastic interpretation of the classical drama. Here, the future comedian was inoculated with a passion for the histrionic art, and when Molière, later in life, became an actor, his father shuddered at the notion of so vast a descent from the level of respectability and prosperity to which the family had risen.

The young Poquelin was brought up at the College de Clermont, at that time (1637) the best and most popular school in Paris. Amongst its four hundred scholars were many members of the first families in France; and during this attendance on its classes, tradition mentions that he was the schoolfellow of the Prince de Conti, the poet Hesnaut, the rollicking Chapelle, Bernier the traveller, and the astronomer Gassendi. Poquelin distinguished himself at the College, both in classics and in philosophy; and afterwards, following the usual course of a complete education, he proceeded to Orleans to attend a series of lectures on civil law.[1]

The period of Molière's life was the period of France's greatest glory. Louis XIII. died in 1643, and gave place to Louis le Grand – then only five years old, but destined to be a patron of literature, science, and art; and in particular, the unvarying, though selfish protector of Molière. Corneille had written some of his most famous tragedies before Molière came of age, La Fontaine wrote his charming allegories, Pascal and Bossuet added the sparkle of literature to the dignity of religion, Descartes and Gassendi advanced the limits of scientific knowledge, Madame de Sévigné combined the masculine strength of her intellect with feminine grace, whilst Racine in his tragedies, and Boileau in his satires, aimed at raising and sustaining the literary taste of the age of Louis XIV. Port Royal, within three leagues of Versailles, made its conscientious effort after moral and ethical reform; whilst in Paris itself, the hôtel de Rambouillet—the domain of three generations of magnificent women—gathered to its alcove the wits, fops, and littérateurs of the Metropolis, until Molière, in 1659, gave a death-blow to the *Précieuses*. The court of Louis

[1] Grimarest (*La Vie de M. de Molière*, 1705, p. 14), says, "*quand Molière eut achevé ses études, il fut obligé à cause du grand âge de son père, d'exercer sa charge pendant quelque temps, et même il fit le voyage de Narbonne à la suite de Louis XIII.*" This journey was in 1642, at which time Beffara (*Dissertation sur J. B. Poquelin-Molière*, 1821, p. 25), has conclusively proved that the elder Poquelin was no more than forty-seven years old. It is also said that Jean Baptiste Poquelin studied at Orleans in 1642. Others of his biographers mention that Molière performed temporarily the duties of valet-tapissier to Louis XIII. The circumstance appears hardly probable; but our knowledge is not sufficiently definite to warrant us in describing it as absolutely impossible.

the Grand was by far more splendid than the court of Louis Treize. The new and gorgeous palace at Versailles welcomed all who offered a fresh entertainment to the self-indulgent monarch and his crowd of pleasure-seeking courtiers. Amongst such entertainments none was more acceptable to the cultivated taste of the Parisians than the drama. Even in the time of Louis XIII. the earlier plays of Corneille obtained the first recognition of their merit, but before Molière came French comedy was meagre in the extreme. The court and the people were addicted to the rounded periods and sonorous enunciation of the hôtel de Bourgogne; and Torelli's Italian farces at the Petit Bourbon were never sufficiently popular to excite in the tragedians the envy and alarm afterwards aroused by Molière.

In the latter part of the year 1643 a number of young men and women, members of certain well to-do families of Parisian bourgeois, established in Paris a dramatic company, to which they gave the high-sounding name of *L'Illustre Théâtre.*[2] One Madeleine Béjart,[3] the daughter of a procureur, was the life and soul of the undertaking. At the time when she commenced her rôle of impressario and manageress she was twenty-seven years old, and had been the mistress of Esprit de Raymond de Moirmoiron, Marquess of Modène, gentilhomme ordinaire de Monsieur (Gaston duke of Orléans), brother of Louis XIII. With her were her brother Joseph,[4] and a sister Geneviève, scarcely twenty years old; Clérin, Pinel, Bonenfant, Madeleine Malingre, Catherine des Urlis and Catherine Bourgeois, Denis or Charles Beys, and Desfontaines, two writers of comedies, and Jean Baptiste Poquelin, who, on adopting the career of an actor, no doubt in deference to the scruples of his family, assumed the sur-

---

[2] The biographers of Molière are not agreed about the date of the opening of the *Illustre Théâtre.* Moland and several others say 1645; Soulié, in his *Recherches sur Molière*, 1863, proves by official documents that it was either December 31st, 1643, or at the very beginning of 1644.

[3] Béjart is sometimes written "Béjard." Soulié always spells it thus, though the members of that family generally wrote it with a *t*.

[4] Several commentators say he was called Jacques, Soulié says Joseph.

name of Molière. He never explained the reason for this assumption in particular; but the name of a popular dancer and musician, attached to the private chapel of the king, Louis de Mollier, was often written Molière; a novel-writer, who at that time enjoyed a certain reputation, was also called François de Molière, whilst the name itself was not uncommon.

Molière was on terms of intimate friendship with Madeleine Béjart, and it is natural that he should at once have obtained a supreme influence over the company. After trying their fortune successively on three stages—one near the Tour de Nesle, another in the rue des Barrés, a third in the faubourg St. Germain—and meeting with scant fortune, seven of them quitted Paris in 1646, and for nearly twelve years were engaged in a tour through the provinces. Before leaving Paris they had run considerably into debt, and that in spite of the fact that they were partially supported by Gaston, duke of Orléans. The widowed mother of the Béjarts, Marie Hervé, became surety for her children, and for Molière; whilst the other associates gave bonds to their creditors for a considerable amount. For the non-payment of one obligation Molière was arrested and imprisoned; nor does this seem to have been the only debt which brought about the like result during the career of the *Illustre Théâtre* in Paris. Documents have been discovered which show that he was successively arrested at the suit of a number of tradesmen who had furnished or supplied the different theatres. Over and over again he was rescued by his friends; often at the cost of his entering into new engagements, bearing more or less exorbitant interest. Fourteen years later we find him discharging one of those debts, with interest, expenses, and "*loyaux coûts*" which had in the meantime accumulated.[5]

The plays with which the undaunted company commenced their histrionic career were of indifferent merit. Amongst them were the comedies of Scarron, and no doubt, of Denis Beys, such as *l'Hôpital des fous*, and of Desfontaines, such as *Eurymédon ou l'illustre Pirate*, and *l'illustre Comédien, ou le Martyre de Saint-Genest*. It would be difficult to fix the exact

[5] Eud. Soulié, *Recherches sur Molière*, 1863, p. 42.

date at which Molière's earliest plays were produced, but it is probable that he began to write for his company as soon as he had enlisted in it. He seems, like Shakespeare, to have in part at least adapted the plays of others; but in the year 1653, if not earlier, he had produced *l'Étourdi* and in 1656 *le Dépit amoureux*.

In 1648 we hear of the Béjart-Molière company at Nantes, Limoges, and Bordeaux. From Bourdeaux they went to Toulouse; and in 1650 they were at Narbonne; after which time they appear to have peregrinated to the south of France, until in 1653 we find them at Lyons, where *l'Étourdi*, Molière's earliest important venture in verse, is supposed to have been represented for the first time, and where Berthelot, generally known as Duparc, and Gros-René, joined them. Here the tide of their fortune was caught at the flood. The whole town flocked to hear them; and during the next two or three years they made Lyons their head-quarters, from whence they visited the populous places in the south-east of France. Occasionally they were invited to the castles of the nobility, as for instance, in 1653, to the country-seat of the Prince de Conti, near Pézenas. *Le Dépit amoureux* was produced in 1656 at Béziers, during the meeting of the States of Languedoc in that town. It was at Grenoble, in the early spring of 1658, that Molière's friends—among them the painter Mignard—persuaded him once more to try his fortune in Paris. After a summer trip to Rouen, he returned to Paris in the autumn, where he was introduced to Cardinal Mazarin, and renewed his acquaintance with the Prince de Conti. Through the latter's friend, the bishop of Valence, he was brought under the notice of the king's brother, Philippe, then Duke of Anjou, who was at that time but eighteen years of age, but who had already formed the design of supporting a dramatic company. The *Illustre Théâtre* acted before him, and pleased him; he invited Molière to repeat the experiment before the court. This was what the company most desired; the opportunity for which they had been conscientiously labouring through their twelve years' apprenticeship. They accepted the offer with gratitude.

The company was not precisely the same on its return to Paris as it had been in 1646. There were now four ladies, Madeleine Béjart, Geneviève Béjart, Duparc and Debrie; the two brothers Béjart, Duparc, Debrie, Dufresne, and Croisac, making, with Molière himself, eleven persons. It may be concluded that their tour—or at all events the part of it which dated from Lyons—had been very successful; for we find that Joseph Béjart, who died early in 1659, left behind him a fortune of twenty-four thousand golden crowns. So at least we are told by the physician, Guy-Patin, in a letter dated May 27, 1659; and he adds, "Is it not enough to make one believe that Peru is no longer in America, but in Paris?"

It was on the 24th of October, 1658—about the same time, in fact, as Sir William D'Avenant was establishing his theatre in London—that Molière and his fellow-actors played before Louis le Grand in a theatre which had been raised in the "salle des Gardes" of the Louvre. The piece chosen was Corneille's *Nicomède*, and after that Molière's farce *le Docteur amoureux*. From that time forward the *Illustre Théâtre* was called the *Comédiens de Monsieur;* and the company was allowed the use of the Petit Bourbon on alternate days with Torelli's Italians. Molière paid Torelli 1500 livres a-year for the monopoly of four days in the week. On November 3d *l'Étourdi* was given, with Molière in the part of Mascarille; and *le Dépit amoureux* followed in December. The success of those pieces was so great that the prices of admission had to be raised; and at the close of the season each actor's share of the profits amounted to about 800 livres.

There were in Paris at this time at least six theatres; one at the hôtel de Bourgogne, one at the Marais, the companies of Monsieur, of which Molière was the manager, and of Mademoiselle,[6] a Spanish company, and Torelli's. The latter was

---

[6] *Mademoiselle* was the title given to Madlle de Montpensier, the daughter of Gaston, duke of Orleans, uncle of Louis XIV. She was sometimes called *la grande Mademoiselle* to distinguish her from the daughter of Philip of Orleans, brother of Louis XIV. See also note 14, page xxxii.

broken up at the Easter of 1659, when Molière had the Petit Bourbon to himself. This theatre was 108 feet long, by 48 broad and high, the stage being raised six feet above the floor.

The taste of the age, before Molière's plays had cultivated an appreciation for high-class comedy, was centred in the tragedies of Corneille and his school, or in the grotesque farces of Scarron and Scudéry. Molière's own earliest efforts were in the latter vein, and his first encouragement arose from the discovery that his intermezzos were more successful on the stage than those of his juvenile models. Several of his best comedies were founded upon the less ambitious efforts which had laid the basis of his company's fame, such as *le Docteur amoureux*, *les trois Docteurs rivaux*, *le Maitre d'école*, *Gorgibus dans le sac*, *le Fagoteux*, *le Docteur pédant*, *la Casaque*, *la Jealousie du Barbouillé*, and *le Médecin volant*. The fourth farce appears to be the foundation of a scene of *les Fourberies de Scapin*, the fifth as well as the last that of the *Médecin malgré lui*, and the eighth that of *George Dandin*.

At the commencement of the next season, November 18, 1659, appeared *les Précieuses ridicules*. This admirably conceived satire upon the imitations of the hôtel de Rambouillet was Molière's first grand hit in the metropolis. Paris was entranced by the novelty and precision of the delineation, and flocked to see it. The *Précieux* and *Précieuses* themselves went down to the theatre of the Petit Bourbon, in order to criticise their critics. Madame de Rambouillet, the head of that famous coterie, Madame de Grignan, Chapelle and Ménage, Scudéry and Benserade, all were compelled to praise the author who ridiculed them. Chapelle sought out his old schoolfellow, and facilitated his good reception by the Parisians. Ménage, quitting the theatre on the first night is reputed to have said to Chapelle, "Now, like Clovis, we must burn what we have adored and adore what we have burnt." According to tradition, a spectator was so overcome by admiration that he called out in the middle of the piece, "*Courage Molière! Voilà la bonne comédie!*" The king, who disliked the Rambouillet coterie, but who was at this time at the foot of the Pyrénées, commanded that the play should be represented before him.

Molière's success was unequivocal, but the incisiveness of his satire had raised up many enemies, and the shrinking receipts of the other theatres added many more. Those who were in authority during the king's absence were induced to forbid *les Précieuses ridicules;* but the Parisians would not consent to lose the best comedy in the language. In fourteen days the prohibition was removed; and then, although the prices of nearly the whole house was raised by about one half, public curiosity would hardly be satisfied.[7]

As we have already mentioned, Joseph Béjart died in 1659, ere he had recognized to what a height of fame and fortune the company was destined to reach, but having already succeeded in amassing a competence. In 1660 another member of the company, Jodelet, died; and Duparc and his wife, who had withdrawn, again placed themselves at Molière's disposal for a time.

In the month of May, 1660, was produced *Sganarelle ou le Cocu Imaginaire*, the poet again taking the leading part. It is recorded that one Neufvillenaine, after a few representations of this one-act comedy, had learned it thoroughly by heart. He wrote it down, had it printed, and put it up for sale through the bookseller Ribou. Molière was advised to invoke the law in defence of his copyright, and he did so successfully. He did not, however, publish his play before 1663, and then it was found word for word the same with Neufvillenaine's copy.

---

[7] In general people have not a correct idea about the prices of admittance to the theatre in Molière's time. In the theatre of the Palais Royal, where all his pieces were played, with the exception of the first four, the prices for the *billets de théâtre* (tickets admitting on the stage) were five livres ten sous, representing about eighteen francs at the present time; those for the boxes four livres; those for the amphitheatre three livres; for the boxes on the second tier, one livre ten sous; for the upper boxes, one livre; and for the pit, fifteen sous. In representations *au double* or *a l' extraordinaire* all the prices are raised except those of five livres ten sous. During ordinary representations, the salle du Petit-Bourbon could hold 1400 livres, that of the Palais Royal 2860 livres; the Comédie Française can at present hold 6000 francs: so that, considering tne relative value of money, the latter place cannot make more, though it has room for 1650 persons.

In August 1660 Louis le Grand returned to Paris with his young wife, and the Louvre being committed to Claude Perrault for renovation and re-decoration, the theatre of the Petit Bourbon was doomed. Molière's company was transferred to the Palais Royal, the great hall being capable of holding four thousand spectators [8] Whilst this building was preparing, the actors played several times at the houses and seats of the nobility, and even in the Louvre itself, where, on the 26th of October, the *Étourdi* and the *Précieuses* were performed before the king and Cardinal Mazarin, the latter being carried in on his sick-bed. On this occasion the company was presented with 3000 livres. The Palais Royal was ready by the 20th of January 1661, and opened with the *Dépit amoureaux* and *Sganarelle.* In honour of the King's Spanish spouse the poet now wrote an inflated piece called *Don Garcie de Navarre.* It met with no success, and was dropped after five representations. A few of the scenes were afterwards adopted in the *Misanthrope*, *Amphitryon*, the *Fâcheux*, *Tartuffe*, and the *Femmes savantes.*

The office of "tapissier valet de chambre," which had been held by Molière's father, was probably transferred by the latter to his younger son, Jean Poquelin, who exercised it during his elder brother's absence from Paris. Jean Poquelin the younger died in 1660, and Molière then assumed the office to himself. Apart from the emoluments attached to this position, the poet no doubt found it extremely useful in bringing him constantly into the presence of the king, and in providing him with abundant opportunities for making the necessary studies of the foibles of humanity. That he suffered somewhat in his dignity as a poet we may well imagine; but Molière's mind was sufficiently strong to bear the rebuffs of smaller men with equanimity. On one occasion a fellow-valet declined to assist the comedian in making the king's bed. Bellocq, a courtier,

[8] Sauval in his *Histoire et Recherches des Antiquités de la ville de Paris*, 1724, 3 vols., iii., p. 47, says the theatre of the Palais Royal could contain 4000 persons, M. Taschereau states 1000; the last number appears to be the most probable, considering the money the room could hold. See also note 7, page xxv.

known by some pretty verses, heard this remark, and walking towards them, said, "M. de Molière, permit me to have the honour of making his majesty's bed with you." But the king himself delighted to honour Molière; and the latter made his own position wherever he went. He was recognised not only as an admirable actor, but as an author of the first rank; from this time forward, although he wrote a few complimentary or farcical pieces which were not quite worthy of his genius, he continued to throw off, with great rapidity and yet with marvellous finish, the series of comedies on which his fame is securely built. Well might he say, "I need no longer study Plautus and Terence, and filch the fragments of Menander; my models henceforth are the world and the living."

In June 1661 Molière produced his *École des Maris*, and in August, at a grand entertainment given by Fouquet to the king and queen, to the former duke of Anjou, who had become duke of Orleans, and to the Princess Henrietta of England, a few days before he was replaced by Colbert, *les Fâcheux* made another good impression. It was during the representation of this play that Louis XIV. pointed out to Molière his future Master of the Hunt, the marquis de Soyecourt, as a character well worthy of his attention. In a few days the piece was richer by a part: though some critics maintained that Molière did not actually write the principal scene which sprang out of this suggestion of the king, but that he merely versified what had been supplied to him by another.

On the 20th February 1662 Molière married Armande-Grésinde-Claire-Elizabeth Béjart, the youngest sister of Madeleine Béjart, and at this time aged about twenty years.[9] Her dowry was ten thousand livres; her widow's portion four thousand. The marriage-contract and other documents relating to this period of Molière's life, which were discovered by Beffara,[10] the most able of his earlier biographers, show clearly that

[9] Some of Molière's biographers state that Armande de Béjart, at the time of her marriage, was not yet seventeen years old; Soulié gives the very marriage-contract, which proves that she was twenty or thereabout. This contract is dated January 23. 1662.

[10] *Dissertation sur J. B. Poquelin-Molière*, 1821, p. 7.

Armande's mother, brother, and eldest sister were present at and consenting to the ceremony—so that Grimarest, and several of Molière's early biographers must have been mistaken in saying that Madeleine was opposed to this union, and that it was kept secret for some time. Geneviève Béjart, however, the second daughter of Marie Hervé, does not seem to have been present at the marriage; and it is surmised by Soulié that whatever opposition existed may have come from her, and that Molière's connection with her may have dated back to the time at which he first resolved to follow the career of an actor. Geneviève married two years after her younger sister. The affection between Molière and Armande had been sincere from the beginning. Armande was brought up, if not born, in the company; and her wit and manners seem to have secured for her in after-life the tenderness which the poet displayed towards her when a child. Molière's enemies have coupled his name injuriously with those of Madeleine and Geneviève Béjart. There is hardly any evidence in support of such suggestions; but there is abundant proof of his love and respect for his wife. His happiness with her was not, however, as great as he had hoped to find it. Armande was fond of pleasure and admiration; Molière, amidst the avocations and anxieties of his position, could not always attend upon her with the devotion and ardour of a lover; and she sought and found adulation at the hands of others. On the stage, therefore, he acted Sganarelle to the life, and in his most melancholy moods could not hold himself free from the twinges of but too well founded jealousy.

In the latter part of 1662 the *École des Femmes* was performed. This play met with some opposition, and was answered by our author's *La Critique de l' École des Femmes*, which was brought out the 1st of June 1663. The comedians of the hôtel de Bourgogne had long envied and hated Molière, and they took now the opportunity of attacking him. Boursault wrote a piece entitled *le Portrait du Peintre ou la Contra-critique de l'École des Femmes*. Molière replied in *l'Impromptu de Versailles*. De Villiers and Montfleury took up the cudgels on the other side, and wrote *la Vengeance des*

Marquis and *l'Impromptu de l'hôtel de Mondé.* At the same time Montfleury's father was base enough to accuse Molière before the king of having married his own daughter; the insinuation being that Armande was the child of Madeleine Béjart. The court did not listen to this tale, and presently after the king and Henrietta, duchess of Orléans, stood sponsors for Molière's eldest son, who was born on the 19th January, 1664.[11] Molière was satisfied with his triumph, and soon after stopped the sale of the *Impromptu de Versailles.*

Molière regarded himself henceforth as the court dramatist *par excellence*, and he was anxious to show by every means in his power the gratitude aroused in him by the king's favour. In January 1664 he wrote, for a court high festival, *le Mariage forcé* a one-act piece with eight *entreés de ballet*,[12] and in which Sganarelle re-appears; who had figured in several previous plays. Louis himself danced in one of the acts. In May of the same year the Grand Monarque gave a grand festival in honour of Louise de Vallière, lasting over a week, to which Molière contributed the *Princesse d'Élide*, a five-act piece, strung together in such haste that only the first act was in verse, and—a far more ambitious flight of the Muse, which had no doubt been for some time past in preparation—the first three acts of *Tartuffe.*

Tartuffe was a protest and satire against the ecclesiastical intolerance and religious hypocrisy which were amongst the characteristics of the day. A revival of orthodoxy had followed upon the restless period of the Ligue and the Fronde; and this reaction had brought in its train more of the outward show than of the reality of religion. Molière hated cant with

[11] Eud. Soulié, *Recherches sur Molière*, p. 59. "This child died in the same year,"

[12] The *ballets de cour*, according to M. Bazin's *Notes historiques sur la vie de Molière*, 1851, were composed of *entrées*, *vers*, and *récits*. The *entrées* were represented by persons who said nothing, but whose gestures, dancing, and dress sufficiently showed what the author intended to represent; this was, moreover, elucidated by the *vers*, which were not spoken on the stage, but only printed in the libretto. The *récits* were verses spoken, or couplets sung, generally by professional actors or actresses.

an unfeigned hatred; and besides, he had a private quarrel of his own against the ecclesiastics, who had excommunicated himself and his brother actors. In *Tartuffe* he hit the priests and the hypocrites very hard, and multiplied the number of his enemies. The play seems to have been acted tentatively from the first, and then only before the king, or certain select audiences at Versailles, Villers-Cotterets, and Raincy. Paris did not see it at the Palais Royal for years after; but this partial publicity was sufficient to secure for it the abhorrence of those who regarded themselves as the guardians of popular morality and orthodoxy. Their objection to *Tartuffe*, and to *le Festin de Pierre*, which was first acted in February 1665, and which treated hypocrisy in the like ungentle fashion, was much akin to those raised against Paul by the coppersmiths of Ephesus. But it was successful; and both pieces were interdicted, after the last-named had been represented for fifteen days before crowded houses. Pierre Roulès, curé of St. Barthélemy, and another clergyman, de Rochemont,[13] wrote treatises to counteract the evil effects of Molière's works; and the enemies of the latter produced a disreputable pasquinade in his name, wherein he was made to cast shameful reflections against the priests. He subsequently thought it worth his while to expose this trick in the fifth act of the *Misanthrope*. The king hardly dared to withstand the Church in the then existing condition of the public mind. Unwilling to remove the prohibition by his royal fiat, he paid Molière the compliment of permitting his troupe to be styled "Comédiens du Roi," which title they held from this time forward: and they were subsidized by a yearly pension of seven thousand livres.

An intermittent source of trouble and anxiety to Molière was found in the ingratitude of his company, who now and again forgot that he had made the fortunes of every one of them. When a play did not draw, or when the public found a mo-

[13] In the re-impression of *Observations sur le Festin de Pierre par de Rochemont et Réponses aux Observations*, edited by the bibliophile Jacob, Genève, 1869, it is stated, p. 11, that though de Rochemont may have been an advocate, as many of Molière's biographers had said, he was a clergyman at the time he wrote his *Observations*.

mentary attraction elsewhere, they seem generally to have laid the blame upon their manager. Such was the case when "Scaramouch" (Torelli), the manager of the Italian farce-company, who had earned enough to buy an estate at Florence of about ten thousand livres per annum, being driven from his retirement by his wife and children, returned to Paris and resumed his career as an actor. The public had not lost their appreciation of the Italian harlequinades,—the receipts of Molière's theatre began to fall off, and his company—especially one of the Béjarts and Maddle.[14] Duparc—pretended that the cause of the failure originated with him.

Molière's path was by no means an easy one to tread; the following anecdote may serve as another illustration of the fact. The king's body guards, and other household troops, had formerly been allowed to see the play for nothing, and Molière, who was doubtless more troubled by the abuse of "paper" than are the managers of to-day, was urged by his company to obtain the removal of this privilege from the king. His request was granted; but the change gave great umbrage to the soldiers. They came down to the house in a body, killed the door-keeper, and uttered loud threats against the actors. On the next day the king had them drawn up on parade, and sent for Molière to harangue them. This he did with so much tact and good humour, and he gave them such excellent reasons why they should pay for their seats like gentlemen, and leave the free admissions for such as could not afford a trifle, that they made no further difficulty in the matter.

Like many comic actors, Molière was often melancholy, morose, and timid off the stage; and the lack of sympathy from the young wife he loved so much tended to aggravate those symptoms. He was, moreover, afflicted by a spasmodic cough and pulmonary attacks, very possibly due to frequent

---

[14] All ladies who were not of noble birth, or those of inferior nobility, were in Molière's time called *Mademoiselle*, the others *Madame;* nevertheless the expressions *une demoiselle*, *une femme demoiselle*, were often used for a noble-born married or unmarried lady. For the use of *Mademoiselle* as a special name see note 6, page xxiv.

exposures during his provincial tours, and compelled to live a most abstemious life. He had taken a house at Auteuil, where he passed all the time that could be spared from his arduous duties; hither his friends were wont to come and visit him, trying, with but little success, to rouse him from his characteristic melancholy. A very touching story is related of one of these visits, which we may quote as an instance of the genuine friendship which existed between the poet and his friends, and of the essentially dramatic constitution of Molière's mind.

Chapelle, La Fontaine, Lulli, director of the Royal Academy of Music, Boileau, Mignard the artist, and Corneille, came one evening to Auteuil to make merry with their friend. Molière was obliged to excuse himself on the ground of ill-health, but he requested Chapelle to do the honours of his house. The guests sat down, and presently, warmed with wine, they fell to talking of religion, futurity, the vanity of human life, and such other lofty and inexhaustible topics as are wont to occupy the vinous moments of intellectual men. Chapelle led the conversation, and indulged in a long tirade against the folly of most things counted wise; at length one of them suggested the idea of suicide, and proposed that they should all go and drown themselves in the river. This splendid notion was received with acclamation; the tipsy philosophers hurried down to the bank, and seized upon a boat in order to get into the middle of the stream. Meanwhile Baron, Molière's favourite pupil,[15] who lived in the house with him, and who had been present at the debauch, aroused his master, and sent off the servants in quest of the would-be suicides. The latter were already in the water when assistance arrived, and they were pulled out; but, resenting such an impertinence, they drew their swords on their deliverers, and pursued them to Molière's house. The poet displayed complete presence of mind, and pretended to approve of the plan which had been formed; but he professed to be much annoyed that they should have thought of drowning themselves without him. They admitted their error, and invited him to come back with them and finish

[15] Subsequently the most finished actor in France.

the business. "Nay," said Molière, "that would be very clumsy. So glorious a deed should not be done at night, and in darkness. Early to-morrow, when we have all slept well, we will go, fasting and in public, and throw ourselves in." To this all assented, and Chapelle proposed that in the meantime they should finish the wine that had been left. It need not be added that the next day found them in a different mood.[16]

In September, 1665, *l'Amour Médecin* was written, studied, and rehearsed within a period of five days, and acted first at Versailles, afterwards in Paris. In December the Palais Royal had to be closed on account of Molière's serious illness. It was the beginning of the end, but he fought against his weakness valiantly. The death of Anne of Austria delayed the reopening of the theatre until June, 1666, in which month Molière produced his *Misanthrope*, a play which has been ranked as high in comedy as *Athalie* is ranked in French tragedy. The circumstances under which it was written were such as might almost warrant us in calling it a tragedy itself; for the great satirist, who had spent his life in copying the eccentricities of others, had now employed the season of his illness and convalescence to commit to paper a drama in which he was himself the principal actor. The misanthrope, Alceste, loves the coquette Célimène almost against his will; and we can imagine the feelings with which Molière himself took the rôle of Alceste to his wife's Célimène. The general sarcasm of the piece is very bitter; but Paris heard it eagerly for close upon a month. It was succeeded by the *Médecin malgré lui*; and at the beginning of the next year followed the charming operetta of *le Sicilien ou l'Amour peintre.* Shortly after the appearance of this piece the author was again confined to his bed for upwards of two months.

Philip IV. of Spain died in September 1665, and Louis XIV. claimed Brabant, Flanders, Hainault, and Limburg in the right of his wife. He went in the spring of 1667 with a corps

---

[16] Boileau repeated this story to Racine, whose son has recorded it in his Memoirs. A sceptic might perhaps suspect that the attempted suicide was only a trick to get Molière to join in the revels.

d'armée to take possession of this territory, and with him went the Queen, Madame de Montespan, Mademoiselle de la Vallière, and the whole court. During their absence Molière relying on a previously implied permission of the King, once more produced *Tartuffe*, the name of which he had changed to *l'Imposteur*. It was immediately prohibited by the President de Lamoignon, and Molière sent off two of his company to ask for the King's sanction. The latter gave an evasive reply, undertaking to inquire into the matter on his return. Louis returned on the 7th of September, but his promise was not at once redeemed. In January 1668, *Amphitryon* appeared, and a little later, in the course of a festival given in the honour of Condé's victories in Franche-Comté, *George Dandin*. In the autumn of this year *l'Avare* was first acted, but it was coldly received by the public. It was not until February 1669 that *Tartuffe* finally made its appearance before a Parisian audience, with the full permission and protection of the king. The objections raised against it were as strong as ever, but Louis was less anxious than formerly to please the ecclesiastics. The play had an immense success, and appears to have run for several months. In the same month (February) died Molière's father, and in the papers he left behind him there is a bitter allusion to "Monsieur Molière." In October of the same year Molière played the title-rôle in his new farce *Monsieur de Pourceaugnac*. In reference to this bright play Diderot has remarked that it would be a mistake to suppose that there are many more men capable of writing *Pourceaugnac* than the *Misanthrope*; and the judgment of later critics has confirmed the observation.

As his infirmities increased upon him, and his short life drew to a close, Molière's pen was more fruitful than ever. In the year 1670 he produced in addition to a comedy-ballet, *les Amants magnifiques*, an excellent comedy, *le Bourgeois Gentilhomme*, in which he played the title-rôle. The same year died Marie Hervé, the mother of the Béjarts. Baron took this year also the place of Louis Béjart. In the following year (1671) were brought out *Psyché*, a tragédie-ballet, of which he only wrote a part, and two farces, *les Fourberies de Scapin* and *la Comtesse d'Escarbagnas.* In 1672 was played a satire-comedy in the highest mood of his trenchant mind, *les Femmes savantes*, a sort of sequel to *les Précieuses ridicules*, though with more general application.

In 1671 his friends succeeded in bringing about a better understanding between Molière and his wife, who for some time past had rarely met except on the stage. One cause of disagreement between them had been the absurd jealousy with which Armande regarded the affection of her husband for the young actor, Baron, whom on one occasion she drove from the house by her petulant reproaches. The reconciliation extended to this faithful pupil of the great comedian, and the last scenes of Molière's life were brightened by the affectionate devotion of the two people whom he loved best. The year 1672 was nevertheless a sad one; and as it were by an omen of his approaching end, more than one of the ties which bound him with his earlier career were broken. Madeleine Béjart, the companion of his life-long labours, died in February, leaving many legacies to religious foundations, but the bulk of her property to her favourite sister Armande, with reversion to Madeleine Esprit, Molière's only surviving child, whose second son had died a few days previously. Of the famous company which in 1646 had quited Paris on its twelve years' provincial tour, only two now remained—the poet and Geneviève Béjart.

Bowed down by sorrow and pain, weakened by a racking cough which never left him a day's peace, he could not be persuaded to spare himself. Within a few months of his death he wrote his *Malade Imaginaire*, a happy conception, which must have done much to rob his bodily sufferings of their sting. On the 17th of February 1673, in spite of the dissuasion of his wife and Baron, he played the part of Argan, and acted the piece through, though he was very ill. In the evening of the same day, in his house in the Rue Richelieu, he burst a blood-vessel. Two nuns who had for some time past been living in the house stood by his bed, and to them he expressed his complete resignation to the will of God. They sent in succession for two priests to administer the last consolations of religion, but both refused to come. Before a third could be found, Molière was dead. He was buried four days later, almost without the rites of religion, in a church-yard adjoining the Rue Montmartre.

The daughter of the actor Du Croisy, Madame Poisson, herself an actress, and one who had seen Molière, when she was very young, has left us an exact description of his personal appearance, which she wrote in the *Mercure de France* for May, 1740. "He was neither too stout nor too thin; his stature was rather tall than short; his carriage was noble; and he had a remarkable good leg. He walked measuredly; had a very serious air; a large nose, an ample mouth, with full lips; brown complexion, and eyebrows black and thick; while the varied motion he gave to these latter rendered his physiognomy extremely comic"[17]

---

[17] In that monument of accuracy and erudition, *Dictionaire critique de Biographie et d'Histoire*, by A. Jal, Paris, 1872, it is stated in the article "Poisson," p. 983, that this actress died at St. Germain en Laye, the 12th of December, 1756, at the age of ninety. Molière died in 1673; therefore, if she saw him even in 1672, she must have been six years old, a rather early age to receive impressions of personal appearance. Moland, in his life of Molière, states that she was fifteen years old at our author's death, but Jal is always exact. I suppose Madame Poisson, who in 1740, was seventy-four years old, gave as her own personal impression what she could only have known by hearsay.

L'ÉTOURDI, OU LES CONTRE-TEMPS.

COMÉDIE.

THE BLUNDERER: OR, THE COUNTERPLOTS.

A COMEDY IN FIVE ACTS.

(*THE ORIGINAL IN VERSE.*)

1653. (?)

INTRODUCTORY NOTICE.

The Blunderer is generally believed to have been first acted at Lyons in 1653, whilst Molière and his troupe were in the provinces. In the month of November 1658 it was played for the first time in Paris, where it obtained a great and well-deserved success. It is chiefly based on an Italian comedy, written by Nicolo Barbieri, known as Beltrame, and called *L'Inavvertito* from which the character of Mascarille, the servant, is taken, but differs in the ending, which is superior in the Italian play. An imitation of the classical boasting soldier, Captain Bellorofonte, Martelione, and a great number of *concetti*, have also not been copied by Molière. The fourth scene of the fourth act of *l'Etourdi* contains some passages taken from the *Angelica*, a comedy by Fabritio de Fornaris, a Neapolitan, who calls himself on the title-page of his play "il Capitano Coccodrillo, comico confidente." A few remarks are borrowed from *la Emilia*, a comedy by Luigi Grotto, whilst here and there we find a reminiscence from Plautus, and one scene, possibly suggested by the sixteenth of the *Contes et Discours d'Eutrapel*, written by Nöel du Fail, Lord of la Hérissaye. Some of the scenes remind us of passages in several Italian *Commedia del' arte* between *Arlecchino* and *Pantaleone* the personifications of impudence and ingenuity, as opposed to meekness and stupidity; they rouse the hilarity of the spectators, who laugh at the ready invention of the knave as well as at the gullibility of the old man. Before this comedy appeared the French stage was chiefly filled with plays full of intrigue, but with scarcely any attempt to delineate character or manners. In this piece the plot is carried on, partly in imitation of the Spanish taste, by a servant, Mascarille, who is the first original personage Molière has created; he is not a mere imitation of the valets of the Italian or classical comedy; he has not the coarseness and base feelings of the servants of his contemporaries, but he is a lineal descendant of Villon, a free and easy fellow, not over nice in the choice or execution of his plans, but inventing new ones after each failure, simply to keep in his hand; not too valiant, except perhaps when in his cups, rather jovial and chaffy, making fun of himself and everybody else besides, no respecter of persons or things, and doomed probably not to die in his bed. Molière must have encountered many such a man whilst the wars of the Fronde were raging, during his perigrinations in the provinces. Even at the present time, a Mascarille is no impossibility; for, "like master like man." There are also in *The Blunderer* too many incidents, which take place successively. without necessarily arising one from another. Some of the characters are not distinctly brought out, the style has often been found fault with, by Voltaire and other competent judges,[1] but these defects are partly covered by a variety and vivacity which are only fully displayed when heard on the stage.

In the third volume of the "Select Comedies of M. de Molière, London, 1732." *The Blunderer* is dedicated to the Right Honorable Philip, Earl of Chesterfield, in the following words :—

MY LORD,—The translation of *L'Etourdi*, which, in company with the original, throws itself at your lordship's feet, is a part of a design form'd by some gentlemen, of exhibiting to the public a *Select Collection of Molière's Plays*, in *French* and *English*. This author, my lord, was truly a genius, caress'd by the greatest men of his own time, and honour'd with the patronage of princes. When the translator, therefore, of this piece was to introduce him in an *English* dress in justice he owed him an *English* patron, and was readily determined to your lordship, whom all the world allows to be a genius of the first rank. But he is too sensible of the beauties of his author, and the refined taste your lordship is universally known to have in polite literature, to plead anything but your candour and goodness, for your acceptance of this performance. He persuades himself that your lordship, who best knows how difficult it is to speak like *Molière*, even when we have his sentiments to inspire us, will be readiest to forgive the imperfections of this attempt. He is the rather encouraged, my lord, to hope for a candid reception from your lordship, on account of the usefulness of this design, which he flatters himself will have your approbation. 'Tis to spirit greater numbers of our countrymen to read this author, who wou'd otherwise not have attempted it, or, being foil'd in their attempts, wou'd throw him by in despair. And however generally the *French* language may be read, or spoke in England, there will be still very great numbers, even of those who are said to understand *French*, who, to master this comic writer, will want the help of a translation ; and glad wou'd the publishers of this work be to guide the feebler steps of some such persons, not only till they should want no translation, but till some of them should be able to make a much better than the present. The great advantage of understanding *Molière* your Lordship best knows. What is it, but almost to understand mankind? He has shown such a compass of knowledge in human nature, as scarce to leave it in the power of succeeding writers in comedy to be originals ; whence it has, in fact, appear'd, that they who, since his time, have most excelled in the *Comic* way, have copied *Molière*, and therein were sure of copying nature. In this author, my lord, our youth will find the strongest sense, the purest moral, and the keenest satyr, accompany'd with the utmost politeness ; so that our countrymen may take a *French* polish, without danger of commencing fops and apes, as they sometimes do by an affectation of the dress and manners of that people ; for no man

---

[1] Victor Hugo appears to be of another opinion. M. Paul Stapfer, in his *les Artistes juges et parties* (2e Causerie, the Grammarian of Hauteville House, p. 55), states :—" the opinion of Victor Hugo about Molière is very peculiar. According to him, the best written of all the plays of our great comic author is his first work, *l'Etourdi*. It possesses a brilliancy and freshness of style which still shine in *le Dépit amoureux*, but which gradually fade, because Molière, yielding unfortunately to other inspirations than his own, enters more and more upon a new way."

has better pourtray'd, or in a finer manner expos'd fopperies of all kinds, than this our author hath, in one or other of his pieces. And now, 'tis not doubted, my lord, but your lordship is under some apprehensions, and the reader under some expectation, that the translator should attempt your character, in right of a dedicator, as a refin'd wit, and consummate statesman. But, my lord, speaking the truth to a person of your lordship's accomplishments, wou'd have the appearance of flattery, especially to those who have not the honour of knowing you; and those who have, conceive greater ideas of you than the translator will pretend to express. Permit him, then, my lord, to crave your lordship's acceptance of this piece, which appears to you with a fair and correct copy of the original; but with a translation which can be of no manner of consequence to your lordship, only as it may be of consequence to those who *would* understand Molière if they *could*. Your lordship's countenance to recommend it to such will infinitely oblige, my lord, your lordship's most devoted, and most obedient, humble servant, THE TRANSLATOR."

To recommend to Lord Chesterfield an author on account of "the purest moral," or because "no man has . . . in a finer manner exposed fopperies of all kinds," appears to us now a bitter piece of satire; it may however, be doubted if it seemed so to his contemporaries.[2]

Dryden has imitated *The Blunderer* in *Sir Martin Mar-all; or the Feigned Innocence*, first translated by William Cavendish, Duke of Newcastle, and afterwards adapted for the stage by "glorious John.' It must have been very successful, for it ran no less than thirty-three nights, and was four times acted at court. It was performed at Lincoln's Inn Fields by the Duke of York's servants, probably at the desire of the Duke of Newcastle, as Dryden was engaged to write for the King's Company. It seems to have been acted in 1667, and was published, without the author's name, in 1668. But it cannot be fairly called a translation, for Dryden has made several alterations, generally not for the better, and changed *double entendres* into single ones. The heroine in the English play, Mrs. Millisent, (Celia), marries the roguish servant, Warner (Mascarille), who takes all his master's blunders upon himself, is bribed by nearly everybody, pockets insults and money with the same equanimity, and when married, is at last proved a gentleman, by the disgusting Lord Dartmouth, who "cannot refuse to own him for my (his) kinsman." With a fine stroke of irony Millisent's father becomes reconciled to his daughter having married a serving-man as soon as he hears that the latter has an estate of eight hundred a year. Sir Martin Mar-all is far more conceited and foolish than Lelio; Trufaldin becomes Mr. Moody, a swashbuckler; a compound of Leander and Andrès, Sir John Swallow, a Kentish knight; whilst of the filthy characters of Lord Dartmouth, Lady Dupe, Mrs. Christian, and Mrs. Preparation, no counterparts are found in Molière's play. But the scene in which Warner plays the lute, whilst his master pretends to do so, and which is at last discovered by Sir Martin continuing to play after the servant has finished, is very clev-

[2] Lord Chesterfield appeared not so black to those who lived in his own time as he does to us, for Bishop Warburton dedicated to him his *Necessity and Equity of an Established Religion and a Test-Law Demonstrated*, and says in his preface: "It is an uncommon happiness when an honest man can congratulate a patriot on his becoming minister," and expresses the hope, that "the temper of the times will suffer your Lordship to be instrumental in saving your country by a reformation of the general manners."

er.[3] Dryden is also said to have consulted *l'Amant indiscret* of Quinault, in order to furbish forth the Duke of Newcastle's labours. Sir Walter Scott states in his introduction: "in that part of the play, which occasions its second title of 'the feigned Innocence,' the reader will hardly find wit enough to counterbalance the want of delicacy." Murphy has borrowed from *The Blunderer* some incidents of the second act of his *School for Guardians*, played for the first time in 1767.

[3] According to Geneste, *Some Accounts of the English Stage*, 10 vols., 1832, vol i., p. 76, Bishop Warburton, in his *Alliance of Church and State* (the same work is mentioned in Note 2), and Porson in his *Letters to Travis* alludes to this scene.

DRAMATIS PERSONÆ.[4]

LELIO, *son to* PANDOLPHUS.

LEANDER, *a young gentleman of good birth.*

ANSELMO, *an old man.*

PANDOLPHUS, *an old man.*

TRUFALDIN, *an old man.*

ANDRÈS, *a supposed gipsy.*

MASCARILLE,[5] *servaut to Lelio.*

ERGASTE, *a servant.*

A MESSENGER.

Two Troops of Masqueraders.

CELIA, *slave to* TRUFALDIN.

HIPPOLYTA, *daughter to* ANSELMO.

Scene.—MESSINA.

---

[4] Molière, Racine, and Corneille always call the dramatis personæ *acteurs*, and not *personnages.*

[5] *Mascarille* is a name invented by Molière, and a diminutive of the Spanish *mascara*, a mask. Some commentators of Molière think that the author, who acted this part, may sometimes have played it in a mask, but this is now generally contradicted. He seems, however, to have performed it habitually, for after his death there was taken an inventory of all his dresses, and amongst these, according to M. Eudore Soulié, *Recherches sur Molière*, 1863, p. 278, was: "a . . . dress for *l'Étourdi*, consisting in doublet, knee-breeches, and cloak of satin." Before his time the usual name of the intriguing man-servant was *Philipin.*

THE BLUNDERER: OR, THE COUNTERPLOTS.

(*L'ÉTOURDI, ou LES CONTRE-TEMPS.*)

ACT I.

SCENE I.—LELIO, *alone.*

LEL. Very well! Leander, very well! we must quarrel then,—we shall see which of us two will gain the day; and which, in our mutual pursuit after this young miracle of beauty, will thwart the most his rival's addresses. Do whatever you can, defend yourself well, for depend upon it, on my side no pains shall be spared.

SCENE II.—LELIO, MASCARILLE.

LEL. Ah! Mascarille!

MASC. What's the matter?

LEL. A great deal is the matter. Everything crosses my love. Leander is enamoured of Celia. The Fates have willed it, that though I have changed the object of my passion, he still remains my rival.

MASC. Leander enamoured of Celia!

LEL. He adores her, I tell you.[6]

MASC. So much the worse.

LEL. Yes, so much the worse, and that's what annoys me. However, I should be wrong to despair, for since you aid me, I ought to take courage. I know that your mind can plan many intrigues, and never finds anything

---

[6] In French, *tu, toi,* thee, thou, denote either social superiority or familiarity. The same phraseology was also employed in many English comedies of that time, but sounds so stiff at present, that the translator has everywhere used "you."

too difficult; that you should be called the prince of servants, and that throughout the whole world. . . .

MASC. A truce to these compliments; when people have need of us poor servants, we are darlings, and incomparable creatures; but at other times, at the least fit of anger, we are scoundrels, and ought to be soundly thrashed.

LEL. Nay, upon my word, you wrong me by this remark. But let us talk a little about the captive. Tell me, is there a heart so cruel, so unfeeling, as to be proof against such charming features? For my part, in her conversation as well as in her countenance, I see evidence of her noble birth. I believe that Heaven has concealed a lofty origin beneath such a lowly station.

MASC. You are very romantic with all your fancies. But what will Pandolphus do in this case? He is your father, at least he says so. You know very well that his bile is pretty often stirred up; that he can rage against you finely, when your behaviour offends him. He is now in treaty with Anselmo about your marriage with his daughter, Hippolyta; imagining that it is marriage alone that mayhap can steady you: now, should he discover that you reject his choice, and that you entertain a passion for a person nobody knows anything about; that the fatal power of this foolish love causes you to forget your duty and disobey him; Heaven knows what a storm will then burst forth, and what fine lectures you will be treated to.

LEL. A truce, I pray, to your rhetoric.

MASC. Rather a truce to your manner of loving, it is none of the best, and you ought to endeavour . . .

LEL. Don't you know, that nothing is gained by making me angry, that remonstrances are badly rewarded by me, and that a servant who counsels me acts against his own interest?

MASC. (*Aside*). He is in a passion now. (*Aloud*). All that I said was but in jest, and to try you. Do I look so very much like a censor, and is Mascarille an enemy to pleasure? You know the contrary, and that it is only too certain people can tax me with nothing but being too good-natured. Laugh at the preachings of an old greybeard of a father; go on, I tell you, and mind them not.

Upon my word, I am of opinion that these old, effete and grumpy libertines come to stupify us with their silly stories, and being virtuous, out of necessity, hope through sheer envy to deprive young people of all the pleasures of life! You know my talents; I am at your service.

LEL. Now, this is talking in a manner I like. Moreover, when I first declared my passion, it was not ill received by the lovely object who inspired it; but, just now, Leander has declared to me that he is preparing to deprive me of Celia; therefore let us make haste; ransack your brain for the speediest means to secure me possession of her; plan any tricks, stratagems, rogueries, inventions, to frustrate my rival's pretensions.

MASC. Let me think a little upon this matter. (*Aside*). What can I invent upon this urgent occasion?

LEL. Well, the stratagem?

MASC. What a hurry you are in! My brain must always move slowly. I have found what you want; you must . . . No, that's not it; but if you would go . . .

LEL. Whither?

MASC. No, that's a flimsy trick. I thought that . . .

LEL What is it?

MASC. That will not do either. But could you not . . ?

LEL. Could I not what?

MASC. No, you could not do anything. Speak to Anselmo.

LEL. And what can I say to him?

MASC. That is true; that would be falling out of the frying-pan into the fire. Something must be done however. Go to Trufaldin.

LEL. What to do?

MASC. I don't know.

LEL. Zounds! this is too much. You drive me mad with this idle talk.

MASC. Sir, if you could lay your hand on plenty of pistoles,[7] we should have no need now to think of and try to find out what means we must employ in compassing

---

[7] The pistole is a Spanish gold coin worth about four dollars; formerly the French pistole was worth in France ten *livres*—about ten francs—they were struck in Franche-Comté.

our wishes; we might, by purchasing this slave quickly, prevent your rival from forestalling and thwarting you. Trufaldin, who takes charge of her, is rather uneasy about these gipsies, who placed her with him. If he could get back his money, which they have made him wait for too long, I am quite sure he would be delighted to sell her; for he always lived like the veriest curmudgeon; he would allow himself to be whipped for the smallest coin of the realm. Money is the God he worships above everything, but the worst of it is that . . .

LEL. What is the worst of it? . . .

MASC. That your father is just as covetous an old hunk, who does not allow you to handle his ducats, as you would like; that there is no way by which we could now open ever so small a purse, in order to help you. But let us endeavour to speak to Celia for a moment, to know what she thinks about this affair; this is her window.

LEL. But Trufaldin watches her closely night and day; Take care.

MASC. Let us keep quiet in this corner. What luck! Here she is coming just in the nick of time.

SCENE III.—CELIA, LELIO, MASCARILLE.

LEL. Ah! madam, what obligations do I owe to Heaven for allowing me to behold those celestial charms you are blest with! Whatever sufferings your eyes may have caused me, I cannot but take delight in gazing on them in this place.

CEL. My heart, which has good reason to be astonished at your speech, does not wish my eyes to injure any one; if they have offended you in anything, I can assure you I did not intend it.

LEL. Oh! no, their glances are too pleasing to do me an injury. I count it my chief glory to cherish the wounds they give me; and . . .

MASC. You are soaring rather too high; this style is by no means what we want now; let us make better use of our time; let us know of her quickly what . . .

TRUF. (*Within*). Celia!

MASC. (*To Lelio*). Well, what do you think now?

LEL. O cruel mischance! What business has this wretched old man to interrupt us!

MASC. Go, withdraw, I'll find something to say to him.

SCENE IV.—TRUFALDIN, CELIA, MASCARILLE, *and* LELIO *in a corner.*

TRUF. (*To Celia*). What are you doing out of doors? And what induces you to go out,—you, whom I have forbidden to speak to any one?

CEL. I was formerly acquainted with this respectable young man; you have no occasion to be suspicious of him.

MASC. Is this Signor Trufaldin?

CEL. Yes, it is himself.

MASC. Sir, I am wholly yours; it gives me extreme pleasure to have this opportunity of paying my most humble respects to a gentleman who is everywhere so highly spoken of.

TRUF. Your most humble servant.

MASC. Perhaps I am troublesome, but I have been acquainted with this young woman elsewhere; and as I heard about the great skill she has in predicting the future, I wished to consult her about a certain affair.

TRUF. What! Do you dabble in the black art?

CEL. No, sir, my skill lies entirely in the white.[8]

MASC. The case is this. The master whom I serve languishes for a fair lady who has captivated him. He would gladly disclose the passion which burns within him to the beauteous object whom he adores, but a dragon that guards this rare treasure, in spite of all his attempts, has hitherto prevented him. And what torments him still more and makes him miserable, is that he has just discovered a formidable rival; so that I have come to consult you to know whether his love is likely to meet with any success, being well assured that from your mouth I may learn truly the secret which concerns us.

CEL. Under what planet was your master born?

MASC. Under that planet which never alters his love.

---

[8] The white art (*magie blanche*) only dealt with beneficent spirits, and wished to do good to mankind; the black art (*magie noire*) invoked evil spirits.

CEL. Without asking you to name the object he sighs for, the science which I possess gives me sufficient information. This young woman is high-spirited, and knows how to preserve a noble pride in the midst of adversity; she is not inclined to declare too freely the secret sentiments of her heart. But I know them as well as herself, and am going with a more composed mind to unfold them all to you, in a few words.

MASC. O wonderful power of magic virtue!

CEL. If your master is really constant in his affections, and if virtue alone prompts him, let him be under no apprehension of sighing in vain: he has reason to hope, the fortress he wishes to take is not averse to capitulation, but rather inclined to surrender.

MASC. That's something, but then the fortress depends upon a governor whom it is hard to gain over.

CEL. There lies the difficulty.

MASC. (*Aside, looking at Lelio*). The deuce take this troublesome fellow, who is always watching us.

CEL. I am going to teach you what you ought to do.

LEL. (*Joining them*). Mr. Trufaldin, give yourself no farther uneasiness; it was purely in obedience to my orders that this trusty servant came to visit you; I dispatched him to offer you my services, and to speak to you concerning this young lady, whose liberty I am willing to purchase before long, provided we two can agree about the terms.

MASC. (*Aside*). Plague take the ass!

TRUF. Ho! ho! Which of the two am I to believe? This story contradicts the former very much.

MASC. Sir, this gentleman is a little bit wrong in the upper story: did you not know it?

TRUF. I know what I know, and begin to smell a rat. Get you in (*to Celia*), and never take such a liberty again. As for you two, arrant rogues, or I am much mistaken, if you wish to deceive me again, let your stories be a little more in harmony.

SCENE V.—LELIO, MASCARILLE.

MASC. He is quite right. To speak plainly, I wish he

had given us both a sound cudgelling. What was the good of showing yourself, and, like a Blunderer, coming and giving the lie to all that I had been saying?

LEL. I thought I did right.

MASC. To be sure. But this action ought not to surprise me. You possess so many counterplots that your freaks no longer astonish anybody.

LEL. Good Heavens! How I am scolded for nothing! Is the harm so great that it cannot be remedied? However, if you cannot place Celia in my hands, you may at least contrive to frustrate all Leander's schemes, so that he cannot purchase this fair one before me. But lest my presence should be further mischievous, I leave you.

MASC. (*Alone*). Very well. To say the truth, money would be a sure and staunch agent in our cause; but as this mainspring is lacking, we must employ some other means.

SCENE VI.—ANSELMO, MASCARILLE.

ANS. Upon my word, this is a strange age we live in; I am ashamed of it; there was never such a fondness for money, and never so much difficulty in getting one's own. Notwithstanding all the care a person may take, debts now-a-days are like children, begot with pleasure, but brought forth with pain. It is pleasant for money to come into our purse; but when the time comes that we have to give it back, then the pangs of labour seize us. Enough of this, it is no trifle to receive at last two thousand francs which have been owing upwards of two years. What luck!

MASC. (*Aside*). Good Heavens! What fine game to shoot flying! Hist, let me see if I cannot wheedle him a little. I know with what speeches to soothe him. (*Joining him*). Anselmo I have just seen. . . .

ANS. Who, prithee?

MASC. Your Nerina.

ANS. What does the cruel fair one say about me?

MASC. Say? that she is passionately fond of you.

ANS. Is she?

MASC. She loves you so that I very much pity her.

ANS. How happy you make me!

MASC. The poor thing is nearly dying with love. "Oh, my dearest Anselmo," she cries every minute, 'when shall marriage unite our two hearts? When will you vouchsafe to extinguish my flames?"

ANS. But why has she hitherto concealed this from me? Girls, in troth, are great dissemblers! Mascarille, what do you say, really? Though in years, yet I look still well enough to please the eye.

MASC. Yes, truly, that face of yours is still very passable; if it is not of the handsomest in the world, it is very agreeable.[9]

ANS. So that . . . . .

MASC. (*Endeavouring to take the purse*). So that she dotes on you; and regards you no longer . . . . .

ANS. What?

MASC. But as a husband: and fully intends . . . .

ANS. And fully intends . . . . ?

MASC. And fully intends, whatever may happen, to steal your purse. . . . .

ANS. To steal . . . . ?

MASC. (*Taking the purse, and letting it fall to the ground*). To steal a kiss from your mouth.[10]

ANS. Ah! I understand you. Come hither! The next time you see her, be sure to say as many fine things of me as possible.

MASC. Let me alone.

ANS. Farewell.

MASC. May Heaven guide you!

ANS. (*Returning*). Hold! I really should have committed a strange piece of folly; and you might justly have accused me of neglect. I engage you to assist me in serving my passion. You bring good tidings, and I do not give you the smallest present to reward your zeal. Here, be sure to remember . . . . .

---

[9] The original has a play on words which cannot be translated, as, *ce visage est encore fort mettable. . . . s'il n'est pas des plus beaux, il est des agreables;* which two last words, according to pronunciation, can also mean disagreeable. This has been often imitated in French. After the Legion of Honour was instituted in France in 1804, some of the wits of the time asked the Imperialists: *etes-vous des honores?*

[10] There is here again, in the original, a play on the words *bourse,* purse, and *bouche,* mouth, which cannot be rendered in English.

MASC. O, pray, don't.[11]

ANS. Permit me . . . .

MASC. I won't, indeed: I do not act thus for the sake of money.

ANS. I know you do not. But however . . . .

MASC. No, Anselmo, I will not. I am a man of honour; this offends me.

ANS. Farewell then, Mascarille.

MASC. (*Aside*). How long-winded he is!

ANS. (*Coming back*). I wish you to carry a present to the fair object of my desires. I will give you some money to buy her a ring, or any other trifle, as you may think will please her most.

MASC. No, there is no need of your money; without troubling yourself, I will make her a present; a fashionable ring has been left in my hands, which you may pay for afterwards, if it fits her.

ANS. Be it so; give it her in my name; but above all, manage matters in such a manner that she may still desire to make me her own.

SCENE VII.—LELIO, ANSELMO, MASCARILLE.

LEL. (*Taking up the purse*). Whose purse is this? [12]

ANS. Oh Heavens! I dropt it, and might have afterwards believed somebody had picked my pocket. I am very much obliged to you for your kindness, which saves me a great deal of vexation, and restores me my money. I shall go home this minute and get rid of it.

SCENE VIII.—LELIO, MASCARILLE.

MASC. Od's death! You have been very obliging, very much so.

LEL. Upon my word! if it had not been for me he would have lost his money.

---

11 Compare in Shakspeare's *Winter's Tale* Autolycus' answer to Camillo (Act IV., Scene 3), who gives him money, "I am a poor fellow, sir, . . . I cannot with conscience take it."

12 During the whole of the preceding scene Mascarille has quietly kicked the purse away, so as to be out of sight of Anselmo, intending to pick it up when the latter has gone.

MASC. Certainly, you do wonders, and show to-day a most exquisite judgment and supreme good fortune. We shall prosper greatly; go on as you have begun.

LEL. What is the matter now? What have I done?

MASC. To speak plainly as you wish me to do, and as I ought, you have acted like a fool. You know very well that your father leaves you without money; that a formidable rival follows us closely; yet for all this, when to oblige you I venture on a trick of which I take all the shame and danger upon myself . . .

LEL. What? was this . . . ?

MASC. Yes, ninny; it was to release the captive that I was getting the money, whereof your officiousness took care to deprive us.

LEL. If that is the case, I am in the wrong. But who could have imagined it?

MASC. It really required a great deal of discernment.

LEL. You should have made some signs to warn me of what was going on.

MASC. Yes, indeed; I ought to have eyes in my back. By Jove,[13] be quiet, and let us hear no more of your nonsensical excuses. Another, after all this, would perhaps abandon everything; but I have planned just now a master-stroke, which I will immediately put into execution, on condition that if . . .

LEL. No, I promise you henceforth not to interfere either in word or deed.

MASC. Go away, then, the very sight of you kindles my wrath.

LEL. Above all, don't delay, for fear that in this business . . .

MASC. Once more, I tell you, begone! I will set about it. (*Exit Lelio*). Let us manage this well; it will be a most exquisite piece of roguery; if it succeeds, as I think it must. We'll try. . . . But here comes the very man I want.

---

[13] The play is supposed to be in Sicily; hence Pagan oaths are not out of place. Even at the present time Italians say, *per Jove! per Bacco!*

SCENE IX.—PANDOLPHUS, MASCARILLE.

PAND. Mascarille!

MASC. Sir?

PAND. To tell you the truth, I am very dissatisfied with my son.

MASC. With my master? You are not the only one who complains of him. His bad conduct which has grown unbearable in everything, puts me each moment out of patience.

PAND. I thought, however, you and he understood one another pretty well.

MASC. I? Believe it not, sir. I am always trying to put him in mind of his duty: we are perpetually at daggers drawn. Just now we had a quarrel again about his engagement with Hippolyta, which, I find he is very averse to. By a most disgraceful refusal he violates all the respect due to a father.

PAND. A quarrel?

MASC. Yes, a quarrel, and a desperate one too.

PAND. I was very much deceived then, for I thought you supported him in all he did.

MASC. I? See what this world is come to! How is innocence always oppressed! If you knew but my integrity, you would give me the additional salary of a tutor, whereas I am only paid as his servant. Yes, you yourself could not say more to him than I do in order to make him behave better. "For goodness' sake, sir," I say to him very often, "cease to be driven hither and thither with every wind that blows,—reform; look what a worthy father Heaven has given you, what a reputation he has. Forbear to stab him thus to the heart, and live, as he does, as a man of honour."

PAND. That was well said; and what answer could he make to this?

MASC. Answer? Why only nonsense, with which he almost drives me mad. Not but that at the bottom of his heart he retains those principles of honour which he derives from you; but reason, at present, does not sway him. If I might be allowed to speak freely, you should soon see him submissive without much trouble.

PAND. Speak out.

MASC. It is a secret which would have serious consequences for me, should it be discovered; but I am quite sure I can confide it to your prudence

PAND. You are right.

MASC. Know then that your wishes are sacrificed to the love your son has for a certain slave.

PAND. I have been told so before; but to hear it from your mouth pleases me.

MASC. I leave you to judge whether I am his secret confidant . . .

PAND. I am truly glad of it.

MASC. However, do you wish to bring him back to his duty, without any public scandal? You must . . . (I am in perpetual fear lest anybody should surprise us. Should he learn what I have told you, I should be a dead man.) You must, as I was saying, to break off this business, secretly purchase this slave, whom he so much idolizes, and send her into another country. Anselmo is very intimate with Trufaldin; let him go and buy her for you this very morning. Then, if you put her into my hands, I know some merchants, and promise you to sell her for the money she costs you, and to send her out of the way in spite of your son. For, if you would have him disposed for matrimony, we must divert this growing passion. Moreover, even if he were resolved to wear the yoke you design for him, yet this other girl might revive his foolish fancy, and prejudice him anew against matrimony.

PAND. Very well argued. I like this advice much. Here comes Anselmo; go, I will do my utmost quickly to obtain possession of this troublesome slave, when I will put her into your hands to finish the rest.

MASC. (*Alone*). Bravo, I will go and tell my master of this. Long live all knavery, and knaves also!

SCENE X.—HIPPOLYTA, MASCARILLE.

HIPP. Ay, traitor, is it thus that you serve me? I overheard all, and have myself been a witness of your treachery. Had I not, could I have suspected this? You are an arrant rogue, and you have deceived me. You promised me, you miscreant, and I expected, that you would assist me in my passion for Leander, that your skill and your management should find means to break off my match with Lelio ; that you would free me from my father's project ; and yet you are doing quite the contrary. But you will find yourself mistaken. I know a sure method of breaking off the purchase you have been urging Pandolphus to make, and I will go immediately . . . .

MASC. How impetuous you are ! You fly into a passion in a moment ; without inquiring whether you are right or wrong, you fall foul of me. I am in the wrong, and I ought to make your words true, without finishing what I began, since you abuse me so outrageously.

HIPP. By what illusion do you think to dazzle my eyes, traitor ? Can you deny what I have just now heard ?

MASC. No ; but you must know that all this plotting was only contrived to serve you ; that this cunning advice, which appeared so sincere, tends to make both old men fall into the snare ; that all the pains I have taken for getting Celia into my hands, through their means, was to secure her for Lelio, and to arrange matters so that Anselmo, in the very height of passion, and finding himself disappointed of his son-in-law, might make choice of Leander.

HIPP. What ! This admirable scheme, which has angered me so much, was all for my sake, Mascarille ?

MASC. Yes, for your sake ; but since I find my good offices meet with so bad a return,—since I have thus to bear your caprices, and as a reward for my services, you come here with a haughty air, and call me knave, cur, and cheat, I shall presently go, correct the mistake I have committed, and undo what I had undertaken to perform.

HIPP. (*Holding him.*) Nay, do not be so severe upon me, and forgive these outbursts of a sudden passion.

MASC. No, no ; let me go. I have it yet in my power to set aside the scheme which offends you so much. Henceforth you shall have no occasion to complain of my zeal. Yes, you shall have my master, I promise you.

HIPP. My good Mascarille, be not in such a passion. I judged you ill ; I was wrong ; I confess I was. (*Pulls out her purse*). But I intend to atone for my fault with this. Could you find it in your heart to abandon me thus?

MASC. No, I cannot, do what I will. But your impetuosity was very shocking. Let me tell you that nothing offends a noble mind so much as the smallest imputation upon its honour.

HIPP. It is true; I treated you to some very harsh language, but here are two louis to heal your wounds.

MASC. Oh! all this is nothing. I am very sensitive on this point; but my passion begins to cool a little already. We must bear with the failings of our friends.

HIPP. Can you, then, bring about what I so earnestly wish for? Do you believe your daring projects will be as favourable to my passion as you imagine?

MASC. Do not make yourself uneasy on that account. I have several irons in the fire, and though this stratagem should fail us, what this cannot do, another shall.

HIPP. Depend upon it, Hippolyta will at least not be ungrateful

MASC. It is not the hope of gain that makes me act.

HIPP. Your master beckons and wishes to speak with you. I will leave you, but remember to do what you can for me.

SCENE XI.—LELIO, MASCARILLE.

LEL. What the deuce are you doing there? You promised to perform wonders, but I am sure your dilatory ways are unparalleled. Had not my good genius inspired me, my happiness had been already wholly overthrown. There was an end to my good fortune, my joy. I should have been a prey to eternal grief; in short, had I not gone to this place in the very nick of time, Anselmo would have got possession of the captive, and I should have been deprived of her. He was carrying her home, but I parried the thrust, warded off the blow, and so worked upon Trufaldin's fears as to make him keep the girl.

MASC. This is the third time! When we come to ten we will score. It was by my contrivance, incorrigible scatterbrains, that Anselmo undertook this desirable purchase; she should have been placed into my own hands, but your cursed officiousness knocks everything on the head again. Do you think I shall still labour to serve your love? I would sooner a hundred times become a fat old woman, a dolt, a cabbage, a lantern, a wehrwolf, and that Satan should twist your neck!

LEL. (*Alone.*) I must take him to some tavern and let him vent his passion on the bottles and glasses.

ACT II.

SCENE I.—LELIO, MASCARILLE.

MASC. I have at length yielded to your desires. In spite of all my protestations I could hold out no longer; I am going to venture upon new dangers, to promote your interest, which I intended to abandon. So tender-hearted am I! If dame nature had made a girl of Mascarille, I leave you to guess what would have happened. However, after this assurance, do not deal a back stroke to the project I am about to undertake; do not make a blunder and frustrate my expectations. Then, as to Anselmo, we shall anew present your excuses to him, in order to get what we desire. But should your imprudence burst forth again hereafter, then you may bid farewell to all the trouble I take for the object of your passion.

LEL. No, I shall be careful, I tell you; never fear; you shall see. . . .

MASC. Well, mind that you keep your word. I have planned a bold stratagem for your sake. Your father is very backward in satisfying all your wishes by his death. I have just killed him (in words, I mean); I have spread a report that the good man, being suddenly smitten by a fit of apoplexy, has departed this life. But first, so that I might the better pretend he was dead, I so managed that he went to his barn. I had a person ready to come and tell him that the workmen employed on his house accidentally discovered a treasure, in digging the foundations. He set out in an instant, and as all his people, except us two, have gone with him into the country, I shall kill him to-day in everybody's imagination and produce some image which I shall bury under his name. I have already told you what I wish you to do; play your part well; and as to the character I have to keep up, if you perceive that I miss one word of it, tell me plainly I am nothing but a fool.

SCENE II.—LELIO, *alone.*

It is true, he has found out a strange way to accomplish my wishes fully; but when we are very much in love with a fair lady, what would we not do to be made happy? If love is said to be an excuse for a crime, it may well serve for a slight piece of imposture, which love's ardour to-day compels me to comply with, in expectation of the happy consequences that may result from it. Bless me! How expeditious they are. I see them already talking together about it; let us prepare to act our part.

SCENE III.—MASCARILLE, ANSELMO.

MASC. The news may well surprise you.

ANS. To die in such a manner!

MASC. He was certainly much to blame. I can never forgive him for such a freak.

ANS. Not even to take time to be ill.

MASC. No, never was a man in such a hurry to die.

ANS. And how does Lelio behave?

MASC. He raves, and has lost all command over his temper; he has beaten himself till he is black and blue in several places, and wishes to follow his father into the grave. In short, to make an end of this, the excess of his grief has made me with the utmost speed wrap the corpse in a shroud, for fear the sight, which fed his melancholy, should tempt him to commit some rash act.

ANS. No matter, you ought to have waited until evening. Besides, I should have liked to see Pandolphus once more. He who puts a shroud on a man too hastily very often commits murder; for a man is frequently thought dead when he only seems to be so.

MASC. I warrant him as dead as dead can be. But now, to return to what we were talking about, Lelio has resolved (and it will do him good) to give his father a fine funeral, and to comfort the deceased a little for his hard fate, by the pleasure of seeing that we pay him such honours after his death. My master inherits a goodly estate, but as he is only a novice in business, and does not see his way clearly in his affairs, since the greater part of his property lies in another part of the country, or what he has here consists in paper, he would beg of you, after having entreated you to excuse the too great violence which he has shewn of late, to lend him for this last duty at least. . . .

ANS. You have told me so already, and I will go and see him.

MASC. (*Alone*). Hitherto, at least, everything goes on swimmingly; let us endeavour to make the rest answer as well; and lest we should be wrecked in the very harbour, let us steer the ship carefully and keep a sharp look out.

SCENE IV.—ANSELMO, LELIO, MASCARILLE.

ANS. (*Coming out of Pandolphus' house*). Let us leave the house. I cannot, without great sorrow, see him wrapped up in this strange manner. Alas! in so short a time! He was alive this morning.

MASC. We go sometimes over a good deal of ground in a short time.

LEL. (*Weeping*). Oh!

ANS. Dear Lelio, he was but a man after all; even Rome can grant no dispensation from death.

LEL. Oh!

ANS. Death smites men without giving warning, and always has bad designs against them.

LEL. Oh!

ANS. That merciless foe would not loosen one grip of his murderous teeth, however we may entreat him. Everybody must feel them.

LEL. Oh!

MASC. Your preaching will all be in vain; this sorrow is too deep-rooted to be plucked up.

ANS. If, notwithstanding all these arguments, you will not cast aside your grief, at least, my dear Lelio, endeavour to moderate it.

LEL. Oh!

MASC. He will not moderate it; I know his temper.

ANS. However, according to your servant's message, I have brought you the money you want, so that you might celebrate your father's funeral obsequies!

LEL. Oh! oh!

MASC. How his grief increases at these words! It will kill him to think of his misfortune.

ANS. I know you will find by the good man's books that I owe him a much larger sum, but even if I should not owe anything, you could freely command my purse. Here it is; I am entirely at your service, and will show it.

LEL. (*Going away*). Oh!

MASC. How full of grief is my master!

ANS. Mascarille, I think it right he should give me some kind of receipt under his hand.

MASC. Oh!

ANS. Nothing in this world is certain.

MASC. Oh! oh!

ANS. Get him to sign me the receipt I require.

MASC. Alas! How can he comply with your desire in the condition he now is? Give him but time to get rid of his sorrow; and, when his troubles abate a little, I shall take care immediately to get you your security. Your servant, sir, my heart is over full of grief, and I shall go to take my fill of weeping with him. Hi! Hi!

ANS. (*Alone*). This world is full of crosses; we meet with them every day in different shapes, and never here below . . .

SCENE V.—PANDOLPHUS, ANSELMO.

ANS. Oh Heavens! how I tremble! It is Pandolphus who has returned to the earth! God grant nothing disturbed his repose! How wan his face is grown since his death! Do not come any nearer, I beseech you; I very much detest to jostle a ghost.

PAND. What can be the reason of this whimsical terror?

ANS. Keep your distance, and tell me what business brings you here. If you have taken all this trouble to bid me farewell, you do me too much honour; I could really have done very well without your compliment. If your soul is restless, and stands in need of prayers. I promise you you shall have them, but do not frighten me. Upon the word of a terrified man, I will immediately set prayers agoing for you, to your very heart's content.

"Oh, dead worship, please to go!
Heaven, if now you disappear,
Will grant you joy down there below,
And health as well, for many a year."[14]

PAND. (*Laughing*). In spite of my indignation, I cannot help laughing.

ANS. It is strange, but you are very merry for a dead man.

PAND. Is this a joke, pray tell me, or is it downright madness to treat a living man as if he were dead?

ANS. Alas! you must be dead; I myself just now saw you.

PAND. What? Could I die without knowing it?

ANS. As soon as Mascarille told me the news, I was ready to die of grief.

PAND. But, really, are you asleep or awake? Don't you know me?

ANS. You are clothed in an aerial body which imitates your own, but which may take another shape at any moment. I am mightily afraid to see you swell up to the size of a giant, and your countenance become frightfully distorted. For the love of God, do not assume any hideous form; you have scared me sufficiently for the nonce.

PAND. At any other time, Anselmo, I should have considered the simplicity which accompanies your credulity an excellent joke, and I should have carried on the pleasant conceit a little longer; but this story of my death, and the news of the supposed treasure, which I was told upon the road had not been found at all, raises in my mind a strong suspicion that Mascarille is a rogue, and an arrant rogue, who is proof against fear or remorse, and who invents extraordinary stratagems to compass his ends.

ANS. What! Am I tricked and made a fool of? Really, this would be a compliment to my good sense! Let me touch him and be satisfied. This is, indeed, the very man. What an ass I am! Pray, do not spread this story about, for they will write a farce about it, and shame me

---

[14] This seems to be an imitation of a spell, charm, or incantation to lay the supposed ghost, which Anselmo says kneeling and hardly able to speak for terror.

for ever. But, Pandolphus, help me to get the money back which I lent them to bury you.

PAND. Money, do you say? Oh! that is where the shoe pinches; that is the secret of the whole affair! So much the worse for you. For my part, I shall not trouble myself about it, but will go and lay an information against this Mascarille, and if he can be caught he shall be hanged, whatever the cost may be.

ANS. (*Alone*). And I, like a ninny, believe a scoundrel, and must in one day lose both my senses and my money. Upon my word, it well becomes me to have these gray hairs and to commit an act of folly so readily, without examining into the truth of the first story I hear . . . ! But I see . . . .

SCENE VI.—LELIO, ANSELMO.

LEL. Now, with this master-key, I can easily pay Trufaldin a visit.

ANS. As far as I can see, your grief has subsided.

LEL. What do you say? No; it can never leave a heart which shall ever cherish it dearly.

ANS. I came back to tell you frankly of a mistake I made in the money I gave you just now; amongst these louis-d'or, though they look very good, I carelessly put some which I think are bad. I have brought some money with me to change them. The intolerable audacity of our coiners is grown to such a height in this state, that no one can receive any money now without danger of his being imposed upon. It would be doing good service to hang them all!

LEL. I am very much obliged to you for being willing to take them back, but I saw none among them that were bad, as I thought.

ANS. Let me see the money; let me see it; I shall know them again. Is this all?

LEL. Yes.

ANS. So much the better. Are you back again? my dear money! get into my pocket. As for you, my gallant sharper, you have no longer got a penny of it. You kill people who are in good health, do ye? And what would you have done, then, with me, a poor infirm father-in-law?

Upon my word, I was going to get a nice addition to my family, a most discreet son-in-law. Go, go, and hang yourself for shame and vexation.

LEL. (*Alone*). I really must admit I have been bit this time. What a surprise this is! How can he have discovered our stratagem so soon?

SCENE VII.—LELIO, MASCARILLE.

MASC. What, you were out? I have been hunting for you everywhere. Well, have we succeeded at last? I will give the greatest rogue six trials to do the like. Come, give me the money that I may go and buy the slave; your rival will be very much astonished at this.

LEL. Ah! my dear boy, our luck has changed. Can you imagine how ill fortune has served me?

MASC. What? What can it be?

LEL. Anselmo having found out the trick, just now got back every sou he lent us, pretending some of the gold-pieces were bad, and that he was going to change them.

MASC. You do but joke, I suppose?

LEL. It is but too true.

MASC. In good earnest?

LEL. In good earnest; I am very much grieved about it. It will put you into a furious passion.

MASC. Me, sir! A fool might, but not I! Anger hurts, and I am going to take care of myself, come what will. After all, whether Celia be captive or free, whether Leander purchases her or whether she remains where she is, I do not care one stiver about it.

LEL. Ah! do not show such indifference, but be a little more indulgent to my slight imprudence. Had this last misfortune not happened, you would have confessed that I did wonders, and that in this pretended decease I deceived everybody, and counterfeited grief so admirably that the most sharp-sighted would have been taken in.

MASC. Truly you have great reason to boast.

LEL. Oh! I am to blame, and I am willing to acknowledge it; but if ever you cared for my happiness, repair this mishap, and help me.

MASC. I kiss your hands, I cannot spare the time.

LEL. Mascarille, my dear boy!

MASC. No.

LEL. Do me this favour.

MASC. No, I will not.

LEL. If you are inflexible, I shall kill myself

MASC. Do so—you may.

LEL. Can I not soften your hard heart?

MASC. No.

LEL. Do you see my sword ready drawn?

MASC. Yes.

LEL. I am going to stab myself.

MASC. Do just what you please.

LEL. Would you not regret to be the cause of my death?

MASC. No.

LEL. Farewell, Mascarille.

MASC. Good bye, Master Lelio.

LEL. What . . . ?

MASC. Kill yourself quick. You are a long while about it.

LEL. Upon my word, you would like me to play the fool and kill myself, so that you might get hold of my clothes.

MASC. I knew all this was nothing but a sham; whatever people may swear they will do, they are not so hasty now-a-days in killing themselves.

SCENE VIII.—TRUFALDIN, LEANDER, LELIO, MASCARILLE.

(*Trufaldin taking Leander aside and whispering to him*).

LEL. What do I see? my rival and Trufaldin together! He is going to buy Celia. Oh! I tremble for fear.

MASC. There is no doubt that he will do all he can; and if he has money, he can do all he will. For my part I am delighted. This is a just reward for your blunders, your impatience.

LEL. What must I do? Advise me.

MASC. I don't know.

LEL. Stay, I will go and pick a quarrel with him.

MASC. What good will that do?

LEL. What would you have me do to ward off this blow?

MASC. Well, I pardon you; I will yet cast an eye of

pity on you. Leave me to watch them; I believe I shall discover what he intends to do by fairer means. (*Exit Lelio*).

TRUF. (*To Leander*). When you send by and by, it shall be done.

MASC. (*Aside and going out*). I must trap him and become his confidant, in order to baffle his designs the more easily.

LEAND. (*Alone*). Thanks to Heaven, my happiness is complete. I have found the way to secure it, and fear nothing more. Whatever my rival may henceforth attempt, it is no longer in his power to do me any harm.

SCENE IX.—LEANDER, MASCARILLE.

MASC. (*Speaking these words within, and then coming on the stage*). Oh! oh! Help! Murder! Help! They are killing me! Oh! oh! oh! oh! Traitor! Barbarian!

LEAND. Whence comes that noise? What is the matter? What are they doing to you?

MASC. He has just given me two hundred blows with a cudgel.

LEAND. Who?

MASC. Lelio.

LEAND. And for what reason?

MASC. For a mere trifle he has turned me away and beats me most unmercifully.

LEAND. He is really much to blame.

MASC. But, I swear, if ever it lies in my power I will be revenged on him. I will let you know, Mr. Thrasher, with a vengeance, that people's bones are not to be broken for nothing! Though I am but a servant, yet I am a man of honour. After having been in your service for four years you shall not pay me with a switch, nor affront me in so sensible a part as my shoulders! I tell you once more, I shall find a way to be revenged! You are in love with a certain slave, you would fain induce me to get her for you, but I will manage matters so that somebody else shall carry her off; the deuce take me if I don't!

LEAND. Hear me, Mascarille, and moderate your passion. I always liked you, and often wished that a young fellow, faithful and clever like you, might one day or other take a fancy to enter my service. In a word, if you think my offer worthy of acceptance, and if you have a mind to serve me, from this moment I engage you.

MASC. With all my heart, sir, and so much the rather because good fortune in serving you offers me an opportunity of being revenged, and because in my endeavours to please you I shall at the same time punish that wretch. In a word, by my dexterity, I hope to get Celia for . . .

LEAND. My love has provided already for that. Smitten by a faultless fair one, I have just now bought her for less than her value.

MASC. What! Celia belongs to you, then?

LEAND. You should see her this minute, if I were the master of my own actions. But alas! it is my father who is so; since he is resolved, as I understand by a letter brought me, to make me marry Hippolyta. I would not have this affair come to his knowledge lest it should exasperate him. Therefore in my arrangement with Trufaldin (from whom I just now parted), I acted purposely in the name of another. When the affair was settled, my ring was chosen as the token, on the sight of which Trufaldin is to deliver Celia. But I must first arrange the ways and means to conceal from the eyes of others the girl who so much charms my own, and then find some retired place where this lovely captive may be secreted.

MASC. A little way out of town lives an old relative of mine, whose house I can take the freedom to offer you; there you may safely lodge her, and not a creature know anything of the matter.

LEAND. Indeed! so I can: you have delighted me with the very thing I wanted. Here, take this, and go and get possession of the fair one. As soon as ever Trufaldin sees my ring, my girl will be immediately delivered into your hands. You can then take her to that house, when . . . But hist! here comes Hippolyta.

SCENE X.—HIPPOLYTA, LEANDER, MASCARILLE.

HIPP. I have some news for you, Leander, but will you be pleased or displeased with it?

LEAND. To judge of that, and make answer off-hand, I should know it.

HIPP. Give me your hand, then, as far as the church,[15] and I will tell it you as we go.

LEAND. (*To Mascarille*). Go, make haste, and serve me in that business without delay.

SCENE XI.—MASCARILLE, *alone*.

Yes, I will serve you up a dish of my own dressing. Was there ever in the world so lucky a fellow. How delighted Lelio will be soon! His mistress to fall into our hands by these means! To derive his whole happiness from the man he would have expected to ruin him! To become happy by the hands of a rival! After this great exploit, I desire that due preparations be made to paint me as a hero crowned with laurel, and that underneath the portrait be inscribed in letters of gold: *Vivat Mascarillus, rogum imperator.*

SCENE XII.—TRUFALDIN, MASCARILLE.

MASC. Soho, there!

TRUF. What do you want?

MASC. This ring, which you know, will inform you what business brings me hither.

TRUF. Yes, I recognise that ring perfectly; stay a little, I will fetch you the slave.

SCENE XIII.—TRUFALDIN, A MESSENGER, MASCARILLE.

MESS. (*To Trufaldin*). Do me the favor, sir, to tell me where lives a gentleman . . . .

TRUF. What gentleman?

MESS. I think his name is Trufaldin.

TRUF. And what is your business with him, pray? I am he.

MESS. Only to deliver this letter to him.

TRUF. (*Reads*). "*Providence, whose goodness watches over my life, has just brought to my ears a most welcome report, that my daughter, who was stolen from me by some robbers when she was four years old, is now a slave at your*

---

15 Generally it was thought preferable, during Molière's lifetime, to use the word *temple* for "church," instead of *église*.

house, under the name of Celia. If ever you knew what it was to be a father, and if natural affection makes an impression on your heart, then keep in your house this child so dear to me, and treat her as if she were your own flesh and blood. I am preparing to set out myself in order to fetch her. You shall be so well rewarded for your trouble, that in everything that relates to your happiness (which I am determined to advance) you shall have reason to bless the day in which you caused mine."

DON PEDRO DE GUSMAN,
From Madrid. Marquess of MONTALCANA.

Though the gipsies can be seldom believed, yet they who sold her to me told me she would soon be fetched by somebody, and that I should have no reason to complain. Yet here I was going, all through my impatience, to lose the fruits of a great expectation. (*To the Messenger*). Had you come but one moment later, your journey would have been in vain; I was going, this very instant, to give the girl up into this gentleman's hands; but it is well, I shall take great care of her. (*Exit Messenger*). (*To Mascarille*). You yourself have heard what this letter says, so you may tell the person who sent you that I cannot keep my word, and that he had better come and receive his money back.

MASC But the way you insult him . . .

TRUF. Go about your business, and no more words.

MASC. (*Alone*). Oh, what a curse that this letter came now! Fate is indeed against me. What bad luck for this messenger to come from Spain when he was not wanted! May thunder and hail go with him! Never, certainly, had so happy a beginning such a sad ending in so short a time.

SCENE XIV.—LELIO *laughing*, MASCARILLE.

MASC. What may be the cause of all this mirth?

LEL. Let me have my laugh out before I tell you.

MASC. Let us laugh then heartily, we have abundant cause so to do.

LEL. Oh! I shall no longer be the object of your expostulations: you who always reproach me shall no longer say that I am marrying all your schemes, like a busy-body as I am. I myself have played one of the cleverest tricks in the world. It is true I am quick-tempered, and now and then rather too hasty; but yet, when I have a mind to it, I can plan as many tricks as any man alive; even you shall own that what I have done shows an amount of sharpness rarely to be met with.

MASC. Let us hear what tricks you have invented.

LEL. Just now, being terribly frightened on seeing Trufaldin along with my rival, I was casting about to find a remedy for that mischief, when, calling all my invention to my aid, I conceived, digested, and perfected a stratagem, before which all yours, however vain you may be of them, ought undoubtedly to lower their colours.

MASC. But what may this be?

LEL. May it please you to have a little patience. Without much delay I invented a letter, written by an imaginary nobleman to Trufaldin, setting forth that, having fortunately heard that a certain slave, who lives in the latter's house, and is named Celia, was this grandee's daughter formerly kidnapped by thieves, it was his intention to come and fetch her; and he entreats him at least to keep her and take great care of her; for, that on her account he was setting out from Spain, and would acknowledge his civility by such handsome presents, that he should never regret being the means of making him happy.

MASC. Mighty well.

LEL. Hear me out; here is something much cleverer still. The letter I speak of was delivered to him, but can you imagine how? Only just in time, for the messenger told me, had it not been for this droll device, a fellow, who looked very foolish, was waiting to carry her off that identical moment.

MASC. And you did all this without the help of the devil?

LEL. Yes. Would you have believed me capable of such a subtle piece of wit? At least praise my skill, and the dexterity with which I have utterly disconcerted the scheme of my rival.

MASC. To praise you as you deserve, I lack eloquence; and feel unequal to the task. Yes, sufficiently to commend this lofty effort, this fine stratagem of war achieved before our eyes, this grand and rare effect of a mind which plans as many tricks as any man, which for smartness yields to none alive, my tongue wants words. I wish I had the abilities of the most refined scholars, so that I might tell you in the noblest verse, or else in learned prose, that you will always be, in spite of everything that may be done, the very same you have been all your life; that is to say, a scatter-brain, a man of distempered reason, always perplexed, wanting common sense, a man of left-handed judgment, a meddler, an ass, a blundering, hare-brained, giddy fellow,—what can I think of? A . . . a hundred times worse than anything I can say. This is only an abridgement of your panegyric.

LEL. Tell me, what puts you in such a passion with me? Have I done anything? Clear up this matter.

MASC. No, you have done nothing at all; but do not come after me.

LEL. I will follow you all over the world to find out this mystery.

MASC. Do so. Come on, then; get your legs in order, I shall give you an opportunity to exercise them.

LEL. (*Alone*). He has got away from me! O misfortune which cannot be allayed! What am I to understand by his discourse? And what harm can I possibly have done to myself?

ACT III.

SCENE I.—MASCARILLE, *alone*.[16]

Silence, my good nature, and plead no more; you are a fool, and I am determined not to do it. Yes, my anger, you are right, I confess it! To be for ever doing what a meddler undoes, is showing too much patience, and I ought to give it up after the glorious attempts he has marred. But let us argue the matter a little without passion; if I should now give way to my just impatience the world will say I sank under difficulties, that my cunning was completely exhausted. What then becomes of that public esteem,

---

[16] Compare Launcelot Gobbo's speech about his conscience in Shakspeare's *Merchant of Venice* (ii. 2).

which extols you everywhere as a first-rate rogue, and which you have acquired upon so many occasions, because you never yet were found wanting in inventions? Honour, Mascarille, is a fine thing; do not pause in your noble labours; and whatever a master may have done to incense you, complete your work, for your own glory, and not to oblige him. But what success can you expect, if you are thus continually crossed by your evil genius? You see he compels you every moment to change your tone; you may as well hold water in a sieve as try to stop that resistless torrent, which in a moment overturns the most beautiful structures raised by your art. Well, once more, out of kindness, and whatever may happen, let us take some pains, even if they are in vain; yet, if he still persists in baffling my designs, then I shall withdraw all assistance. After all, our affairs are not going on badly, if we could but supplant our rival, and if Leander, at last weary of his pursuit, would leave us one whole day for my intended operations. Yes, I have a most ingenious plot in my head, from which I expect a glorious success, if I had no longer that obstacle in my way. Well, let us see if he still persists in his love.

SCENE II.—LEANDER, MASCARILLE.

MASC. Sir, I have lost my labour; Trufaldin will not keep his word.

LEAND. He himself has told me the whole affair; but, what is more, I have discovered that all this pretty rigmarole about Celia being carried off by gypsies, and having a great nobleman for her father, who is setting out from Spain to come hither, is nothing but a mere stratagem, a merry trick, a made-up story, a tale raised by Lelio to prevent my buying Celia.

MASC. Here is roguery for you!

LEAND. And yet this ridiculous story has produced such an impression on Trufaldin, and he has swallowed the bait of this shallow device so greedily, that he will not allow himself to be undeceived.

MASC. So that henceforth he will watch her carefully. I do not see we can do anything more.

LEAND. If at first I thought this girl amiable, I now find her absolutely adorable, and I am in doubt whether I ought not to employ extreme measures to make her my own, thwart her ill fortune by plighting her my troth, and turn her present chains into matrimonial ones.

MASC. Would you marry her?

LEAND. I am not yet determined, but if her origin is somewhat obscure, her charms and her virtue are gentle attractions, which have incredible force to allure every heart.

MASC. Did you not mention her virtue?

LEAND. Ha! what is that you mutter? Out with it; explain what you mean by repeating that word "virtue."

MASC. Sir, your countenance changes all of a sudden; perhaps I had much better hold my tongue.

LEAND. No, no, speak out.

MASC. Well, then, out of charity I will cure you of your blindness. That girl. . . .

LEAND. Proceed.

MASC. So far from being merciless, makes no difficulty in obliging some people in private; you may believe me, after all she is not stony-hearted, to any one who knows how to take her in the right mood. She looks demure, and would fain pass for a prude; but I can speak of her on sure grounds. You know I understand something of the craft, and ought to know that kind of cattle.

LEAND. What! Celia? . . .

MASC. Yes, her modesty is nothing but a mere sham, the semblance of a virtue which will never hold out, but vanishes, as any one may discover, before the shining rays[17] emitted from a purse.

LEAND. Heavens! What do you tell me? Can I believe such words?

MASC. Sir, there is no compulsion; what does it matter to me? No, pray do not believe me, follow your own inclination, take the sly girl and marry her; the whole city, in a body, will acknowledge this favour; you marry the public good in her.

LEAND. What a strange surprise!

---

[17] This is an allusion to the rays of the sun, placed above the crown, and stamped on all golden crown-pieces, struck in France from Louis XI. (November 2, 1475) until the end of the reign of Louis XIII. These crowns were called *écus au soleil.* Louis XIV. took much later for his device the sun shining in full, with the motto, *Nec pluribus impar.*

MASC. (*Aside*). He has taken the bait. Courage, my lad; if he does but swallow it in good earnest, we shall have got rid of a very awkward obstruction on our path.

LEAND. This astonishing account nearly kills me.

MASC. What! Can you . . .

LEAND. Go to the post-office, and see if there is a letter for me. (*Alone, and for a while lost in thought*). Who would not have been imposed upon? If what he says be true, then there never was any countenance more deceiving.

SCENE III.—LELIO, LEANDER.

LEL. What may be the cause of your looking so sad?

LEAND. Who, I?

LEL. Yes, yourself.

LEAND. I have, however, no occasion to be so.

LEL. I see well enough what it is; Celia is the cause of it.

LEAND My mind does not run upon such trifles.

LEL. And yet you had formed some grand scheme to get her into your hands; but you must speak thus, as your stratagem has miscarried.

LEAND. Were I fool enough to be enamoured of her, I should laugh at all your finesse.

LEL. What finesse, pray?

LEAND. Good Heavens! sir, we know all.

LEL. All what?

LEAND. All your actions, from beginning to end.

LEL. This is all Greek to me; I do not understand one word of it.

LEAND. Pretend, if you please, not to understand me; but believe me, do not apprehend that I shall take a property which I should be sorry to dispute with you. I adore a beauty who has not been sullied, and do not wish to love a depraved woman.

LEL. Gently, gently, Leander.

LEAND. Oh! how credulous you are! I tell you once more, you may attend on her now without suspecting anybody. You may call yourself a lady-killer. It is true, her beauty is very uncommon, but, to make amends for that, the rest is common enough.

LEL. Leander, no more of this provoking language. Strive against me as much as you like in order to obtain her; but, above all things, do not traduce her so vilely. I should consider myself a great coward if I could tamely submit to hear my earthly deity slandered. I can much better bear your rivalry than listen to any speech that touches her character.

LEAND. What I state here I have from very good authority.

LEL. Whoever told you so is a scoundrel and a rascal. Nobody can discover the least blemish in this young lady; I know her heart well.

LEAND. But yet Mascarille is a very competent judge in such a cause; he thinks her guilty.

LEL. He?

LEAND. He himself.

LEL. Does he pretend impudently to slander a most respectable young lady, thinking, perhaps, I should only laugh at it? I will lay you a wager he eats his words.

LEAND. I will lay you a wager he does not.

LEL. 'Sdeath! I would break every bone in his body should he dare to assert such lies to me.

LEAND. And I will crop his ears, if he does not prove every syllable he has told me.

SCENE IV.—LELIO, LEANDER, MASCARILLE.

LEL. Oh! that's lucky; there he is. Come hither, cursed hangdog!

MASC. What is the matter?

LEL. You serpent's tongue! so full of lies! dare you fasten your stings on Celia, and slander the most consummate virtue that ever added lustre to misfortune?

MASC. (*In a whisper to Lelio*). Gently; I told him so on purpose.

LEL. No, no; none of your winking, and none of your jokes. I am blind and deaf to all you do or say. If it were my own brother he should pay dear for it; for to dare defame her whom I adore is to wound me in the most tender part. You make all these signs in vain. What was it you said to him?

MASC. Good Heavens! do not quarrel, or I shall leave you.

LEL. You shall not stir a step.

MASC. Oh!

LEL. Speak then; confess.

MASC. (*Whispering to Lelio*). Let me alone. I tell you it is a stratagem.

LEL. Make haste; what was it you said? Clear up this dispute between us.

MASC. (*In a whisper to Lelio*). I said what I said. Pray do not put yourself in a passion.

LEL. (*Drawing his sword*). I shall make you talk in another strain.

LEAND. (*Stopping him*). Stay your hand a little; moderate your ardour.

MASC. (*Aside*). Was there ever in the world a creature so dull of understanding?

LEL. Allow me to wreak my just vengeance on him.

LEAND. It is rather too much to wish to chastise him in my presence.

LEL. What! have I no right, then, to chastise my own servant?

LEAND. What do you mean by saying "your servant?"

MASC. (*Aside*). He is at it again! He will discover all.

LEL. Suppose I had a mind to thrash him within an inch of his life, what then? He is my own servant.

LEAND. At present he is mine.

LEL. That is an admirable joke. How comes he to be yours? Surely . . .

MASC. (*In a whisper*). Gently.

LEL. What are you whispering?

MASC. (*Aside*). Oh! the confounded blockhead. He is going to spoil everything, He understands not one of my signs.

LEL. You are dreaming, Leander. You are telling me a pretty story! Is he not my servant?

LEAND. Did you not discharge him from your service for some fault?

LEL. I do not know what this means.

LEAND. And did you not, in the violence of your passion, make his back smart most unmercifully?

LEL. No such thing. I discharge him! cudgel him! Either you make a jest of me, Leander, or he has been making a jest of you.

MASC. (*Aside*). Go on, go on, numskull; you will do your own business effectually.

LEAND. (*To Mascarille*). Then all this cudgelling is purely imaginary?

MASC. He does not know what he says; his memory . . .

LEAND. No, no; all these signs do not look well for you. I suspect some prettily contrived trick here; but for the ingenuity of the invention, go your ways, I forgive you. It is quite enough that I am undeceived, and see now why you imposed upon me. I come off cheap, because I trusted myself to your hypocritical zeal. A word to the wise is enough. Farewell, Lelio, farewell; your most obedient servant.

SCENE V.—LELIO, MASCARILLE.

MASC. Take courage, my boy, may fortune ever attend us! Let us draw and bravely take the field; let us act *Olibrius, the slayer of the innocents.*[18]

LEL. He accused you of slandering . .

MASC. And you could not let the artifice pass, nor let him remain in his error, which did you good service, and which pretty nearly extinguished his passion. No, honest soul, he cannot bear dissimulation. I cunningly get a footing at his rival's, who, like a dolt, was going to place his mistress in my hands, but he, Lelio, prevents me getting hold of her by a fictitious letter; I try to abate the passion of his rival, my hero presently comes and undeceives him. In vain I make signs to him, and show him it was all a contrivance of mine; it signifies nothing; he continues to the end, and never rests satisfied till he has discovered all. Grand and sublime effect of a mind which is not inferior to any man living! It is an exquisite piece, and worthy, in troth, to be made a present of to the king's private museum.

LEL. I am not surprised that I do not come up to your

18 Olibrius was, according to ancient legends, a Roman governor of Gaul, in the time of the Emp ror Decius, very cruel, and a great boaster.

expectations; if I am not acquainted with the designs you are setting on foot, I shall be for ever making mistakes.

MASC. So much the worse.

LEL. At least, if you would be justly angry with me, give me a little insight into your plan; but if I am kept ignorant of every contrivance, I must always be caught napping.[19]

MASC. I believe you would make a very good fencing-master, because you are so skilful at making feints, and at parrying of a thrust.[20]

LEL. Since the thing is done, let us think no more about it. My rival, however, will not have it in his power to cross me, and provided you will but exert your skill, in which I trust . . .

MASC. Let us drop this discourse, and talk of something else; I am not so easily pacified, not I; I am in too great a passion for that. In the first place, you must do me a service, and then we shall see whether I ought to undertake the management of your amours.

LEL. If it only depends on that, I will do it! Tell me, have you need of my blood, of my sword?

MASC. How crack-brained he is! You are just like those swashbucklers who are always more ready to draw their sword than to produce a tester, if it were necessary to give it.

LEL. What can I do, then, for you?

---

19 The original is, *je suis pris sans vert*, "I am taken without green," because in the month of May, in some parts of France, there is a game which binds him or her who is taken without a green leaf about them to pay a forfeit.

20 In the original we find *prendre les contretemps*, and *rompre les mesures*. In a little and very curious book, "The Scots Fencing Master, or Compleat Smal-Sword Man," printed in Edinburgh 1687, and written by Sir William Hope of Kirkliston, the *contre-temps* is said to be: "When a man thrusts without having a good opportunity, or when he thrusts at the same time his adversarie thrusts, and that each of them at that time receive a thrust." *Breaking of measure* is, according to the same booklet, done thus: "When you perceive your adversary thrusting at you, and you are not very certain of the *parade*, then *break his measure*, or make his thrust short of you, by either stepping a foot or half a foot back, with the *single stepp*, for if you judge your adversary's *distance or measure* well, half a foot will *break his measure* as well as ten ells."

MASC. You must, without delay, endeavour to appease your father's anger.

LEL. We have become reconciled already.

MASC. Yes, but I am not; I killed him this morning for your sake; the very idea of it shocks him. Those sorts of jokes are severely felt by such old fellows as he, which, much against their will, make them reflect sadly on the near approach of death. The good sire, notwithstanding his age, is very fond of life, and cannot bear jesting upon that subject; he is alarmed at the prognostication, and so very angry that I hear he has lodged a complaint against me. I am afraid that if I am once housed at the expense of the king, I may like it so well after the first quarter of an hour, that I shall find it very difficult afterwards to get away. There have been several warrants out against me this good while; for virtue is always envied and persecuted in this abominable age. Therefore go and make my peace with your father.

LEL. Yes, I shall soften his anger, but you must promise me then . . .

MASC. We shall see what there is to be done. (*Exit Lelio*). Now, let us take a little breath after so many fatigues; let us stop for a while the current of our intrigues, and not move about hither and thither as if we were hobgoblins. Leander cannot hurt us now, and Celia cannot be removed, through the contrivance of . . .

SCENE VI.– ERGASTE, MASCARILLE.

ERG. I was looking for you everywhere to render you a service. I have a secret of importance to disclose.

MASC. What may that be?

ERG. Can no one overhear us?

MASC. Not a soul.

ERG. We are as intimate as two people can be; I am acquainted with all your projects, and the love of your master. Mind what you are about by and by; Leander has formed a plot to carry off Celia; I have been told he has arranged everything, and designs to get into Trufaldin's house in disguise, having heard that at this time of the year some ladies of the neighbourhood often visit him in the evening in masks.

MASC. Ay, well! He has not yet reached the height of his happiness; I may perhaps be beforehand with him; and as to this thrust, I know how to give him a counter-thrust, by which he may run himself through. He is not aware with what gifts I am endowed. Farewell, we shall take a cup together next time we meet.

SCENE VII.—MASCARILLE, *alone.*

We must, we must reap all possible benefit from this amorous scheme, and by a dexterous and uncommon counterplot endeavour to make the success our own, without any danger. If I put on a mask and be beforehand with Leander, he will certainly not laugh at us; if we take the prize ere he comes up, he will have paid for us the expenses of the expedition; for, as his project has already become known, suspicion will fall upon him; and we, being safe from all pursuit, need not fear the consequences of that dangerous enterprise Thus we shall not show ourselves, but use a cat's paw to take the chesnuts out of the fire. Now, then, let us go and disguise ourselves with some good fellows; we must not delay if we wish to be beforehand with our gentry. I love to strike while the iron is hot, and can, without much difficulty, provide in one moment men and dresses. Depend upon it, I do not let my skill lie dormant. If Heaven has endowed me with the gift of knavery, I am not one of those degenerate minds who hide the talents they have received.

SCENE VIII.—LELIO, ERGASTE.

LEL. He intends to carry her off during a masquerade!

ERG. There is nothing more certain; one of his band informed me of his design, upon which I instantly ran to Mascarille and told him the whole affair; he said he would spoil their sport by some counter-scheme which he planned in an instant; so meeting with you by chance, I thought I ought to let you know the whole.

LEL. I am very much obliged to you for this piece of news; go, I shall not forget this faithful service.

[*Exit Ergaste.*

SCENE IX.—LELIO, *alone.*

My rascal will certainly play them some trick or other; but I, too, have a mind to assist him in his project. It shall never be said that, in a business which so nearly concerns me, I stirred no more than a post; this is the time; they will be surprised at the sight of me. Why did I not take my blunderbuss with me? But let anybody attack me who likes, I have two good pistols and a trusty sword. So ho! within there; a word with you.

SCENE X.—TRUFALDIN *at his window*, LELIO.

TRUF. What is the matter? Who comes to pay me a visit?

LEL. Keep your door carefully shut to-night.

TRUF. Why?

LEL. There are certain people coming masked to give you a sorry kind of serenade; they intend to carry off Celia.

TRUF. Good Heavens!

LEL. No doubt they will soon be here. Keep where you are, you may see everything from your window. Hey! Did I not tell you so? Do you not see them already? Hist! I will affront them before your face. We shall see some fine fun, if they do not give way.[21]

SCENE XI. — LELIO, TRUFALDIN, MASCARILLE, *and his company masked.*

TRUF. Oh, the funny blades, who think to surprise me.

LEL. Maskers, whither so fast? Will you let me into the secret? Trufaldin, pray open the door to these gentry, that they may challenge us for a throw with the dice.[22] (*To*

[21]This is one of the passages of Molière about which commentators do not agree; the original is, *nous allons voir beau jeu, si la corde ne rompt.* Some maintain that *corde* refers to the tight rope of a rope dancer; others that *corde* means the string of a bow, as in the phrase *avoir deux cordes a son arc*, to have two strings (resources) to one's bow. Mons. Eugène Despois, in his carefully edited edition of Moliere, (i., 187), defends the latter reading, and I agree with him.

[22] The original has *jouer un momon.* Guy Miege, in his Dictionary of barbarous French. London, 1679 has "*Mommon,* a mummer, also a company of mummers; also a visard, or mask; also a let by a mummer at dice."

Mascarille, disguised as a woman). Good Heavens! What a pretty creature! What a darling she looks! How now! What are you mumbling? Without offence, may I remove your mask and see your face.

TRUF. Hence! ye wicked rogues; begone, ye ragamuffins! And you, sir, good night, and many thanks.

SCENE XII.—LELIO, MASCARILLE.

LEL. (*After having taken the mask from Mascarille's face*). Mascarille, is it you?

MASC. No, not at all; it is somebody else.

LEL. Alas! How astonished I am! How adverse is our fate! Could I possibly have guessed this, as you did not secretly inform me that you were going to disguise yourself? Wretch that I am, thoughtlessly to play you such a trick, while you wore this mask. I am in an awful passion with myself, and have a good mind to give myself a sound beating.

MASC. Farewell, most refined wit, unparalleled inventive genius.

LEL. Alas! If your anger deprives me of your assistance, what saint shall I invoke?

MASC. Beelzebub.

LEL. Ah! If your heart is not made of stone or iron, do once more at least forgive my imprudence; if it is necessary to be pardoned that I should kneel before you, behold . . .

MASC. Fiddlesticks! Come, my boys, let us away; I hear some other people coming closely behind us.

SCENE XIII. — LEANDER *and his company masked;* TRUFALDIN *at the window.*

LEAND. Softly, let us do nothing but in the gentlest manner.

TRUF. (*At the window*). How is this? What! mummers besieging my door all night. Gentlemen, do not catch a cold gratuitously; every one who is catching it here must have plenty of time to lose. It is rather a little too late to take Celia along with you; she begs you will excuse her to-night; the girl is in bed and cannot speak to you; I am very sorry; but to repay you for all the trouble you have taken for her sake, she begs you will be pleased to accept this pot of perfume.

LEAND. Faugh! That does not smell nicely. My clothes are all spoiled; we are discovered; let us be gone this way.

ACT IV.

SCENE I.—LELIO, *disguised as an Armenian;* MASCARILLE.

MASC. You are dressed in a most comical fashion.

LEL. I had abandoned all hope, but you have revived it again by this contrivance.

MASC. My anger is always too soon over; it is vain to swear and curse, I can never keep to my oaths.

LEL. Be assured that if ever it lies in my power you shall be satisfied with the proofs of my gratitude, and though I had but one piece of bread . . .

MASC. Enough: Study well this new project; for if you commit now any blunder, you cannot lay the blame upon ignorance of the plot; you ought to know your part in the play perfectly by heart.

LEL. But how did Trufaldin receive you?

MASC. I cozened the good fellow with a pretended zeal for his interests. I went with alacrity to tell him that, unless he took very great care, some people would come and surprise him; that from different quarters they had designs upon her of whose origin a letter had given a false account; that they would have liked to draw me in for a share in the business, but that I kept well out of it; and that, being full of zeal for what so nearly concerned him, I came to give him timely notice that he might take his precautions. Then, moralizing, I discoursed solemnly about the many rogueries one sees every day here below; that, as for me, being tired with the world and its infamies, I wished to work out my soul's salvation, retire from all its noise, and live with some worthy honest man, with whom I could spend the rest of my days in peace; that, if he had no objection, I should desire nothing more than to pass the remainder of my life with him; that I had taken such a liking to him, that, without asking for any wages to serve him, I was ready to place in his hands, knowing it to be safe there, some property my father had left me, as well as my savings, which I was fully determined to leave to him alone, if it pleased Heaven to take me hence. That was the right way to gain his affection. You and your beloved should decide what means to use to attain your wishes. I was anxious to arrange a secret interview between you two; he himself has contrived to show me a most excellent method, by which you may fairly and openly stay in her house. Happening to talk to me about a son he had lost, and whom he dreamt last night had come to life again, he told me the following story, upon which, just now, I founded my stratagem.

LEL. Enough; I know it all; you have told it me twice already.[23]

MASC. Yes, yes; but even if I should tell it thrice, it may happen still, that with all your conceit, you might break down in some minor detail.

LEL. I long to be at it already.

MASC. Pray, not quite so fast, for fear we might stumble. Your skull is rather thick, therefore you should be perfectly well instructed in your part. Some time ago Trufaldin left Naples; his name was then Zanobio Ruberti. Being suspected in his native town of having participated in a certain rebellion, raised by some political faction (though really he is not a man to disturb any state), he was obliged to quit it stealthily by night, leaving behind him his daughter, who was very young, and his wife. Some time afterwards he received the news that they were both dead, and in this perplexity, wishing to take with him to some other town, not only his property, but also the only one who was left of all his family, his young son, a schoolboy, called Horatio, he wrote to Bologna, where a certain tutor, named Alberto, had taken the boy when very young, to finish there his education; but though for two whole years he appointed several times to meet them, they never made their appearance. Believing them to be

[23] Though Lelio says to Mascarille, "Enough, I know it all," he has not been listening to the speech of his servant, but, in the meanwhile, is arranging his dress, and smoothing his ruffles, and making it clear to the spectator that he knows nothing, and that he will be a bad performer of the part assigned to him. This explains the blunders he makes afterwards in the second and fifth scenes of the same act.

dead, after so long a time, he came to this city, where he took the name he now bears, without for twelve years ever having discovered any traces of this Alberto, or of his son Horatio. This is the substance of the story, which I have repeated so that you may better remember the groundwork of the plot. Now, you are to personate an Armenian merchant, who has seen them both safe and sound in Turkey. If I have invented this scheme, in preference to any other, of bringing them to life again according to his dream, it is because it is very common in adventures for people to be taken at sea by some Turkish pirate, and afterwards restored to their families in the very nick of time, when thought lost for fifteen or twenty years. For my part, I have heard a hundred of that kind of stories. Without giving ourselves the trouble of inventing something fresh, let us make use of this one; what does it matter? You must say you heard the story of their being made slaves from their own mouths, and also that you lent them money to pay their ransom; but that as urgent business obliged you to set out before them, Horatio asked you to go and visit his father here, whose adventures he was acquainted with, and with whom you were to stay a few days till their arrival. I have given you a long lesson now.

LEL. These repetitions are superfluous. From the very beginning I understood it all.

MASC. I shall go in and prepare the way.

LEL. Listen, Mascarille, there is only one thing that troubles me; suppose he should ask me to describe his son's countenance?

MASC. There is no difficulty in answering that! You know he was very little when he saw him last. Besides it is very likely that increase of years and slavery have completely changed him.

LEL. That is true. But pray, if he should remember my face, what must I do then?

MASC. Have you no memory at all? I told you just now, that he has merely seen you for a minute, that therefore you could only have produced a very transient impression on his mind; besides, your beard and dress disguise you completely.

LEL. Very well. But, now I think of it, what part of Turkey . . . ?

MASC. It is all the same, I tell you, Turkey or Barbary.

LEL. But what is the name of the town I saw them in?

MASC. Tunis. I think he will keep me till night. He tells me it is useless to repeat that name so often, and I have already mentioned it a dozen times.

LEL. Go, go in and prepare matters; I want nothing more.

MASC. Be cautious at least, and act wisely. Let us have none of your inventions here.

LEL. Let me alone! Trust to me, I say, once more.

MASC. Observe, Horatio, a schoolboy in Bologna; Trufaldin, his true name Zanobio Ruberti, a citizen of Naples; the tutor was called Alberto . . .

LEL. You make me blush by preaching so much to me; do you think I am a fool?

MASC. No, not completely, but something very like it.

SCENE II.—LELIO, *alone.*

When I do not stand in need of him he cringes, but now, because he very well knows of how much use he is to me, his familiarity indulges in such remarks as he just now made. I shall bask in the sunshine of those beautiful eyes, which hold me in so sweet a captivity, and, without hindrance, depict in the most glaring colours the tortures I feel. I shall then know my fate. . . . But here they are.

SCENE III.—TRUFALDIN, LELIO, MASCARILLE.

TRUF. Thanks, righteous heaven, for this favourable turn of my fortune!

MASC. You are the man to see visions and dream dreams, since you prove how untrue is the saying that dreams are falsehoods.[24]

TRUF. How can I thank you? what returns can I make you, sir? You, whom I ought to style the messenger sent from Heaven to announce my happiness!

---

[24] In French there is a play on words between *songes*, dreams, and *mensonges*, falsehoods, which cannot be rendered into English.

LEL. These compliments are superfluous; I can dispense with them.

TRUF. (*To Mascarille*). I have seen somebody like this Armenian, but I do not know where.

MASC. That is what I was saying, but one sees surprising likenesses sometimes.

TRUF. You have seen that son of mine, in whom all my hopes are centred?

LEL. Yes, Signor Trufaldin, and he was as well as well can be.

TRUF. He related to you his life and spoke much about me, did he not?

LEL. More than ten thousand times.

MASC. (*Aside to Lelio*). Not quite so much, I should say.

LEL. He described you just as I see you, your face, your gait.

TRUF. Is that possible? He has not seen me since he was seven years old. And even his tutor, after so long a time, would scarcely know my face again.

MASC. One's own flesh and blood never forget the image of one's relations; this likeness is imprinted so deeply, that my father . . .

TRUF. Hold your tongue. Where was it you left him?

LEL. In Turkey, at Turin.

TRUF. Turin! but I thought that town was in Piedmont.

MASC. (*Aside*). Oh the dunce! (*To Trufaldin*). You do not understand him; he means Tunis; it was in reality there he left your son; but the Armenians always have a certain vicious pronunciation, which seems very harsh to us; the reason of it is because in all their words they change *nis* into *rin;* and so, instead of saying *Tunis*, they pronounce *Turin.*

TRUF. I ought to know this in order to understand him. Did he tell you in what way you could meet with his father?

MASC. (*Aside*). What answer will he give?[25] (*To

---

[25] Trufaldin having found out that Mascarille makes signs to his master, the servant pretends to fence.

Trufaldin, after pretending to fence). I was just practising some passes; I have handled the foils in many a fencing school.

TRUF. (*To Mascarille*). That is not the thing I wish to know now. (*To Lelio*). What other name did he say I went by?

MASC. Ah, Signor Zanobio Ruberti. How glad you ought to be for what Heaven sends you!

LEL. That is your real name; the other is assumed.

TRUF. But where did he tell you he first saw the light?

MASC. Naples seems a very nice place, but you must feel a decided aversion to it.

TRUF. Can you not let us go on with our conversation, without interrupting us?

LEL. Naples is the place where he first drew his breath.

TRUF. Whither did I send him in his infancy, and under whose care?

MASC. That poor Albert behaved very well, for having accompanied your son from Bologna, whom you committed to his care.

TRUF. Pshaw!

MASC. (*Aside*). We are undone if this conversation lasts long.

TRUF. I should very much like to know their adventures; aboard what ship did my adverse fate . . . ?

MASC. I do not know what is the matter with me, I do nothing but yawn. But, Signor Trufaldin, perhaps this stranger may want some refreshment; besides, it grows late.

LEL. No refreshment for me.

MASC. Oh sir, you are more hungry than you imagine.

TRUF. Please to walk in then.

LEL. After you, sir.[26]

MASC. (*To Trufaldin*). Sir, in Armenia, the masters of the house use no ceremony. (*To Lelio, after Trufaldin has gone in*). Poor fellow, have you not a word to say for yourself?

---

[26] It shows that Lelio knows not what he is about when he does the honours of the house to the master of the house himself, and forgets that as a stranger he ought to go in first.

LEL. He surprised me at first; but never fear, I have rallied my spirits, and am going to rattle away boldly . .

MASC. Here comes our rival, who knows nothing of our plot. (*They go into Trufaldin's house*).

SCENE IV.—ANSELMO, LEANDER.

ANS. Stay, Leander, and allow me to tell you something which concerns your peace and reputation. I do not speak to you as the father of Hippolyta, as a man interested for my own family, but as your father, anxious for your welfare, without wishing to flatter you or to disguise anything; in short, openly and honestly, as I would wish a child of mine to be treated upon the like occasion. Do you know how everybody regards this amour of yours, which in one night has burst forth? How your yesterday's undertaking is everywhere talked of and ridiculed? What people think of the whim which, they say, has made you select for a wife a gipsy outcast, a strolling wench, whose noble occupation was only begging? I really blushed for you, even more than I did for myself, who am also compromised by this public scandal. Yes, I am compromised, I say, I whose daughter, being engaged to you, cannot bear to see her slighted, without taking offence at it. For shame, Leander; arise from your humiliation; consider well your infatuation; if none of us are wise at all times, yet the shortest errors are always the best. When a man receives no dowry with his wife, but beauty only, repentance follows soon after wedlock; and the handsomest woman in the world can hardly defend herself against a lukewarmness caused by possession. I repeat it, those fervent raptures, those youthful ardours and ecstacies, may make us pass a few agreeable nights, but this bliss is not at all lasting, and as our passions grow cool, very unpleasant days follow those pleasant nights; hence proceed cares, anxieties, miseries, sons disinherited through their fathers' wrath.

LEAND. All that I now hear from you is no more than what my own reason has already suggested to me. I know how much I am obliged to you for the great honour you are inclined to pay me, and of which I am unworthy. In spite of the passion which sways me, I have ever retained a just sense of your daughter's merit and virtue: therefore I will endeavour . . .

ANS. Somebody is opening this door; let us retire to a distance, lest some contagion spreads from it, which may attack you suddenly.

SCENE V.—LELIO, MASCARILLE.

MASC. We shall soon see our roguery miscarry if you persist in such palpable blunders.

LEL. Must I always hear your reprimands? What can you complain of? Have I not done admirably since . . . ?

MASC. Only middling; for example, you called the Turks heretics, and you affirmed, on your corporal oath, that they worshipped the sun and moon as their gods. Let that pass. What vexes me most is that, when you are with Celia, you strangely forget yourself; your love is like porridge, which by too fierce a fire swells, mounts up to the brim, and runs over everywhere.

LEL. Could any one be more reserved? As yet I have hardly spoken to her.

MASC. You are right! but it is not enough to be silent; you had not been a moment at table till your gestures roused more suspicion than other people would have excited in a whole twelvemonth.

LEL. How so?

MASC. How so? Everybody might have seen it. At table, where Trufaldin made her sit down, you never kept your eyes off her, blushed, looked quite silly, cast sheep's eyes at her, without ever minding what you were helped to; you were never thirsty but when she drank, and took the glass eagerly from her hands; and without rinsing it, or throwing a drop of it away, you drank what she left in it, and seemed to choose in preference that side of the glass which her lips had touched; upon every piece which her slender hand had touched, or which she had bit, you laid your paw as quickly as a cat does upon a mouse, and you swallowed it as glibly as if you were a regular glutton. Then, besides all this, you made an intolerable noise, shuffling with your feet under the table, for which Trufaldin, who received two lusty kicks, twice punished a couple of innocent dogs, who would have growled at you if they dared; and yet, in spite of all this, you say you behaved finely! For my part I sat upon thorns all the time; notwithstanding the cold, I feel even now in a perspiration. I hung over you just as a bowler does over his bowl after he has thrown it, and thought to restrain your actions by contorting my body ever so many times.

LEL Lack-a day! how easy it is for you to condemn things of which you do not feel the enchanting cause. In order to humour you for once I have, nevertheless, a good mind to put a restraint upon that love which sways me. Henceforth . . .

SCENE VI.—TRUFALDIN, LELIO, MASCARILLE.

MASC. We were speaking about your son's adventures.

TRUF. (*To Lelio*). You did quite right. Will you do me the favour of letting me have one word in private with him?

LEL. I should be very rude if I did not. (*Lelio goes into Trufaldin's House*).

SCENE VII.—TRUFALDIN, MASCARILLE.

TRUF. Hark ye! do you know what I have just been doing?

MASC. No, but if you think it proper, I shall certainly not remain long in ignorance.

TRUF. I have just now cut off from a large and sturdy oak, of about two hundred years old, an admirable branch, selected on purpose, of tolerable thickness, of which immediately, upon the spot, I made a cudgel, about . . . yes, of this size (*showing his arm*); not so thick at one end as at the other, but fitter, I imagine, than thirty switches to belabour the shoulders withal; for it is well poised, green, knotty, and heavy.

MASC. But, pray, for whom is all this preparation?

TRUF. For yourself, first of all; then, secondly, for that fellow, who wishes to palm one person upon me, and trick me out of another; for this Armenian, this merchant in disguise, introduced by a lying and pretended story.

MASC. What! you do not believe . . . ?

TRUF. Do not try to find an excuse; he himself, fortu-

H. Vernet pt. Nargeot sc.

THE BLUNDERER.

nately, discovered his own stratagem, by telling Celia, whilst he squeezed her hand at the same time, that it was for her sake alone he came disguised in this manner. He did not perceive Jeannette, my little god-daughter, who overheard every word he said. Though your name was not mentioned, I do not doubt but you are a cursed accomplice in all this.

MASC. Indeed, you wrong me. If you are really deceived, believe me I was the first imposed upon with his story.

TRUF. Would you convince me you speak the truth? Assist me in giving him a sound drubbing, and in driving him away; let us give it the rascal well, and then I will acquit you of all participation in this piece of rascality.

MASC. Ay, ay, with all my soul. I will dust his jacket for him so soundly, that you shall see I had no hand in this matter. (*Aside*). Ah! you shall have a good licking, Mister Armenian, who always spoil everything.

SCENE VIII.—LELIO, TRUFALDIN, MASCARILLE.

TRUF. (*Knocks at his door, and then addresses Lelio*). A word with you, if you please. So, Mr. Cheat, you have the assurance to fool a respectable man, and make game of him?

MASC. To pretend to have seen his son abroad, in order to get the more easily into his house!

TRUF. (*Beating Lelio*). Go away, go away immediately.

LEL. (*To Mascarille, who beats him likewise*). Oh! you scoundrel!

MASC It is thus that rogues . . .

LEL. Villain!

MASC. Are served here. Keep that for my sake!

LEL. What? Is a gentleman . . . ?

MASC. (*Beating him and driving him off*). March off, begone, I tell you, or I shall break all the bones in your body.

TRUF. I am delighted with this; come in, I am satisfied. (*Mascarille follows Trufaldin into his house*).

LEL. (*Returning*) This to me! To be thus affronted

by a servant! Could I have thought the wretch would have dared thus to ill-treat his master?

MASC. (*From Trufaldin's window*). May I take the liberty to ask how your shoulders are?

LEL. What! Have you the impudence still to address me?

MASC. Now see what it is not to have perceived Jeannette, and to have always a blabbing tongue in your head! However, this time I am not angry with you, I have done cursing and swearing at you; though you behaved very imprudently, yet my hand has made your shoulders pay for your fault.

LEL. Ha! I shall be revenged on you for your treacherous behaviour.

MASC. You yourself were the cause of all this mischief.

LEL. I?

MASC. If you had had a grain of sense when you were talking to your idol you would have perceived Jeannette at your heels, whose sharp ears overheard the whole affair.

LEL. Could anybody possibly catch one word I spoke to Celia?

MASC And what else was the cause why you were suddenly turned out of doors? Yes, you are shut out by your own tittle-tattle. I do not know whether you play often at piquet, but you at least throw your cards away in an admirable manner.

LEL. Oh! I am the most unhappy of all men. But why did you drive me away also?

MASC. I never did better than in acting thus. By these means, at least, I prevent all suspicion of my being the inventor or an accomplice of this stratagem.

LEL. But you should have laid it on more gently.

MASC. I was no such fool! Trufaldin watched me most narrowly; besides, I must tell you, under the pretence of being of use to you, I was not at all displeased to vent my spleen. However, the thing is done, and if you will give me your word of honour, never, directly or indirectly, to be revenged on me for the blows on the back I so heartily gave you, I promise you, by the help of my present station, to satisfy your wishes within these two nights.

LEL. Though you have treated me very harshly, yet what would not such a promise prevail upon me to do?

MASC. You promise, then?

LEL. Yes, I do.

MASC. But that is not all; promise never to meddle in anything I take in hand.

LEL. I do.

MASC. If you break your word may you get the cold shivers!

LEL. Then keep it with me, and do not forget my uneasiness.

MASC. Go and change your dress, and rub something on your back.

LEL. (*Alone*). Will ill-luck always follow me, and heap upon me one misfortune after another?

MASC. (*Coming out of Trufaldin's house*). What! Not gone yet? Hence immediately; but, above all, be sure you don't trouble your head about any thing. Be satisfied, that I am on your side; do not make the least attempt to assist me; remain quiet.

LEL. (*Going*). Yes, to be sure, I will remain quiet.

MASC. (*Alone*). Now let me see what course I am to steer.

SCENE IX.—ERGASTE, MASCARILLE.

ERG. Mascarille, I come to tell you a piece of news, which will give a cruel blow to your projects. At the very moment I am talking to you, a young gipsy, who nevertheless is no black, and looks like a gentleman, has arrived with a very wan-looking old woman, and is to call upon Trufaldin to purchase the slave you wished to redeem. He seems to be very anxious to get possession of her.

MASC. Doubtless it is the lover Celia spoke about. Were ever fortunes so tangled as ours? No sooner have we got rid of one trouble than we fall into another. In vain do we hear that Leander intends to abandon his pursuit, and to give us no further trouble; that the unexpected arrival of his father has turned the scales in favour of Hippolyta; that the old gentleman has employed his parental authority to make a thorough change, and that the marriage contract is going to be signed this very day; as soon as one rival withdraws, another and a more dangerous one starts up to destroy what little hope there was left. However, by a wonderful stratagem, I believe I shall be able to delay their departure and gain what time I want to put the finishing stroke to this famous affair. A great robbery has lately been committed, by whom, nobody knows. These gipsies have not generally the reputation of being very honest; upon this slight suspicion, I will cleverly get the fellow imprisoned for a few days. I know some officers of justice, open to a bribe, who will not hesitate on such an occasion; greedy and expecting some present, there is nothing they will not attempt with their eyes shut; be the accused ever so innocent, the purse is always criminal, and must pay for the offence.

ACT V.

SCENE I.—MASCARILLE, ERGASTE.

MASC. Ah blockhead! numskull! idiot! Will you never leave off persecuting me?

ERG. The constable took great care everything was going on smoothly; the fellow would have been in jail, had not your master come up that very moment, and, like a madman spoiled your plot. "I cannot suffer," says he in a loud voice, "that a respectable man should be dragged to prison in this disgraceful manner; I will be responsible for him, from his very looks, and will be his bail." And as they refused to let him go, he immediately and so vigorously attacked the officers, who are a kind of people much afraid of their carcasses, that, even at this very moment, they are running, and every man thinks he has got a Lelio at his heels.

MASC. The fool does not know that this gipsy is in the house already to carry off his treasure.

ERG. Good-bye, business obliges me to leave you.

SCENE II.—MASCARILLE, *alone.*

Yes, this last marvellous accident quite stuns me. One would think, and I have no doubt of it, that this bungling devil which possesses Lelio takes delight in defying me, and leads him into every place where his presence can do mischief. Yet I shall go on, and notwithstanding all these buffets of fortune, try who will carry the day. Celia has no aversion to him, and looks upon her departure with great regret. I must endeavour to improve this opportunity. But here they come; let me consider how I shall execute my plan. Yonder furnished house is at my disposal, and I can do what I like with it; if fortune but favours us, all will go well; nobody lives there but myself, and I keep the key. Good Heavens! what a great many adventures have befallen us in so short a time, and what numerous disguises a rogue is obliged to put on.

SCENE III.—CELIA, ANDRÈS.

AND. You know it, Celia, I have left nothing undone to prove the depth of my passion. When I was but very young, my courage in the wars gained me some consideration among the Venetians, and one time or other, and without having too great an opinion of myself, I might, had I continued in their service, have risen to some employment of distinction; but, for your sake, I abandoned everything; the sudden change you produced in my heart, was quickly followed by your lover joining the gipsies. Neither a great many adventures nor your indifference have been able to make me abandon my pursuit. Since that time, being by an accident separated from you much longer than I could have foreseen, I spared neither time nor pains to meet with you again. At last I discovered the old gipsy-woman, and heard from her that for a certain sum of money, which was then of great consequence to the gipsies, and prevented the dissolution of the whole band, you were left in pledge in this neighbourhood. Full of impatience, I flew hither immediately to break these mercenary chains, and to receive from you whatever commands you might be pleased to give. But, when I thought to see joy sparkle in your eyes, I find you pensive and melancholy; if quietness has charms for you, I have sufficient means at Venice, of the spoils taken in war, for us both to live there; but if I must still follow you as before, I will do so, and my heart shall have no other ambition than to serve you in whatever manner you please.

CEL. You openly display your affection for me. I

should be ungrateful not to be sensible of it. Besides, just now, my countenance does not bear the impress of the feelings of my heart; my looks show that I have a violent headache. If I have the least influence over you, you will delay our voyage for at least three or four days, until my indisposition has passed away.

AND. I shall stay as long as you like; I only wish to please you; let us look for a house where you may be comfortable. Ho! here is a bill up just at the right time.

SCENE IV.—CELIA, ANDRÈS, MASCARILLE, *disguised as a Swiss.*

AND. Monsieur Swiss, are you the master of the house?

MASC. I am at your service."[27]

AND. Can we lodge here?

MASC. Yes, I let furnished lodgings to strangers, but only to respectable people.

AND. I suppose your house has a very good reputation?

MASC. I see by your face you are a stranger in this town.

AND. I am.

MASC. Are you the husband of this lady?

AND. Sir?

MASC. Is she your wife or your sister?

AND. Neither.

MASC. Upon my word, she is very pretty! Do you come on business, or have you a la wsuit going on before the court? A lawsuit is a very bad thing, it costs so much money; a solicitor is a thief, and a barrister a rogue.

AND. I do not come for either of these.

MASC. You have brought this young lady then to walk about and to see the town?

AND. What is that to you? (*To Celia*). I shall be

---

[27]In the original, Mascarille speaks a kind of gibberish, which is only amusing when the play is acted; but it can serve no purpose to translate "*moi, pour serfir a fous,*" "*Oui, moi pour d'estrancher chappon champre garni, mais che non point locher te gent te mechant vi,*" etc., by "me be at your serfice," "yes. me have de very goot shambers, ready furnish for stranger, but me no loge de people scandaluse,' etc. A provincial pronunciation, an Irish brogue, or a Scotch tongue, are no equivalent for this mock Swiss German-French

with you again in one moment; I am going to fetch the old woman presently, and tell them not to send the travelling-carriage which was ready.

MASC. Is the lady not quite well?

AND. She has a headache.

MASC I have some good wine and cheese within; walk in, go into my small house. (*Celia, Andrès and Mascarille go into the house*).

SCENE V.—LELIO, *alone*.

However impatient and excited I may feel, yet I have pledged my word to do nothing but wait quietly, to let another work for me, and to see, without daring to stir, in what manner Heaven will change my destiny.

SCENE VI.—ANDRÈS, LELIO.

LEL. (*Addressing Andrès, who is coming out of the house*). Do you want to see anybody in this house?

AND. I have just taken some furnished apartments there.

LEL. The house belongs to my father, and my servant sleeps there every night to take care of it.

AND. I know nothing of that; the bill, at least, shows it is to be let; read it.

LEL. Truly this surprises me, I confess. Who the deuce can have put that bill up, and why . . . ? Ho, faith, I can guess, pretty near, what it means; this cannot possibly proceed but from the quarter I surmise.

AND. May I ask what affair this may be?

LEL. I would keep it carefully from anybody else, but it can be of no consequence to you, and you will not mention it to any one. Without doubt, that bill can be nothing else but an invention of the servant I spoke of; nothing but some cunning plot he has hatched to place into my hands a certain gipsy girl, with whom I am smitten, and of whom I wish to obtain possession. I have already attempted this several times, but until now in vain.

AND. What is her name?

LEL. Celia.

AND. What do you say? Had you but mentioned this,

no doubt I should have saved you all the trouble this project costs you.

LEL. How so? Do you know her?

AND. It is I who just now bought her from her master.

LEL. You surprise me!

AND. As the state of her health did not allow her to leave this town, I just took these apartments for her; and I am very glad that on this occasion you have acquainted me with your intentions.

LEL. What! shall I obtain the happiness I hope for by your means? Could you . . . ?

AND. (*Knocks at the door*). You shall be satisfied immediately.

LEL. What can I say to you? And what thanks . . . ?

AND. No, give me none; I will have none.

SCENE VII.—LELIO, ANDRÈS, MASCARILLE.

MASC. (*Aside*). Hallo! Is this not my mad-cap master? He will make another blunder.

LEL. Who would have known him in this grotesque dress? Come hither, Mascarille, you are welcome.

MASC. I am a man of honour; I am not Mascarille,[28] I never debauched any married or unmarried woman.

LEL. What funny gibberish! It is really very good!

MASC. Go about your business, and do not laugh at me.

LEL. You can take off your dress; recognise your master.

MASC. Upon my word! by all the saints, I never knew you!

LEL. Everything is settled, disguise yourself no longer.

MASC. If you do not go away I will give you a slap in the face.

LEL. Your Swiss jargon is needless, I tell you, for we are agreed, and his generosity lays me under an obligation. I have all I can wish for; you have no reason to be under any farther apprehension.

MASC. If you are agreed, by great good luck, I will no longer play the Swiss, and become myself again.

---

[28] Mascarille answers in his gibberish, "*Moi non point Masquerille*," an allusion to *maquerelle* a female pander; hence his further remarks.

AND. This valet of yours serves you with much zeal; stay a little; I will return presently.

SCENE VIII.—LELIO, MASCARILLE.

LEL. Well, what do you say now?

MASC. That I am delighted to see our labours crowned with success.

LEL. You were hesitating to doff your disguise, and could hardly believe me.

MASC. As I know you I was rather afraid, and still find the adventure very astonishing.

LEL. But confess, however, that I have done great things—at least I have now made amends for all my blunders—mine will be the honour of having finished the work.

MASC. Be it so; you have been much more lucky than wise.

SCENE IX.—CELIA, ANDRÈS, LELIO, MASCARILLE.

AND. Is not this the lady you were speaking of to me?

LEL. Heavens! what happiness can be equal to mine!

AND. It is true; I am indebted to you for the kindness you have shown me; I should be much to blame if I did not acknowledge it; but this kindness would be too dearly bought were I to repay it at the expense of my heart. Judge, by the rapture her beauty causes me, whether I ought to discharge my debt to you at such a price. You are generous, and would not have me act thus. Farewell. Let us return whence we came, and stay there for a few days. (*He leads Celia away*).

SCENE X.—LELIO, MASCARILLE.

MASC. I am laughing, and yet I have little inclination to it. You two are quite of the same mind; he gives Celia to you. Hem! . . . You understand me, sir?

LEL. This is too much. I am determined no longer to ask you to assist me; it is useless; I am a puppy, a wretch, a detestable blockhead, not worthy of any one taking any trouble for me, incapable of doing anything. Abandon all endeavours to aid an unfortunate wretch, who will not allow himself to be made happy; after so many misfortunes, after all my imprudent actions, death alone should aid me.

SCENE XI.—MASCARILLE, *alone.*

That is the true way of putting the finishing stroke to his fate; he wants nothing now but to die, to crown all his follies. But in vain his indignation, for all the faults he has committed urges him to renounce my aid and my support. I intend, happen what will, to serve him in spite of himself, and vanquish the very devil that possesses him. The greater the obstacle, the greater the glory; and the difficulties which beset us are but a kind of tire-women who deck and adorn virtue.

SCENE XII.—CELIA, MASCARILLE.

CELIA. (*To Mascarille, who has been whispering to her*). Whatever you may say, and whatever they intend doing, I have no great expectation from this delay. What we have seen hitherto may indeed convince us that they are not as yet likely to agree. I have already told you that a heart like mine will not for the sake of one do an injustice to another, and that I find myself strongly attached to both, though by different ties. If Lelio has love and its power on his side, Andrès has gratitude pleading for him, which will not permit even my most secret thoughts ever to harbour anything against his interests. Yes; if he has no longer a place in my heart, if the gift of my hand must not crown his love, I ought at least to reward that which he has done for me, by not choosing another, in contempt of his flame, and suppress my own inclinations in the same manner as I do his. You have heard the difficulties which duty throws in my way, and you can judge now whether your expectations will be realized.

MASC. To speak the truth, they are very formidable obstacles in our way, and I have not the knack of working miracles; but I will do my utmost, move Heaven and earth, leave no stone unturned to try and discover some happy expedient. I shall soon let you know what can be done.

SCENE XIII.—HIPPOLYTA, CELIA.

HIPP. Ever since you came among us, the ladies of this neighbourhood may well complain of the havoc caused by your eyes, since you deprive them of the greatest part of their conquests, and make all their lovers faithless. There is not a heart which can escape the darts with which you pierce them as soon as they see you; many thousands load themselves with your chains, and seem to enrich you daily at our expense. However, as regards myself, I should make no complaints of the irresistible sway of your exquisite charms, had they left me one of all my lovers to console me for the loss of the others; but it is inhuman in you that without mercy you deprive me of all; I cannot forbear complaining to you.

CEL. You rally in a charming manner, but I beseech you to spare me a little. Those eyes, those very eyes of yours, know their own power too well ever to dread anything that I am able to do; they are too conscious of their own charms, and will never entertain similar feelings of fear.

HIPP. Yet I advance nothing in what I have said which has not already entered the mind of every one, and without mentioning anything else, it is well known that Celia has made a deep impression on Leander and on Lelio.

CEL. I believe you will easily console yourself about their loss, since they have become so infatuated; nor can you regret a lover who could make so ill a choice.

HIPP. On the contrary, I am of quite a different opinion, and discover such great merits in your beauty, and see in it so many reasons sufficient to excuse the inconstancy of those who allow themselves to be attracted by it, that I cannot blame Leander for having changed his love and broken his plighted troth. In a short time, and without either hatred or anger, I shall see him again brought under my sway, when his father shall have exercised his authority.

SCENE XIV.—CELIA, HIPPOLYTA, MASCARILLE.

MASC. Great news! great news! a wonderful event which I am now going to tell you!

CEL. What means this?

MASC. Listen. This is, without any compliments. . .

CEL. What?

MASC. The last scene of a true and genuine comedy. The old gipsy-woman was, but this very moment . . .

CEL. Well?

MASC. Crossing the market-place, thinking about nothing at all, when another old woman, very haggard-looking, after having closely stared at her for some time, hoarsely broke out in a torrent of abusive language, and thus gave the signal for a furious combat, in which, instead of swords, muskets, daggers, or arrows, nothing was seen but four withered paws, brandished in the air, with which these two combatants endeavoured to tear off the little flesh old age had left on their bones. Not a word was heard but drab, wretch, trull. Their caps, to begin with, were flying about, and left a couple of bald pates exposed to view, which rendered the battle ridiculously horrible. At the noise and hubbub, Andrès and Trufaldin, as well as many others, ran to see what was the matter, and had much ado to part them, so excited were they by passion. Meanwhile each of them, when the storm was abated, endeavoured to hide her head with shame. Everybody wished to know the cause of this ridiculous fray. She who first began it having, notwithstanding the warmth of her passion, looked for some time at Trufaldin, said in a loud voice,—"It is you, unless my sight misgives me, who, I was informed, lived privately in this town; most happy meeting! Yes, Signor Zanobio Ruberti, fortune made me find you out at the very moment I was giving myself so much trouble for your sake. When you left your family at Naples, your daughter, as you know, remained under my care. I brought her up from her youth. When she was only four years old she showed already in a thousand different ways what charms and beauty she would have. That woman you see there—that infamous hag—who had become rather intimate with us, robbed me of that treasure. Your good lady, alas! felt so much grief at this misfortune, that, as I have reason to believe it shortened her days; so that, fearing your severe reproaches because your daughter had been stolen from me, I sent you word that both were dead; but now, as I have found out the thief, she must tell us what has become of your child." At the name of Zanobio Ruberti, which she repeated several times throughout the story, Andrès, after changing colour often, addressed to the surprised Trufaldin these words: "What! has Heaven most happily brought me to him whom I have hitherto sought in vain! Can I possibly have beheld my father, the author of my being, without knowing him? Yes, father, I am Horatio, your son; my tutor, Albert, having died, I felt anew certain uneasiness in my mind, left Bologna, and abandoning my studies, wandered about for six years in different places, according as my curiosity led me. However, after the expiration of that time, a secret impulse drove me to revisit my kindred and my native country; but in Naples, alas! I could no longer find you, and could only hear vague reports concerning you; so that having in vain tried to meet with you, I ceased to roam about idly, and stopped for a while in Venice. From that time to this I have lived without receiving any other information about my family, except knowing its name." You may judge whether Trufaldin was not more than ordinarily moved all this while; in one word (to tell you shortly that which you will have an opportunity of learning afterwards more at your leisure, from the confession of the old gipsy-woman), Trufaldin owns you (*to Celia*) now for his daughter; Andrès is your brother; and as he can no longer think of marrying his sister, and as he acknowledges he is under some obligation to my master, Lelio, he has obtained for him your hand. Pandolphus being present at this discovery, gives his full consent to the marriage; and to complete the happiness of the family, proposes that the newly-found Horatio should marry his daughter. See how many incidents are produced at one and the same time!

CEL. Such tidings perfectly amaze me.

MASC. The whole company follow me, except the two female champions, who are adjusting their toilet after the fray. Leander and your father are also coming. I shall go and inform my master of this, and let him know that when we thought obstacles were increasing, Heaven almost wrought a miracle in his favour. (*Exit Mascarille*).

HIPP. This fortunate event fills me with as much as joy as if it were my own case. But here they come.

SCENE XV.—TRUFALDIN, ANSELMO, ANDRÈS, CELIA, HIPPOLYTA, LEANDER.

TRUF. My child!

CEL. Father!

TRUF. Do you already know how Heaven has blest us?

CEL. I have just now heard this wonderful event.

HIPP. (*To Leander*). You need not find excuses for your past infidelity. The cause of it, which I have before my eyes, is a sufficient excuse.

LEAND. I crave nothing but a generous pardon. I call Heaven to witness that, though I return to my duty suddenly, my father's authority has influenced me less than my own inclination.

AND. (*To Celia*). Who could ever have supposed that so chaste a love would one day be condemned by nature? However, honour swayed it always so much, that with a little alteration it may still continue.

CEL. As for me, I blamed myself, and thought I was wrong, because I felt nothing but a very sincere esteem for you. I could not tell what powerful obstacle stopped me in a path so agreeable and so dangerous, and diverted my heart from acknowledging a love which my senses endeavoured to communicate to my soul.

TRUF. (*To Celia*). But what would you say of me if, as soon as I have found you, I should be thinking of parting with you? I promised your hand to this gentleman's son.

CEL. I know no will but yours

SCENE XVI.—TRUFALDIN, ANSELMO, PANDOLPHUS, CELIA, HIPPOLYTA, LELIO, LEANDER, ANDRÈS, MASCARILLE.

MASC. Now, let us see whether this devil of yours will have the power to destroy so solid a foundation as this; and whether your inventive powers will again strive against this great good luck that befalls you. Through a most unexpected favourable turn of fortune your desires are crowned with success, and Celia is yours.

LEL. Am I to believe that the omnipotence of Heaven . . . ?

TRUF. Yes, son-in-law, it is really so.

PAND. The matter is settled.

AND. (*To Lelio*). By this I repay the obligation you lay me under.

LEL. (*To Mascarille*). I must embrace you ever so many times in this great joy . . .

MASC. Oh! oh! gently, I beseech you; he has almost choked me. I am very much afraid for Celia if you embrace her so forcibly. One can do very well without such proofs of affection.

TRUF. (*To Lelio*). You know the happiness with which Heaven has blessed me; but since the same day has caused us all to rejoice, let us not part until it is ended, and let Leander's father also be sent for quickly.

MASC. You are all provided for. Is there not some girl who might suit poor Mascarille? As I see, every Jack has his Gill, I also want to be married.

ANS. I have a wife for you.

MASC. Let us go, then; and may propitious Heaven give us children, whose fathers we really are.

LE DÉPIT AMOUREUX.

COMÉDIE.

THE LOVE-TIFF.

A COMEDY IN FIVE ACTS.

(*THE ORIGINAL IN VERSE.*)

1656.

INTRODUCTORY NOTICE.

The Love-tiff (*Le Dépit-amoureux*) is composed of two pieces joined together. The first and longest is a comparatively modest imitation of a very coarse and indecent Italian comedy, *L'Interesse*, by Signor Nicolo Secchi; its intrigue depends chiefly on the substitution of a female for a male child, a change which forms the groundwork of many plays and novels, and of which Shakespeare has also made use. The second and best part of the *Love-tiff* belongs to Molière alone, and is composed chiefly of the whole of the first act, the first six verses of the third scene, and the whole of the fourth scene of the second act; these, with a few alterations and a few lines added, form the comedy which the *Théâtre Française* plays at the present time. It was first represented at Béziers towards the end of 1656, when the States General of Languedoc were assembled in that town, and met with great success; a success which continued when it was played in Paris at the Théâtre du Petit-Bourbon in 1658. Why in some of the former English translations of Molière the servant Gros-René is called "Gros-Renard" we are unable to understand, for both names are thoroughly French. Mr. Ozell, in his translation, gives him the unmistakably English, but not very euphonious name of "punch-gutted Ben, *alias* Renier," whilst Foote calls him "Hugh." The incidents of the *Love-tiff* are arranged artistically, though in the Spanish taste; the plot is too complicated, and the ending very unnatural. But the characters are well delineated, and fathers, lovers, mistresses, and servants all move about amidst a complication of errors from which there is no visible disentangling. The conversation between Valère and Ascanio in man's clothes, the mutual begging pardon of Albert and Polydore, the natural astonishment of Lucile, accused in the presence of her father, and the stratagem of Éraste to get the truth from his servants, are all described in a masterly manner, whilst the tiff between Éraste and Lucile, which gives the title to the piece, as well as their reconciliation, are considered among the best scenes of this play.

Nearly all actors in France who play either the *valets* or the *soubrettes* have attempted the parts of Gros-René and Marinette, and even the great tragédienne Madlle. Rachel ventured, on the 1st of July, 1844, to act Marinette, but not with much success.

Dryden has imitated, in the fourth act of *An Evening's Love*, a small part of the scene between Marinette and Éraste, the quarrelling scene between Lucile, Éraste, Marinette, and Gros-René, as well as in the third act of the same play, the scene between Albert and Metaphrastus. Vanbrugh has very closely followed Molière's play in the *Mistake*, but has laid the scene in Spain. This is the principal difference I can perceive. He has paraphased the French with a spirit and ease which a mere translation can hardly ever acquire. The epilogue to his play, written by M. Motteux, a Frenchman, whom the revocation of the Edict of Nantes brought into England, is filthy in the extreme. Mr. J. King has curtailed Vanbrugh's play into an interlude, in one act, called *Lover's Quarrels*, or *Like Master Like Man*.

Another imitator of Molière was Edward Ravenscroft, of whom Baker says in his *Biographia Dramatica*, that he was "a writer or compiler of plays, who lived in the reigns of Charles II. and his two successors." He was descended from the family of the Ravenscrofts, in Flintshire; a family, as he himself, in a dedication asserts, so ancient that when William the Conqueror came into England, one of his nobles married into it. He was some time a member of the Middle Temple; but, looking on the dry study of the law as greatly beneath the attention of a man of genius, quitted it. He was an arrant plagiary. Dryden attacked one of his plays, *The Citizen turned Gentleman*, an imitation of Molière's *Bourgeois-Gentilhomme*, in the Prologue to *The Assignation*. Ravenscroft wrote "*The Wrangling Lovers, or the Invisible Mistress*. Acted at the Duke's Theatre, 1677. London, Printed for William Crook, at the sign of the *Green Dragon*, without *Temple-Bar*, 1677." Though the plot was partly taken from a Spanish novel, the author has been inspired by Molière's *Dépit amoureux*. The scene is in Toledo: Éraste is called Don Diego de Stuniga, Valère Don Gusman de Haro, "a well-bred cavaliere," Lucile is Octavia de Pimentell, and Ascanio is Elvira; Gros-René's name is Sanco, "vallet to Gusman, a simple pleasant fellow," and Mascarille is Ordgano, "a cunning knave;" Marinette is called Beatrice and Frosine Isabella. The English play is rather too long. Don Gusman courts Elvira veiled, whilst in the French play Ascanio, her counterpart, is believed to be a young man. There is also a brother of Donna Elvira, Don Ruis de Moncade, who is a rival of Don Diego, whilst in *le Dépit-amoureux* Valère is not the brother but the husband of Ascanio and the rival of Éraste (Don Diego) as well. The arrangement of the English comedy differs greatly from the French. Though the plot in both plays is nearly identical, yet the words and scenes in *The Wrangling Lovers* are totally different, and not so amusing. Mascarille and Gros-René are but faintly attempted; Marinette and Frosine only sketched in outline; and in the fifth act the ladies appear to have nothing else to do but to pop in and out of closets. The scenes of the French play between Albert and Metaphrastus (ii. 7); the very comical scene between Albert and Polydore (iii. 4) and the reconciliation scene between Lucile and Éraste (iv. 3), are also not rendered in the English comedy. There are very few scenes which can be compared with those of *le Dépit amoureux*.

DRAMATIS PERSONÆ.

ÉRASTE, *in love with Lucile.*
ALBERT, *father to Lucile.*[1]
GROS-RENÉ, *servant to Éraste.*
VALÈRE, *son to Polydore.*
POLYDORE, *father to Valère.*
MASCARILLE, *servant to Valère.*
METAPHRASTUS, *a pedant.*
LA RAPIÉRE, *a bully.*

LUCILE, *daughter to Albert.*
ASCANIO, *Albert's daughter, in man's clothes.*
FROSINE, *confidant to Ascanio.*
MARINETTE, *maid to Lucile.*

---

[1] This part was played by Moliére himself.

THE LOVE-TIFF.

(*LE DÉPIT AMOUREUX.*)

ACT I.

SCENE I.—ÉRASTE, GROS-RENÉ.

ERAS. Shall I declare it to you? A certain secret anxiety never leaves my mind quite at rest. Yes, whatever remarks you make about my love, to tell you the truth, I am afraid of being deceived; or that you may be bribed in order to favour a rival; or, at least, that you may be imposed upon as well as myself.

GR-RE. As for me, if you suspect me of any knavish trick, I will say, and I trust I give no offence to your honour's love, that you wound my honesty very unjustly, and that you show but small skill in physiognomy. People of my bulk are not accused, thank Heaven! of being either rogues or plotters. I scarcely need protest against the honour paid to us, but am straightforward in every thing.[1] As for my being deceived that may be; there is a better foundation for that idea; nevertheless, I do not believe it can be easily done. I may be a fool, but I do not see yet why you vex yourself thus. Lucile, to my

---

[1] Du Parc, the actor who played this part, was very stout; hence the allusion in the original, "*et suis homme fort rond de toutes les manieres.*" I have, of course, used in the translation the word "straightforward" ironically, and with an eye to the rotundity of stomach of the actor. Molière was rather fond of making allusions in his plays to the infirmities or peculiarities of some of his actors. Thus, in the Miser (*l'Avare*) Act I, Scene 3, he alludes to the lameness of the actor Béjart, "*Je ne me plais point a voir ce chien de boiteux-la.*" "I do not like to see that lame dog;" in the Citizen who apes the Nobleman (*le Bourgeois gentilhomme*), Act iii. sc, 9, he even gives a portrait of his wife.

thinking, shows sufficient love for you; she sees you and talks to you, at all times; and Valère, after all, who is the cause of your fear, seems only to be allowed to approach her because she is compelled so to act.

ERAS. A lover is often buoyed up by false hope. He who is best received is not always the most beloved. The affection a woman displays is often but a veil to cover her passion for another. Valère has lately shown too much tranquillity for a slighted lover; and the joy or indifference he displays at those favours, which you suppose bestowed upon me, embitters continually their greatest charms, causes this grief, which you cannot understand, holds my happiness in suspense, and makes it difficult for me to trust completely anything Lucile says to me. I should feel delighted if I saw Valère animated by a little more jealousy; his anxiety and impatience would then reassure my heart. Do you as yourself think it possible for any one to see a rival caressed and be as satisfied as he is; if you do not believe it, tell me, I conjure you, if I have not a cause to be perplexed?

GR.-RE. Perhaps he has changed his inclination, upon finding that he sighed in vain.

ERAS. When love has been frequently repelled it frees itself, and wishes to flee from the object it was charmed with; nor does it break its chain so quietly as to be able to continue at peace. When once we have been fond of anyone who influenced our destiny we are never afterwards indifferent in her presence; if our dislike does not increase when we behold her our love is upon the point of returning again. Believe me, however much a passion may be extinguished, a little jealousy still dwells in our breast; no one can see, without feeling some pang, the heart he has lost possessed by another.

GR.-RE. For my part, I do not understand so much philosophy. I candidly believe what my eyes see, and am not such a mortal enemy to myself as to become melancholy without any cause. Why should I try to split hairs, and labour hard to find out reasons to be miserable? Shall I alarm myself about castles in the air? Let Lent come before we keep it! I think grief an uncomfortable thing; and, for my part, I never foster it without good and just cause. I might frequently find a hundred opportunities to become sad, but I do not want to see them. I run the same risk in love as you do; I share in your bad or good luck. The mistress cannot deceive you but the maid will do the same by me; yet I carefully avoid thinking about it. I like to believe people when they say "I love you." In order to be happy, I do not try to find out whether Mascarille tears the hair out of his head or not. Let Marinette allow herself to be kissed and caressed by Gros-René[2] as much as he likes, and let my charming rival laugh at it like a fool, I will laugh too as much as I like, and follow his example; we shall then see who will laugh the heartiest.

ERAS. That is like your talk.

GR. RE. But here she comes.

SCENE II.—MARINETTE, ÉRASTE, GROS-RENÉ.

GR.-RE. Hist! Marinette.

MAR. Hallo! what are you doing there?

GR.-RE. Faith! do you ask? We were just talking about you.

MAR. Are you there too, sir? Upon my word you have made me trot about like a flunkey for this hour past.

ERAS. How so?

MAR. I have walked ten miles to look for you, and give you my word that . . .

ERAS. What?

MAR. That you were neither at church, in the fashionable walk, at home, nor in the market-place.

GR.-RE. You may swear to that.

ERAS. But pray, tell me who sent you?

MAR. One, in good truth, who bears you no great ill-will; in a word, my mistress.

ERAS. Ah! dear Marinette, do your words really express what she feels? Do not hide some ominous secret from me. I should not dislike you for this. For Heaven's

---

[2] In several editions of Molière we find, instead of Gros-René the name of Jodelet. The latest, and if I might be permitted to say so, the most careful editor of our author, Mons. E. Despois, thinks that "Gros-René" ought to be mentioned here. The sense shows he is right.

sake tell me if your charming mistress does not merely pretend to love me?

MAR. Ha! ha! ha! What has put that funny notion into your head? Does she not sufficiently show her inclination? What further security does your love demand? What does it require?

GR.-RE. Unless Valère hangs himself, or some such trifle, he will not be reassured.

MAR. How so?

GR.-RE. He is so very jealous.

MAR. Of Valère? Ha! a pretty fancy indeed! It could only be hatched in your brain. I thought you a man of sense, and until now had a good opinion of your intellect; but I see I was very much deceived. Have you also got a touch of this distemper in your head?

GR.-RE. I jealous? Heaven forbid! and keep me from being so silly as to go and make myself lean with any such grief. Your heart guarantees your fidelity; besides, I have too good an opinion of myself to believe that any other could please you after me. Where the deuce could you find any one equal to me?

MAR. You really are right; that is as it should be. A jealous man should never show his suspicions! All that he gains by it is to do himself harm, and in this manner furthers the designs of his rival. Your distrust often is the cause that a mistress pays attention to a man, before whose merits your own have paled. I know a certain person who, were it not for the preposterous jealousy of a rival, had never been so happy as he now is. But, in any case, to show suspicion in love is acting a foolish part, and after all is to make one's-self miserable for nothing. This, sir (*to Eraste*), I mean as a hint to you.

ERAS. Very well, let us talk no more about it. What have you to say to me?

MAR. You deserve to be kept in suspense. In order to punish you, I ought to keep from you the great secret which has made me hunt for you so long. Here, read this letter, and doubt no more. Read it aloud, nobody listens.

ERAS. (*Reads*). *"You told me that your love was capable of doing anything. It may be crowned this very day, if you can but get my father's consent. Acquaint him with the power you have over my heart; I give you leave so to do; if his reply be favourable, I can answer for it that I shall obey.*" Ah! how happy am I! I ought to look upon you, the bearer of this letter, as a divine creature.

GR.-RE. I told you so. Though you do not believe it, I am seldom deceived in the things I ponder on.

ERAS. (*Reading the letter again*). "*Acquaint him with the power you have over my heart; I give you leave so to do; if his reply be favourable, I can answer for it that I shall obey.*"

MAR. If I should tell her you are weak-minded enough to be jealous, she would immediately disown such a letter as this.

ERAS. I beseech you, conceal from her a momentary fear, for which I thought I had some slight foundation; or, if you do tell it her, say to her at the same time that I am ready to atone for my fit of madness with my life, and would die at her feet, if I have been capable of displeasing her.

MAR. Let us not talk of dying; this is no time for it.

ERAS. However, you have laid me under a great obligation; I intend shortly to acknowledge in a handsome manner the trouble so gentle and so lovely a messenger has taken.

MAR. That reminds me. Do you know where I looked for you just now?

ERAS. Well?

MAR. Quite near the market-place; you know where that is.

ERAS. Where did you say?

MAR. There . . . in that shop where last month you generously and freely promised me a ring.

ERAS. Um! I understand you.

GR.-RE. What a cunning jade!

ERAS. It is true; I have delayed too long to make good my promise to you, but . . .

MAR. What I said, sir, was not because I wished you to make haste.

GR.-RE. Oh, no!

ERAS. (*Giving her his ring*). Perhaps this ring may please you; accept it instead of the one I owe.

MAR. You are only jesting, sir; I should be ashamed to take it.

GR.-RE. Poor shame-faced creature! Take it without more ado; only fools refuse what is offered them.

MAR. I will only accept it so that I may have something to remember you by.

ERAS. When may I return thanks to that lovely angel?

MAR. Endeavour to gain over her father.

ERAS. But if he rejects me, should I . . . ?

MAR. We will think about that when he does so! We will do our utmost for you: one way or another she must be yours; do your best, and we will do ours.

ERAS. Farewell! we shall know our fate to-day. (*Eraste reads the letter again to himself*).

MAR. (*To Gros-René*). Well, what shall we say of our love? You do not speak to me of it.

GR.-RE. If such people as we wish to be married, the thing is soon done. I will have you. Will you have me?

MAR. Gladly.

GR.-RE. Shake hands, that is enough.

MAR. Farewell, Gros-René, my heart's delight.

GR.-RE. Farewell, my star.

MAR. Farewell, fair fire-brand of my flame.

GR.-RE. Farewell, dear comet, rainbow of my soul. (*Exit Marinette*). Heaven be praised, our affairs go on swimmingly. Albert is not a man to refuse you anything.

ERAS. Valère is coming here.

GR.-RE. I pity the poor wretch, knowing what I do know.

SCENE III.—ÉRASTE, VALÈRE, GROS-RENÉ.

ERAS. Well, Valère?

VAL. Well, Eraste?

ERAS. How does your love prosper?

VAL. And how does yours?

ERAS. It grows stronger and stronger every day.

VAL. So does mine.

ERAS. For Lucile?

VAL. For her.

ERAS. Certainly, I must own, you are a pattern of uncommon constancy.

VAL. And your perseverance will be a rare example to posterity.

ERAS. As for me, I am not very fond of that austere kind of love which is satisfied with looks only; nor do I possess feelings lofty enough to endure ill-treatment with constancy. In one word, when I really love, I wish to be beloved again.

VAL. It is very natural, and I am of the same opinion. I would never do homage to the most perfect object by whom I could be smitten, if she did not return my passion.

ERAS. However, Lucile . . .

VAL. Lucile does willingly everything my passion can desire.

ERAS. You are easily satisfied then.

VAL. Not so easily as you may think.

ERAS. I, however, may, without vanity, believe that I am in her favour.

VAL. And I know that I have a very good share of it.

ERAS. Do not deceive yourself; believe me.

VAL. Believe me, do not be too credulous, and take too much for granted.

ERAS. If I might show you a certain proof that her heart . . . but no, it would too much distress you.

VAL. If I might discover a secret to you . . . but it might grieve you, and so I will be discreet.

ERAS. You really urge me too far, and though much against my will, I see I must lower your presumption. Read that.

VAL. (*After having read the letter*). These are tender words.

ERAS. You know the handwriting?

VAL. Yes, it is Lucile's.

ERAS. Well! where is now your boasted certainty . . . ?

VAL. (*Smiling and going away*). Farewell, Eraste.

GR.-RE. He is mad, surely. What reason has he to laugh?

ERAS. He certainly surprises me, and between ourselves I cannot imagine what the deuce of a mystery is hidden under this.

GR.-RE. Here comes his servant, I think.

ERAS. Yes, it is he; let us play the hypocrite, to set him talking about his master's love.

SCENE IV.—ÉRASTE, MASCARILLE, GROS-RENÉ.

MASC. (*Aside*). No, I do not know a more wretched situation, than to have a young master, very much in love.

GR.-RE. Good morning.

MASC. Good morning.

GR.-RE. Where is Mascarille going just now? What is he doing? Is he coming back? Is he going away? Or does he intend to stay where he is?

MASC. No, I am not coming back, because I have not yet been where I am going; nor am I going, for I am stopped; nor do I design to stay, for this very moment I intend to be gone.

ERAS. You are very abrupt, Mascarille; gently.

MASC. Ha! Your servant, sir.

ERAS. You are in great haste to run away from us: what! do I frighten you?

MASC. You are too courteous to do that.

ERAS. Shake hands; all jealousy is now at an end between us; we will be friends; I have relinquished my love; henceforth you can have your own way to further your happiness.

MASC. Would to Heaven it were true!

ERAS. Gros-René knows that I have already another flame elsewhere.

GR.-RE. Certainly; and I also give up Marinette to you.

MASC. Do not let us touch on that point; our rivalry is not likely to go to such a length. But is it certain, sir, that you are no longer in love, or do you jest?

ERAS. I have been informed that your master is but too fortunate in his amours; I should be a fool to pretend any longer to gain the same favours which that lady grants to him alone.

MASC. Certainly, you please me with this news. Though I was rather afraid of you, with regard to our plans, yet you do wisely to slip your neck out of the collar. You have done well to leave a house where you were only caressed for form's sake; I, knowing all that was going on, have many times pitied you, because you were allured by expectations, which could never be realized. It is a sin and a shame to deceive a gentleman! But how the deuce, after all, did you find out the trick? For when they plighted their faith to each other there were no witnesses but night, myself, and two others; and the tying of the knot, which satisfies the passion of our lovers, is thought to have been kept a secret till now.

ERAS. Ha! What do you say?

MASC. I say that I am amazed, sir, and cannot guess who told you, that under this mask, which deceives you and everybody else, a secret marriage unites their matchless love.

ERAS. You lie.

MASC. Sir, with all my heart.

ERAS. You are a rascal.

MASC. I acknowledge I am.

ERAS. And this impudence deserves a sound beating on the spot.

MASC. I am completely in your power,

ERAS. Ha! Gros-René.

GR.-RE. Sir?

ERAS. I contradict a story, which I much fear is but too true. (*To Mascarille*). You wanted to run away.

MASC. Not in the least.

ERAS. What! Lucile is married to . . .

MASC. No, sir, I was only joking.

ERAS. Hey! you were joking, you wretch?

MASC. No, I was not joking.

ERAS. Is it true then?

MASC. No, I do not say that.

ERAS. What do you say then?

MASC. Alas! I say nothing, for fear of saying something wrong.

ERAS. Tell me positively, whether you have spoken the truth, or deceived me.

MASC. Whatever you please. I do not come here to contradict you.

ERAS. (*Drawing his sword*). Will you tell me? Here is something that will loosen your tongue without more ado.

MASC. It will again be saying some foolish speech or other. I pray you, if you have no objection, let me quickly have a few stripes, and then allow me to scamper off.

ERAS. You shall suffer death, unless you tell me the whole truth without disguise.

MASC. Alas! I will tell it then; but perhaps, sir, I shall make you angry.

ERAS. Speak: but take great care what you are doing; nothing shall save you from my just anger, if you utter but one single falsehood in your narration.

MASC. I agree to it; break my legs, arms, do worse to me still, kill me, if I have deceived you in the smallest degree, in anything I have said.

ERAS. It is true then that they are married?

MASC. With regard to this, I can now clearly see that my tongue tripped; but, for all that, the business happened just as I told you. It was after five visits paid at night, and whilst you were made use of as a screen to conceal their proceedings, that they were united the day before yesterday. Lucile ever since tries still more to hide the great love she bears my master, and desires he will only consider whatever he may see, and whatever favours she may show you, as the results of her deep-laid scheme, in order to prevent the discovery of their secrets. If, notwithstanding my protestations, you doubt the truth of what I have told you, Gros-René may come some night along with me, and I will show him, as I stand and watch, that we shall be admitted into her house, after dark.

ERAS. Out of my sight, villain.

MASC. I shall be delighted to go; that is just what I want. (*Exit.*

SCENE V.—ÉRASTE, GROS-RENÉ.

ERAS. Well?

GR.-RE. Well! Sir, we are both taken in if this fellow speaks the truth.

ERAS. Alas! The odious rascal has spoken the truth too well. All that he has said is very likely to have happened; Valère's behaviour, at the sight of this letter, denotes that there is a collusion between them, and that it is a screen to hide Lucile's love for him.

SCENE VI.—ÉRASTE, MARINETTE, GROS-RENÉ.

MAR. I come to tell you that this evening my mistress permits you to see her in the garden.

ERAS. How dare you address me, you hypocritical traitress? Get out of my sight, and tell your mistress not to trouble me any more with her letters; that is the regard, wretch, I have for them.

(*He tears the letter and goes out.*

MAR. Tell me, Gros-René, what ails him?

GR.-RE. Dare you again address me, iniquitous female, deceitful crocodile, whose base heart is worse than a satrap or a Lestrigon?[3] Go, go, carry your answer to your lovely mistress, and tell her short and sweet, that in spite of all her cunning, neither my master nor I are any longer fools, and that henceforth she and you may go to the devil together. (*Exit.*

MAR. My poor Marinette, are you quite awake? What demon are they possessed by? What? Is it thus they receive our favours? How shocked my mistress will be when she hears this!

ACT II.

SCENE I.—ASCANIO, FROSINE.

FROS. Thank Heaven! I am a girl who can keep a secret, Ascanio.

ASC. But is this place private enough for such a conversation? Let us take care that nobody surprises us, or that we be not overheard from some corner or other.

FROS. We should be much less safe within the house; here we can easily see anybody coming, and may speak in perfect safety.

ASC. Alas! how painful it is for me to begin my tale!

FROS. Sure, this must be an important secret then?

ASC. Too much so, since I even entrust it to you with reluctance; even you should not know it, if I could keep it concealed any longer.

FROS. Fie! you insult me when you hesitate to trust in me, whom you have ever found so reserved in everything

---

[3] See Homer's Odyssey, X., v. 81–132.

that concerns you—me, who was brought up with you, and have kept secret things of so great an importance to you; me, who know . . .

ASC. Yes, you are already acquainted with the secret reason which conceals from the eyes of the world my sex and family. You know that I was brought into this house, where I have passed my infancy, in order to preserve an inheritance which, on the death of young Ascanio (whom I personate), should have fallen to others; that is why I dare to unbosom myself to you with perfect confidence. But before we begin this conversation, Frosine, clear up a doubt which continually besets me. Can it be possible that Albert should know nothing of the secret, which thus disguises my sex, and makes him my father?

FROS. To tell you the truth, what you now wish to know has also greatly puzzled me. I have never been able to get at the bottom of this intrigue, nor could my mother give me any further insight. When Albert's son died, who was so much beloved, and to whom a very rich uncle bequeathed a great deal of property, even before his birth; his mother kept his death secret, fearing that her husband, who was absent at the time, would have gone distracted, had he seen that great inheritance, from which his family would have reaped such advantage, pass into the hands of another. She, I say, in order to conceal this misfortune formed the plan of putting you into the place of her lost son; you were taken from our family, where you were brought up. Your mother gave her consent to this deceit; you took the son's place, and every one was bribed to keep the secret. Albert has never known it through us, and as his wife kept it for more than twelve years, and died suddenly, her unexpected death prevented her from disclosing it. I perceive, however, that he keeps up an acquaintance with your real mother, and that, in private, he assists her; perhaps all this is not done without a reason. On the other hand, he commits a blunder by urging you to marry some young lady! Perhaps he knows that you took the place of his son, without knowing that you are a girl. But this digression might gradually carry us too far; let us return to that secret which I am impatient to hear.

ASC. Know then that Cupid cannot be deceived, that I have not been able to disguise my sex from love's eyes, and that his subtle shafts have reached the heart of a weak woman beneath the dress I wear. In four words, I am in love!

FROS. You in love!

ASC. Gently, Frosine; do not be quite so astonished; it is not time yet; this love-sick heart has something else to tell you that will surprise you.

FROS. What is it?

ASC. I am in love with Valère.

FROS. Ha! I really am surprised. What! you love a man whose family your deceit has deprived of a rich inheritance, and who, if he had the least suspicion of your sex, would immediately regain everything. This is a still greater subject of astonishment.

ASC. I have a more wonderful surprise for you yet in store—I am his wife.

FROS. Oh, Heavens! his wife!

ASC. Yes, his wife.

FROS. Ha! this is worse than all, and nearly drives me mad.

ASC. And yet this is not all.

FROS. Not all!

ASC. I am his wife, I say, and he does not think so, nor has he the least idea of what I really am.

FROS. Go on, I give it up, and will not say any thing more, so much every word amazes me. I cannot comprehend anything of these riddles.

ASC I shall explain if you will but hear me. Valère who admired my sister, seemed to me a lover worthy of being listened to; I could not bear to see his addresses slighted without feeling a certain interest in him. I wished that Lucile should take pleasure in his conversation, I blamed her severity, and blamed it so effectually, that I myself, without being able to help it, became affected with that passion which she could not entertain. He was talking to her, and persuaded me; I suffered myself to be overcome by the very sighs he breathed; and the love, rejected by the object of his flame, entered, like a conqueror, into my heart, which was wounded by an arrow, not aimed at it, and paid another's debt with heavy interest. At last, my dear, the love I felt for him forced me to declare myself, but under a borrowed name. One night I spoke to him, disguising my voice as if it were Lucile's, and this too amiable lover thought she returned his love; I managed the conversation so well that he never found out the deception. Under that disguise which pleased so much his deluded imagination, I told him that I was enamoured of him, but that, finding my father opposed to my wishes, I ought at least to pretend to obey him; that therefore it behooved us to keep our love secret, with which the night alone should be acquainted; that all private conversation should be avoided during the day, for fear of betraying everything; that he should behold me with the same indifference as he did before we had come to an understanding; and that on his part, as well as mine, no communication should take place either by gesture, word, or writing. In short, without dwelling any longer upon all the pains I have taken to bring this deception to a safe termination, I went on with my bold project as far as it was possible to go, and secured the husband I mentioned to you.

FROS. Upon my word, you possess great talents. Would any one think so, on seeing her passionless countenance? However, you have been pretty hasty, and though I grant that the affair has succeeded until now, what do you think will be the end of it, for it cannot be long concealed?

ASC. When love is strong it overcomes all obstacles, until it is satisfied; provided it reaches the wished-for goal, it looks upon everything else as a mere trifle. I have told you all to-day, so that your advice . . . But here comes my husband.

SCENE II.—VALÈRE, ASCANIO, FROSINE.

VAL. If you are conversing, and if my presence is any interruption, I shall withdraw.

ASC. No; you may well interrupt it, since we were talking about you.

VAL. About me?

ASC. About yourself.

VAL. How so?

ASC. I was saying, that if I had been a woman, Valère would have been able to please me but too well, and that if I had been beloved by him, I should not have delayed long to make him happy.

VAL. This declaration does not cost you much, as there is such an *if* in the way; but you would be finely caught if some miraculous event should put to the proof the truth of so obliging a declaration.

ASC. Not in the least; I tell you that if I reigned in your heart, I would very willingly crown your passion.

VAL. And what, if you might contribute to my happiness, by assisting me to further my love?

ASC. I should then, certainly, disappoint you.

VAL. This admission is not very polite.

ASC. What, Valère? Supposing I were a woman and loved you tenderly, would you be so cruel as to make me promise to aid you in your love for another lady? I could not perform such a painful task.

VAL. But you are not a woman.

ASC. What I said to you I said in the character of a woman, and you ought to take it so.

VAL. Thus I ought not to imagine you like me, Ascanio, unless Heaven works a miracle in you. Therefore, as you are not a woman, I bid farewell to your affection; you do not care in the least for me.

ASC. My feelings are far more nice than people imagine, and the smallest misgiving shocks me when love is in the case. But I am sincere; I will not promise to aid you, Valère, unless you assure me that you entertain precisely the same sentiments for me; that you feel the same warmth of friendship for me as I feel for you; and that if I were a woman you would love no one better than me.

VAL. I never before heard of such a jealous scruple, but though quite unexpected, this affection obliges me to make some return for it; I here promise you all you require of me.

ASC. But sincerely?

VAL. Yes, sincerely.

ASC. If this be true, I promise you that henceforth your interests shall be mine.

VAL. I have a secret of the utmost consequence to reveal to you by and by, and then I shall remind you of your words.

ASC. And I have likewise a secret to discover to you, wherein your affection for me may show itself.

VAL. Indeed! what can that be?

ASC. I have a love affair which I dare not reveal, and you have influence enough over the object of my passion to promote my happiness

VAL. Explain yourself, Ascanio, and be assured beforehand that, if your happiness lies in my power, it is certain.

ASC. You promise more than you imagine.

VAL. No, no; tell me the name of the person whom I have to influence.

ASC. It is not yet time, but it is a person who is nearly related to you.

VAL. Your words amaze me; would to Heaven my sister . . .

ASC. This is not the proper time to explain myself, I tell you.

VAL. Why so?

ASC. For a certain reason. You shall know my secret when I know yours.

VAL. I must have another person's permission before I can discover it to you.

ASC. Obtain it then; and when we shall have explained ourselves we shall see which of us two will best keep his word.

VAL. Farewell, I accept your offer.

ASC. And I will be bound by it, Valère. (*Exit Valère.*)

FROS. He thinks you will help him as a brother.

SCENE III.—LUCILE, ASCANIO, MARINETTE, FROSINE.

LUC. (*Saying the first words to Marinette*). I have done it; it is thus I can revenge myself; if this step torments him, it will be a great consolation to me . . . Brother, you perceive a change in me; I am resolved to love Valère, after so much ill-usage; he shall become the object of my affection.

ASC. What do you say, sister? How do you change so suddenly? This inconstancy seems to me very strange.

LUC. Your change of disposition has more cause to surprise me. You formerly used always to plead in favour of Valère; for his sake you have accused me of caprice, blind cruelty, pride and injustice; and now, when I wish to love him, my intention displeases you, and I find you speaking against his interest.

ASC. I abandon his interest, sister, out of regard to yours. I know he is under the sway of another fair one; it will be a discredit to your charms if you call him back, and he does not come.

LUC. If that is all, I shall take care not to suffer a defeat; I know what I am to believe of his passion; he has shown it very clearly, at least so I think; you may safely discover my sentiments to him: or if you refuse to do it, I, myself shall let him know that his passion has touched me. What! you stand thunderstruck, brother, at those words!

ASC. Oh, sister, if I have any influence over you, if you will listen to a brother's entreaties, abandon such a design; do not take away Valère from the love of a young creature, in whom I feel great interest, and for whom, upon my word, you ought to feel some sympathy. The poor unfortunate woman loves him to distraction; to me alone she has disclosed her passion; I perceive in her heart such a tender affection, that it might soften even the most relentless being. Yes, you yourself will pity her condition when she shall become aware with what stroke you threaten to crush her love; so sure am I of the excess of her grief, that I am certain, sister, she will die, if you rob her of the man she adores. Eraste is a match that ought to satisfy you, and the mutual affection you have for one another . . .

LUC. Brother, it is sufficient! I do not know in whom you take such an interest; but let us not continue this conversation, I beg of you; leave me a little to my own thoughts.

ASC. Cruel sister, you will drive me to despair if you carry your design into execution.

SCENE IV.—LUCILE, MARINETTE.

MAR. Your resolution, madam, is very sudden.

LUC. A heart considers nothing when it is once affronted, but flies to its revenge, and eagerly lays hold of whatever it thinks can minister to its resentment. The wretch! To treat me with such extreme insolence!

MAR. You see I have not yet recovered the effects; though I were to brood over it to all eternity, I cannot understand it, and all my labour is in vain. For never did a lover express more delight on receiving good news; so pleased was he with your kind note that he called me nothing less than a divine creature; and yet, when I brought him the other message, there was never a poor girl treated so scurvily. I cannot imagine what could happen in so short a time to occasion so great a change.

LUC. Do not trouble yourself about what may have happened, since nothing shall secure him against my hatred. What! do you think there is any secret reason for this affront but his own baseness? Does the unfortunate letter I sent him, and for which I now blame myself, present the smallest excuse for his madness?

MAR. Indeed, I must say you are right; this quarrel is downright treachery; we have both been duped, and yet, madam, we listen to these faithless rascals who promise everything; who, in order to hook us, feign so much tenderness; we let our severity melt before their fine speeches, and yield to their wishes, because we are too weak! A shame on our folly, and a plague take the men!

LUC. Well, well! let him boast and laugh at us; he shall not long have cause to triumph; I will let him see that in a well-balanced mind hatred follows close on slighted favours.

MAR. At least, in such a case, it is a great happiness to know that we are not in their power. Notwithstanding all that was said, Marinette was right the other night to interfere when some people were in a very merry mood. Another, in hopes of matrimony, would have listened to the temptation, but *nescio vos*, quoth I.[4]

LUC. How foolishly you talk; how ill you choose your

[4] These two Latin words, which were in very common use in France, during Molière's time, are taken from the Vulgate, Matthew xxv. 12: "*Domine, domine, aperi nobis.*"—*At ille respondens ait:* "*Amen dico vobis, nescio vos.*"

time to joke! My heart is full of grief. If ever fate wills it that this false lover,—but I am in the wrong to conceive at present any such expectation; for Heaven has been too well pleased to afflict me to put it in my power to be revenged on him,—but if ever a propitious fate, I say, should cause Eraste to come back to me, and lay down his life as a sacrifice at my feet, as well as declare his sorrow for what he has done to-day, I forbid you, above all things, to speak to me in his favour. On the contrary, I would have you show your zeal by setting fully before me the greatness of his crime; if my heart should be tempted ever to degrade itself so far, let your affection then show itself; spare me not, but support my anger as is fit.

MAR. Oh! do not fear! leave that to me; I am at least as angry as you; I would rather remain a maid all my life than that my fat rascal should give me any inclination for him again. If he comes . . .

SCENE V.—MARINETTE, LUCILE, ALBERT.

ALB. Go in, Lucile, and tell the tutor to come to me; I wish to have a little talk with him; and as he is the master of Ascanio, find out what is the cause that the latter has been of late so gloomy.

SCENE VI.—ALBERT, *alone.*

Into what an abyss of cares and perplexities does one unjust action precipitate us. For a long time I have suffered a great deal because I was too avaricious, and passed off a stranger for my dead son. When I consider the mischief which followed I sincerely wish I had never thought of it. Sometimes I dread to behold my family in poverty and covered with shame, when the deception will be found out; at other times I fear a hundred accidents that may happen to this son whom it concerns me so much to preserve. If any business calls me abroad, I am afraid of hearing, on my return, some such melancholy tidings as these: "You know, I suppose? Have they not told you? Your son has a fever; or he has broken his leg or his arm." In short, every moment, no matter what I do, all kinds of apprehensions are continually entering into my head. Ha!

SCENE VII.—ALBERT, METAPHRASTUS.

MET. *Mandatum tuum curo diligenter.*[5]

ALB. Master, I want to . . .

MET. Master is derived from *magis ter;* it is as though you say "thrice greater."

ALB. May I die if I knew that; but, never mind, be it so. Master, then . . .

MET. Proceed.

ALB. So I would, but do not proceed to interrupt me thus. Once more, then, master, for the third time, my son causes me some uneasiness. You know that I love him, and that I always brought him up carefully.

MET. It is true: *filio non potest præferri nisi filius.*

ALB. Master, I do not think this jargon at all necessary in common conversation. I believe you are a great Latin scholar and an eminent doctor, for I rely on those who have told me so; but in a conversation which I should like to have with you, do not display all your learning—do not play the pedant, and utter ever so many words, as if you were holding forth in a pulpit. My father, though he was a very clever man, never taught me anything but my prayers; and though I have said them daily for fifty years, they are still High-Dutch to me. Therefore, do not employ your prodigious knowledge, but adapt your language to my weak understanding.

MET. Be it so.

ALB. My son seems to be afraid of matrimony; whenever I propose a match to him, he seems indifferent, and draws back.

MET. Perhaps he is of the temper of Mark Tully's brother, whom he writes about to Atticus. This is what the Greeks call *athanaton* . . . .[7]

ALB. For Heaven's sake! you ceaseless teacher, I pray you have done with the Greeks, the Albanians, the Scla-

---

5 "I hasten to obey your order."

6 "To a son one can only prefer a son." An allusion to an article of feudal law.

7 Immortal.

vonians, and all the other nations you have mentioned; they have nothing to do with my son.

MET. Well then, your son . . . ?

ALB. I do not know whether a secret love does not burn within him. Something disturbs him, or I am much deceived; for I saw him yesterday, when he did not see me, in a corner of the wood, where no person ever goes.

MET. In a recess of a grove, you mean, a remote spot, in Latin *secessus*. Virgil says, *est in secessu locus* . . . [8]

ALB. How could Virgil say that, since I am certain that there was not a soul in that quiet spot except us two?

MET. I quote Virgil as a famous author, who employed a more correct expression than the word you used, and not as a witness of what you saw yesterday.

ALB. I tell you I do not need a more correct expression, an author, or a witness, and that my own testimony is sufficient.

MET. However, you ought to choose words which are used by the best authors; *tu vivendo bonos, scribendo sequare peritos*,[9] as the saying is.

ALB. Man or devil, will you hear me without disputing?

MET. That is Quintilian's rule.

ALB. Hang the chatterbox!

MET. He has a very learned sentence upon a similar subject, which, I am sure, you will be very glad to hear.

ALB. I will be the devil to carry you off, you wretch. Oh! I am very much tempted to apply something to those chops.

MET. Sir, what is the reason that you fly in such a passion! What do you wish me to do?

ALB. I have told you twenty times; I wish you to listen to me when I speak.

MET. Oh! undoubtedly, you shall be satisfied if that is all. I am silent.

ALB. You act wisely.

MET. I am ready to hear what you have to say.

ALB. So much the better.

---

[8] There is a remote spot.

[9] "Regulate your conduct after the example of good people your style after good authors."

MET. May I be struck dead if I say another word!

ALB. Heaven grant you that favour.

MET. You shall not accuse me henceforth of talkativeness.

ALB. Be it so.

MET. Speak whenever you please

ALB. I am going to do so.

MET. And do not be afraid of my interrupting you.

ALB. That is enough.

MET. My word is my bond.

ALB. I believe so.

MET. I have promised to say nothing.

ALB. That is sufficient.

MET. From this moment I am dumb.

ALB. Very well.

MET. Speak; go on; I will give you a hearing at least; you shall not complain that I cannot keep silent; I will not so much as open my mouth.

ALB. (*Aside*). The wretch!

MET. But pray, do not be prolix. I have listened already a long time, and it is reasonable that I should speak in my turn.

ALB. Detestable torturer!

MET. Hey! good lack! would you have me listen to you for ever? Let us share the talk, at least, or I shall be gone.

ALB. My patience is really . . .

MET. What, will you proceed? You have not done yet? By Jove, I am stunned.

ALB. I have not spoken . . .

MET. Again! good Heavens! what exuberant speechifying! Can nothing be done to stop it?

ALB. I am mad with rage.

MET. You are talking again! What a peculiar way of tormenting people! Let me say a few words, I entreat you; a fool who says nothing cannot be distinguished from a wise man who holds his tongue.

ALB. Zounds! I will make you hold yours. (*Exit.*

SCENE VIII.—METAPHRASTUS, *alone.*

Hence comes very properly that saying of a philosopher, "Speak, that I may know thee." Therefore, if the liberty of speaking is taken from me, I, for my part, would as soon be divested of my humanity, and exchange my being for that of a brute. I shall have a headache for a week Oh! how I detest these eternal talkers! But if learned men are not listened to, if their mouths are for ever to be stopped, then the order of events must be changed; the hens in a little time will devour the fox; young children teach old men; little lambs take a delight in pursuing the wolf; fools make laws; women go to battle; judges be tried by criminals; and masters whipped by pupils; a sick man prescribe for a healthy one; a timorous hare . . .

SCENE IX.—ALBERT, METAPHRASTUS.

(*Albert rings a bell in the ears of Metaphrastus, and drives him off*).

MET. Mercy on me! Help! help!

ACT III.

SCENE I.—MASCARILLE, *alone*.

Heaven sometimes favours a bold design; we must get out of a bad business as well as we can. As for me, after having imprudently talked too much, the quickest remedy I could employ was to go on in the same way, and immediately to tell to our old master the whole intrigue. His son is a giddy-brained mortal, who worries me; but if the other tells what I have discovered to him, then I had better take care, for I shall get a beating. However, before his fury can be kindled, some lucky thing may happen to us, and the two old men may arrange the business between themselves. That is what I am going to attempt; without losing a moment I must, by my master's order, go and see Albert. (*Knocks at Albert's door*).

SCENE II.—ALBERT, MASCARILLE.

ALB. Who knocks?

MASC. A friend.

ALB. What brings you hither, Mascarille?

MASC. I come, sir, to wish you good-morning.

ALB. Hah! you really take a great deal of pains. Good-morning, then, with all my heart. (*He goes in*).

MASC. The answer is short and sweet. What a blunt old fellow he is. (*Knocks*).

ALB. What, do you knock again?

MASC. You have not heard me, sir.

ALB. Did you not wish me good-morning?

MASC. I did.

ALB. Well, then, good morning I say.

(*Is going; Mascarille stops him.*

MASC. But I likewise come to pay Mr. Polydore's compliments to you.

ALB. Oh! that is another thing. Has your master ordered you to give his compliments to me?

MASC. Yes.

ALB. I am obliged to him; you may go; tell him I wish him all kind of happiness. (*Exit*).

MASC. This man is an enemy to all ceremony. (*Knocks*). I have not finished, sir, giving you his whole message; he has a favour to request of you.

ALB. Well, whenever he pleases, I am at his service.

MASC. (*Stopping him*). Stay, and allow me to finish in two words. He desires to have a few minutes' conversation with you about an important affair, and he will come hither.

ALB. Hey! what affair can that be which makes him wish to have some conversation with me?

MASC. A great secret, I tell you, which he has but just discovered, and which, no doubt, greatly concerns you both. And now I have delivered my message.

SCENE III.—ALBERT, *alone*.

ALB. Righteous Heavens! how I tremble! Polydore and I have had little acquaintance together; my designs will all be overthrown; this secret is, no doubt, that of which I dread the discovery. They have bribed somebody to betray me; so there is a stain upon my honour which can never be wiped off. My imposture is found out. Oh! how difficult it is to keep the truth concealed for any length of time! How much better would it have been for me and my reputation had I followed the dictates of a well-founded apprehension! Many times and oft have I been tempted to give up to Polydore the wealth I withhold from him, in order to prevent the outcry that will be raised against me when everything shall be known, and so get the whole business quietly settled. But, alas! it is now too late; the opportunity is gone; and this wealth, which wrongfully came into my family, will be lost to them, and sweep away the greatest part of my own property with it.

SCENE IV.—ALBERT, POLYDORE.

POL. (*Not seeing Albert*). To be married in this fashion, and no one knowing anything about it! I hope it may all end well! I do not know what to think of it; I much fear the great wealth and just anger of the father. But I see him alone.

ALB. Oh, Heavens! yonder comes Polydore.

POL. I tremble to accost him.

ALB. Fear keeps me back.

POL. How shall I begin?

ALB. What shall I say?

POL. He is in a great passion.

ALB. He changes colour.

POL. I see, Signor Albert, by your looks, that you know already what brings me hither.

ALB. Alas! yes.

POL. The news, indeed, may well surprise you, and I could scarcely believe what I was told just now.

ALB. I ought to blush with shame and confusion.

POL. I think such an action deserves great blame, and do not pretend to excuse the guilty.

ALB. Heaven is merciful to miserable sinners.

POL. You should bear this in mind.

ALB. A man ought to behave as a Christian.

POL. That is quite right.

ALB. Have mercy; for Heaven's sake, have mercy, Signor Polydore.

POL. It is for me to implore it of you.

ALB. Grant me mercy; I ask it on my bended knees.

POL. I ought to be in that attitude rather than you.[10]

---

[10] The two old men are kneeling opposite to one another.

ALB. Pity my misfortune.

POL. After such an outrage I am the postulant.

ALB. Your goodness is heart-rending.

POL. You abash me with so much humility.

ALB. Once more, pardon.

POL. Alas! I crave it of you.

ALB. I am extremely sorry for this business.

POL. And I feel it greatly.

ALB. I venture to entreat you not to make it public.

POL. Alas, Signor Albert, I desire the very same.

ALB. Let us preserve my honour.

POL. With all my heart.

ALB. As for money, you shall determine how much you require.

POL. I desire no more than you are willing to give; you shall be the master in all these things, I shall be but too happy if you are so.

ALB. Ha! what a God-like man! how very kind he is!

POL. How very kind you are yourself, and that after such a misfortune.

ALB. May you be prosperous in all things!

POL. May Heaven preserve you!

ALB. Let us embrace like brothers.

POL. With all my heart! I am overjoyed that everything has ended so happily,

ALB. I thank Heaven for it.

POL. I do not wish to deceive you; I was afraid you would resent that Lucile has committed a fault with my son; and as you are powerful, have wealth and friends. . .

ALB. Hey! what do you say of faults and Lucile?

POL. Enough, let us not enter into a useless conversation. I own my son is greatly to blame; nay, if that will satisfy you, I will admit that he alone is at fault; that your daughter was too virtuous, and would never have taken a step so derogatory to honour, had she not been prevailed upon by a wicked seducer; that the wretch has betrayed her innocent modesty, and thus frustrated all your expectations. But since the thing is done, and my prayers have been granted, since we are both at peace and amity, let it be buried in oblivion, and repair the offence by the ceremony of a happy alliance.

ALB. (*Aside*). Oh, Heavens! what a mistake I have been under! What do I hear! I get from one difficulty into another as great. I do not know what to answer amidst these different emotions; if I say one word, I am afraid of betraying myself.

POL. What are you thinking of, Signor Albert?

ALB. Of nothing. Let us put off our conversation for a while, I pray you. I have become suddenly very unwell, and am obliged to leave you.

SCENE V.—POLYDORE, *alone*.

I can look into his soul and discover what disturbs him; though he listened to reason at first, yet his anger is not quite appeased. Now and then the remembrance of the offence flashes upon him; he endeavours to hide his emotion by leaving me alone. I feel for him, and his grief touches me. It will require some time before he regains his composure, for if sorrow is suppressed too much, it easily becomes worse. O! here comes my foolish boy, the cause of all this confusion.

SCENE VI.—POLYDORE, VALÈRE.

POL. So, my fine fellow, shall your nice goings-on disturb your poor old father every moment? You perform something new every day, and we never hear of anything else.

VAL. What am I doing every day that is so very criminal? And how have I deserved so greatly a father's wrath?

POL. I am a strange man, and very peculiar to accuse so good and discreet a son. He lives like a saint, and is at prayers and in the house from morning to evening. It is a great untruth to say that he perverts the order of nature, and turns day into night! It is a horrible falsehood to state that upon several occasions he has shown no consideration for father or kindred; that very lately he married secretly the daughter of Albert, regardless of the great consequences that were sure to follow; they mistake him for some other! The poor innocent creature does not even know what I mean! Oh, you villain! whom Heaven has sent me as a punishment for my sins, will you always do as you like, and shall I never see you act discreetly as long as I live? (*Exit.*

VAL. (*Alone, musing*). Whence comes this blow? I am perplexed, and can find none to think of but Mascarille, he will never confess it to me; I must be cunning, and curb my well-founded anger a little.

SCENE VII.—VALÈRE, MASCARILLE.

VAL. Mascarille, my father whom I just saw knows our whole secret.

MASC. Does he know it?

VAL. Yes.

MASC. How the deuce could he know it?

VAL. I do not know whom to suspect; but the result has been so successful, that I have all the reason in the world to be delighted. He has not said one cross word about it; he excuses my fault, and approves of my love; I would fain know who could have made him so tractable. I cannot express to you the satisfaction it gives me.

MASC. And what would you say, sir, if it was I who had procured you this piece of good luck?

VAL. Indeed! you want to deceive me.

MASC. It is I, I tell you, who told it to your father, and produced this happy result for you.

VAL. Really, without jesting?

MASC. The devil take me if I jest, and if it is not as I tell you.

VAL. (*Drawing his sword*). And may he take me if I do not this very moment reward you for it.

MASC. Ha, sir! what now? Don't surprise me.

VAL. Is this the fidelity you promised me? If I had not deceived you, you would never have owned the trick which I rightly suspected you played me. You rascal! your tongue, too ready to wag, has provoked my father's wrath against me, and utterly ruined me. You shall die without saying another word.

MASC. Gently; my soul is not in a fit condition to die. I entreat you, be kind enough to await the result of this affair. I had very good reasons for revealing a marriage which you yourself could hardly conceal. It was a masterpiece of policy; you will not find your rage justified by the issue. Why should you get angry if, through me, you get all you desire, and are freed from the constraint you at present lie under?

VAL. And what if all this talk is nothing but moonshine?

MASC. Why, then, it will be time enough to kill me; but my schemes may perchance succeed. Heaven will assist his own servants; you will be satisfied in the end, and thank me for my extraordinary management.

VAL. Well, we shall see. But Lucile . . .

MASC. Hold, here comes her father

SCENE VIII.—ALBERT, VALÈRE, MASCARILLE.

ALB. (*Not seeing Valère*). The more I recover from the confusion into which I fell at first, the more I am astonished at the strange things Polydore told me, and which my fear made me interpret in so different a manner to what he intended. Lucile maintains that it is all nonsense, and spoke to me in such a manner as leaves no room for suspicion . . . Ha! sir, it is you whose unheard-of impudence sports with my honour, and invents this base story?

MASC. Pray, Signor Albert, use milder terms, and do not be so angry with your son-in-law.

ALB. How! son-in-law, rascal? You look as if you were the main-spring of this intrigue, and the originator of it.

MASC. Really I see no reason for you to fly in such a passion.

ALB. Pray, do you think it right to take away the character of my daughter, and bring such a scandal upon a whole family?

MASC. He is ready to do all you wish.

ALB. I only want him to tell the truth. If he had any inclination for Lucile, he should have courted her in an honourable and open way; he should have acted as he ought, and asked her father's leave; and not have had recourse to this cowardly contrivance, which offends modesty so much.

MASC. What! Lucile is not secretly engaged to my master?

ALB. No, rascal, nor ever will be.

MASC. Not quite so fast! If the thing is already done, will you give your consent to ratify that secret engagement?

ALB. And if it is certain that it is not so, will you have your bones broken?

VAL. It is easy, sir, to prove to you that he speaks the truth.

ALB. Good! there is the other! Like master, like man. O! what impudent liars!

MASC. Upon the word of a man of honour, it is as I say.

VAL. Why should we deceive you?

ALB. (*Aside*) They are two sharpers that know how to play into each other's hands.

MASC. But let us come to the proof, and without quarrelling. Send for Lucile, and let her speak for herself.

ALB. And what if she should prove you a liar?

MASC. She will not contradict us, sir; of that I am certain. Promise to give your consent to their engagement; and I will suffer the severest punishment if, with her own mouth, she does not confess to you that she is engaged to Valère, and shares his passion.

ALB. We shall see this presently.

(*He knocks at his door*).

MASC. (*To Valère*). Courage, Sir; all will end well.

ALB. Ho! Lucile, one word with you.

VAL. (*To Mascarille*). I fear . . .

MASC. Fear nothing.

SCENE IX.—VALÈRE, ALBERT, LUCILE, MASCARILLE.

MASC. Signor Albert, at least be silent. At length, madam, everything conspires to make your happiness complete. Your father, who is informed of your love, leaves you your husband and gives his permission to your union, provided that, banishing all frivolous fears, a few words from your own mouth corroborate what we have told him.

LUC. What nonsense does this impudent scoundrel tell me?

MASC. That is all right. I am already honoured with a fine title.

LUC. Pray, sir, who has invented this nice story which has been spread about to-day?

VAL. Pardon me, charming creature. My servant has been babbling; our marriage is discovered, without my consent.

LUC. Our marriage?

VAL. Everything is known, adorable Lucile; it is vain to dissemble.

LUC. What! the ardour of my passion has made you my husband?

VAL. It is a happiness which causes a great many heart-burnings. But I impute the successful result of my courtship less to your great passion for me than to your kindness of heart. I know you have cause to be offended, that it was the secret which you would fain have concealed. I myself have put a restraint on my ardour, so that I might not violate your express commands; but . . .

MASC. Yes, it was I who told it. What great harm is done?

LUC. Was there ever a falsehood like this? Dare you mention this in my very presence, and hope to obtain my hand by this fine contrivance? What a wretched lover you are—you, whose gallant passion would wound my honour, because it could not gain my heart; who wish to frighten my father by a foolish story, so that you might obtain my hand as a reward for having vilified me. Though everything were favourable to your love—my father, fate, and my own inclination—yet my well-founded resentment would struggle against my own inclination, fate, and my father, and even lose life rather than be united to one who thought to obtain my hand in this manner. Begone! If my sex could with decency be provoked to any outburst of rage, I would let you know what it was to treat me thus.

VAL. (*To Mascarille*). It is all over with us; her anger cannot be appeased.

MASC. Let me speak to her. Prithee, madam, what is the good of all these excuses? What are you thinking of? And what strange whim makes you thus oppose your own happiness? If your father were a harsh parent, the case would be different, but he listens to reason; and he himself has assured me that if you would but confess the truth, his affection would grant you everything. I believe you are a little ashamed frankly to acknowledge that you have yielded to love; but if you have lost a trifling amount of freedom, everything will be set to rights again by a good marriage. Your great love for Valère may be blamed a little, but the mischief is not so great as if you had murdered a man. We all know that flesh is frail, and that a maid is neither stock nor stone. You were not the first, that is certain; and you will not be the last, I dare say.

LUC. What! can you listen to this shameless talk, and make no reply to these indignities?

ALB. What would you have me say? This affair puts me quite beside myself.

MASC. Upon my word, madam, you ought to have confessed all before now.

LUC. What ought I to have confessed?

MASC. What? Why, what has passed between my master and you. A fine joke, indeed!

LUC. Why, what has passed between your master and me, impudent wretch?

MASC. You ought, I think, to know that better than I; you passed that night too agreeably, to make us believe you could forget it so soon.

LUC. Father, we have too long borne with the insolence of an impudent lackey. (*Gives him a box on the ear*).

SCENE X.—ALBERT, VALÈRE, MASCARILLE.

MASC. I think she gave me a box on the ear.

ALB. Begone! rascal, villain! Her father approves the way in which she has made her hand felt upon your cheek.

MASC. May be so; yet may the devil take me if I said anything but what was true!

ALB. And may I lose an ear if you carry on this impudence any further!

MASC. Shall I send for two witnesses to testify to the truth of my statements?

ALB. Shall I send for two of my servants to give you a sound thrashing?

MASC. Their testimony will corroborate mine.

ALB. Their arms may make up for my want of strength.

MASC. I tell you, Lucile behaves thus because she is ashamed.

ALB. I tell you, you shall be answerable for all this.

MASC. Do you know Ormin, that stout and clever notary?

ALB. Do you know Grimpant, the city executioner?

MASC. And Simon, the tailor, who used formerly to work for all the people of fashion?

ALB. And the gibbet set up in the middle of the market-place?

MASC. You shall see they will confirm the truth of this marriage.

ALB. You shall see they will make an end of you.

MASC. They were the witnesses chosen by them.

ALB. They shall shortly revenge me on you.

MASC. I myself saw them at the altar.

ALB. And I myself shall see you with a halter.

MASC. By the same token, your daughter had a black veil on.

ALB. By the same token, your face foretells your doom.

MASC. What an obstinate old man.

ALB. What a cursed rascal! You may thank my advanced years, which prevent me from punishing your insulting remarks upon the spot; but I promise you, you shall be paid with full interest.

SCENE XI.—VALÈRE, MASCARILLE.

VAL. Well, where is now that fine result you were to produce . . . ?

MASC. I understand what you mean. Everything goes against me: I see cudgels and gibbets preparing for me on every side. Therefore, so that I may be at rest amidst this chaos, I shall go and throw myself headlong from a rock, if, in my present despair, I can find one high enough to please me. Farewell, sir.

VAL. No, no; in vain you wish to fly. If you die, I expect it to be in my presence.

MASC. I cannot die if anybody is looking on: it would only delay my end.

VAL. Follow me traitor; follow me. My maddened love will soon show whether this is a jesting matter or not.

MASC. (*Alone*). Unhappy Mascarille, to what misfortunes are you condemned to-day for another's sin!

ACT IV.

SCENE I.—ASCANIO, FROSINE.

FROS. What has happened is very annoying.

ASC. My dear Frosine, fate has irrevocably decreed my ruin. Now the affair has gone so far, it will never stop there, but will go on; Lucile and Valère, surprised at such a strange mystery, will, one day, try to find their way amidst this darkness, and thus all my plans will miscarry. For, whether Albert is acquainted with the deception, or whether he himself is deceived, as well as the rest of the world, if ever it happens that my family is discovered, and all the wealth he has wrongfully acquired passes into the hands of others, judge if he will then endure my presence; for, not having any interest more in the matter, he will abandon me, and his affection for me will be at an end. Whatever, then, my lover may think of my deception, will he acknowledge as his wife a girl without either fortune or family?

FROS. I think you reason rightly; but these reflections should have come sooner. What has prevented you from seeing all this before? there was no need to be a witch to foresee, as soon as you fell in love with Valère, all that your genius never found out until to-day. It is the natural consequence of what you have done; as soon as I was made acquainted with it I never imagined it would end otherwise.

ASC. But what must I do? There never was such a misfortune as mine. Put yourself in my place, and give me advice.

FROS. If I put myself in your place, you will have to give me advice upon this ill-success; for I am you, and you are I. Counsel me, Frosine, in the condition I am in. Where can we find a remedy? Tell me, I beg of you.

ASC. Alas! do not make fun of me. You show but

little sympathy with my bitter grief, if you laugh in the midst of my distress.

FROS. Really, Ascanio, I pity your distress, and would do my utmost to help you. But what can I do, after all? I see very little likelihood of arranging this affair so as to satisfy your love.

ASC. If no assistance can be had, I must die.

FROS. Die! Come, come; it is always time enough for that. Death is a remedy ever at hand; we ought to make use of it as late as possible.

ASC. No, no, Frosine. If you and your invaluable counsels do not guide me amidst all these breakers, I abandon myself wholly to despair.

FROS. Do you know what I am thinking about? I must go and see the . . . .[11] But here comes Eraste; he may interrupt us. We will talk this matter over as we go along. Come, let us retire.

SCENE II.—ÉRASTE, GROS-RENÉ.

ERAS. You have failed again?

GR.-RE. Never was an ambassador less listened to. No sooner had I told her that you desired to have a moment's conversation with her, than, drawing herself up, she answered haughtily, "Go, go, I value your master just as much as I do you; tell him he may go about his business;" and after this fine speech she turned her head away from me and walked off. Marinette, too, imitating her mistress, said, with a disdainful sneer, "Begone, you low fellow,"[12] and then left me; so that your fortune and mine are very much alike.

ERAS. What an ungrateful creature, to receive with so much haughtiness the quick return of a heart justly in-

---

[11] Frosine means by "the . . . , " the woman who knows the secret of all this intrigue, and who is supposed to be the mother of Ascanio, This is explained later on, in Act V., Scene 4, page 125.

[12] In the original it is *beau valet de carreau*. Littré, in his "Dictionnaire de la langue francaise," says that this word which means literally "knave of diamonds, was considered an insult, because in the old packs of cards of the beginning of the seventeenth century, that knave was called *valet de ch sse*, hunting servant, a rather menial situation; while the knave of spades, *valet de pique*, was called *valet de noblesse*, nobleman's servant: the knave of hearts, *valet de cœur*, *valet de cour*, court servant; and the knave of clubs, *valet de trefle*, *valet de pied*, foot-servant.

censed. Is the first outburst of a passion, which with so much reason thought itself deceived, unworthy of excuse? Could I, when burning with love, remain insensible, in that fatal moment, to the happiness of a rival? Would any other not have acted in the same way as I did, or been less amazed at so much boldness? Was I not quick in abandoning my well-founded suspicions? I did not wait till she swore they were false. When no one can tell as yet what to think of it, my heart, full of impatience, restores Lucile to her former place, and seeks to find excuses for her. Will not all these proofs satisfy her of the ardour of my respectful passion? Instead of calming my mind, and providing me with arms against a rival who wishes to alarm me, this ungrateful woman abandons me to all the tortures of jealousy, and refuses to receive my messages and notes, or to grant me an interview. Alas! that love is certainly very lukewarm which can be extinguished by so trifling an offence; that scornful rigour, which is displayed so readily, sufficiently shows to me the depth of her affection. What value ought I to set now upon all the caprices with which she fanned my love? No! I do not pretend to be any longer the slave of one who has so little love for me; since she does not mind whether she keeps me or not, I will do the same.

GR.-RE. And so will I. Let us both be angry, and put our love on the list of our old sins; we must teach a lesson to that wayward sex, and make them feel that we possess some courage. He that will bear their contempt shall have enough of it. If we had sense enough not to make ourselves too cheap, women would not talk so big. Oh! how insolent they are through our weakness! May I be hanged if we should not see them fall upon our neck more often than we wished, if it was not for those servilities with which most men, now-a-days, continually spoil them.

ERAS. As for me, nothing vexes me so much as contempt; and to punish her's by one as great, I am resolved to cherish a new passion.

GR.-RE. So will I, and never trouble my head about women again. I renounce them all, and believe honestly you could not do better than to act like me. For, master, people say that woman is an animal hard to be known, and naturally very prone to evil; and as an animal is always an animal, and will never be anything but an animal, though it lived for a hundred thousand years, so, without contradiction, a woman is always a woman, and will never be anything but a woman as long as the world endures.[13] Wherefore, as a certain Greek author says: a woman's head is like a quicksand; for pray, mark well this argument, which is most weighty: As the head is the chief of the body, and as the body without a chief is worse than a beast, unless the chief has a good understanding with the body, and unless everything be as well regulated as if it were measured with a pair of compasses, we see certain confusions arrive; the animal part then endeavours to get the better of the rational, and we see one pull to the right, another to the left; one wants something soft, another something hard; in short, everything goes topsy turvy. This is to show that here below, as it has been explained to me, a woman's head is like a weathercock on the top of a house, which veers about at the slightest breeze; that is why cousin Aristotle often compares her to the sea; hence people say that nothing in the world is so stable as the waves.[14] Now, by comparison—for comparison makes us comprehend an argument distinctly,—and we learned men love a comparison better than a similitude,—by comparison, then, if you please, master, as we see that the sea, when a storm rises, begins to rage, the wind roars and destroys, billows dash against billows with a great hullabaloo, and the ship, in spite of the mariner, goes sometimes down to the cellar and sometimes up into the garret; so, when a woman gets whims and crotchets into her head, we see a tempest in the form of a violent storm, which will break out by certain . . .

---

[13] This passage is paraphrased from Erasmus, *Colloquia familiaria et Encomium Moriæ*, in which, after having called a woman *animal stultum atque ineptum verum ridiculum, et suave*, Folly adds, *Quemadmodum, juxta Græcorum proverbium, simia semper est simia, etiamsi purpura vestiatur, ita mulier semper mulier est, hoc est stulta, quamcunque personam induxerit.*

[14] Though "stable" is here used, it is only employed to show the confusion of Gros-René's ideas, who, of course, wishes to say "unstable."

words, and then a . . . certain wind, which by . . . certain waves in . . . a cert in manner, like a sand-bank . . . when . . . In short, woman is worse than the devil.[15]

ERAS. You have argued that very well.

GR.-RE. Pretty well, thanks to Heaven ; but I see them coming this way, sir,—stand firm.

ERAS. Never fear.

GR.-RE. I am very much afraid that her eyes will ensnare you again.

SCENE III. — ÉRASTE, LUCILE, MARINETTE, GROS-RENÉ.

MAR. He is not gone yet, but do not yield.

LUC. Do not imagine I am so weak.

MAR. He comes towards us.

ERAS. No, no, madam, do not think that I have come to speak to you again of my passion ; it is all over ; I am resolved to cure myself. I know how little share I have in your heart. A resentment kept up so long for a slight offence shows me your indifference but too plainly, and I must tell you that contempt, above all things, wounds a lofty mind. I confess I saw in you charms which I never found in any other ; the delight I took in my chains would have made me prefer them to sceptres, had they been offered to me. Yes, my love for you was certainly very great ; my life was centred in you ; I will even own that, though I am insulted, I shall still perhaps have difficulty enough to free myself. Maybe, notwithstanding the cure I am attempting, my heart may for a long time smart with this wound. Freed from a yoke which I was happy to bend under, I shall take a resolution never to love again. But no matter, since your hatred repulses a heart which

---

15 This long speech of Gros-René ridicules the pedantic arguments of some of the philosophers of the time of Molière. It also attributes to the ancients some sayings of authors of the day ; for example, the comparison, from a Greek author, "that a woman's head is like a quicksand,' is from a contemporary ; the saying from Aristotle, comparing woman to the sea, is from Malherbe. Words very familiar look more homely when employed with high-flown language, and Gros-René's speech is no bad example of this, whilst at the same time it becomes more muddled the longer it goes on. There exists also a tradition that the actor who performs the part of Gros-René should in order to show his confusion, when he says "goes sometimes down the cellar, ' point to his head, and when he mentions "up into the garret," point to his feet.

Desenne del.

THE LOVE TIFF.

Act IV sc 3.

love brings back to you, this is the last time you shall ever be troubled by the man you so much despise.

LUC. You might have made the favour complete, sir, and spared me also this last trouble.

ERAS. Very well, madam, very well, you shall be satisfied. I here break off all acquaintance with you, and break it off for ever, since you wish it; may I lose my life if ever again I desire to converse with you!

LUC. So much the better, you will oblige me.

ERAS. No, no, do not be afraid that I shall break my word! For, though my heart may be weak enough not to be able to efface your image, be assured you shall never have the pleasure of seeing me return.

LUC. You may save yourself the trouble.

ERAS. I would pierce my breast a hundred times should I ever be so mean as to see you again, after this unworthy treatment.

LUC. Be it so; let us talk no more about it.

ERAS. Yes, yes; let us talk no more about it; and to make an end here of all unnecessary speeches, and to give you a convincing proof, ungrateful woman, that I forever throw off your chain, I will keep nothing which may remind me of what I must forget. Here is your portrait; it presents to the eye many wonderful and dazzling charms, but underneath them lurk as many monstrous faults; it is a delusion which I restore to you.

GR.-RE. You are right.

LUC. And I, not to be behind-hand with you in the idea of returning everything, restore to you this diamond which you obliged me to accept.

MAR. Very well.

ERAS. Here is likewise a bracelet of yours.[16]

LUC. And this agate seal is yours.

ERAS. (*Reads*). "You love me with the most ardent passion, Eraste, and wish to know if I feel the same. If I do not love Eraste as much, at least I am pleased that

---

[16] Formerly lovers used to wear bracelets generally made of each others hair, which no doubt were hidden from the common view, Shakespeare, in his *Mid-summer Night's Dream*, Act i., Scene I. says, "Thou, Lysander, thou hast . . . stol'n th' impression of her fantasy with bracelets of thy hair."

Eraste should thus love me.—LUCILE." You assure me by this letter that you accept my love; it is a falsehood which I punish thus. (*Tears the letter*).

LUC. (*Reading*). "I do not know what may be the fate of my ardent love, nor how long I shall suffer; but this I know, beauteous charmer, that I shall always love you.—ERASTE." This is an assurance of everlasting love; both the hand and the letter told a lie. (*Tears the letter*).

GR.-RE. Go on.

ERAS. (*Showing another letter*). This is another of your letters; it shall share the same fate.

MAR. (*To Lucile*). Be firm.

LUC. (*Tearing another letter*). I should be sorry to keep back one of them.

GR.-RE. (*To Eraste*). Do not let her have the last word.

MAR. (*To Lucile*). Hold out bravely to the end.

LUC. Well, there are the rest.

ERAS. Thank Heaven, that is all! May I be struck dead if I do not keep my word!

LUC. May it confound me if mine be vain.

ERAS. Farewell, then.

LUC. Farewell, then.

MAR. (*To Lucile*). Nothing could be better.

GR.-RE. (*To Eraste*). You triumph.

MAR. (*To Lucile*). Come, let us leave him.

GR.-RE. (*To Eraste*). You had best retire after this courageous effort.

MAR. (*To Lucile*). What are you waiting for?

GR.-RE. (*To Eraste*). What more do you want?

ERAS. Ah, Lucile, Lucile! you will be sorry to lose a heart like mine, and I know it.

LUC. Eraste, Eraste, I may easily find a heart like yours.

ERAS. No, no, search everywhere; you will never find one so passionately fond of you, I assure you. I do not say this to move you to pity; I should be in the wrong now to wish it; the most respectful passion could not bind you. You wanted to break with me; I must think of you no more. But whatever any one may pretend, nobody will ever love you so tenderly as I have done.

LUC. When a woman is really beloved she is treated differently, and is not condemned so rashly.

ERAS. Those who love are apt to be jealous on the slightest cause of suspicion, but they can never wish to lose the object of their adoration, and that you have done.

LUC. Pure jealousy is more respectful

ERAS. An offence caused by love is looked upon with more indulgence.

LUC. No, Eraste, your flame never burnt very bright.

ERAS. No, Lucile, you never loved me.

LUC. Oh! that does not trouble you much, I suppose; perhaps it would have been much better for me if . . . But no more of this idle talk; I do not say what I think on the subject.

ERAS. Why?

LUC. Because, as we are to break, it would be out of place, it seems to me.

ERAS. Do we break, then?

LUC. Yes, to be sure; have we not done so already?

ERAS. And you can do this calmly?

LUC. Yes; so can you.

ERAS. I?

LUC. Undoubtedly. It is weakness to let people see that we are hurt by losing them.

ERAS. But, hard-hearted woman, it is you who would have it so.

LUC. I? not at all; it was you who took that resolution.

ERAS. I? I thought it would please you.

LUC. Me; not at all; you did it for your own satisfaction.

ERAS. But what if my heart should wish to resume its former chain? If, though very sad, it should sue for pardon . . . ?[17]

LUC. No, no; do no such thing; my weakness is too great. I am afraid I might too quickly grant your request.

ERAS. Oh! you cannot grant it, nor I ask for it, too soon, after what I have just heard. Consent to love me

---

[17] An imitation from Horace, book iii., ode ix., vers. 17 and 18.

Quid? si prisca redet Venus
Diductosque jugo cogit aheneo?

still, madam; so pure a flame ought to burn for ever, for your own sake. I ask for it, pray grant me this kind pardon.

LUC. Lead me home.

SCENE IV.—MARINETTE, GROS-RENÉ.

MAR. Oh! cowardly creature,

GR.-RE. Oh! weak courage.

MAR. I blush with indignation.

GR.-RE. I am swelling with rage; do not imagine I will yield thus.

MAR. And do not think to find such a dupe in me.

GR.-RE. Come on, come on; you shall soon see what my wrath is capable of doing.

MAR. I am not the person you take me for; you have not my silly mistress to deal with. It is enough to look at that fine phiz to be smitten with the man himself! Should I fall in love with your beastly face? Should I hunt after you? Upon my word, girls like us are not for the like of you.

GR.-RE. Ay! and you address me in such a fashion? Here, here, without any further compliments, there is your bow of tawdry lace, and your narrow ribbon; it shall not have the honour of being on my ear any more.

MAR. And to show you how I despise you, here, take back your half hundred of Paris pins, which you gave me yesterday with so much bragging.

GR.-RE. Take back your knife too; a thing most rich and rare; it cost you about twopence when you made me a present of it.

MAR. Take back your scissors with the pinchbeck chain.

GR.-RE. I forgot the piece of cheese you gave me the day before yesterday – here it is; I wish I could bring back the broth you made me eat, so that I might have nothing belonging to you.

MAR. I have none of your letters about me now, but I shall burn every one of them.

GR.-RE. And do you know what I shall do with yours?

MAR. Take care you never come begging to me again to forgive you.

GR. RE. (*Picking up a bit of straw*). To cut off every

way of being reconciled, we must break this straw between us; when a straw is broken, it settles an affair between people of honour.[18] Cast none of your sheep's eyes at me;[19] I will be angry.

MAR. Do not look at me thus; I am too much provoked.

GR.-RE. Here, break this straw; this is the way of never recanting again; break. What do you laugh at, you jade?

MAR. Yes, you make me laugh.

GR.-RE. The deuce take your laughing! all my anger is already softened. What do you say? shall we break or not?

MAR. Just as you please.

GR.-RE. Just as you please.

MAR. Nay, it shall be as you please.

GR.-RE. Do you wish me never to love you?

MAR. I? As you like.

GR.-RE. As you yourself like; only say the word.

MAR. I shall say nothing.

GR.-RE. Nor I.

MAR. Nor I.

GR.-RE. Faith! we had better forswear all this nonsense; shake hands, I pardon you.

MAR. And I forgive you.

GR.-RE. Bless me! how you bewitch me with your charms.

---

[18] A wisp of straw, or a stick, was formerly used as a symbol of investiture of a feudal fief. According to some authors the breaking of the straw or stick was a proof that the vassals renounced their homage; hence the allusion of Molière. The breaking of a staff was also typical of the voluntary or compulsory abandonment of power. Formerly, after the death of the kings of France, the *grand maitre* (master of the household) broke his wand of office over the grave, saying aloud three times, *le roi est mort* and then *Vive le roi.* Hence also, most likely, the saying of Prospero, in Shakespeare's "Tempest" Act v. Sc. 1, "I'll break my staff," *i. e.*, I voluntarily abandon my power. Sometimes the breaking of a staff betokened dishonour, as in Shakespeare's second part of "Henry VI." Act i. Sc. 2, when Gloster says: "Methought this staff, mine office-badge in court was broke in twain."

[19] According to tradition, Gros-René and Marinette stand on the stage back to back; from time to time they look to the right and to the left; when their looks meet they turn their heads abruptly away, whilst Gros-René presents over his shoulder to Marinette the piece of straw, which the latter takes very good care not to touch.

MAR. What a fool is Marinette when her Gros-René is by.

ACT V.

SCENE I.—MASCARILLE, *alone*.

"As soon as darkness has invaded the town, I will enter Lucile's room; go, therefore, and get ready immediately the dark lantern, and whatever arms are necessary." When my master said these words, it sounded in my ears as if he had said, "Go quickly and get a halter to hang yourself." But come on, master of mine, for I was so astonished when first I heard your order, that I had no time to answer you; but I shall talk with you now, and confound you; therefore defend yourself well, and let us argue without making a noise. You say you wish to go and visit Lucile to-night? "Yes, Mascarille." And what do you propose to do? "What a lover does who wishes to be convinced." "What a man does who has very little brains, who risks his carcass when there is no occasion for it. "But do you know what is my motive? Lucile is angry." Well, so much the worse for her. "But my love prompts me to go and appease her." But love is a fool, and does not know what he says: will this same love defend us against an enraged rival, father, or brother? "Do you think any of them intend to harm us?" Yes, really, I do think so; and especially this rival. "Mascarille, in any case, what I trust to is, that we shall go well armed, and if anybody interrupts us we shall draw." Yes, but that is precisely what your servant does not wish to do. I draw! Good Heavens! am I a Roland, master, or a Ferragus?[20] You hardly know me.

---

[20] Roland, or Orlando in Italian, one of Charlemagne's paladins and nephew is represented as brave, loyal, and simple-minded. On the return of Charlemagne from Spain, Roland who commanded the rear-guard, fell into an ambuscade at Roncezvalles, in the Pyrenées (778), and perished, with the flower of French chivalry. He is the hero of Ariosto's poem, "Orlando Furioso." In this same poem Cant. xii. is also mentioned Ferragus, or Ferrau in Italian, a Saracen giant, who dropped his helmet into the river, and vowed he would never wear another till he had won that worn by Orlando; the latter slew him in the only part where he was vulnerable.

When I, who love myself so dearly, consider that two inches of cold steel in this body would be quite sufficient to send a poor mortal to his last home, I am particularly disgusted. "But you will be armed from head to foot." So much the worse. I shall be less nimble to get into the thicket; besides, there is no armour so well made but some villainous point will pierce its joints. "Oh! you will then be considered a coward." Never mind; provided I can but always move my jaws. At table you may set me down for as good as four persons, if you like; but when fighting is going on, you must not count me for anything. Moreover, if the other world possesses charms for you, the air of this world agrees very well with me. I do not thirst after death and wounds; if you have a mind to play the fool, you may do it all by yourself, I assure you.

SCENE II.—VALÈRE, MASCARILLE.

VAL. I never felt a day pass more slowly; the sun seems to have forgotten himself; he has yet such a course to run before he reaches his bed, that I believe he will never accomplish it; his slow motion drives me mad.

MASC. What an eagerness to go in the dark, to grope about for some ugly adventure! You see that Lucile is obstinate in her repulses. . . .

VAL. A truce to these idle remonstrances. Though I were sure to meet a hundred deaths lying in ambush, yet I feel her wrath so greatly, that I shall either appease it, or end my fate. I am resolved on that.

MASC. I approve of your design; but it is unfortunate, sir, that we must get in secretly.

VAL. Very well.

MASC. And I am afraid I shall only be in the way.

VAL. How so?

MASC. I have a cough which nearly kills me, and the noise it makes may betray you. Every moment . . . (*He coughs*). You see what a punishment it is.

VAL. You will get better; take some liquorice.

MASC. I do not think, sir, it will get better. I should be delighted to go with you, but I should be very sorry if any misfortune should befall my dear master through me.

SCENE III.—VALÈRE, LA RAPIÈRE, MASCARILLE.

LA RA. Sir, I have just now heard from good authority that Eraste is greatly enraged against you, and that Albert talks also of breaking all the bones in Mascarille's body, on his daughter's account.

MASC. I? I have nothing to do with all this confusion. What have I done to have all the bones in my body broken? Am I the guardian of the virginity of all the girls in the town, that I am to be thus threatened? Have I any influence with temptation? Can I help it, I, poor fellow, if I have a mind to try it?

VAL. Oh! they are not so dangerous as they pretend to be; however courageous love may have made Eraste, he will not have so easy a bargain with us.

LA RA. If you should have any need for it, my arm is entirely at your service. You know me to be at all times staunch.[21]

VAL. I am much obliged to you, M. de la Rapière.

LA RA. I have likewise two friends I can procure, who will draw against all comers, and upon whom you may safely rely.

MASC. Accept their services, sir.

VAL. You are too kind.

LA RA. Little Giles might also have assisted us, if a sad accident had not taken him from us. Oh, sir, it is a great pity! He was such a handy fellow, too! You know the trick justice played him; he died like a hero; when the executioner broke him on the wheel, he made his exit without uttering a word.

VAL. M. de la Rapière, such a man ought to be lamented, but, as for your escort, I thank you, I want them not.

LA RA. Be it so, but do not forget that you are sought after, and may have some scurvy trick played upon you.

VAL. And I, to show you how much I fear him, will

---

[21] It is thought the introduction of Mons. de la Rapière contains an allusion to the poor noblemen of Languedoc, who formerly made a kind of living by being seconds at duels, and whom the Prince de Conti compelled to obey the edicts of Louis XIV. against duelling. *The Love-tiff* was first played in 1656 at Béziers, where the States of Languedoc were assembled.

offer him the satisfaction he desires, if he seeks me; I will immediately go all over the town, only accompanied by Mascarille.

SCENE IV.—VALÈRE, MASCARILLE.

MASC. What, sir? will you tempt Heaven? Do not be so presumptuous! Lack-a-day! you see how they threaten us. How on every side . . .

VAL. What are you looking at yonder?

MASC. I smell a cudgel that way. In short, if you will take my prudent advice, do not let us be so obstinate as to remain in the street; let us go and shut ourselves up.

VAL. Shut ourselves up, rascal? How dare you propose to me such a base action? Come along, and follow me, without any more words.

MASC. Why, sir, my dear master, life is so sweet! One can die but once, and it is for such a long time!

VAL. I shall half kill you, if I hear anything more. Here comes Ascanio; let us leave him; we must find out what side he will choose. However, come along with me into the house, to take whatever arms we may want.

MASC. I have no great itching for fighting. A curse on love and those darned girls, who will be tasting it, and then look as if butter would not melt in their mouth.

SCENE V.—ASCANIO, FROSINE.

ASC. Is it really true, Frosine, do I not dream? Pray tell me all that has happened, from first to last.

FROS. You shall know all the particulars in good time; be patient; such adventures are generally told over and over again, and that every moment. You must know then that after this will, which was on condition of a male heir being born, Albert's wife who was *enceinte*, gave birth to you. Albert, who had stealthily and long beforehand laid his plan, changed you for the son of Inez, the flower-woman, and gave you to my mother to nurse, saying it was her own child. Some ten months after, death took away this little innocent, whilst Albert was absent; his wife being afraid of her husband, and inspired by maternal love, invented a new stratagem. She secretly took her own daughter back; you received the name of the boy, who had taken your place, whilst the death of that pretended son was kept a secret from Albert, who was told that his daughter had died. Now the mystery of your birth is cleared up, which your supposed mother had hitherto concealed. She gives certain reasons for acting in this manner, and may have others to give, for her interests were not the same as yours. In short, this visit,[22] from which I expected so little, has proved more serviceable to your love than could have been imagined. This Inez has given up all claim to you. As it became necessary to reveal this secret, on account of your marriage, we two informed your father of it; a letter of his deceased wife has confirmed all. Pursuing our reasoning yet farther, and being rather fortunate as well as skilful, we have so cunningly interwoven the interests of Albert and of Polydore, so gradually unfolded all this mystery to the latter, that we might not make things appear too terrible to him in the beginning, and, in a word, to tell you all, so prudently led his mind step by step to a reconciliation, that Polydore is now as anxious as your father to legitimize that connection which is to make you happy.

ASC. Ah! Frosine, what happiness you prepare for me. . . . What do I not owe to your fortunate zeal?

FROS. Moreover, the good man is inclined to be merry, and has forbidden us to mention anything of this affair to his son.

SCENE VI.—POLYDORE, ASCANIO, FROSINE.

POL. Come hither, daughter, since I may give you this name now, for I know the secret which this disguise conceals. You have shown so much resolution, ingenuity, and archness in your stratagem, that I forgive you; I think my son will esteem himself happy when he knows that you are the object of his love. You are worth to him more than all the treasures in this world; and I will tell him so. But here he comes: let us divert ourselves with this event. Go and tell all the people to come hither immediately.

ASC. To obey you, sir, shall be the first compliment I pay you.

---

[22] That is the visit of which Frosine speaks, Act iv., Scene 1, p. 113.

SCENE VII.—MASCARILLE, POLYDORE, VALÈRE.

MASC. Misfortunes are often revealed by Heaven: I dreamt last night of pearls unstrung and broken eggs,[23] sir. This dream depresses my spirits.

VAL. Cowardly rascal!

POL. Valère, an encounter awaits you, wherein all your valour will be necessary: you are to cope with a powerful adversary.

MASC. Will nobody stir to prevent people from cutting each other's throats? As for me, I do not care about it; but if any fatal accident should deprive you of your son, do not lay the blame on me.

POL. No, no; in this case I myself urge him to do what he ought.

MASC. What an unnatural father!

VAL. This sentiment, sir, shows you to be a man of honour; I respect you the more for it. I know I have offended you, I am to blame for having done all this without a father's consent; but however angry you may be with me, Nature always will prevail. You do what is truly honourable, in not believing that I am to be terrified by the threats of Eraste.

POL. They just now frightened me with his threats, but since then things have changed greatly; you will be attacked by a more powerful enemy, without being able to flee from him.

MASC. Is there no way of making it up?

VAL! I flee!—Heaven forbid! And who can this be?

POL. Ascanio.

VAL. Ascanio?

POL. Yes; you shall see him appear presently.

VAL. He, who has pledged his word to serve me!

POL. Yes, it is he who says he has a quarrel with you; he, who is determined to decide the quarrel by single combat, to which he challenges you.

MASC. He is a good fellow: he knows that generous minds do not endanger other people's lives by their quarrels.

[23] In a little book still sold on the quays of Paris, and called *la Cle des Songes*, it is said that to dream of pearls denotes "embarrassed affairs," and of broken eggs, "loss of place and lawsuits."

POL. He accuses you of deceit. His anger appears to me to have so just a cause, that Albert and I have agreed you should give Ascanio satisfaction for this affront, but publicly, and without any delay, according to the formalities requisite in such a case.

VAL. What! father; and did Lucile obstinately . . . ?

POL. Lucile is to marry Eraste, and blames you too; and the better to prove your story to be false, is resolved to give her hand to Eraste before your very face.

VAL. Ha! this impudence is enough to drive me mad. Has she lost, then, all sense, faith, conscience, and honour?

SCENE VIII. — ALBERT, POLYDORE, LUCILE, ÉRASTE, VALÈRE, MASCARILLE.

ALB. Well! where are the combatants? They are bringing ours. Have you prepared yours for the encounter?

VAL. Yes, yes; I am ready, since you compel me to it; if I at all hesitated, it was because I still felt a little respect, and not on account of the valour of the champion who is to oppose me. But I have been urged too far. This respect is at an end; I am prepared for any catastrophe! I have been treated so strangely and treacherously, that my love must and shall be revenged. (*To Lucile*). Not that I still pretend to your hand: my former love is now swallowed up in wrath; and when I have made your shame public, your guilty marriage will not in the least disturb me. Lucile, your behaviour is infamous: scarcely can I believe my own eyes. You show yourself so opposed to all modesty, that you ought to die for shame.

LUC. Such reproaches might affect me, if I had not one at hand to avenge my cause. Here comes Ascanio; he shall soon have the pleasure, and without giving himself much trouble, of making you change your language.

SCENE IX. — ALBERT, POLYDORE, ASCANIO, LUCILE, ÉRASTE, VALÈRE, FROSINE, MARINETTE, GROS-RENÉ, MASCARILLE.

VAL. He shall not make me change my language,

though he had twenty arms besides his own. I am sorry he defends a guilty sister; but since he is foolish enough to pick a quarrel with me, I shall give him satisfaction, and you also, my valiant gentleman.

ERAS. A short time ago I took an interest in this, but as Ascanio has taken the affair upon himself, I will have nothing more to do with it, but leave it to him.

VAL. You do well; prudence is always timely, but . .

ERAS. He shall give you satisfaction for us all.

VAL. He?

POL. Do not deceive yourself; you do not yet know what a strange fellow Ascanio is.

ALB. He is blind to it now, but Ascanio will let him know in a little time.

VAL. Come on, then; let him do so now.

MAR. What! before everybody?

GR.-RE. That would not be decent.

VAL. Are you making fun of me? I will break the head of any fellow who laughs. But let us see what Ascanio is going to do.

ASC. No, no. I am not so bad as they make me out; in this adventure, in which every one has put me forward, you shall see my weakness appear more than anything else; you will discover that Heaven, to which we must all submit, did not give me a heart to hold out against you, but that it reserved for you the easy triumph of putting an end to Lucile's brother. Yes; far from boasting of the power of his arm, Ascanio shall receive death from your hands; nay, would gladly die, if his death could contribute to your satisfaction, by giving you, in the presence of all this company, a wife who lawfully belongs to you.

VAL. No, even the whole world, after her perfidy and shamelessness . . .

ASC. Ah! Valère, allow me to tell you that the heart which is pledged to you is guilty of no crime against you; her love is still pure, and her constancy unshaken; I call your own father himself to witness that I speak the truth.

POL. Yes, son, we have laughed enough at your rage; I see it is time to undeceive you; she to whom you are bound by oath is concealed under the dress you here behold. Some question about property was the cause of this disguise, which from her earliest youth deceived so many people. Lately love was the cause of another which deceived you, whilst it made of the two families but one. Yes, in a word, it is she whose subtle skill obtained your hand at night, who pretended to be Lucile, and by this contrivance, which none discovered, has perplexed you all so much. But since Ascanio now gives place to Dorothea, your love must be free from every appearance of deceit, and be strengthened by a more sacred knot.

ALB. This is the single combat by which you were to give us satisfaction for your offence, and which is not forbidden by any laws.[24]

POL. Such an event amazes you, but all hesitation is now too late.

VAL. No, no, I do not hesitate; if this adventure astonishes me, it is a flattering surprise; I find myself seized with admiration, love, and pleasure. Is it possible that those eyes . . . ?

ALB. This dress, dear Valère, is not a proper one to hear your fine speeches in. Let her go and put on another, and meanwhile you shall know the particulars of the event.

VAL. Pardon me, Lucile, if my mind, duped by . . .

LUC. It is easy to forget that.

ALB. Come, these compliments will do as well at home; we shall then have plenty of time to pay them to one another.

ERAS. But in talking thus you do not seem to think that there is still occasion for manslaughter here. Our loves are indeed crowned, but who ought to obtain the hand of Marinette, his Mascarille or my Gros-René? This affair must end in blood.

MASC. No, no, my blood suits my body too well; let him marry her in peace, it will be nothing to me. I know Marinette too well to think marriage will be any bar to my courting her.

MAR. And do you think I will make my gallant of you? A husband does not matter; anything will do for that. We do not stand, then, upon so much ceremony; but a

[24] Severe laws were promulgated in the preceding reign against duelling; Louis XIV. also published two edicts against it in 1643 and in 1651. *The Love-Tiff* was first performed in 1656.

gallant should be well made enough to make one's mouth water.

GR.-RE. Listen! When we are united by marriage, I insist that you should turn a deaf ear to all sparks.

MASC. Do you think, brother, to marry her for yourself alone?

GR.-RE. Of course; I will have a virtuous wife, or else I shall kick up a fine row.

MASC. Ah! lack-a-day, you shall do as others, and become more gentle. Those people who are so severe and critical before marriage, often degenerate into pacific husbands.

MAR. Make yourself easy, my dear husband, and do not have the least fear about my fidelity; flattery will produce no impression on me, and I shall tell you everything.

MASC. Oh! what a cunning wench to make of a husband a confidant.

MAR. Hold your tongue, you knave of clubs.[25]

ALB. For the third time, I say, let us go home, and continue at leisure such an agreeable conversation.

---

[25]The original has *as de pique*, and different commentators have of course given various explanations. But why, says M. Despois, should Marinette, who appears to be fond of cards, not call people by names derived from her favourite game? She calls Gros-René in another place *beau valet de carreau*. (See Note 12, page 113.)

LES PRÉCIEUSES RIDICULES;

COMÉDIE EN UN ACTE.

1659.

THE PRETENTIOUS YOUNG LADIES:

A COMEDY IN ONE ACT.

(*THE ORIGINAL IN PROSE.*)

1659.

INTRODUCTORY NOTICE.

Molière began in *The Pretentious Young Ladies* to paint men and women as they are; to make living characters and existing manners the ground-work of his plays. From that time he abandoned all imitation of Italian or Spanish imbroglios and intrigues.

There is no doubt that aristocratic society attempted, about the latter years of the reign of Louis XIII., to amend the coarse and licentious expressions, which, during the civil wars had been introduced into literature as well as into manners. It was praiseworthy of some high-born ladies in Parisian society to endeavour to refine the language and the mind. But there was a very great difference between the influence these ladies exercised from 1620 until 1640, and what took place in 1658, the year when Molière returned to Paris. The Hôtel de Rambouillet, and the aristocratic drawing-rooms, had then done their work, and done it well; but they were succeeded by a clique which cared only for what was nicely said, or rather what was out of the common. Instead of using an elegant and refined diction, they employed only a pretentious and conceitedly affected style, which became highly ridiculous; instead of improving the national idiom they completely spoilt it. Where formerly D'Urfe, Malherbe, Racan, Balzac, and Voiture reigned, Chapelain, Scudéry, Ménage, and the Abbé Cotin, "the father of the French Riddle,' ruled in their stead. Moreover, every lady in Paris, as well as in the provinces, no matter what her education was, held her drawing-room, where nothing was heard but a ridiculous, exaggerated, and what was worse, a borrowed phraseology. The novels of Mdlle. de Scudéry became the text-book of the *précieux* and the *précieuses*, for such was the name given to these gentlemen and ladies who set up for wits, and thought they displayed exquisite taste, refined ideas, fastidious judgment, and consummate and critical discrimination, whilst they only uttered vapid and blatant nonsense. What other language can be used when we find that they called the sun *l'aimable éclairant le plus beau du monde*, *l'époux de la nature*, and that when speaking of an old gentleman with grey hair, they said, not as a joke, but seriously, *il a des quittances d'amour*. A few of their expressions, however, are employed even at the present time, such as, *châtier son style;* to correct one's style; *dépenser une heure*, to spend an hour; *revêtir ses pensées d' expressions nobles*, to clothe one's thoughts in noble expressions, etc.

Though the *précieux and précieuses* had been several times attacked before, it remained for Molière to give them their death blow, and after the performance of his comedy the name became a term of ridicule and contumely. What enhanced the bitterness of the attack was the difference between Molière s natural style and the affected tone of the would-be elegants he brought upon the stage.

This comedy, in prose, was first acted at Paris, at the Théâtre du Petit Bourbon, on the 18th of November, 1659, and met with great success. Through the influence of some noble *précieux* and *précieuses* it was forbidden until the 2d of December, when the concourse of spectators was so great that it had to be performed twice a day, that the prices of nearly all the places were raised (See Note 7, page xxv.), and that it ran for four months together. We have referred in our prefatory memoir of Molière to some of the legendary anecdotes connected with this play.

It has also been said that our author owed perhaps the first idea of this play to a scarcely-known work, *le Cercle des Femmes, ou le Secret du Lit Nuptial; entretiens comiques,* written by a long-forgotten author, Samuel Chapuzeau, in which a servant, dressed in his master's clothes, is well received by a certain lady who had rejected the master. But as the witty dialogue is the principal merit in Molière's play, it is really of no great consequence who first suggested the primary idea.

The piece, though played in 1659, was only printed on the 29th of January, 1660, by Guillaume de Luyne, a bookseller in Paris, with a preface by Molière, which we give here below:

A strange thing it is, that People should be put in print against their Will. I know nothing so unjust, and should pardon any other Violence much sooner than that.

Not that I here intend to personate the bashful Author, and out of a point of Honour undervalue my Comedy. I should very unseasonably disoblige all the People of Paris, should I accuse them of having applauded a foolish Thing: as the Public is absolute Judge of such sort of Works, it would be Impertinence in me to contradict it; and even if I should have had the worst Opinion in the World of my *Pretentious Young Ladies* before they appeared upon the Stage, I must now believe them of some Value, since so many People agree to speak in their behalf. But as great part of the Pleasure it gave depends upon the Action and Tone of the Voice, it behooved me, not to let them be deprived of those Ornaments; and that success they had in the representation, was, I thought, sufficiently favorable for me to stop there. I was, I say, determined, to let them only be seen by Candlelight, that I might give no room for any one to use the Proverb;[1] nor was I willing they should leap from the Theatre de Bourbon into the *Galerie du Palais.*[2] Notwithstanding, I have been unable to avoid it, and am fallen under the Misfortune of seeing a surreptitious Copy of my Play in the Hands of the Booksellers, together with a Privilege, knavishly obtained, for printing it. I cried out in vain, O Times! O Manners! They showed me that there was a Necessity for me to be in print, or have a Law-suit; and the last evil is even worse than the first. Fate therefore must be submitted to, and I must consent to a Thing, which they would not fail to do without me.

Lord, the strange Perplexity of sending a book abroad! and what an awkward Figure an Author makes the first time he appears in print! Had they allowed me time, I should have thought it over better, and have taken all those Precautions which the Gentlemen Authors, who are now my Brethren, commonly make use of upon the like Occasions. Besides, some noble Lord, whom I should have chosen, in spite of his Teeth, to be the Patron of my Work, and whose Generosity I should have excited by an Epistle Dedicatory very elegantly composed, I should have endeavoured to make a fine and learned Preface; nor do I want books which would have supplied me with all that can be said in a scholarly Manner upon Tragedy and Comedy; the Etymology of them both, their Origin, their Definition, and so forth. I should likewise have spoken to my friends, who to recommend my Performance, would not have refused me Verses, either in French or Latin. I have even some

[1] In Moliere's time it was proverbially said of a woman, "*Elle est belle a la chandelle, mais le grand jour gate tout.*" She is beautiful by candle-light, but day-light spoils everything.

[2] The *Galerie du Palais* was the place where Moliere's publisher lived.

that would have praised me in Greek, and Nobody is ignorant, that a Commendation in Greek is of a marvellous efficacy at the Beginning of a Book. But I am sent Abroad without giving me time to look about me; and I can't so much as obtain the Liberty of speaking two words, to justify my Intention, as to the subject of this Comedy. I would willingly have shewn that it is confined throughout within the Bounds of allowable and decent Satire, that Things the most excellent are liable to be mimicked by wretched Apes, who deserve to be ridiculed; that these absurd Imitations of what is most perfect, have been at all times the Subject of Comedy; and that, for the same Reason, that the truly Learned and truly Brave never yet thought fit to be offended at the Doctor or the Captain in a Comedy, no more than Judges, Princes, and Kings at seeing Trivelin,[3] or any other upon the Stage, ridiculously act the Judge, the Prince, or King; so the true *Precieuses* would be in the wrong to be angry, when the pretentious Ones are exposed, who imitate them awkwardly. In a Word, as I said, I am not allowed breathing time; Mr. de Luyne is going to bind me up this Instant: . . . let it be so, since the Fates so ordain it.

In the third volume of the "Select Comedies of M. de Molière," this comedy is called "The Conceited Ladies." It is dedicated to Miss Le Bas in the following words:—

Madam,

Addresses of this Nature are usually fill'd with Flattery: And it is become so general and known a Practice for Authors of every kind to bedeck with all Perfections Those to whom they present their Writings, that Dedications are, by most People, at Present, interpreted like Dreams, directly backwards. I dare not, therefore, attempt Your Character, lest even Truth itself should be suspected—— Thus far, however, I'll venture to declare, that if sprightly blooming Youth, endearing sweet Good-nature, flowing gentile Wit, and an easy unaffected Conversation, may be reckon'd Charms,—*Miss* Le Bas is exquisitely charming.

The following Comedy of *Monsieur* Moliere, that celebrated Dramatick Writer, was, by him, intended to reprove a vain, fantastical, conceited and preposterous Humour, which about that time prevailed very much in *France*. It had the desir'd good Effect, and conduced a great deal towards rooting out a Taste so unreasonable and ridiculous.—As Pride, Conceit, Vanity, and Affectation, are Foibles so often found amongst the Fair Sex at present, I have attempted this Translation, in hopes of doing service to my pretty Country-Women.———And, certainly, it must have a double efficacy, under the Patronage of one who is so bright an Example of the contrary fine Accomplishments, which a large Fortune makes her not the less careful to improve.

I am not so presumptuous to imagine that my *English* can do sufficient Justice to the sense of this admir'd Author; and, therefore, have caused the Original to be placed against it Page for Page, hoping that, both together, may prove an agreeable and useful Entertainment.———But I have detain'd you too long already, and shall only add, that I am, with much respect, and every good Wish, Madam, *Your most Obedient Humble Servant,*

THE TRANSLATOR.

The *Précieuses Ridicules* have been partly imitated in "*The Damoiselles à la Mode*, Compos'd and Written by Richard Flecknoe. London: Printed for the Author, 1667. To their graces the Duke and Duchess of Newcastle, the Author dedicates this his comedy more humbly than by way of epistle." This gentleman, who was "so distinguished as a wretched poet, that his name had almost become proverbial," and who gave the title to Dryden's *Mac-Flecknoe*, is said to have been originally a Jesuit. Langbaine states "that his acquaintance with the nobility was more than with the Muses." In the preface our author says: "This *Comedy* is taken out of several excellent pieces of *Molière*. The main

[3] The Doctor and the Captain were traditional personages of the Italian stage; their parts need no further explanation; Trivelin was a popular Italian actor, who in a humorous and exaggerated way played the parts of Judges, Princes, and Kings.

plot out of his *Pretieusee's Ridiculee's;* the Counterplot of *Sganarelle* out of his *Escole des Femmes*, and out of the *Escole des Marys*, the two *Naturals;* all which, like so many *Pretieuse* stones, I have brought out of *France;* and as a Lapidary set in one Jewel to adorn our English stage."

This motley play was never acted; at least the author says: "for the Acting it, those who have the Governing of the Stage, have their Humours, and wou'd be intreated; and I have mine and won't intreat them; and were all Dramatick Writers of my mind, they shou'd wear their old *Playes* Thred-bare. e're they shou'd have any *New*, till they better understood their own Interest, and how to distinguish betwixt good and bad."

The "Prologue intended for the overture of the Theater 1666," opens thus:—

> "In these sad Times[4] our Author has been long
> Studying to give you some diversion;
> And he has ta'en the way to do't, which he
> Thought most diverting, mirth and Comedy;
> And now he knows there are inough i' the Town
> At name of mirth and Comedy will frown,
> And sighing say, the times are bad; what then?
> Will their being sad and heavy better them?"

According to the list of "The Representers, as they were first design'd." I see that Nell Gwyn should have played the part of "*Lysette*, the *Damoiselle's* waiting Woman."

James Miller, a well-known dramatist, and joint-translator of Molière, with H. Baker, has also imitated part of "the *Pretentious Young Ladies*," and with another part borrowed from Molière's *School for Husbands*, two characters taken from Molière's *Learned Ladies*, and some short speeches borrowed from the *Countess of Escarbagnas*, he composed a comedy, which was played at Drury Lane, March 6th, 1735, under the title of *The Man of Taste, or, The Guardians.* Mr. Miller appears to have been a man of indomitable spirit and industry. Being a clergyman, with a very small stipend, he wrote plays to improve his circumstances, but offended both his bishop and the public. At last he was presented to the very valuable living of Upcerne, in Dorsetshire, and was also successful with a translation of *Mahomet* of Voltaire, but died within the year after his induction. *The Man of Taste* was printed for J. Watts, MDCCXXXV., and is dedicated to Lord Weymouth. We give part of the dedication:

> "As to the Attempt here made to expose the several Vices and Follies that at present flourish in Vogue, I hope your Lordship will think it confined within the bounds of a modest and wholesome Chastisement. That it is a very seasonable one, I believe, every Person will acknowledge. When what is set up for the Standard of Taste, is but just the Reverse of Truth and Common Sense; and that which is dignify'd with the Name of Politeness, is deficient in nothing—but Decency and Good Manners: When all Distinctions of Station and Fortune are broke in upon, so that a *Peer* and a *Mechanick* are cloathed in the same Habits, and indulge in the same Diversions and Luxuries: When Husbands are ruin'd, Children robb'd, and Tradesmen starv'd, in order to give Estates to a *French* Harlequin, and *Italian* Eunuch, for a Shrug or a Song;[5] shall not fair and fearless Satire oppose this Out-

---

[4] In 1665 the plague broke out in London, and in the succeeding year the great fire took place; only at Christmas 1666 theatrical performances began again.

[5] Farinelli, an eminent Italian soprano, went to England in 1734, remained there three years, sang chiefly at the Theatre of Lincoln's-Inn-Fields, then under the direction of Porpora, his old Master, became a great favorite, and made about £5,000 a year. As *The Man of Taste* was performed at a rival house, Drury Lane, the bitterness of the allusion may be easily understood. The French Comedians acted

rage upon all Reason and Discretion. Yes, My Lord, resentment can never better be shown, nor Indignation more laudably exerted than on such an occasion."

The Prologue, spoken by Mr. Cibber, is racy. We give the first half of it:—

" Wit springs so slow in our bleak Northern Soil,
It scarce, at best, rewards the Planter's Toil.
But now, when all the Sun-shine, and the Rain,
Are turn'd to cultivate a Foreign grain;
When, what should cherish, preys upon the Tree,
What generous Fruit can you expect to see?
Our Bard, to strike the Humour of the Times,
Imports these Scenes from kindlier Southern Climes;
Secure his Pains will with Applause be crown'd,
If you're as fond of Foreign sense as . . . sound:
And since their Follies have been bought so dear,
We hope their Wit a moderate Price may bear.
Terence, Great Master! who, with wond'rous Art,
Explor'd the deepest Secrets of the Heart;
That best Old Judge of Manners and of Men,
First grac'd this Tale with his immortal Pen.[6]
Molière, the Classick of the Gallick Stage,
First dar'd to modernize the Sacred Page;
Skilful, the one thing wanting to supply,
Humour, that Soul of Comic Poesy.
The Roman Fools were drawn so high . . . the Pit
Might take 'em now for Modern Men of Wit.
But Molière painted with a bolder Hand,
And mark'd his Oafs with the Fool's-Cap and Band:
To ev'ry Vice he tagged the just Reproach,
Shew'd Worth on Foot, and Rascals in a Coach."

Mrs. Aphra Behn, a voluminous writer of plays, novels, poems, and letters, all of a lively and amorous turn, was the widow of a Dutch merchant, and partly occupied the time not engaged in literary pursuits in political or gallant intrigues. Her comedies are her best works, and although some of her scenes are often indecent, and not a few of her expressions indelicate, yet her plots are always lively and well sustained and her dialogues very witty. The date of her birth is unknown, but she died on the 16th of April, 1689, and was buried in the cloisters of Westminster Abbey.

In 1682, was performed, at the Theatre, Dorset Garden, her play. *The False Count, or a New Way to Play an Old Game.* The prologue attacks the Whigs most furiously, and the epilogue, spoken by Mrs. Barry, is very indecent. The plot of this play, or rather farce, is very improbable, and the language is more than free. Julia, in love with Don Carlos, afterwards Governor of Cadiz, was forced by her father to marry Francisco, a rich old man, formerly a leather-seller; the latter going with his family to sea on a party of pleasure, are taken prisoners by Carlos and his servants, disguised as Turks. They are carried to a country house, and made to believe they are in the Grand Turk's seraglio. There is also an underplot, in which Isabella, Francisco's proud and vain daughter, is courted by Guilion, a supposed Count, but in reality

at the Haymarket from November 22, 1734 to June 1735, hence the allusion to a French Harlequin.

[6] The plot of *The Man of Taste*, as we have said before, was partly borrowed from Molière's *School for Husbands*, partly from the *Pretentious Young Ladies*, and other of his plays. The first-mentioned French comedy owes part of its plot to Terence's *Adelphi*, hence the allusion.

a chimney-sweep, whose hand she accepts. In the end everything is discovered, and Guilion comes to claim his wife in his sooty clothes.

Thomas Shadwell, a dramatist, and the poet-laureate of William III., who has been flagellated by Dryden in his *MacFlecknoe* and in the second part of *Absalom* and *Achitophel,* and been mentioned with contempt by Pope in his *Dunciad,* took from the *Précieuses Ridicules* Mascarille and Jodelet, and freely imitated and united them in the character of La Roch, a sham Count, in his *Bury-Fair*, acted by His Majesty's servants in 1689. This play, dedicated to Charles, Earl of Dorset and Middlesex, was written "during eight months' painful sickness." In the Prologue Shadwell states:

> That every Part is Fiction in his Play;
> Particular Reflections there are none;
> Our Poet knows not one in all your Town.
> If any has so very little Wit,
> To think a Fop's Dress can his Person fit,
> E'en let him take it, and make much of it.

Whilst, in *The Pretentious Young Ladies*, Mascarille and Jodelet impose upon two provincial girls, in *Bury-Fair*, La Roch, "a French peruke-maker," succeeds in deceiving Mrs. Fantast and Mrs. Gertrude under the name of Count de Cheveux. The Count is very amusing, and though a coward to boot, pretends to be a great warrior. His description of war is characteristic; he states that "de great Heros always burne and killè de Man, Woman, and Shilde for deir Glory."

DRAMATIS PERSONÆ.

LA GRANGE, } *repulsed Lovers.*
DU CROISY, }

GORGIBUS,[7] *a good citizen.*

THE MARQUIS DE MASCARILLE, *valet to La Grange.*[8]

THE VISCOUNT JODELET, *valet to Du Croisy.*

ALMANZOR, *footman to the pretentious ladies.*

TWO CHAIRMEN.

MUSICIANS.

MADELON, *daughter to Gorgibus,* } *The pretentious young ladies.*
CATHOS, *niece to Gorgibus,* }

MAROTTE, *maid to the pretentious young ladies.*

LUCILE. } *two female neighbours.*
CÉLIMÈNE. }

SCENE—GORGIBUS' HOUSE, PARIS.

---

7 Gorgibus was the name of certain characters in old comedies. The actor, L'Epy, who played this part, had a very loud voice; hence Molière gave him probably this name.

8 *Mascarille* was played by Molière, and has a personality quite distinct from the servant of the same name in the *Blunderer* and the *Love-Tiff.* The dress in which he acted this part, has not been mentioned in the inventory taken after his death, but in a pamphlet, published in 1660, he is described as wearing an enormous wig, a very small hat, a ruff like a morning gown, rolls in which children could play hide-and-seek, tassels like cornucopiæ, ribbons that covered his shoes, with heels half a foot in height.

THE PRETENTIOUS YOUNG LADIES.

(*LES PRÉCIEUSES RIDICULES.*)

ACT I.

SCENE I.—LA GRANGE, DU CROISY.

DU. CR. Mr. La Grange.

LA. GR. What?

DU. CR. Look at me for a moment without laughing.

LA. GR. Well?

DU. CR. What do you say of our visit? Are you quite pleased with it?

LA. GR. Do you think either of us has any reason to be so?

DU. CR. Not at all, to say the truth.

LA. GR. As for me, I must acknowledge I was quite shocked at it. Pray now, did ever anybody see a couple of country wenches giving themselves more ridiculous airs, or two men treated with more contempt than we were? They could hardly make up their mind to order chairs for us. I never saw such whispering as there was between them; such yawning, such rubbing of the eyes, and asking so often what o'clock it was. Did they answer anything else but "yes," or "no," to what we said to them? In short, do you not agree with me that if we had been the meanest persons in the world, we could not have been treated worse?

DU. CR. You seem to take it greatly to heart.

LA. GR. No doubt I do; so much so, that I am resolved to be revenged on them for their impertinence. I know well enough why they despise us. Affectation has not alone infected Paris, but has also spread into the country, and our ridiculous damsels have sucked in their share of it. In a word, they are a strange medley of coquetry and affectation. I plainly see what kind of persons will be well received by them; if you will take my advice, we will play them such a trick as shall show them their folly, and teach them to distinguish a little better the people they have to deal with.

DU. CR. How can you do this?

LA. GR. I have a certain valet, named Mascarille, who, in the opinion of many people, passes for a kind of wit; for nothing now-a-days is easier than to acquire such a reputation. He is an extraordinary fellow, who has taken it into his head to ape a person of quality. He usually prides himself on his gallantry and his poetry, and despises so much the other servants that he calls them brutes.

DU. CR. Well, what do you mean to do with him?

LA. GR. What do I mean to do with him? He must . . . but first, let us be gone.

SCENE II. GORGIBUS, DU CROISY, LA GRANGE.

GORG. Well, gentlemen, you have seen my niece and my daughter. How are matters going on? What is the result of your visit?

LA. GR. They will tell you this better than we can. All we say is that we thank you for the favour you have done us, and remain your most humble servants.

DU. CR. Your most humble servants.

GORG. (*Alone*). Hoity-toity! Methinks they go away dissatisfied. What can be the meaning of this? I must find it out. Within there!

SCENE III.—GORGIBUS, MAROTTE.

MAR. Did you call, sir?

GORG. Where are your mistresses?

MAR. In their room.

GORG. What are they doing there?

MAR. Making lip salve.

GORG. There is no end of their salves. Bid them come down. (*Alone*). These hussies with their salves have, I think, a mind to ruin me. Everywhere in the house I see nothing but whites of eggs, lac virginal, and a thousand other fooleries I am not acquainted with. Since we have been here they have employed the lard of a dozen hogs at least, and four servants might live every day on the sheep's trotters they use.

SCENE IV.—MADELON, CATHOS, GORGIBUS.

GORG. Truly there is great need to spend so much money to grease your faces. Pray tell me, what have you done to those gentlemen, that I saw them go away with so much coldness. Did I not order you to receive them as persons whom I intended for your husbands?

MAD. Dear father, what consideration do you wish us to entertain for the irregular behaviour of these people?

CAT. How can a woman of ever so little understanding, uncle, reconcile herself to such individuals?

GORG. What fault have you to find with them?

MAD. Their's is fine gallantry, indeed. Would you believe it? they began with proposing marriage to us.

GORG. What would you have them begin with—with a proposal to keep you as mistresses? Is not their proposal a compliment to both of you, as well as to me? Can anything be more polite than this? And do they not prove the honesty of their intentions by wishing to enter these holy bonds?

MAD. O, father! Nothing can be more vulgar than what you have just said. I am ashamed to hear you talk in such a manner; you should take some lessons in the elegant way of looking at things.

GORG. I care neither for elegant ways nor songs.[9] I tell you marriage is a holy and sacred affair; to begin with that is to act like honest people.

MAD. Good Heavens! If everybody was like you a love-story would soon be over. What a fine thing it would

---

[9] The original has a play on words. Madelon says, in addressing her father, *vous devriez un peu vous faire apprendre le bel air des choses*, upon which he answers, *je n'ai que faire ni d'air ni de chanson*. *Air* means tune as well as look, appearance.

have been if Cyrus had immediately espoused Mandane, and if Aronce had been married all at once to Clélie.[10].

GORG. What is she jabbering about?

MAD. Here is my cousin, father, who will tell as well as I that matrimony ought never to happen till after other adventures. A lover, to be agreeable, must understand how to utter fine sentiments, to breathe soft, tender, and passionate vows; his courtship must be according to the rules. In the first place, he should behold the fair one of whom he becomes enamoured either at a place of worship,[11] or when out walking, or at some public ceremony; or else he should be introduced to her by a relative or a friend, as if by chance, and when he leaves her he should appear in a pensive and melancholy mood. For some time he should conceal his passion from the object of his love, but pay her several visits, in every one of which he ought to introduce some gallant subject to exercise the wits of all the company. When the day comes to make his declarations—which generally should be contrived in some shady garden-walk while the company is at a distance—it should be quickly followed by anger, which is shown by our blushing, and which, for a while, banishes the lover from our presence. He finds afterwards means to pacify us, to accustom us gradually to hear him depict his passion, and to draw from us that confession which causes us so much pain. After that come the adventures, the rivals who thwart mutual inclination, the persecutions of fathers, the jealousies arising without any foundation, complaints, despair, running away with, and its consequences. Thus things are carried on in fashionable life, and veritable gallantry cannot dispense with these forms. But to come out point-blank with a proposal of marriage,—to make no love but with a marriage-contract, and begin a novel at the wrong end! Once more, father, nothing can be more tradesmanlike, and the mere thought of it makes me sick at heart.

---

10 *Cyrus* and *Mandane* are the two principal charactersof Mademoiselle de Scudéry's novel *Artamene, on the Grand Cyrus; Aronce* and *Clelie* of the novel *Clelie*, by the same author.

11 See note 15, page 33.

GORG. What deuced nonsense is all this? That is high-flown language with a vengeance!

CAT. Indeed, uncle, my cousin hits the nail on the head. How can we receive kindly those who are so awkward in gallantry. I could lay a wager they have not even seen a map of the country of *Tenderness*, and that *Love-letters*, *Trifling attentions*, *Polite epistles*, and *Sprightly verses*, are regions to them unknown.[12] Do you not see that the whole person shews it, and that their external appearance is not such as to give at first sight a good opinion of them. To come and pay a visit to the object of their love with a leg without any ornaments, a hat without any feathers, a head with its locks not artistically arranged, and a coat that suffers from a paucity of ribbons. Heavens! what lovers are these! what stinginess in dress! what barrenness of conversation! It is not to be allowed; it is not to be borne. I also observed that their ruffs[13] were not made by the fashionable milliner, and that their breeches were not big enough by more than half-a-foot.

GORG. I think they are both mad, nor can I understand anything of this gibberish. Cathos, and you Madelon . . .

MAD. Pray, father, do not use those strange names, and call us by some other.

GORG. What do you mean by those strange names? Are they not the names your godfathers and godmothers gave you?

MAD. Good Heavens! how vulgar you are! I confess I wonder you could possibly be the father of such an intelligent girl as I am. Did ever anybody in genteel style talk of Cathos or of Madelon? And must you not admit that either of these names would be sufficient to disgrace the finest novel in the world?

---

[12] The map of the country of Tenderness (*la carte de Tendre*) is found in the first part of *Clelie* (see note 2, page 146); Love-letter (*Billet-doux*); Polite epistle (*Billet galant*); Trifling attentions (*Petit Soins*); Sprightly verses (*Jolis vers*), are the names of villages to be found in the map, which is a curiosity in its way.

[13] The ruff (*rabat*) was at first only the shirt-collar pulled out and worn outside the coat. Later ruffs were worn, which were not fastened to the shirt, sometimes adorned with lace, and tied in front with two strings with tassels. The *rabat* was very fashionable during the youthful years of Louis XIV.

CAT. It is true, uncle, an ear rather delicate suffers extremely at hearing these words pronounced, and the name of Polixena, which my cousin has chosen, and that of Amintha, which I took, possesses a charm, which you must needs acknowledge.[14]

GORG. Hearken; one word will suffice. I do not allow you to take any other names than those that were given you by your godfathers and godmothers; and as for those gentlemen we are speaking about, I know their families and fortunes, and am determined they shall be your husbands. I am tired of having you upon my hands. Looking after a couple of girls is rather too weighty a charge for a man of my years.

CAT. As for me, uncle, all I can say is, that I think marriage a very shocking business. How can one endure the thought of lying by the side of a man, who is really naked?

MAD. Give us leave to take breath for a short time among the fashionable world of Paris, where we are but just arrived. Allow us to prepare at our leisure the groundwork of our novel, and do not hurry on the conclusion too abruptly.

GORG. (*Aside*). I cannot doubt it any longer; they are completely mad. (*Aloud*). Once more, I tell you, I understand nothing of all this gibberish; I will be master, and to cut short all kinds of arguments, either you shall both be married shortly, or, upon my word, you shall be nuns; that I swear.[15]

SCENE VI.—CATHOS, MADELON.

CAT. Good Heavens, my dear, how deeply is your father still immersed in material things! how dense is his understanding, and what gloom overcasts his soul!

MAD. What can I do, my dear? I am ashamed of him.

---

[14] The *precieuses* often changed their names into more poetical and romantic appellations. The Marquise de Rambouillet, whose real name was Catherine, was known under the anagram of Arthenice.

[15] This scene is the mere outline of the well known quarrel between Chrysale, Philaminte, and Belinda in the "*Femmes Savantes*" (see vol. iii.) but a husband trembling before his wife, and only daring to show his temper to his sister, is a much more tempting subject for a dramatic writer than a man addressing in a firm tone his daughter and niece.

I can hardly persuade myself I am indeed his daughter; I believe that an accident, some time or other, will discover me to be of a more illustrious descent.

CAT. I believe it; really, it is very likely; as for me, when I consider myself . . .

SCENE VII.—CATHOS, MADELON, MAROTTE.

MAR. Here is a footman asks if you are at home, and says his master is coming to see you.

MAD. Learn, you dunce, to express yourself a little less vulgarly. Say, here is a necessary evil inquiring if it is commodious for you to become visible.[16]

MAR. I do not understand Latin, and have not learned philosophy out of Cyrus,[17] as you have done.

MAD. Impertinent creature! How can this be borne! And who is this footman's master?

MAR. He told me it was the Marquis de Mascarille.

MAD. Ah, my dear! A marquis! a marquis! Well, go and tell him we are visible. This is certainly some wit who has heard of us.

CAT. Undoubtedly, my dear.

MAD. We had better receive him here in this parlour than in our room. Let us at least arrange our hair a little and maintain our reputation. Come in quickly, and reach us the Counsellor of the Graces.

MAR. Upon my word, I do not know what sort of a beast that is; you must speak like a Christian if you would have me know your meaning.

CAT. Bring us the looking-glass, you blockhead! and take care not to contaminate its brightness by the communication of your image.

SCENE VIII.—MASCARILLE, TWO CHAIRMEN.

MASC. Stop, chairman, stop. Easy does it! Easy, easy! I think these boobies intend to break me to pieces by bumping me against the walls and the pavement.

---

[16] All these and similar sentences were really employed by the *precieuses*.

[17] *Artamene, ou le Grand Cyrus*, (1649-1653) a novel in ten volumes by Madle. de Scudéry.

1 CHAIR. Ay, marry, because the gate is narrow and you would make us bring you in here.

MASC. To be sure, you rascals! Would you have me expose the fulness of my plumes to the inclemency of the rainy season, and let the mud receive the impression of my shoes? Begone; take away your chair.

2 CHAIR. Then please to pay us, sir.

MASC. What?

2 CHAIR. Sir, please to give us our money, I say.

MASC. (*Giving him a box on the ear*). What, scoundrel, to ask money from a person of my rank!

2 CHAIR. Is this the way poor people are to be paid? Will your rank get us a dinner?

MASC. Ha, ha! I shall teach you to keep your right place. Those low fellows dare to make fun of me!

1 CHAIR. (*Taking up one of the poles of his chair*). Come, pay us quickly

MASC. What?

1 CHAIR. I mean to have my money at once.

MASC. That is a sensible fellow.

1 CHAIR. Make haste, then.

MASC. Ay, you speak properly, but the other is a scoundrel, who does not know what he says. There, are you satisfied?

1 CHAIR. No, I am not satisfied; you boxed my friend's ears, and . . . (*holding up his pole*).

MASC. Gently; there is something for the box on the ear. People may get anything from me when they go about it in the right way. Go now, but come and fetch me by and by to carry me to the Louvre to the *petit coucher*.[18]

SCENE IX.—MAROTTE, MASCARILLE.

MAR. Sir, my mistresses will come immediately.

---

[18] Louis XIV. and several other Kings of France, received their courtiers when rising or going to bed. This was called *lever* and *coucher*. The *lever* as well as the *coucher* was divided into *petit* and *grand*. All persons received at court had a right to come to the *grand lever* and *coucher*, but only certain noblemen of high rank and the princes of the royal blood could remain at the *petit lever* and *coucher*, which was the time between the king putting on either a day or night shirt, and the time he went to bed or was fully dressed. The highest person of rank always claimed the right of handing to the king his shirt.

MASC. Let them not hurry themselves; I am very comfortable here, and can wait.

MAR. Here they come.

SCENE X.—MADELON, CATHOS, MASCARILLE, ALMAZOR.

MASC. (*After having bowed to them*). Ladies, no doubt you will be surprised at the boldness of my visit, but your reputation has drawn this disagreeable affair upon you; merit has for me such potent charms, that I run everywhere after it.

MAD. If you pursue merit you should not come to us.

CAT. If you find merit amongst us, you must have brought it hither yourself.

MASC. Ah! I protest against these words. When fame mentioned your deserts it spoke the truth, and you are going to make *pic*, *repic*, and *capot*[19] all the gallants from Paris.

MAD. Your complaisance goes a little too far in the liberality of its praises, and my cousin and I must take care not to give too much credit to your sweet adulation.

CAT. My dear, we should call for chairs.

MAD. Almanzor!

ALM. Madam.

MAD. Convey to us hither, instantly, the conveniences of conversation.

MASC. But am I safe here? (*Exit Almanzor.*

CAT. What is it you fear?

MASC. Some larceny of my heart; some massacre of liberty. I behold here a pair of eyes that seem to be very naughty boys, that insult liberty, and use a heart most barbarously. Why the deuce do they put themselves on their guard, in order to kill any one who comes near them? Upon my word! I mistrust them; I shall either scamper away, or expect very good security that they do me no mischief.

MAD. My dear, what a charming facetiousness he has!

---

[19] Dryden, in his *Sir Martin Mar-all* (Act i. sc. 1), makes Sir Martin say: "If I go to picquet . . . he will picque and repicque, and capot me twenty times together." I believe that these terms in Molière's and Dryden's times had a different meaning from what they have now.

CAT. I see, indeed, he is an Amilcar.[20]

MAD. Fear nothing, our eyes have no wicked designs, and your heart may rest in peace, fully assured of their innocence.

CAT. But, pray, Sir, be not inexorable to the easy chair, which, for this last quarter of an hour, has held out its arms towards you; yield to its desire of embracing you.

MASC. (*After having combed himself,*[21] *and adjusted the rolls of his stockings*).[22] Well, ladies, and what do you think of Paris?

MAD. Alas! what can we think of it? It would be the very antipodes of reason not to confess that Paris is the grand cabinet of marvels, the centre of good taste, wit, and gallantry.

MASC. As for me, I maintain that, out of Paris, there is no salvation for the polite world.

CAT. Most assuredly.

MASC. Paris is somewhat muddy; but then we have sedan chairs.

MAD. To be sure; a sedan chair is a wonderful protection against the insults of mud and bad weather.

MASC. I am sure you receive many visits. What great wit belongs to your company?

MAD. Alas! we are not yet known, but we are in the way of being so; for a lady of our acquaintance has promised us to bring all the gentlemen who have written for the Miscellanies of Select Poetry.[23]

CAT. And certain others, whom, we have been told, are likewise the sovereign arbiters of all that is handsome.

MASC. I can manage this for you better than any one;

---

[20] Amilcar is one of the heroes of the novel *Clélie*, who wishes to be thought sprightly.

[21] It was at that time the custom for men of rank to comb their hair or periwigs in public.

[22] The rolls (*canons*) were large round pieces of linen, often adorned with lace or ribbons, and which were fastened below the breeches, just under the knee.

[23] Molière probably alludes to a Miscellany of Select Poetry, published in 1653, by de Sercy, under the title of *Poésies choisies de M. M. Corneille Benserade, de Scudéry, Boisrobert, Sarrazin, Desmarets, Baraud, Saint-Laurent, Colletet, Lamesnardière, Montreuil, Viguier, Chevreau, Malleville, Tristan, Testu, Maucroy, de Prade, Girard et de L'Age.* A great number of such miscellanies appeared in France, and in England also, about that time.

they all visit me; and I may say that I never rise without having half-a-dozen wits at my levee.

MAD. Good Heavens! you will place us under the greatest obligation if you will do us the kindness; for, in short, we must make the acquaintance of all those gentlemen if we wish to belong to the fashion. They are the persons who can make or unmake a reputation at Paris; you know that there are some, whose visits alone are sufficient to start the report that you are a *Connaisseuse*, though there should be no other reason for it. As for me, what I value particularly is, that by means of these ingenious visits, we learn a hundred things which we ought necessarily to know, and which are the quintessence of wit. Through them we hear the scandal of the day, or whatever niceties are going on in prose or verse. We know, at the right time, that Mr. So-and-so has written the finest piece in the world on such a subject; that Mrs. So-and-so has adapted words to such a tune; that a certain gentleman has written a madrigal upon a favour shown to him; another stanzas upon a fair one who betrayed him; Mr. Such-a-one wrote a couplet of six lines yesterday evening to Miss Such-a-one, to which she returned him an answer this morning at eight o'clock; such an author is engaged on such a subject; this writer is busy with the third volume of his novel; that one is putting his works to press.] Those things procure you consideration in every society, and if people are ignorant of them, I would not give one pinch of snuff for all the wit they may have.

CAT. Indeed, I think it the height of ridicule for any one who possesses the slightest claim to be called clever not to know even the smallest couplet that is made every day; as for me, I should be very much ashamed if any one should ask me my opinion about something new, and I had not seen it.

MASC. It is really a shame not to know from the very first all that is going on; but do not give yourself any farther trouble, I will establish an academy of wits at your house, and I give you my word that not a single line of poetry shall be written in Paris, but what you shall be able to say by heart before anybody else. As for me, such as you see me, I amuse myself in that way when I am in the humour, and you may find handed about in the fashionable assemblies[24] of Paris two hundred songs, as many sonnets, four hundred epigrams, and more than a thousand madrigals all made by me, without counting riddles and portraits.[25]

MAD. I must acknowledge that I dote upon portraits; I think there is nothing more gallant.

MASC. Portraits are difficult, and call for great wit; you shall see some of mine that will not displease you.

CAT. As for me, I am awfully fond of riddles.

MASC. They exercise the intelligence; I have already written four of them this morning, which I will give you to guess.

MAD. Madrigals are pretty enough when they are neatly turned.

MASC. That is my special talent; I am at present engaged in turning the whole Roman history into madrigals.[26]

MAD. Goodness gracious! that will certainly be superlatively fine; I should like to have one copy at least, if you think of publishing it.

MASC. I promise you each a copy, bound in the handsomest manner. It does not become a man of my rank to scribble, but I do it only to serve the publishers, who are always bothering me.

MAD. I fancy it must be a delightful thing to see one's self in print.

MASC. Undoubtedly; but, by the by, I must repeat to

---

[24] In the original French the word is *ruelle*, which means literally "a small street," "a lane," hence any narrow passage, hence the narrow opening between the wall and the bed. The *Précieuses* at that time received their visitors lying dressed in a bed, which was placed in an alcove and upon a raised platform. Their fashionable friends (*alcovistes*) took their places between the bed and the wall, and thus the name *ruelle* came to be given to all fashionable assemblies. In Dr. John Ash's New and Complete Dictionary of the English Language, published in London 1755, I still find *ruelle* defined: "a little street, a circle, an assembly at a private house."

[25] This kind of literature, in which one attempted to write a portrait of one's self or of others, was then very much in fashion. La Bruyère and de Saint-Simon in France, as well as Dryden and Pope in England, have shown what a literary portrait may become in the hands of men of talent.

[26] Seventeen years after this play was performed, Benserade published *les Métamorphoses d' Ovide mises en rondeaux.*

you some extempore verses I made yesterday at the house of a certain duchess, an acquaintance of mine. I am deuced clever at extempore verses.

CAT. Extempore verses are certainly the very touchstone of genius.

MASC. Listen then.

MAD. We are all ears.

MASC. *Oh! oh! quite without heed was I,*
As harmless you I chanced to spy,
Slily your eyes
My heart surprise,
Stop thief! stop thief! stop thief I cry!

CAT. Good Heavens! this is carried to the utmost pitch of gallantry.

MASC. Everything I do shows it is done by a gentleman; there is nothing of the pedant about my effusions.

MAD. They are more than two thousand miles removed from that.

MASC. Did you observe the beginning, *oh! oh?* there is something original in that *oh! oh!* like a man who all of a sudden thinks about something, *oh! oh!* Taken by surprise as it were, *oh! oh!*

MAD. Yes, I think that *oh! oh!* admirable.

MASC. It seems a mere nothing.

CAT. Good Heavens! How can you say so? It is one of these things that are perfectly invaluable.

MAD. No doubt on it; I would rather have written that *oh! oh!* than an epic poem.

MASC. Egad, you have good taste.

MAD. Tolerably; none of the worst, I believe.

MASC. But do you not also admire *quite without heed was I? quite without heed was I,* that is, I did not pay attention to anything; a natural way of speaking, *quite without heed was I, of no harm thinking,* that is, as I was going along, innocently, without malice, like a poor sheep, *you I chanced to spy,* that is to say, I amused myself with looking at you, with observing you, with contemplating you. *Slily your eyes. . . .* What do you think of that word *slily*—is it not well chosen?

CAT. Extremely so.

MASC. *Slily*, stealthily; just like a cat watching a mouse—*slily*.

MAD. Nothing can be better.

MASC. *My heart surprise*, that is, carries it away from me, robs me of it. *Stop thief! stop thief! stop thief!* Would you not think a man were shouting and running after a thief to catch him? *Stop thief! stop thief! stop thief!*[27]

MAD. I must admit the turn is witty and sprightly.

MASC. I will sing you the tune I made to it.

CAT. Have you learned music?

MASC. I? Not at all.

CAT. How can you make a tune then?

MASC. People of rank know everything without ever having learned anything.

MAD. His lordship is quite in the right, my dear.

MASC. Listen if you like the tune: *hem, hem, la, la.* The inclemency of the season has greatly injured the delicacy of my voice; but no matter, it is in a free and easy way. (*He sings*). *Oh! Oh! quite without heed was I*, etc.

CAT. What a passion there breathes in this music. It is enough to make one die away with delight!

MAD. There is something plaintive in it.

MASC. Do you not think that the air perfectly well expresses the sentiment, *stop thief, stop thief?* And then as if some one cried out very loud, *stop, stop, stop, stop, stop, stop thief!* Then all at once like a person out of breath, *Stop thief!*

MAD. This is to understand the perfection of things, the grand perfection, the perfection of perfections. I declare it is altogether a wonderful performance. I am quite enchanted with the air and the words.

CAT. I never yet met with anything so excellent.

---

[27] The scene of Mascarille reading his extempore verses is something like Trissotin in *Les Femmes savantes* (see vol. III.) reading his sonnet for the Princess Uranie. But Mascarille comments on the beauties of his verses with the insolent vanity of a man who does not pretend to have even one atom of modesty; Trissotin, a professional wit, listens in silence, but with secret pride, to the ridiculous exclamations of the admirers of his genius.

MASC. All that I do comes naturally to me; it is without study.

MAD. Nature has treated you like a very fond mother; you are her darling child.

MASC. How do you pass away the time, ladies?

CAT. With nothing at all.

MAD. Until now we have lived in a terrible dearth of amusements.

MASC. I am at your service to attend you to the play, one of those days, if you will permit me. Indeed, a new comedy is to be acted which I should be very glad we might see together.

MAD. There is no refusing you anything.

MASC. But I beg of you to applaud it well, when we shall be there; for I have promised to give a helping hand to the piece. The author called upon me this very morning to beg me so to do. It is the custom for authors to come and read their new plays to people of rank, that they may induce us to approve of them and give them a reputation. I leave you to imagine if, when we say anything, the pit dares contradict us. As for me, I am very punctual in these things, and when I have made a promise to a poet, I always cry out "Bravo" before the candles are lighted.

MAD. Do not say another word; Paris is an admirable place. A hundred things happen every day which people in the country, however clever they may be, have no idea of.

CAT. Since you have told us, we shall consider it our duty to cry up lustily every word that is said.

MASC. I do not know whether I am deceived, but you look as if you had written some play yourself.

MAD. Eh! there may be something in what you say.

MASC. Ah! upon my word, we must see it. Between ourselves, I have written one which I intend to have brought out.

CAT. Ay! to what company do you mean to give it?

MASC. That is a very nice question, indeed. To the actors of the hôtel de Bourgogne; they alone can bring things into good repute; the rest are ignorant creatures who recite their parts just as people speak in every-day life; they do not understand to mouth the verses, or to pause at a beautiful passage; how can it be known where the fine lines are, if an actor does not stop at them, and thereby tell you to applaud heartily?[28]

CAT. Indeed! that is one way of making an audience feel the beauties of any work; things are only prized when they are well set off.

MASC. What do you think of my top-knot, sword-knot, and rosettes?[29] Do you find them harmonize with my coat?

CAT. Perfectly.

MASC. Do you think the ribbon well chosen?

MAD. Furiously well. It is real Perdrigeon.[30]

MASC. What do you say of my rolls?[31]

MAD. They look very fashionable.

MASC. I may at least boast that they are a quarter of a yard wider than any that have been made.

MAD. I must own I never saw the elegance of dress carried farther.

MASC. Please to fasten the reflection of your smelling faculty upon these gloves.

MAD. They smell awfully fine.

CAT. I never inhaled a more delicious perfume.

MASC. And this? (*He gives them his powdered wig to smell*).

MAD. It has the true quality odour; it titillates the nerves of the upper region most deliciously.

MASC. You say nothing of my feathers. How do you like them?

CAT. They are frightfully beautiful.

---

28 The company of actors at the hôtel de Bourgogne were rivals to the troop of Molière; it appears, however, from contemporary authors, that the accusations brought by our author against them were well-founded.

29 In the original *petite oie;* this was first, the name given to the giblets of a goose, *oie;* next it came to mean all the accessories of dress, ribbons, laces, feathers, and other small ornaments. In one of the old translations of Molière *petite oie* is rendered by "muff," and *Perdrigeon* (see note 30), I suppose, with a faint idea of *perdrix*, a partridge, by "bird of paradise feathers!!"

30 Perdrigeon was the name of a fashionable linen-draper in Paris at that time.

31 See note 21, page 152. According to Ash's Dictionary, 1775, *canons*, are "cannions, a kind of boot hose, an ancient dress for the legs."

MASC. Do you know that every single one of them cost me a Louis-d'or? But it is my hobby to have generally everything of the very best.

MAD. I assure you that you and I sympathize. I am furiously particular in everything I wear; I cannot endure even stockings, unless they are bought at a fashionable shop.[32]

MASC. (*Crying out suddenly*). O! O! O! gently. Damme, ladies, you use me very ill; I have reason [33] to complain of your behaviour; it is not fair.

CAT. What is the matter with you?

MASC. What! two at once against my heart! to attack me thus right and left! Ha! This is contrary to the law of nations, the combat is too unequal, and I must cry out, "Murder!"

CAT. Well, he does say things in a peculiar way.

MAD. He is a consummate wit.

CAT. You are more afraid than hurt, and your heart cries out before it is even wounded.

MASC. The devil it does! it is wounded all over from head to foot.

SCENE XI.—CATHOS, MADELON, MASCARILLE, MAROTTE.

MAR. Madam, somebody asks to see you.

MAD. Who!

MAR. The Viscount de Jodelet.

MASC. The Viscount de Jodelet?

MAR. Yes, sir.

CAT. Do you know him?

MASC. He is my most intimate friend.

---

[32] Without going into details about the phraseology of the *précieuses*, of which the ridiculousness has appeared sufficiently in this scene, it will be observed that they used adverbs, as "furiously, terribly, awfully, extraordinarily, horribly, greatly," and many more, in such a way that they often appear absurd, as, "I love you horribly," or, "he was greatly small." Such a way of speaking is not unknown even at the present time in England; we sometimes hear, "I like it awfully," "it is awfully jolly."

[33] I employ here the words "to have reason," because that verb, in the sense of "to have a right, to be right," seems to have been a courtly expression in Dryden's time. Old Moody answers to Sir Martin Marall (Act iii., Scene 3), "You have reason, sir. There he is again, too; the town phrase; a great compliment I wis! *you have reason*, sir; that is, you are no beast, sir."

MAD. Shew him in immediately.

MASC. We have not seen each other for some time; I am delighted to meet him.

CAT. Here he comes.

SCENE XII.—CATHOS, MADELON, JODELET, MASCARILLE, MAROTTE, ALMANZOR.

MASC. Ah, Viscount!

JOD. Ah, Marquis! (*Embracing each other*).

MASC. How glad I am to meet you!

JOD. How happy I am to see you here.

MASC. Embrace me once more, I pray you.[34]

MAD. (*To Cathos*). My dearest, we begin to be known; people of fashion find the way to our house.

MASC. Ladies, allow me to introduce this gentleman to you. Upon my word, he deserves the honour of your acquaintance.

JOD. It is but just we should come and pay you what we owe; your charms demand their lordly rights from all sorts of people.

MAD. You carry your civilities to the utmost confines of flattery.

CAT. This day ought to be marked in our diary as a red-letter day.

MAD. (*To Almanzor*). Come, boy, must you always be told things over and over again? Do you not observe there must be an additional chair?

MASC. You must not be astonished to see the Viscount thus; he has but just recovered from an illness, which, as you perceive, has made him so pale.[35]

JOD. The consequence of continual attendance at court and the fatigues of war.

MASC. Do you know, ladies, that in the Viscount you

---

[34] It was then the fashion for young courtiers to embrace each other repeatedly with exaggerated gestures, uttering all the while loud exclamations. The Viscount de Jodelet is the caricature of a courtier of a former reign; he is very old, very pale, dressed in sombre colours, speaks slowly and through the nose. Geoffrin, the actor, who played this part, was at least seventy years old.

[35] Molière here alludes to the complexion of the actor Geoffrin. See Note 1, page 79.

THE PRETENTIOUS YOUNG LADIES

behold one of the heroes of the age. He is a very valiant man.[36]

JOD. Marquis, you are not inferior to me; we also know what you can do.

MASC. It is true we have seen one another at work when there was need for it.

JOD. And in places where it was hot.

MASC. (*Looking at Cathos and Madelon*). Ay, but not so hot as here. Ha, ha, ha!

JOD. We became acquainted in the army; the first time we saw each other he commanded a regiment of horse aboard the galleys of Malta.

MASC. True, but for all that you were in the service before me; I remember that I was but a young officer when you commanded two thousand horse.

JOD. War is a fine thing; but, upon my word, the court does not properly reward men of merit like us.

MASC. That is the reason I intend to hang up my sword.

CAT. As for me, I have a tremendous liking for gentlemen of the army.[37]

MAD. I love them, too; but I like bravery seasoned with wit.

MASC. Do you remember, Viscount, our taking that half-moon from the enemy at the siege of Arras?[38]

JOD. What do you mean by a half-moon? It was a complete full moon.

MASC. I believe you are right.

JOD. Upon my word, I ought to remember it very well. I was wounded in the leg by a hand-grenade, of which I still carry the marks. Pray, feel it, you can perceive what sort of a wound it was.

CAT. (*Putting her hand to the place*). The scar is really large.

---

[36] In the original *un brave à trois poils*, literally, "a brave man with three hairs." This is an allusion to the moustache and pointed beard on the chin, then called *royale*. We have seen the fashion revived in our days by the late emperor of the French, Napoleon III. and his courtiers; of course, the *royale* was then called *impériale*.

[37] Cathos, who only repeats what her cousin says, and has observed that Mascarille admires Madelon, is resolved to worship more particularly the Viscount de Jodelet.

[38] Turenne compelled the Prince de Condé and the Spanish army to raise the siege of Arras in 1654.

MASC. Give me your hand for a moment, and feel this; there, just at the back of my head. Do you feel it?

MAD. Ay, I feel something.

MASC. A musket shot which I received the last campaign I served in.

JOD. (*Unbuttoning his breast*). Here is a wound which went quite through me at the attack of Gravelines.[39]

MASC. (*Putting his hand upon the button of his breeches*). I am going to show you a tremendous wound.

MAD. There is no occasion for it, we believe it without seeing it.

MASC They are honour's marks, that show what a man is made of.

CAT. We have not the least doubt of the valour of you both.

MASC. Viscount, is your coach in waiting?

JOD. Why?

MASC. We shall give these ladies an airing, and offer them a collation.

MAD. We cannot go out to-day.

MASC. Let us send for musicians then, and have a dance.

JOD. Upon my word, that is a happy thought.

MAD. With all our hearts, but we must have some additional company.

MASC. So ho! Champagne, Picard, Bourguignon, Cascaret, Basque, La Verdure, Lorrain, Provençal, La Violette.[40] I wish the deuce took all these footmen! I do not think there is a gentleman in France worse served than I am! These rascals are always out of the way.

MAD. Almanzor, tell the servants of my lord marquis to go and fetch the musicians, and ask some of the gentlemen and ladies hereabouts to come and people the solitude of our ball. (*Exit Almanzor.*

MASC. Viscount, what do you say of those eyes?

---

[39] In 1658, the Marshal de la Ferté took this town from the Spaniards.

[40] These names, with the exception of *Cascaret, La Verdure* and *La Violette* are those of natives of different provinces. and were often given to footmen, according to the place where they were born. *Cascaret* is of Spanish origin, and not seldom used as a name for servants; *La Verdure* means, verdure; *La Violette*, violet.

JOD. Why, Marquess, what do you think of them yourself?

MASC. I? I say that our liberty will have much difficulty to get away from here scot free. At least mine has suffered most violent attacks; my heart hangs by a single thread.

MAD. How natural is all he says! he gives to things a most agreeable turn.

CAT. He must really spend a tremendous deal of wit.

MASC. To show you that I am in earnest, I shall make some extempore verses upon mv passion. (*Seems to think.*

CAT. O! I beseech you by all that I hold sacred, let us hear something made upon us.

JOD. I should be glad to do so too, but the quantity of blood that has been taken from me lately, has greatly exhausted my poetic vein.

MASC. Deuce take it! I always make the first verse well, but I find the others more difficult. Upon my word, this is too short a time; but I will make you some extempore verses at my leisure, which you shall think the finest in the world.

JOD. He is devilish witty.

MAD. He—his wit is so gallant and well expressed.

MASC. Viscount, tell me, when did you see the Countess last?

JOD. I have not paid her a visit these three weeks.

MASC. Do you know that the duke came to see me this morning; he would fain have taken me into the country to hunt a stag with him?

MAD. Here come our friends.

SCENE XIII.—LUCILE, CÉLIMÈNE, CATHOS, MADELON, MASCARILLE, JODELET, MAROTTE, ALMANZOR, AND MUSICIANS.

MAD. Lawk! my dears, we beg your pardon. These gentlemen had a fancy to put life into our heels; we sent for you to fill up the void of our assembly.

LUC. We are certainly much obliged to you for doing so.

MASC. This is a kind of extempore ball, ladies, but one

of these days we shall give you one in form. Have the musicians come?

ALM. Yes, sir, they are here.

CAT. Come then, my dears, take your places.

MASC. (*Dancing by himself and singing*). La, la, la, la, la, la, la, la.

MAD. What a very elegant shape he has.

CAT. He looks as if he were a first-rate dancer.

MASC. (*Taking out Madelon to dance*). My freedom will dance a Couranto[41] as well as my feet. Play in time, musicians, in time. O what ignorant wretches! There is no dancing with them. The devil take you all, can you not play in time? La, la, la, la, la, la, la, la? Steady, you country-scrapers!

JOD. (*Dancing also*). Hold, do not play so fast. I have but just recovered from an illness.

SCENE XIV.—DU CROISY, LA GRANGE, CATHOS, MADELON, LUCILE, CÉLIMÈNE, JODELET, MASCARILLE, MAROTTE, AND MUSICIANS.

LA GR. (*With a stick in his hand*). Ah! ah! scoundrels, what are you doing here? We have been looking for you these three hours. (*He beats Mascarille*).

MASC. Oh! oh! oh! you did not tell me that blows should be dealt about.

JOD. (*Who is also beaten*). Oh! oh! oh!

LA GR. It becomes you well, you rascal, to pretend to be a man of rank.

DU CR. This will teach you to know yourself.

SCENE XV.—CATHOS, MADELON, LUCILE, CÉLIMÈNE, MASCARILLE, JODELET, MAROTTE, AND MUSICIANS.

MAD. What is the meaning of this?

JOD. It is a wager.

CAT. What, allow yourselves to be beaten thus?

MASC. Good Heavens! I did not wish to appear to take any notice of it; because I am naturally very violent, and should have flown into a passion.

MAD. To suffer an insult like this in our presence!

---

[41] A Couranto was a very grave, Spanish dance, or rather march, but in which the feet did not rise from the ground.

MASC. It is nothing. Let us not leave off. We have known one another for a long time, and among friends one ought not to be so quickly offended for such a trifle.

SCENE XVI.—DU CROISY. LA GRANGE, MADELON, CATHOS, LUCILE, CÉLIMÈNE, MASCARILLE, JODELET, MAROTTE, AND MUSICIANS.

LA GR.—Upon my word, rascals, you shall not laugh at us, I promise you. Come in, you there. (*Three or four men enter*).

MAD. What means this impudence to come and disturb us in our own house?

DU CR. What, ladies, shall we allow our footmen to be received better than ourselves? Shall they come to make love to you at our expense, and even give a ball in your honour?

MAD. Your footmen?

LA GR. Yes, our footmen; and you must give me leave to say that it is not acting either handsome or honest to spoil them for us, as you do.

MAD. O Heaven! what insolence!

LA GR. But they shall not have the advantage of our clothes to dazzle your eyes. Upon my word, if you are resolved to like them, it shall be for their handsome looks only. Quick, let them be stripped immediately.

JOD. Farewell, a long farewell to all our fine clothes.[42]

MASC. The marquisate and viscountship are at an end.

DU. CR. Ah! ah! you knaves, you have the impudence to become our rivals. I assure you, you must go somewhere else to borrow finery to make yourselves agreeable to your mistresses.

LA GR. It is too much to supplant us, and that with our own clothes.

MASC. O fortune, how fickle you are!

DU CR. Quick, pull off everything from them.

LA GR. Make haste and take away all these clothes.

[42] The original has *braverie*; brave, and bravery, had formerly also the meaning of showy, gaudy, rich, in English. Fuller in *The Holy State*, bk. ii., c. 18, says: "If he (the good yeoman) chance to appear in clothes above his rank, it is to grace some great man with his service, and then he blusheth at his own bravery."

Now, ladies, in their present condition you may continue your amours with them as long as you please; we leave you perfectly free; this gentleman and I declare solemnly that we shall not be in the least degree jealous.

SCENE XVII.—MADELON, CATHOS, JODELET, MASCARILLE, AND MUSICIANS.

CAT. What a confusion!

MAD. I am nearly bursting with vexation.

1 MUS. (*To Mascarille*). What is the meaning of this? Who is to pay us?

MASC. Ask my lord the viscount.

1 MUS. (*To Jodelet*). Who is to give us our money?

JOD. Ask my lord the marquis.

SCENE XVIII.—GORGIBUS, MADELON, CATHOS, JODELET, MASCARILLE, AND MUSICIANS.

GORG. Ah! you hussies, you have put us in a nice pickle, by what I can see; I have heard about your fine goings on from those two gentlemen who just left.

MAD. Ah, father! they have played us a cruel trick.

GORG. Yes, it is a cruel trick, but you may thank your own impertinence for it, you jades. They have revenged themselves for the way you treated them; and yet, unhappy man that I am, I must put up with the affront.

MAD. Ah! I swear we will be revenged, or I shall die in the attempt. And you, rascals, dare you remain here after your insolence?

MASC. Do you treat a marquis in this manner? This is the way of the world; the least misfortune causes us to be slighted by those who before caressed us. Come along, brother, let us go and seek our fortune somewhere else; I perceive they love nothing here but outward show, and have no regard for worth unadorned. (*They both leave.*

SCENE XIX.—GORGIBUS, MADELON, CATHOS, AND MUSICIANS.

1 MUS. Sir, as they have not paid us, we expect you to do so, for it was in this house we played.

GORG. (*Beating them*). Yes, yes, I shall satisfy you; this is the coin I will pay you in. As for you, you sluts,

I do not know why I should not serve you in the same way; we shall become the common talk and laughing-stock of everybody; this is what you have brought upon yourselves by your fooleries. Out of my sight and hide yourselves, you jades; go and hide yourselves forever. (*Alone*). And you, that are the cause of their folly, you stupid trash, mischievous amusements for idle minds, you novels, verses, songs, sonnets, and sonatas, the devil take you all.

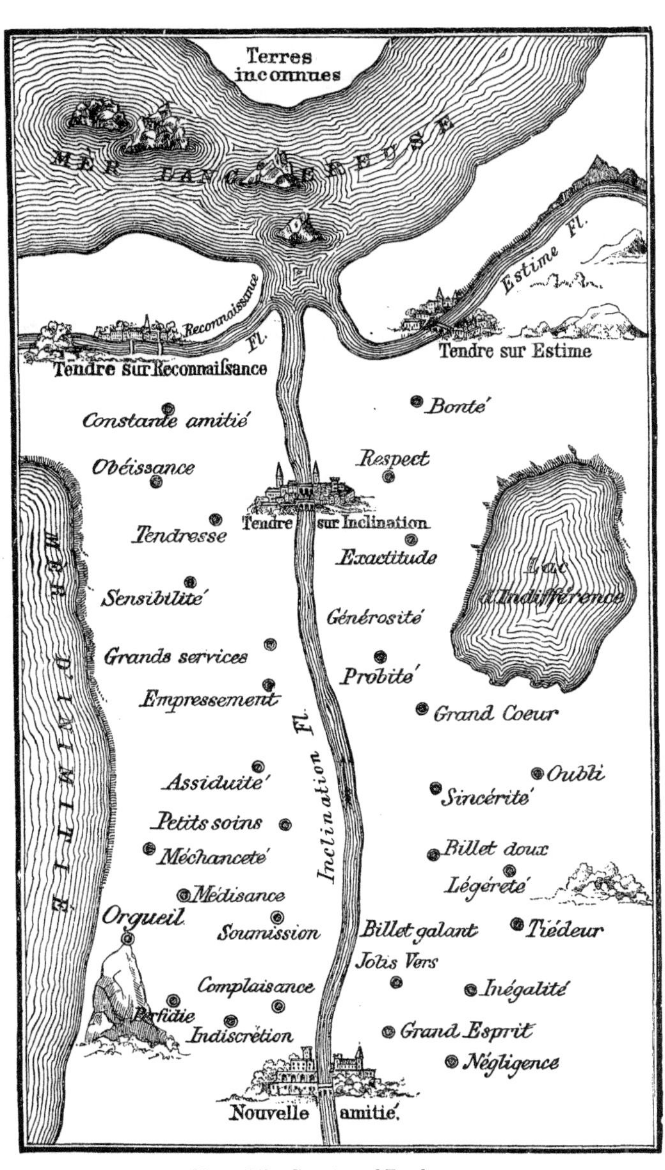

Map of the Country of Tenderness.

SGANARELLE; OU, LE COCU IMAGINAIRE.

COMÉDIE EN UN ACTE.

SGANARELLE:

OR THE SELF-DECEIVED HUSBAND.

A COMEDY IN ONE ACT.

(*THE ORIGINAL IN VERSE.*)

28TH MAY, 1660.

INTRODUCTORY NOTICE.

SIX months after the brilliant success of the *Précieuses Ridicules*, Molière brought out at the Théâtre du Petit-Bourbon a new comedy, called *Sganarelle, ou le Cocu Imaginaire*, which I have translated by *Sganarelle, or the self-deceived Husband*. It has been said that Molière owed the first idea of this piece to an Italian farce, *Il Ritratto ovvero Arlichino cornuto per opinione*, but, as it has never been printed, it is difficult to decide at the present time whether or not this be true. The primary idea of the play is common to many *commedia dell' arte*, whilst Molière has also been inspired by such old authors as Noël Du Fail, Rabelais, those of the *Quinze joyes de Mariage*, of the *Cent nouvelles Nouvelles*, and perhaps others.

The plot of *Sganarelle* is ingenious and plausible; every trifle becomes circumstantial evidence, and is received as conclusive proof both by the husband and wife. The dialogue is sprightly throughout, and the anxious desire of Sganarelle to kill his supposed injurer, whilst his cowardice prevents him from executing his valorous design, is extremely ludicrous. The chief aim of our author appears to have been to show how dangerous it is to judge with too much haste, especially in those circumstances where passion may either augment or diminish the view we take of certain objects. This truth, animated by a great deal of humour and wit, drew crowds of spectators for forty nights, though the play was brought out in summer and the marriage of the young king kept the court from Paris.

The style is totally different from that employed in the *Précieuses Ridicules*, and is a real and very good specimen of the *style gaulois* adapted to the age in which Molière lived. He has often been blamed for not having followed up his success of the *Précieuses Ridicules* by a comedy in the same style, but Molière did not want to make fresh enemies. It appears to have been a regular and set purpose with him always to produce something farcical after a creation which provoked either secret or open hostility, or even violent opposition.

Sganarelle appears in this piece for the first time, if we except the farce, or rather sketch, of the *Médecin volant*, where in reality nothing is developed, but everything is in mere outline. But in Sganarelle Molière has created a character that is his own just as much as Falstaff belongs to Shakespeare, Sancho Panza to Cervantes, or Panurge to Rabelais. Whether Sganarelle is a servant, a husband, the father of Lucinde, the brother of Ariste, a guardian, a faggot-maker, a doctor, he always represents the ugly side of human nature, an antiquated, grumpy, sullen, egotistical, jealous, grovelling, frightened character, ever and anon raising a laugh on account of his boasting, mean, morose, odd qualities. Molière was, at the time he wrote *Sganarelle*, more than thirty years old, and could therefore no longer successfully represent Mascarille as the rollicking servant of the *Biunderer*.

This farce was published by a certain Mr. Neufvillenaine, who was so smitten by it that, after having seen it represented several times, he knew it by heart, wrote it out, and published it, accompanied by a running commentary, which is not worth much, and preceded by a letter to a friend in which he extols its beauties. Molière got, in 1663, his name inserted, instead of that of Neufvillenaine, in the *privilége du roi*.

Mr. Henry Baker, the translator of this play, in the "Select Comedies of M. de Molière, London, 1732," oddly dedicates it to Miss Wolstenholme[1] in the following words:—

MADAM,

Be so good to accept this little Present as an Instance of my high Esteem. Whoever has any Knowledge of the French Language, or any Taste for COMEDY, must needs distinguish the Excellency of *Molière's* Plays: one of which is here translated. What the *English* may be, I leave others to determine; but the ORIGINAL, which you receive along with it, is, I am certain, worthy your Perusal.

Tho' what You read, at present, is called a DEDICATION, it is, perhaps, the most unlike one of any thing You ever saw: for, You'll find not one Word, in Praise, either of Your blooming Youth, Your agreeable Person, Your genteel Behaviour, Your easy Temper, or Your good Sense . . . and, the Reason is, that I cannot for my Life bring myself to such a Degree of Impertinence, as to sit down with a solemn Countenance, and Take upon me to inform the World, that the Sun is bright, and that the Spring is lovely.

My Knowledge of You from Your Infancy, and the many Civilities I am obliged for to Your Family, will, I hope, be an Excuse for this Presumption in,

MADAM, *Your most obedient humble servant*,

H. B.

Enfield,
Jan. 1st 1731-2.

This play seems to have induced several English playwrights to imitate it. Fiist, we have Sir William D'Avenant's *The Playhouse to be Let*, of which the date of the first performance is uncertain. According to the Biographia Britannica, it was "a very singular entertainment, composed of five acts, each being a distinct performance. The first act is introductory, shows the distress of the players in the time of vacation, that obliges them to let their house, which several offer to take for different purposes; amongst the rest a Frenchman, who had brought over a troop of his countrymen to act a farce. This is performed in the second act, which is a translation of Molière's *Sganarelle, or the Cuckold Conceit;* all in broken French to make the people laugh. The third act is a sort of comic opera, under the title of The History of Sir Francis Drake. The fourth act is a serious opera, representing the cruelties of the Spaniards in Peru. The fifth act is a burlesque in Heroicks on the Amours of Cæsar and Cleopatra, has a great deal of wit and humour, and was often acted afterwards by itself."

---

[1] I suppose the lady was a descendant of Sir John Wolstenholme, mentioned in one of the notes of Pepy's Diary, Sept. 5, 1662, as created a baronet, 1664, an intimate friend of Lord Clarendon's, and collector outward for the Port of London—ob. 1679.

With the exception of the first act, all the others, which are separate and distinct, but short dramatic pieces, were written in the time of Oliver Cromwell, and two of them at least were performed at the Cockpit, when Sir William D'Avenant had obtained permission to present his entertainments of music and perspective in scenes.

The second imitation of *Sganarelle* is "*Tom Essence, or the Modish Wife*, a Comedy as it is acted at the Duke's Theatre, 1677. London, printed by T. M. for W. Cademan, at the *Pope's Head*, in the Lower Walk of the *New Exchange* in the *Strand*, 1677." This play is written by a Mr. Thomas Rawlins, printer and engraver to the Mint, under Charles the First and Second, and is founded on two French comedies—viz., Molière's *Sganarelle*, and Thomas Corneille's *Don César d' Avalos*. The prologue is too bad to be quoted, and I doubt if it can ever have been spoken on any stage. This play is written partly in blank verse, partly in prose; though very coarse, it is, on the whole, clever and witty. Old Moneylove, a credulous fool, who has a young wife (Act ii., Scene 1), reminds one at times of the senator Antonio in Otway's *Venice Preserved*, and is, of course, deceived by the gallant Stanley; the sayings and doings of Mrs. Moneylove, who is "what she ought not to be," and the way she tricks her husband, are very racy, perhaps too much so for the taste of the present times. I do not think any dramatist would now bring upon the stage a young lady like Theodocia, daughter of old Moneylove, reading the list about Squire Careless. Tom Essence is a seller of perfumes, a "jealous coxcomb of his wife;" and Courtly is "a sober gentleman, servant to Theodocia;" these are imitations of Sganarelle and Lelio. Loveall, "a wilde debaucht blade," and Mrs. Luce, "a widdow disguis'd, and passes for Theodocia's maid," are taken from Corneille.

In the epilogue, the whole of which cannot be given, Mrs. Essence speaks the following lines:

"But now methinks a Cloak-Cabal I see,
Whose Prick-ears glow, whilst they their Jealousie
In *Essence* find; but Citty-Sirs, I fear,
Most of you have more cause to be severe.
We yield you are the truest Character."

Nearly all the scenes imitated in this play from Molière's *Sganarelle* contain nothing which merits to be reproduced.

The Perplexed Couple, or Mistake upon Mistake, as it is acted at the New Theatre in Lincolns-Inn-Fields, by the Company of Comedians, acting under Letters Patent granted by King Charles the Second. London, Printed for *W. Meares* at the *Lamb*, and *J. Brown*, at the *Black Swan* without *Temple-Bar*, 1715, is the third imitation of Molière's *Sganarelle*. This comedy, printed for two gentlemen, with zoological signs, was written by a Mr. Charles Molloy, who for a long time was the editor of a well-known paper, *Common Sense*, in defence of Tory principles. This play had little success, and deserved to have had none, for it has no merit whatever. Our author states in the prologue:—

"The injur'd Muses, who with savage Rage,
Of late have often been expell'd a Tyrant Stage,
Here fly for Refuge; where, secure from Harms,
By you protected, shall display their Charms . . .
No Jest profane the guilty scene deforms,
That impious way of being dull he scorns;
No Party Cant shall here inflame the Mind,
And poison what for Pleasure was designed."

Mr. Molloy admits in the preface that "the Incident of the Picture in the Third act, something in the Fourth, and one Hint in the last Act, are taken from the *Cocu Imaginaire;* the rest I'm forced to subscribe to myself, for I can lay it to no Body else." I shall only remark on this, that nearly the whole play is a mere paraphrasing of Molière's *Cocu Imaginaire,* and several other of his plays. The scene between Leonora, the heroine, and Sterling, the old usurer and lover (Act I.), is imitated from Madelon's description in the art of making love in the *Pretentious Young Ladies,* and so are many others. The servant Crispin is a medley of Mascarille from *The Blunderer,* of Gros-René from *The Love-Tiff,* and of the servant of the same name in the *Cocu Imaginaire;* the interfering uncle of Lady Thinwit, is taken from *George Dandin,* whilst Sir Anthony Thinwit becomes Sganarelle. The only thing new I have been able to discover in *The Perplexed Couple* is the lover Octavio disguising himself as a pedlar to gain admittance to the object of his love; and old Sterling, the usurer, marrying the maid instead of the mistress. Molière's farce has been lengthened by those means into a five-act comedy, and though "no jest profane" may be found in it it is more full than usual of coarse and lewd sayings, which can hardly be called inuendoes. The play is a mistake altogether; perhaps that is the reason its second name is called *Mistake upon Mistake.*

The Picture, or the Cuckold in Conceit, a Comedy in one act, by Js. Miller, is founded on Molière, and is the fourth imitation of *Sganarelle.* London, MDCCXLV. This play is, on the whole, a free translation of Molière's, interspersed with some songs set to music by Dr. Arne. Sganarelle is called Mr. Timothy Dotterel, grocer and common councilman; Gorgibus, Mr. Per-cent; Lelio, Mr. Heartly; Gros-René, John Broad, whilst Celia's maid is called Phillis. The Prologue, spoken by Mr. Havard, ends thus:

"... To-night we serve
A Cuckold, that the Laugh does well deserve;
A Cuckold in Conceit, by Fancy made
As mad, as by the common Course of Trade:
And more to please ye, and his Worth enhance,
He's carbonado'd a la mode de France;
Cook'd by Molière, great Master of his Trade,
From whose Receipt this Harrico was made.
But if that poignant Taste we fail to take,
That something, that a mere Receipt can't make;
Forgive the Failure—we're but Copies all,
And want the Spirit of th' Original."

The fifth and best imitation is Arthur Murphy's *All in the Wrong,* a comedy in five acts, first performed during the summer season of 1761, at the Theatre Royal, in Drury Lane. Though the chief idea and several of the scenes are taken from *Sganarelle,* yet the characters are well drawn, and the play, as a whole, very entertaining. The Prologue, written and spoken by Samuel Foote, is as follows:

"To-night, be it known to Box, Gall'ry, and Pit,
Will be open'd the best Summer-Warehouse for Wit;[2]
The New Manufacture, Foote and Co., Undertakers;
Play, Pantomime, Opera, Farce,—by the Makers!

---

[2] Mr. Garrick, at this time, had let his playhouse for the summer months.

We scorn, like our brethren, our fortunes to owe
To Shakespeare and Southern, to Otway and Rowe.
Though our judgment may err, yet our justice is shewn,
For we promise to mangle no works but our own.
And moreover on this you may firmly rely,
If we can't make you laugh, that we won't make you cry.
For Roscius, who knew we were mirth-loving souls,
Has lock'd up his lightning, his daggers, and bowls.
Resolv'd that in buskins no hero shall stalk,
He has shut us quite out of the Tragedy walk.
No blood, no blank verse !——and in short we're undone,
Unless you're contented with Frolic and Fun.
If tired of her round in the Ranelagh-mill,
There should be but one female inclined to sit still;
If blind to the beauties, or sick of the squall,
A party should shun to catch cold at Vauxhall;
If at Sadler's sweet Wells the made wine should be thick,
The cheese-cakes turn sour, or Miss Wilkinson sick;
If the fume of the pipes should oppress you in June,
Or the tumblers be lame, or the bells out of tune;
I hope you will call at our warehouse in Drury;
We've a curious assortment of goods, I assure you;
Domestic and foreign, and all kinds of wares;
English cloths, Irish linnen, and French petenlairs!
If for want of good custom, or losses in trade,
The poetical partners should bankrupts be made;
If from dealings too large, we plunge deeply in debt,
And Whereas issue out in the Muses Gazette;
We'll on you our assigns for Certificates call;
Though insolvent, we're honest, and give up our all."

Otway in his very indecent play, *The Soldier's Fortune*, performed at Dorset Garden, 1681, has borrowed freely from Molière; namely: one scene from *Sganarelle*, four scenes from *The School for Husbands*, and a hint from *The School for Wives*.

The joke from *The Pretentious Young Ladies*, Scene xii., page 162, about "the half moon and the full moon" is repeated in the conversation between Fourbin and Bloody-Bones in *The Soldier's Fortune*.

Sir John Vanbrugh also translated Molière's *Sganarelle*, which was performed at the Queen's Theatre in the Haymarket, 1706, but has not been printed.

There was also a ballad opera played at Drury Lane April 11, 1733, called the *Imaginary Cuckold*, which is an imitation of *Sganarelle*.

DRAMATIS PERSONÆ.

GORGIBUS, *a citizen of Paris.*

LELIO, *in love with Celia.*

SGANARELLE,[3] *a citizen of Paris and the self-deceived husband.*

VILLEBREQUIN, *father to Valère.*

GROS-RENÉ, *servant to Lelio.*

A RELATIVE OF SGANARELLE'S WIFE.

CELIA, *daughter of Gorgibus.*

SGANARELLE'S WIFE.

CELIA'S MAID.

Scene.—A PUBLICK PLACE IN PARIS.

---

[3] Molière acted this part himself. In the inventory of his dresses taken after his death, and given by M. Eudore Soulié in his *Recherches sur Molière*, 1863, we find: "a . . . dress for the *Cocu imaginaire*, consisting of knee-breeches, doublet, cloak, collar, and shoes, all in crimson red satin."

SGANARELLE:

OR THE SELF-DECEIVED HUSBAND.

(*SGANARELLE: OU LE COCU IMAGINAIRE.*)

SCENE I.—GORGIBUS, CELIA, CELIA'S MAID.

CEL. (*Coming out in tears, her father following her*). Ah! never expect my heart to consent to that.

GORG. What do you mutter, you little impertinent girl? Do you suppose you can thwart my resolution? Have I not absolute power over you? And shall your youthful brain control my fatherly discretion by foolish arguments? Which of us two has most right to command the other? Which of us two, you or I, is, in your opinion, best able to judge what is advantageous for you? Zounds, do not provoke me too much, or you may feel, and in a very short time too, what strength this arm of mine still possesses! Your shortest way, you obstinate minx, would be to accept without any more ado the husband intended for you; but you say, "I do not know what kind of temper he has, and I ought to think about it beforehand, if you will allow me." I know that he is heir to a large fortune; ought I therefore to trouble my head about anything else? Can this man, who has twenty thousand golden charms in his pocket to be beloved by you, want any accomplishments? Come, come, let him be what he will, I promise you that with such a sum he is a very worthy gentleman!

CEL. Alas!

GORG. Alas, indeed! What is the meaning of that?

A fine alas you have uttered just now! Look ye! If once you put me in a passion you will have plenty of opportunities for shouting alas! This comes of that eagerness of yours to read novels day and night; your head is so full of all kinds of nonsense about love, that you talk of God much less than of Clélie. Throw into the fire all these mischievous books, which are every day corrupting the minds of so many young people; instead of such trumpery, read, as you ought to do, the Quatrains of Pibrac[4] and the learned memorandum-books of Councillor Matthieu,[5] a valuable work and full of fine sayings for you to learn by heart; the Guide for Sinners[6] is also a good book. Such writings teach people in a short time how to spend their lives well, and if you had never read anything but such moral books you would have known better how to submit to my commands.

CEL. Do you suppose, dear father, I can ever forget that unchangeable affection I owe to Lelio? I should be wrong to dispose of my hand against your will, but you yourself engaged me to him.

GORG. Even if you were engaged ever so much, another man has made his appearance whose fortune annuls your engagement. Lélio is a pretty fellow, but learn that there is nothing that does not give way to money, that gold will make even the most ugly charming, and that without it everything else is but wretchedness. I believe you are not very fond of Valère, but though you do not

---

[4] Gui du Faur de Pibrac (1528–1584) was a distinguished diplomatist, magistrate, and orator, who wrote several works, of which the *Cinquante quatrains contenant préceptes et enseignements utiles pour la vie de l'homme, composés à l'imitation de Phocylides, Epicharmus, et autres poëtes grecs*, and which number he afterwards increased to 126, are the best known. These quatrains, or couplets of four verses, have been translated into nearly all European and several Eastern languages. A most elegant reprint has been published of them, in 1874, by M. A. Lemerre, of Paris.

[5] Pierre Matthieu (1563–1621), a French historian and poet wrote, among other works, his *Tablettes de la vie et de la mort, quatrains de la Vanité du Monde*, a collection of 274 moral quatrains, divided in three parts, each part of which was published separately in an oblong shape, like a memorandum book; hence the name *Tablettes.*

[6] *La guide des pécheurs*, the Guide for Sinners, is a translation in French of an ascetic Spanish work, *la guia de pecadores*, written by a Dominican friar, Lewis, of Granada.

like him as a lover, you will like him as a husband. The very name of husband endears a man more than is generally supposed, and love is often a consequence of marriage. But what a fool I am to stand arguing when I possess the absolute right to command. A truce then, I tell you, to your impertinence; let me have no more of your foolish complaints. This evening Valère intends to visit you, and if you do not receive him well, and look kindly upon him, I shall . . . but I will say no more on this subject.

SCENE II.—CELIA, CELIA'S MAID.

MAID. What, madam! you refuse positively what so many other people would accept with all their heart! You answer with tears a proposal for marriage, and delay for a long time to say a "yes" so agreeable to hear! Alas! why does some one not wish to marry me? I should not need much entreaty: and so far from thinking it any trouble to say "yes" once, believe me I would very quickly say it a dozen times. Your brother's tutor was quite right when, as we were talking about worldly affairs, he said, "A woman is like the ivy, which grows luxuriantly whilst it clings closely to the tree, but never thrives if it be separated from it." Nothing can be truer, my dear mistress, and I, miserable sinner, have found it out. Heaven rest the soul of my poor Martin! when he was alive my complexion was like a cherub's; I was plump and comely, my eyes sparkled brightly, and I felt happy: now I am doleful. In those pleasant times, which flew away like lightning, I went to bed, in the very depth of winter, without kindling a fire in the room; even airing the sheets appeared then to me ridiculous; but now I shiver even in the dogdays. In short, madam, believe me there is nothing like having a husband at night by one's side, were it only for the pleasure of hearing him say, "God bless you," whenever one may happen to sneeze.

CEL. Can you advise me to act so wickedly as to forsake Lelio and take up with this ill-shaped fellow?

MAID. Upon my word, your Lelio is a mere fool to stay away the very time he is wanted; his long absence makes me very much suspect some change in his affection.

CEL. (*showing her the portrait of Lelio*). Oh! do not distress me by such dire forebodings! Observe carefully the features of his face; they swear to me an eternal affection; after all, I would not willingly believe them to tell a falsehood, but that he is such as he is here limned by art, and that his affection for me remains unchanged.

MAID. To be sure, these features denote a deserving lover, whom you are right to regard tenderly.

CEL. And yet I must —— Ah! support me.

(*She lets fall the portrait of Lelio.*

MAID. Madam, what is the cause of . . . Heavens! she swoons. Oh! make haste! help! help!

SCENE III.—CELIA, SGANARELLE, CELIA'S MAID.

SGAN. What is the matter? I am here.

MAID. My lady is dying.

SGAN. What! is that all? You made such a noise, I thought the world was at an end. Let us see, however. Madam, are you dead? Um! she does not say one word.

MAID. I shall fetch somebody to carry her in; be kind enough to hold her so long.

SCENE IV. — CELIA, SGANARELLE, SGANARELLE'S WIFE.

SGAN. (*passing his hand over Celia's bosom*). She is cold all over, and I do not know what to say to it. Let me draw a little nearer and try whether she breathes or not. Upon my word, I cannot tell, but I perceive still some signs of life.

SGAN.'s WIFE. (*looking from the window*). Ah! what do I see? My husband, holding in his arms . . . But I shall go down; he is false to me most certainly; I should be glad to catch him.

SGAN. She must be assisted very quickly; she would certainly be in the wrong to die. A journey to another world is very foolish, so long as a body is able to stay in this. (*He carries her in*).

SCENE V.—SGANARELLE'S WIFE, *alone.*

He has suddenly left this spot; his flight has disappointed my curiosity; but I doubt no longer that he is unfaithful to me; the little I have seen sufficiently proves it. I am no longer astonished that he returns my modest love with strange coldness; the ungrateful wretch reserves his caresses for others, and starves me in order to feed their pleasures. This is the common way of husbands; they become indifferent to what is lawful; at the beginning they do wonders, and seem to be very much in love with us, but the wretches soon grow weary of our fondness, and carry elsewhere what is due to us alone. Oh! how it vexes me that the law will not permit us to change our husband as we do our linen! That would be very convenient; and, troth, I know some women whom it would please as much as myself. (*Taking up the picture which Celia had let fall*). But what a pretty thing has fortune sent me here; the enamel of it is most beautiful, the workmanship delightful; let me open it?

SCENE VI.—SGANARELLE, SGANARELLE'S WIFE.

SGAN. (*Thinking himself alone*). They thought her dead, but it was nothing at all! She is already recovering and nearly well again. But I see my wife.

SGAN.'S WIFE. (*Thinking herself alone*). O Heaven! It is a miniature, a fine picture of a handsome man.

SGAN. (*Aside, and looking over his wife's shoulder*). What is this she looks at so closely? This picture bodes my honour little good. A very ugly feeling of jealousy begins to creep over me.

SGAN.'S WIFE. (*Not seeing her husband*). I never saw anything more beautiful in my life! The workmanship is even of greater value than the gold! Oh, how sweet it smells!

SGAN. (*Aside*). The deuce! She kisses it! I am victimized!

SGAN.'S WIFE. (*Continues her Monologue.*) I think it must be a charming thing to have such a fine-looking man for a sweetheart; if he should urge his suit very much the temptation would be great. Alas! why have I not a handsome man like this for my husband instead of my booby, my clod-hopper . . . ?

SGAN. (*Snatching the portrait from her*). What, hussey! have I caught you in the very act, slandering your honourable and darling husband? According to you, most worthy spouse, and everything well considered, the husband is not as good as the wife? In Beelzebub's name (and may he fly away with you), what better match could you wish for? Is there any fault to be found with me? It seems that this shape, this air, which everybody admires; this face, so fit to inspire love, for which a thousand fair ones sigh both night and day; in a word, my own delightful self, by no manner of means pleases you. Moreover, to satisfy your ravenous appetite you add to the husband the relish of a gallant.

SGAN.'s WIFE. I see plainly the drift of your jocular remarks, though you do not clearly express yourself. You expect by these means . . .

SGAN. Try to impose upon others, not upon me, I pray you. The fact is evident; I have in my hands a convincing proof of the injury I complain of.

SGAN.'s WIFE. I am already too angry, and do not wish you to make me more so by any fresh insult. Hark ye, do not imagine that you shall keep this pretty thing; consider . . .

SGAN. I am seriously considering whether I shall break your neck. I wish I had but the original of this portrait in my power as much as I have the copy.

SGAN.'s WIFE. Why?

SGAN. For nothing at all, dear, sweet object of my love! I am very wrong to speak out; my forehead ought to thank you for many favours received. (*Looking at the portrait of Lelio*). There he is, your darling, the pretty bed-fellow, the wicked incentive of your secret flame, the merry blade with whom . . .

SGAN.'s WIFE. With whom? Go on.

SGAN. With whom, I say . . . I am almost bursting with vexation.[7]

SGAN.'s WIFE. What does the drunken sot mean by all this?

---

[7] The original has: "*j'en crève d'ennuis.*" The French word *ennui*, which now only means weariness of mind, signified formerly injury, and the vexation or hatred caused thereby; something like the English word "annoy," as in Shakespeare's Richard III., v. 3:

> "Sleep, Richmond, sleep in peace, and wake in joy;
> Good angels guard thee from the boar's annoy."

SGAN. You know but too well, Mrs. Impudence. No one will call me any longer Sganarelle, but every one will give me the title of Signor Cornutus; my honor is gone, but to reward you, who took it from me, I shall at the very least break you an arm or a couple of ribs.

SGAN.'s WIFE. How dare you talk to me thus?

SGAN. How dare you play me these devilish pranks?

SGAN.'s WIFE. What devilish pranks? Say what you mean.

SGAN. Oh! It is not worth complaining of. A stag's top-knot on my head is indeed a very pretty ornament for everybody to come and look at.

SGAN.'s WIFE. After you have insulted your wife so grossly as to excite her thirst for vengeance, you stupidly imagine you can prevent the effects of it by pretending to be angry? Such insolence was never before known on the like occasion. The offender is the person who begins the quarrel.

SGAN. Oh! what a shameless creature! To see the confident behaviour of this woman, would not any one suppose her to be very virtuous?

SGAN.'s WIFE. Away, go about your business, wheedle your mistresses, tell them you love them, caress them even, but give me back my picture, and do not make a jest of me. (*She snatches the picture from him and runs away*).

SGAN. So you think to escape me; but I shall get hold of it again in spite of you.

SCENE VII.—LELIO, GROS-RENÉ.

GR.-RE. Here we are at last; but, sir, if I might be so bold, I should like you to tell me one thing.

LEL. Well, speak.

GR.-RE. Are you possessed by some devil or other, that you do not sink under such fatigues as these? For eight whole days we have been riding long stages, and have not been sparing of whip and spur to urge on confounded screws, whose cursed trot shook us so very much that, for my part, I feel as if every limb was out of joint; without mentioning a worse mishap which troubles me very much in a place I will not mention. And yet, no sooner are you at your journey's end, than you go out well and hearty. without taking rest, or eating the least morsel.

LEL. My haste may well be excused, for I am greatly alarmed about the report of Celia's marriage. You know I adore her, and, before everything, I wish to hear if there is any truth in this ominous rumour.

GR.-RE. Ay, sir, but a good meal would be of great use to you to discover the truth or falsehood of this report; doubtless you would become thereby much stronger to withstand the strokes of fate. I judge by my own self, for, when I am fasting, the smallest disappointment gets hold of me and pulls me down; but when I have eaten sufficiently my soul can resist anything, and the greatest misfortunes cannot depress it. Believe me, stuff yourself well, and do not be too cautious. To fortify you under whatever misfortune may do, and in order to prevent sorrow from entering your heart, let it float in plenty of wine.[8]

LEL. I cannot eat.

GR.-RE. (*Aside*). I can eat very well indeed; If it is not true may I be struck dead! (*Aloud*). For all that, your dinner shall be ready presently.

LEL. Hold your tongue, I command you.

GR.-RE. How barbarous is that order!

LEL. I am not hungry, but uneasy.

GR.-RE. And I am hungry and uneasy as well, to see that a foolish love-affair engrosses all your thoughts.[9]

LEL. Let me but get some information about my heart's

---

[8] This is an imitation of Plautus' *Curculio, or the Forgery*. The Parasite of Phædromus, who gave his name to the piece, says (ii. 3):—" I am quite undone. I can hardly see; my mouth is bitter; my teeth are blunted; my jaws are clammy through fasting; with my entrails thus lank with abstinence from food, am I come . . . Let's cram down something first; the gammon, the udder, and the kernels; these are the foundations for the stomach, with head and roast-beef, a good-sized cup and a capacious pot, that council enough may be forthcoming."

[9] Shakespeare, in *The Two Gentlemen of Verona* (Act ii., Sc. 1), has the following:

Speed. . . . Why muse you, sir? 'tis dinner-time.

Val. I have dined.

Speed. Ay, but hearken, sir; though the chameleon, love, can feed on the air, I am one that am nourished by my victuals, and would fain have meat. O, be not like your mistress; be moved, be moved.

delight, and without troubling me more, go and take your meal if you like.

GR.-RE. I never say nay when a master commands.

SCENE VIII.—LELIO, *alone.*

No, no, my mind is tormented by too many terrors; the father has promised me Celia's hand, and she has given me such proofs of her love that I need not despair.

SCENE IX.—SGANARELLE, LELIO.

SGAN. (*Not seeing Lelio, and holding the portrait in his hand*). I have got it. I can now at my leisure look at the countenance of the rascal who causes my dishonour. I do not know him at all.

LEL. (*Aside*). Heavens! what do I see? If that be my picture, what then must I believe?

SGAN. (*Not seeing Lelio*). Ah! poor Sganarelle! your reputation is doomed, and to what a sad fate! Must . . (*Perceiving that Lelio observes him he goes to the other side of the stage*).

LEL. (*Aside*). This pledge of my love cannot have left the fair hands to which I gave it, without startling my faith in her.

SGAN. (*Aside*). People will make fun of me henceforth by holding up their two fingers; songs will be made about me, and every time they will fling in my teeth that scandalous affront, which a wicked wife has printed upon my forehead.

LEL. (*Aside*). Do I deceive myself?

SGAN. (*Aside*). Oh! Jade![10] were you impudent enough to cuckold me in the flower of my age? The wife too of a husband who may be reckoned handsome! and must be a monkey, a cursed addle-pated fellow . . .

LEL. (*Aside, looking still at the portrait in Sganarelle's hand*). I am not mistaken; it is my very picture.

SGAN. (*Turning his back towards him*). This man seems very inquisitive.

---

[10] The original is *truande*, which, as well as the masculine *truand*, meant, in old French, a vagabond, a rascal; it is still retained in the English phrase "to play the truant."

LEL. (*Aside*). I am very much surprised.

SGAN. What would he be at?

LEL. (*Aside*). I will speak to him. (*Aloud*). May I . . . (*Sganarelle goes farther off*). I say, let me have one word with you.

SGAN. (*Aside, and moving still farther*). What does he wish to tell me now?

LEL. Will you inform me by what accident that picture came into your hands?

SGAN. (*Aside*). Why does he wish to know? But I am thinking . . . (*Looking at Lelio and at the portrait in his hand*). Oh! upon my word, I know the cause of his anxiety; I no longer wonder at his surprise. This is my man, or rather, my wife's man.

LEL. Pray, relieve my distracted mind, and tell me how you come by . . .

SGAN. Thank Heaven, I know what disturbs you; this portrait, which causes you some uneasiness, is your very likeness, and was found in the hands of a certain acquaintance of yours; the soft endearments which have passed between that lady and you are no secret to me. I cannot tell whether I have the honour to be known by your gallant lordship in this piece of gallantry; but henceforth, be kind enough to break off an intrigue, which a husband may not approve of; and consider that the holy bonds of wedlock . . .

LEL. What do you say? She from whom you received this pledge . . .

SGAN. Is my wife, and I am her husband.

LEL. Her husband?

SGAN. Yes, her husband, I tell you. Though married I am far from merry;[11] you, sir, know the reason of it; this very moment I am going to inform her relatives about this affair.

SCENE X.—LELIO, *alone*.

Alas! what have I heard! The report then was true that

[11] The original has *mari-très-marri;* literally, "husband very sad;" *marri* being the old French for sad: the ancient plays and tales are full of allusions to the connection between these two words, *mari* and *marri.*

her husband was the ugliest of all his sex. Even if your faithless lips had never sworn me more than a thousand times eternal love, the disgust you should have felt at such a base and shameful choice might have sufficiently secured me against the loss of your affection . . But this great insult, and the fatigues of a pretty long journey, produce all at once such a violent effect upon me, that I feel faint, and can hardly bear up under it.

SCENE XI.—LELIO, SGANARELLE'S WIFE.

SGAN.'S WIFE. In spite of me, my wretch . . . (*Seeing Lelio*). Good lack! what ails you? I perceive, sir, you are ready to faint away.

LEL. It is an illness that has attacked me quite suddenly.

SGAN'S WIFE. I am afraid you shall faint; step in here, and stay until you are better.

LEL. For a moment or two I will accept of your kindness.

SCENE XII.—SGANARELLE, A RELATIVE OF SGANARELLE'S WIFE.

REL. I commend a husband's anxiety in such a case, but you take fright a little too hastily. All that you have told me against her, kinsman, does not prove her guilty. It is a delicate subject, and no one should ever be accused of such a crime unless it can be fully proved.

SGAN. That is to say, unless you see it.

REL. Too much haste leads us to commit mistakes. Who can tell how this picture came into her hands, and, after all, whether she knows the man? Seek a little more information, and if it proves to be as you suspect, I shall be one of the first to punish her offence.

SCENE XIII.—SGANARELLE, *alone*.

Nothing could be said fairer; it is really the best way to proceed cautiously. Perhaps I have dreamt of horns without any cause, and the perspiration has covered my brow rather prematurely. My dishonour is not at all proved by that portrait which frightened me so much. Let me endeavour then by care . . .

SCENE XIV. SGANARELLE, SGANARELLE'S WIFE, *standing at the door of her house, with* LELIO.

SGAN. (*Aside seeing them*). Ha! what do I see? Zounds! there can be no more question about the portrait, for upon my word here stands the very man, in *propria persona*.

SGAN.'S WIFE. You hurry away too fast, sir; if you leave us so quickly, you may perhaps have a return of your illness.

LEL. No, no, I thank you heartily for the kind assistance you have rendered me.

SGAN. (*Aside*). The deceitful woman is to the last polite to him. (*Sganarelle's Wife goes into the house again*).

SCENE XV.—SGANARELLE, LELIO.

SGAN. He has seen me, let us hear what he can say to me.

LEL. (*Aside*). Oh! my soul is moved! this sight inspires me with . . . but I ought to blame this unjust resentment, and only ascribe my sufferings to my merciless fate; yet I cannot help envying the success that has crowned his passion. (*Approaching Sganarelle*). O too happy mortal in having so beautiful a wife.

SCENE XVI.—SGANARELLE, CELIA, *at her window, seeing Lelio go away.*

SGAN. (*Alone*). This confession is pretty plain. His extraordinary speech surprises me as much as if horns had grown upon my head. (*Looking at the side where Lelio went off*). Go your way, you have not acted at all like an honourable man.

CEL. (*Aside, entering*). Who can that be? Just now I saw Lelio. Why does he conceal his return from me?

SGAN. (*Without seeing Celia*). "O too happy mortal in having so beautiful a wife!" Say rather, unhappy mortal in having such a disgraceful spouse through whose guilty passion, it is now but too clear, I have been cuckolded without any feeling of compassion. Yet I allow him to go away after such a discovery, and stand with my arms folded like a regular silly-billy! I ought at least to have knocked his hat off, thrown stones at him, or mud on his cloak; to satisfy my wrath I should rouse the whole neighbourhood, and cry, "Stop, thief of my honour!"

CEL. (*To Sganarelle*). Pray, sir, how came you to know this gentleman who went away just now and spoke to you?

SGAN. Alas! madam, it is not I who am acquainted with him; it is my wife.

CEL. What emotion thus disturbs your mind?

SGAN. Do not blame me; I have sufficient cause for my sorrow; permit me to breathe plenty of sighs.

CEL. What can be the reason of this uncommon grief?

SGAN. If I am sad it is not for a trifle: I challenge other people not to grieve, if they found themselves in my condition. You see in me the model of unhappy husbands. Poor Sganarelle's honour is taken from him; but the loss of my honour would be small—they deprive me of my reputation also.

CEL. How do they do that?

SGAN. That fop has taken the liberty to cuckold me—saving your presence, madam—and this very day my own eyes have been witness to a private interview between him and my wife.

CEL. What? He who just now . . .

SGAN. Ay, ay, it is he who brings disgrace upon me; he is in love with my wife, and my wife is in love with him.

CEL. Ah! I find I was right when I thought his returning secretly only concealed some base design; I trembled the minute I saw him, from a sad foreboding of what would happen.

SGAN. You espouse my cause with too much kindness, but everybody is not so charitably disposed; for many, who have already heard of my sufferings, so far from taking my part, only laugh at me.

CEL. Can anything be more base than this vile deed? or can a punishment be discovered such as he deserves? Does he think he is worthy to live, after polluting himself with such treachery? O Heaven! is it possible?

SGAN. It is but too true.

CEL. O traitor, villain, deceitful, faithless wretch!

SGAN. What a kind-hearted creature!

CEL. No, no, hell has not tortures enough to punish you sufficiently for your guilt!

SGAN. How well she talks!

CEL. Thus to abuse both innocence and goodness!

SGAN. (*Sighing aloud*). Ah!

CEL. A heart which never did the slightest action deserving of being treated with such insult and contempt.

SGAN. That's true.

CEL. Who far from . . . but it is too much; nor can this heart endure the thought of it without feeling on the rack.

SGAN. My dear lady, do not distress yourself so much; it pierces my very soul to see you grieve so at my misfortune.

CEL. But do not deceive yourself so far as to fancy that I shall sit down and do nothing but lament; no, my heart knows how to act in order to be avenged; nothing can divert me from it; I go to prepare everything.

SCENE XVII.—SGANARELLE, *alone*.

May Heaven keep her for ever out of harm's way! How kind of her to wish to avenge me! Her anger at my dishonour plainly teaches me how to act. Nobody should bear such affronts as these tamely, unless indeed he be a fool. Let us therefore hasten to hunt out this rascal who has insulted me, and let me prove my courage by avenging my dishonour.[12] I will teach you, you rogue, to laugh at my expense, and to cuckold people without showing them any respect. (*After going three or four steps he comes back again.*) But gently, if you please, this man looks as if he were very hot-headed and passionate; he may, perhaps, heaping one insult upon another, ornament my

---

[12] A similar adventure is told of the renowned fabulist La Fontaine. One day some one informed him that Poignan, a retired captain of dragoons and one of his friends, was by far too intimate with Madame La Fontaine, and that to avenge his dishonour he ought to fight a duel with him. La Fontaine calls upon Poignan at four o'clock in the morning, tells him to dress, takes him out of town, and then coolly says "that he has been advised to fight a duel with him in order to avenge his wounded honour." Soon La Fontaine's sword flies out of his hand, the friends go to breakfast, and the whole affair is at an end.

back as well as he has done my brow.[13] I detest, from the bottom of my heart, these fiery tempers, and vastly prefer peaceable people. I do not care to beat for fear of being beaten; a gentle disposition was always my predominant virtue. But my honour tells me that it is absolutely necessary I should avenge such an outrage as this. Let honour say whatever it likes, the deuce take him who listens. Suppose now I should play the hero, and receive for my pains an ugly thrust with a piece of cold steel quite through my stomach; when the news of my death spreads through the whole town, tell me then, my honour, shall you be the better of it.[14] The grave is too melancholy an abode, and too unwholesome for people who are afraid of the colic; as for me, I find, all things considered, that it is, after all, better to be a cuckold than to be dead. What harm is there in it? Does it make a man's legs crooked? does it spoil his shape? The plague take him who first invented being grieved about such a delusion, linking the honour of the wisest man to anything a fickle woman may do. Since every person is rightly held responsible for his own crimes, how can our honour, in this case, be considered criminal? We are blamed for the actions of other people. If our wives have an intrigue with any man, without our knowledge, all the mischief must fall upon our backs; they commit the crime and we are reckoned guilty. It is a villainous abuse, and indeed Government should remedy such injustice. Have we not enough of other accidents that happen to us whether we like them or not? Do not quarrels, lawsuits, hunger, thirst, and sickness sufficiently disturb the even tenour of our lives? and yet we must stupidly get it into our heads to grieve about something which has no foundation. Let us laugh at it, despise such idle fears, and be above sighs and tears. If my wife has done amiss, let her cry as much as she likes, but why should I weep when I have done no wrong? After all, I am not the only one of my fraternity, and that should

---

[13] In the original there is a play on words which cannot be rendered in English. *Il pourrait bien. . . . charger de bois mon dos comme, il a fait mon front. Bois* means "stick" and "stags' antlers."

[14] Compare in Shakespeare's *Part First of King Henry IV.* v. 1, Falstaff's speech about honour.

console me a little. Many people of rank see their wives cajoled, and do not say a word about it. Why should I then try to pick a quarrel for an affront, which is but a mere trifle? They will call me a fool for not avenging myself, but I should be a much greater fool to rush on my own destruction. (*Putting his hand upon his stomach*). I feel, however, my bile is stirred up here; it almost persuades me to do some manly action. Ay, anger gets the better of me; it is rather too much of a good thing to be a coward too! I am resolved to be revenged upon the thief of my honour. Full of the passion which excites my ardour, and in order to make a beginning, I shall go and tell everywhere that he lies with my wife.

SCENE XVIII.—GORGIBUS, CELIA, CELIA'S MAID.

CEL. Yes, I will yield willingly to so just a law, father; you can freely dispose of my heart and my hand; I will sign the marriage contract whenever you please, for I am now determined to perform my duty. I can command my own inclinations, and shall do whatever you order me.

GORG. How she pleases me by talking in this manner! Upon my word! I am so delighted that I would immediately cut a caper or two, were people not looking on, who would laugh at it. Come hither, I say, and let me embrace you; there is no harm in that; a father may kiss his daughter whenever he likes, without giving any occasion for scandal. Well, the satisfaction of seeing you so obedient has made me twenty years younger.

SCENE XIX.—CELIA, CELIA'S MAID.

MAID. This change surprises me.

CEL. When you come to know why I act thus, you will esteem me for it.

MAID. Perhaps so.

CEL. Know then that Lelio has wounded my heart by his treacherous behaviour, and has been in this neighbourhood without . . .

MAID. Here he comes.

SCENE XX.—LELIO, CELIA, CELIA'S MAID.

LEL. Before I take my leave of you for ever, I will at least here tell you that . . .

CEL. What! are you insolent enough to speak to me again?

LEL. I own my insolence is great, and yet your choice is such I should not be greatly to blame if I upbraided you. Live, live contented, and laugh when you think of me, as well as your worthy husband, of whom you have reason to be proud.

CEL. Yes, traitor, I will live so, and I trust most earnestly that the thought of my happiness may disturb you.

LEL. Why this outbreak of passion?

CEL. You pretend to be surprised, and ask what crimes you have committed?

SCENE XXI.—CELIA, LELIO, SGANARELLE *armed cap-a-pie*, CELIA'S MAID.

SGAN. I wage war, a war of extermination against this robber of my honour, who without mercy has sullied my fair name.

CEL. (*To Lelio, pointing to Sganarelle*). Look on this man, and then you will require no further answer.

LEL. Ah! I see.

CEL. A mere glance at him is sufficient to abash you.

LEL. It ought rather to make you blush.

SGAN. My wrath is now disposed to vent itself upon some one; my courage is at its height; if I meet him, there will be blood shed. Yes, I have sworn to kill him, nothing can keep me from doing so. Wherever I see him I will dispatch him. (*Drawing his sword halfway and approaching Lelio*). Right through the middle of his heart I shall thrust . . .

LEL. (*Turning round*). Against whom do you bear such a grudge?

SGAN. Against no one.

LEL. Why are you thus in armour?

SGAN. It is a dress I put on to keep the rain off. (*Aside*). Ah! what a satisfaction it would be for me to kill him! Let us pluck up courage to do it.

LEL. (*Turning round again*). Hey?

SGAN. I did not speak. (*Aside, boxing his own ears, and thumping himself to raise his courage*). Ah! I am enraged at my own cowardice! Chicken-hearted poltroon!

CEL. What you have seen ought to satisfy you, but it appears to offend you.

LEL. Yes through him I know you are guilty of the greatest faithlessness that ever wronged a faithful lover's heart, and for which no excuse can be found.

SGAN. (*Aside*). Why have I not a little more courage?

CEL. Ah, traitor, speak not to me in so unmanly and insolent a manner.

SGAN. (*Aside*). You see, Sganarelle, she takes up your quarrel: courage, my lad, be a trifle vigorous. Now, be bold, try to make one noble effort and kill him whilst his back is turned.

LEL. (*Who has moved accidentally a few steps back, meets Sganarelle, who was drawing near to kill him. The latter is frightened, and retreats*). Since my words kindle your wrath, madam, I ought to show my satisfaction with what your heart approves, and here commend the lovely choice you have made.

CEL. Yes, yes, my choice is such as cannot be blamed.

LEL. You do well to defend it.

SGAN. No doubt, she does well to defend my rights, but what you have done, sir, is not according to the laws; I have reason to complain; were I less discreet, much blood would be shed.

LEL. Of what do you complain? And why this . . .

SGAN. Do not say a word more. You know too well where the shoe pinches me. But conscience and a care for your own soul should remind you that my wife is my wife, and that to make her yours under my very nose is not acting like a good Christian.

LEL. Such a suspicion is mean and ridiculous! Harbour no scruples on that point: I know she belongs to you; I am very far from being in love with . . .

CEL. Oh! traitor! how well you dissemble!

LEL. What! do you imagine I foster a thought which need disturb his mind? Would you slander me by accusing me of such a cowardly action?

CEL. Speak, speak to himself; he can enlighten you.

SGAN. (*To Celia*). No, no, you can argue much better than I can, and have treated the matter in the right way.

SCENE XXII.—CELIA, LELIO, SGANARELLE, SGANARELLE'S WIFE, CELIA'S MAID.

SGAN.'S WIFE. (*To Celia*). I am not inclined, Madam, to show that I am over-jealous; but I am no fool, and can see what is going on. There are certain amours which appear very strange; you should be better employed than in seducing a heart which ought to be mine alone.

CEL. This declaration of her love is plain enough.[15]

SGAN. (*To his wife*). Who sent for you, baggage? You come and scold her because she takes my part, whilst you are afraid of losing your gallant.

CEL. Do not suppose anybody has a mind to him. (*Turning towards Lelio*). You see whether I have told a falsehood, and I am very glad of it.

LEL. What can be the meaning of this?

MAID. Upon my word, I do not know when this entanglement will be unravelled. I have tried for a pretty long time to comprehend it, but the more I hear the less I understand. Really I think I must interfere at last. (*Placing herself between Lelio and Celia*). Answer me one after another, and (*To Lelio*) allow me to ask what do you accuse this lady of?

LEL. That she broke her word and forsook me for another. As soon as I heard she was going to be married I hastened hither, carried away by an irrepressible love, and not believing I could be forgotten; but discovered, when I arrived here, that she was married.

MAID. Married! To whom?

LEL. (*Pointing to Sganarelle*). To him.

MAID. How! to him?

LEL. Yes, to him.

MAID. Who told you so?

LEL. Himself, this very day.

MAID. (*To Sganarelle*). Is this true?

SGAN. I? I told him I was married to my own wife.

---

15 Some commentators think it is Lelio who utters these words, but they are clearly Celia's.

LEL. Just now, whilst you looked at my picture, you seemed greatly moved.

SGAN. True, here it is.

LEL. (*To Sganarelle*). You also told me that she, from whose hands you had received this pledge of her love, was joined to you in the bonds of wedlock.

SGAN. No doubt (*pointing to his wife*), for I snatched it from her, and should not have discovered her wickedness had I not done so.

SGAN.'s WIFE. What do you mean by your groundless complaint? I found this portrait at my feet by accident. After you had stormed without telling me the cause of your rage, I saw this gentleman (*pointing to Lelio*) nearly fainting, asked him to come in, but did not even then discover that he was the original of the picture.

CEL. I was the cause of the portrait being lost; I let it fall when swooning, and when you (*to Sganarelle*) kindly carried me into the house.

MAID. You see that without my help you had still been at a loss, and that you had some need of hellebore.[16]

SGAN. (*Aside*). Shall we believe all this? I have been very much frightened for my brow.

SGAN.'s WIFE. I have not quite recovered from my fear; however agreeable credulity may be, I am loth to be deceived.

SGAN. (*To his wife*). Well, let us mutually suppose ourselves to be people of honour. I risk more on my side than you do on yours; accept, therefore, without much ado, what I propose.

SGAN.'s WIFE. Be it so, but wo be to you if I discover anything.

CEL. (*To Lelio, after whispering together*). Ye heavens! if it be so, what have I done? I ought to fear the consequences of my own anger! Thinking you false, and wishing to be avenged, I in an unhappy moment complied with my father's wishes, and but a minute since engaged myself to marry a man whose hand, until then, I always had refused. I have made a promise to my father, and what grieves me most is . . . But I see him coming.

---

[16] Among the ancients the *helleborus officinalis* or *orientalis* was held to cure insanity; hencc the allusion.

LEL. He shall keep his word with me.

SCENE XXIII.—GORGIBUS, CELIA, LELIO, SGANARELLE, SGANARELLE'S WIFE, CELIA'S MAID.

LEL. Sir, you see I have returned to this town, inflamed with the same ardour, and now I suppose you will keep your promise, which made me hope to marry Celia, and thus reward my intense love.

GORG. Sir, whom I see returned to this town inflamed with the same ardour, and who now supposes I will keep my promise, which made you hope to marry Celia, and thus reward your intense love, I am your lordship's very humble servant.

LEL. What, sir, is it thus you frustrate my expectations?

GORG. Ay, sir, it is thus I do my duty, and my daughter obeys me too.

CEL. My duty compels me, father, to make good your promise to him.

GORG. Is this obeying my commands as a daughter ought to do? Just now you were very kindly disposed towards Valère, but you change quickly . . . I see his father approaching, who certainly comes to arrange about the marriage.

SCENE XXIV.—VILLEBREQUIN, GORGIBUS, CELIA, LELIO, SGANARELLE, SGANARELLE'S WIFE, CELIA'S MAID.

GORG. What brings you hither, M. Villebrequin?

VILL. An important secret, which I only discovered this morning, and which completely prevents me from keeping the engagement I made with you. My son, whom your daughter was going to espouse, has deceived everybody, and been secretly married these four months past to Lise. Her friends, her fortune, and her family connections, make it impossible for me to break off this alliance; and hence I come to you . . .

GORG. Pray, say no more. If Valère has married some one else without your permission, I cannot disguise from you, that I myself long ago, promised my daughter Celia to Lelio, endowed with every virtue, and that his return to-day prevents me from choosing any other husband for her.

VILL. Such a choice pleases me very much.

LEL. This honest intention will crown my days with eternal bliss.

GORG. Let us go and fix the day for the wedding.

SGAN. (*Alone*). Was there ever a man who had more cause to think himself victimized? You perceive that in such matters the strongest probability may create in the mind a wrong belief. Therefore remember, never to believe anything even if you should see everything.

DON GARCIE DE NAVARRE;

OU,

LE PRINCE JALOUX.

COMEDIE HÉROÏQUE EN CINQ ACTES.

DON GARCIA OF NAVARRE

OR,

THE JEALOUS PRINCE.

A HEROIC COMEDY IN FIVE ACTS.

(*THE ORIGINAL IN VERSE.*)

FEB. 4TH, 1661.

INTRODUCTORY NOTICE.

NOTHING can be more unlike *The Pretentious Young Ladies* or *Sganarelle* than Molière's *Don Garcia of Navarre.* The Théâtre du Palais-Royal had opened on the 20th January, 1661, with *The Love-Tiff* and *Sganarelle,* but as the young wife of Louis XIV., Maria Theresa, daughter of Philip IV., King of Spain, had only lately arrived, and as a taste for the Spanish drama appeared to spring up anew in France, Molière thought perhaps that a heroic comedy in that style might meet with some success, the more so as a company of Spanish actors had been performing in Paris the plays of Lope de Vega and Calderon, since the 24th of July, 1660. Therefore, he brought out, on the 4th of February, 1661, his new play of *Don Garcia of Navarre.* It is said that there exists a Spanish play of the same name, of which the author is unknown; Molière seems to have partly followed an Italian comedy, written by Giacinto Andrea Cicognini, under the name of *Le Gelosie fortunata del principe Rodrigo;* the style, loftiness and delicacy of expression are peculiar to the French dramatist.

Don Garcia of Navarre met with no favourable reception, though the author played the part of the hero. He withdrew it after five representations, but still did not think its condemnation final, for he played it again before the King on the 29th of September, 1662, in October, 1663, at Chantilly, and twice at Versailles. He attempted it anew on the theatre of the Palace-Royal in the month of November, 1663; but as it was everywhere unfavourably received, he resolved never to play it more, and even would not print it, for it was only published after his death in 1682. He inserted some parts of this comedy in the *Misanthrope,* the *Femmes Savantes, Amphitryon, Tartuffe,* and *les Fâcheux,* where they produced great effect.

Though it has not gained a place on the French stage, it nevertheless possesses some fine passages. Molière wished to create a counterpart of *Sganarelle,* the type of ridiculous jealousy, and to delineate passionate jealousy, its doubts, fears, perplexities and anxieties, and in this he has succeeded admirably. However noble-minded Don Garcia may be, there rages within his soul a mean passion which tortures and degrades him incessantly. When at last he is banished from the presence of the fair object of his love, he resolves to brave death by devoting himself to the destruction of her foe; but he is forestalled by his presumed rival, Don Alphonso, who turns out to be the brother of his mistress, and she receives him once again and for ever in her favour. The delineation of all these passions is too fine-spun, too argumentative to please the general public; the style is sometimes stilted, yet passages of great beauty may be found in it. Moreover the jealousy expressed by Don Garcia is neither sufficiently terrible to frighten, nor ridiculous enough to amuse the audience; he always speaks and acts as a prince, and hence, he sometimes becomes royally monotonous.

Some scenes of this play have been imitated in *The Masquerade*, a comedy, acted at the Theatre Royal, Drury Lane, 1719, London, "printed for Bernard Linton, between the Temple Gate," which was itself partly borrowed from Shirley's *Lady of Pleasure*. The comedy was written by Mr. Charles Johnson, who "was originally bred to the law, and was a member of the Middle Temple; but being a great admirer of the Muses, and finding in himself a strong propensity to dramatic writing, he quitted the studious labour of the one, for the more spirited amusements of the other; and by contracting an intimacy with Mr. Wilks, found means, through that gentleman's interest, to get his plays on the stage without much difficulty . . . he, by a polite and modest behaviour formed so extensive an acquaintance and intimacy, as constantly ensured him great emoluments on his benefit night; by which means, being a man of economy, he was enabled to subsist very genteelly. He at length married a young widow, with a tolerable fortune; on which he set up a tavern in Bow Street, Covent Garden, but quitted business at his wife's death, and lived privately on an easy competence he had saved. . . . He was born in 1679 . . . but he did not die till March 11, 1748."[1]

The Masquerade is a clever comedy, rather free in language and thought, chiefly about the danger of gambling. Some of the sayings are very pointed. It has been stated that the author frequented the principal coffee-houses in town, and picked up many pungent remarks there; however this may be, the literary men who at the present time frequent clubs, have, I am afraid, not the same chance. As a specimen of free and easy—rather too easy—wit, let me mention the remarks of Mr. Smart (Act I.) on the way he passed the night, and in what manner. "Nine persons are kept handsomely out of the sober income of one hundred pounds a year." I also observe the name of an old acquaintance in this play. Thackeray's hero in the Memoirs of Mr. Charles J. Yellowplush is "the Honourable Algernon Percy Deuceace, youngest and fifth son of the Earl of Crabs," and in *The Masquerade* (Act III. Sc. 1) Mr. Ombre says: "Did you not observe an old decay'd rake that stood next the box-keeper yonder . . . they call him *Sir Timothy Deuxace;* that wretch has play'd off one of the best families in Europe—he has thrown away all his posterity, and reduced 20,000 acres of wood-land, arable, meadow, and pasture within the narrow circumference of an oaken table of eight foot." *The Masquerade* as the title of the play is a misnomer, for it does not conduce at all to the plot.

We give the greater part of the Prologue to *The Masquerade*, spoken by Mr. Wilks:—

> The Poet, who must paint by Nature's Laws,
> If he wou'd merit what he begs, Applause;
> Surveys your changing Pleasures with Surprise,
> Sees each new Day some new Diversion rise;
> Hither, thro' all the Quarters of the Sky, }
> Fresh Rooks in Flocks from ev'ry Nation hye, }
> To us, the Cullies of the Globe, they fly: }

[1] Biographia Dramatica, by Baker, Reed and Jones, 1812, Vol. I. Part 1.

French, Spaniards, Switzers; This Man dines on Fire
And swallows Brimstone to your Heart's Desire;
Another, Handless, Footless, Half a Man,
Does, Wou'd you think it? what no Whole one can,
A Spaniard next, taught an Italian Frown,
Boldly declares he'll stare all Europe down:
His tortured Muscles pleas'd our English Fools; [2]
Why wou'd the Sot engage with English Bulls?
Our English Bulls are Hereticks uncivil,
They'd toss the Grand Inquisitor, the Devil:
'Twas stupidly contrived of Don Grimace,
To hope to fright 'em with an ugly Face.
And yet, tho' these Exotick Monsters please,
We must with humble Gratitude confess,
To you alone 'tis due, that in this Age,
Good Sense still triumphs on the British Stage:
Shakespear beholds with Joy his Sons inherit
His good old Plays, with good old Bess's Spirit.
Be wise and merry, while you keep that Tether;
Nonsense and Slavery must die together.

---

[2] In the rival House, Lincoln's-Inn-Fields Theatre, Rich was bringing out Pantomimes, which, by the fertility of his invention, the excellency of his own performance, and the introduction of foreign performers, drew nightly crowded houses —hence the allusion.

DRAMATIS PERSONÆ.

DON GARCIA, *Prince of Navarre, in love with Elvira*.[3]

DON ALPHONSO, *Prince of Leon, thought to be Prince of Castile, under the name of Don Silvio.*

DON ALVAREZ, *confidant of Don Garcia, in love with Eliza.*

DON LOPEZ, *another confidant of Don Garcia, in love with Eliza.*

DON PEDRO, *gentleman-usher to Inez.*

A PAGE.

DONNA ELVIRA, *Princess of Leon.*

DONNA INEZ, *a Countess, in love with Don Silvio, beloved by Mauregat, the usurper of the Kingdom of Leon.*

ELIZA, *confidant to Elvira.*

Scene.—ASTORGA, *a city of Spain, in the kingdom of Leon.*

---

[3] In the inventory taken after Molière's death mention is made of "Spanish dress, breeches, cloth cloak, and a satin doublet, the whole adorned with silk embroideries." This is probably the dress in which Molière played *Don Garcia*.

DON GARCIA OF NAVARRE;

OR, THE JEALOUS PRINCE.

(*DON GARCIE DE NAVARRE, OU LE PRINCE JALOUX.*)

ACT I.

SCENE I.—DONNA ELVIRA, ELIZA.

ELVIRA. No, the hidden feelings of my heart were not regulated by choice: whatever the Prince may be, there is nothing in him to make me prefer his love. Don Silvio shows, as well as he, all the qualities of a renowned hero. The same noble virtues and the same high birth made me hesitate whom to prefer. If aught but merit could gain my heart, the conqueror were yet to be named; but these chains, with which Heaven keeps our souls enslaved, decide me, and, though I esteem both equally, my love is given to Don Garcia.

ELIZA. The love which you feel for him, seems to have very little influenced your actions, since I, myself, madam, could not for a long time discover which of the two rivals was the favoured one.

ELV. Their noble rivalry in love, Eliza, caused a severe struggle in my breast. When I looked on the one, I felt no pangs, because I followed my own tender inclination; but when I thought I sacrificed the other, I considered I acted very unjustly; and was of opinion, that Don Silvio's passion, after all, deserved a happier destiny. I also reflected that a daughter of the late King of Leon owed some obligation to the house of Castile; that an intimate friendship had long knit together the interests of his father and mine. Thus, the more the one made progress in my heart, the more I lamented the ill success of the other. Full of pity, I listened to his ardent sighs, and received his vows politely; thus in a slight degree I tried to make amends for the opposition his love met with in my heart.

EL. But since you have been informed he previously loved another, your mind ought to be at rest. Before he loved you, Donna Inez had received the homage of his heart. As she is your most intimate friend, and has told you this secret, you are free to bestow your love upon whom you wish, and cover your refusal to listen to him under the guise of friendship for her.

ELV. It is true, I ought to be pleased with the news of Don Silvio's faithlessness, because my heart, that was tormented by his love, is now at liberty to reject it; can justly refuse his addresses, and, without scruple, grant its favours to another. But what delight can my heart feel, if it suffers severely from other pangs; if the continual weakness of a jealous prince receives my tenderness with disdain, compels me justly to give way to anger, and thus to break off all intercourse between us?

EL. But as he has never been told that you love him, how can he be guilty if he disbelieves in his happiness? And does not that which could flatter his rival's expectations warrant him to suspect your affection?

ELV. No, no; nothing can excuse the strange madness of his gloomy and unmanly jealousy; I have told him but too clearly, by my actions, that he can indeed flatter himself with the happiness of being beloved. Even if we do not speak, there are other interpreters which clearly lay bare our secret feelings. A sigh, a glance, a mere blush, silence itself, is enough to show the impulses of a heart. In love, everything speaks: in a case like this, the smallest glimmer ought to throw a great light upon such a subject, since the honour which sways our sex forbids us ever to discover all we feel. I have, I own, endeavoured so to guide my conduct, that I should behold their merits with an unprejudiced eye. But how vainly do we strive against our inclinations! How easy is it to perceive the difference between those favours that are bestowed out of mere politeness, and such as spring from the heart! The first seem always forced; the latter, alas! are granted without thinking, like those pure and limpid streams which spontaneously flow from their native sources. Though the feelings of pity I showed for Don Silvio moved the Prince, yet I unwittingly betrayed their shallowness, whilst my very looks, during this torture, always told him more than I desired they should.

EL. Though the suspicions of that illustrious lover have no foundation—for you tell me so—they at least prove that he is greatly smitten: some would rejoice at what you complain of. Jealousy may be odious when it proceeds from a love which displeases us; but when we return that love, such feelings should delight us. It is the best way in which a lover can express his passion; the more jealous he is the more we ought to love him. Therefore since in your soul a magnanimous Prince . . .

ELV. Ah! do not bring forward such a strange maxim. Jealousy is always odious and monstrous; nothing can soften its injurious attacks; the dearer the object of our love is to us, the more deeply we feel its offensive attempts. To see a passionate Prince, losing every moment that respect with which love inspires its real votaries; to see him, when his whole mind is a prey to jealousy, finding fault either with what I like or dislike, and explaining every look of mine in favour of a rival![4] No, no! such suspicions are too insulting, and I tell you my thoughts without disguise. I love Don Garcia; he alone can fascinate a generous heart; his courage in Leon has nobly proved his passion for me; he dared on my account the greatest dangers, freed me from the toils of cowardly tyrants, and protected me against the horrors of an unworthy alliance by placing me within these strong walls. Nor will I deny but that I should have regretted that I owed my deliverance to any other; for an enamoured heart feels an extreme pleasure, Eliza, in being under some obligations to the object beloved; its faint flame becomes stronger and brighter when it thinks it can discharge them by granting some favours. Yes, I am charmed that he assisted me and

---

[4] Molière has expressed the same thoughts differently in *The Bores*, Act ii. scene 4.

risked his life for me, for this seems to give his passion a right of conquest; I rejoice that the danger I was in threw me into his hands. If common reports be true, and Heaven should grant my brother's return, I wish fervently, and with all my heart, that his arm may aid my brother to recover his throne, and punish a traitor; that his heroic valour may be successful, and thus deserve my brother's utmost gratitude. But for all this, if he continues to rouse my anger; if he does not lay aside his jealousy, and obey me in whatever I command, he in vain aspires to the hand of Donna Elvira. Marriage can never unite us; for I abhor bonds, which, undoubtedly, would then make a hell upon earth for both of us.

EL. Although one may hold different opinions, the Prince, Madam, should conform himself to your desires; they are so clearly set down in your note that, when he sees them thus explained, he . . .

ELV. This letter, Eliza, shall not be employed for such a purpose. It will be better to tell him what I think of his conduct. When we favor a lover by writing to him, we leave in his hands too flagrant proofs of our inclination. Therefore take care that that letter is not delivered to the Prince.

EL. Your will is law; yet I cannot help wondering that Heaven has made people's minds so unlike, and that what some consider an insult should be viewed with a different eye by others. As for me I should think myself very fortunate if I had a lover who could be jealous, for his uneasiness would give me satisfaction. That which often vexes me is to see Don Alvarez give himself no concern about me.

ELV. We did not think he was so near us. Here he comes.

SCENE II.— DONNA ELVIRA, DON ALVAREZ, ELIZA.

ELV. Your return surprises me. What tidings do you bring? Is Don Alphonso coming, and when may we expect him?

ALV. Yes, Madam; the time has arrived when your brother, brought up in Castile, will get his own again. Hitherto, the cautious Don Louis, to whom the late King, on his death-bed, entrusted the care of Don Alphonso, has concealed his rank from every one, in order to save him from the fury of the traitor Mauregat. Though the miserable but successful tyrant has often inquired after him, under pretence of restoring him to the throne, yet Don Louis, who is full of prudence, would never trust to Mauregat's pretended feelings for justice, with which he tried to allure him. But as the people became enraged at the violence which a usurper would have offered you, generous old Don Louis thought it time to try what could be done after twenty years' expectation. He has sounded Leon; his faithful emissaries have sought to influence the minds of great and small. Whilst Castile was arming ten thousand men to restore that Prince so wished for by his people, Don Louis caused a report to be noised abroad that the renowned Don Alphonso was coming, but that he would not produce him save at the head of an army, and completely ready to launch the avenging thunderbolts at the vile usurper's head. Leon is besieged, and Don Silvio himself commands the auxiliary forces, with which his father aids you.

ELV. We may flatter ourselves that our expectations will be realized, but I am afraid my brother will owe Don Silvio too heavy a debt.[5]

ALV. But, Madam, is it not strange that, notwithstanding the storm which the usurper of your throne hears growling over his head, all the advices from Leon agree that he is going to marry the Countess Inez?

ELV. By allying himself to the high-born maiden, he hopes to obtain the support of her powerful family. I am rather uneasy that of late I have heard nothing of her. But she has always shown an inveterate dislike to that tyrant.

EL. Feelings of honour and tenderness will cause her to refuse the marriage they urge upon her, for . . .

ALV. The Prince is coming here.

SCENE III.—DON GARCIA, DONNA ELVIRA, DON ALVAREZ, ELIZA.

GARC. I come, Madam to rejoice with you in the good

[5] Donna Elvira is afraid that Don Alphonso will owe Don Silvio a debt so heavy, that he will only be able to repay it by the gift of her hand.

tidings you have just heard. Your brother, who threatens a tyrant stained with crimes, allows me to hope that my love may one day be returned, and offers to my arm an opportunity to acquire glory in fresh dangers for the sake of your lovely eyes. If Heaven proves propitious I will gain amidst these dangers a victory, which divine justice owes to you, which will lay treachery at your feet, and restore to your family its former dignity. But what pleases me still more amidst these cherished expectations is that Heaven restores you this brother to be King; for now my love may openly declare itself, without being accused of seeking to gain a crown whilst striving to obtain your hand. Yes, my heart desires nothing more than to show before the whole world that in you it values but yourself; if I may say so without giving offence, a hundred times have I wished you were of less rank. Loving you as I do I could have desired that your divine charms had fallen to the lot of some one born in a humbler station, that I might unselfishly proffer my heart, and thus make amends to you for Heaven's injustice, so that you might owe to my love the homage due to your birth.[6] But since Heaven has forestalled me, and deprives me of the privilege of proving my love, do not take it amiss that my amorous flames look for some slight encouragement when I shall have killed the tyrant, whom I am ready to encounter; suffer me by noble services favourably to dispose the minds of a brother and of a whole nation towards me.

ELV I know, Prince, that by avenging our wrongs you can make a hundred deeds of daring speak for your love. But the favour of a brother and the gratitude of a nation are not sufficient to reward you; Elvira is not to be obtained by such efforts; there is yet a stronger obstacle to overcome.

GARC. Yes, Madam, I know what you mean. I know very well that my heart sighs in vain for you; neither do I ignore the powerful obstacle against my love, though you name it not.

ELV. Often we hear badly when we think we hear well.

---

[6] The sentence from "Yes, my heart," &c., until "your birth" is nearly the same as the words addressed by Alceste to Célimène in the *Misanthrope*, Act iv. Sc. 3 (see Vol. II.)

Too much ardour, Prince, may lead us into mistakes. But since I must speak, I will. Do you wish to know how you can please me, and when you may entertain any hope?

GARC. I should consider this, Madam, a very great favour.

ELV. When you know how to love as you ought.

GARC. Alas! Madam, does there exist anything under the canopy of heaven that yields not to the passion with which your eyes have inspired me?

ELV. When your passion displays nothing at which the object of your love can feel offended.

GARC. That is its greatest study.

ELV. When you shall cease to harbour mean unworthy sentiments of me.

GARC. I love you to adoration.

ELV. When you have made reparation for your unjust suspicions, and when you finally banish that hideous monster which poisons your love with its black venom; that jealous and whimsical temper which mars, by its outbreaks, the love you offer, prevents it from ever being favourably listened to, and arms me, each time, with just indignation against it.

GARC. Alas, Madam, it is true, that, notwithstanding my utmost effort, some trifling jealousy lingers in my heart; that a rival, though distant from your divine charms, disturbs my equanimity. Whether it be whimsical or reasonable, I always imagine that you are uneasy when he is absent, and that in spite of my attentions, your sighs are continually sent in search of that too happy rival. But if such suspicions displease you, alas, you may easily cure them; their removal, which I hope for, depends more on you than on me. Yes, with a couple of love-breathing words you can arm my soul against jealousy, and disperse all the horrors with which that monster has enshrouded it, by encouraging me to entertain some expectation of a successful issue. Deign therefore to remove the doubt that oppresses me; and, amidst so many trials, let your charming lips grant me the assurance that you love me,—an assurance, of which, I know, I am utterly unworthy.

ELV. Prince, your suspicions completely master you. The slightest intimation of a heart should be understood; it does not reciprocate a passion that continually adjures the object beloved to explain herself more clearly. The first agitation displayed by our soul ought to satisfy a discreet lover; if he wishes to make us declare ourselves more plainly, he only gives us a reason for breaking our promise. If it depended on me alone, I know not whether I should choose Don Silvio or yourself; the very wish I expressed for you not to be jealous, would have been a sufficient hint to any one but you; I thought this request was worded agreeably enough without needing anything further. Your love, however, is not yet satisfied, and requires a more public avowal. In order to remove any scruples, I must distinctly say that I love you; perhaps even, to make more sure of it, you will insist that I must swear it too.

GARC. Well, Madam, I own I am too bold; I ought to be satisfied with everything that pleases you. I desire no further information. I believe you feel kindly towards me, that my love inspires you even with a little compassion; I am happier than I deserve to be. It is over now; I abandon my jealous suspicions; the sentence which condemns them is very agreeable; I shall obey the decision you so kindly pronounce, and free my heart from their unfounded sway.

ELV. You promise a great deal, Prince, but I very much doubt whether you can restrain yourself sufficiently.

GARC. Ah! Madam, you may believe me; it is enough that what is promised to you ought always to be kept, because the happiness of obeying the being one worships ought to render easy the greatest efforts. May Heaven declare eternal war against me; may its thunder strike me dead at your feet; or, what would be even worse than death, may your wrath be poured upon me, if ever my love descends to such weakness as to fail in the promise I have given, if ever any jealous transport of my soul . . . !

SCENE IV.—DONNA ELVIRA, DON GARCIA, DON ALVAREZ, ELIZA, A PAGE *presenting a letter to Donna Elvira.*

ELV. I was very anxious about this letter, I am very much obliged to you; let the messenger wait.

SCENE V.—DONNA ELVIRA, DON GARCIA, DON ALVAREZ, ELIZA.

ELV. (*Low and aside*). I see already by his looks that this letter disturbs him. What a wonderfully jealous temper he has! (*Aloud*). What stops you, Prince, in the midst of your oath.

GARC. I thought you might have some secret together; I was unwilling to interrupt you.

ELV. It seems to me that you reply in a much altered voice; I see all of a sudden a certain wildness in your looks; this abrupt change surprises me. What can be the cause of it? May I know?

GARC. A sudden sickness at heart.

ELV. Such illnesses have often more serious consequences than one believes; some immediate remedy would be necessary; but, tell me, have you often such attacks?

GARC. Sometimes.

ELV. Alas, weak-minded Prince! Here, let this writing cure your distemper; it is nowhere but in the mind.

GARC. That writing, Madam! No, I refuse to take it. I know your thoughts and what you will accuse me of, if . . .

ELV. Read it, I tell you, and satisfy yourself.

GARC. That you may afterwards call me weak-minded and jealous? No, no, I will prove that this letter gave me no umbrage, and though you kindly allow me to read it, to justify myself, I will not do so.

ELV. If you persist in your refusal, I should be wrong to compel you; it is sufficient, in short, as I have insisted upon it, to let you see whose hand it is.

GARC. I ought always to be submissive to you; if it is your pleasure I should read it for you, I will gladly do so.

ELV. Yes, yes, Prince, here it is; you shall read it for me.

GARC. I only do so, Madam, in obedience to your commands, and I may say . . .

ELV. Whatever you please; but pray make haste.

GARC. It comes from Donna Inez, I perceive.

ELV. It does, and I am glad of it, both for your sake and mine.

GARC. (*Reads*). "*In spite of all that I do to show my contempt for the tyrant, he persists in his love for me; the more effectually to encompass his designs, he has, since your absence, directed against me all that violence with which he pursued the alliance between yourself and his son. Those who perhaps have the right to command me, and who are inspired by base motives of false honour, all approve this unworthy proposal. I do not know yet where my persecution will end; but I will die sooner than give my consent. May you, fair Elvira, be happier in your fate than I am.* DONNA INEZ." A lofty virtue fortifies her mind.

ELV. I will go and write an answer to this illustrious friend. Meanwhile, Prince, learn not to give way so readily to what causes you alarm. I have calmed your emotion by enlightening you, and the whole affair has passed off quietly; but, to tell you the truth, a time may come when I might entertain other sentiments.

GARC. What? you believe then . . .

ELV. I believe what I ought. Farewell, remember what I tell you; if your love for me be really so great as you pretend, prove it as I wish.

GARC. Henceforth this will be my only desire; and sooner than fail in it, I will lose my life.

ACT II.

SCENE I.—ELIZA, DON LOPEZ.

EL. To speak my mind freely to you, I am not much astonished at anything the Prince may do; for it is very natural, and I cannot disapprove of it, that a soul inflamed by a noble passion should become exasperated by jealousy, and that frequent doubts should cross his mind: but what surprises me, Don Lopez, is to hear that you keep alive his suspicions; that you are the contriver of them; that he is sad only because you wish it, jealous only because he looks at everything with your eyes. I repeat it, Don Lopez, I do not wonder that a man who is greatly in love becomes suspicious. But, that a man who is not in love should have all the anxieties of one who is jealous —this is a novelty that belongs to none but you.

LOP. Let everybody comment on my actions as much as they please. Each man regulates his conduct according to the goal he wishes to reach; since my love was rejected by you, I court the favour of the Prince.

EL. But do you not know that no favour will be granted to him if you continue to maintain him in this disposition?

LOP. Pray, charming Eliza, was it ever known that those about great men minded anything but their own interest, or that a perfect courtier wished to increase the retinue of those same grandees by adding to it a censor of their faults? Did he ever trouble himself if his conversation harmed them, provided he could but derive some benefit? All the actions of a courtier only tend to get into their favour, to obtain a place in as short a time as possible; the quickest way to acquire their good graces is by always flattering their weaknesses, by blindly applauding what they have a mind to do, and by never countenancing anything that displeases them. That is the true secret of standing well with them Good advice causes a man to be looked upon as a troublesome fellow, so that he no longer enjoys that confidence which he had secured by an artful subservience. In short, we always see that the art of courtiers aims only at taking advantage of the foibles of the great, at cherishing their errors, and never advising them to do things which they dislike.

EL. These maxims may do well enough for a time: but reverses of fortune have to be dreaded. A gleam of light may at last penetrate the minds of the deceived nobles, who will then justly avenge themselves on all such flatterers for the length of time their glory has been dimmed. Meanwhile I must tell you that you have been a little too frank in your explanations; if a true account of your motives were laid before the Prince, it would but ill serve you in making your fortune.

LOP. I could deny having told you those truths I have just unfolded, and that without being gainsaid; but I know very well that Eliza is too discreet to divulge this private conversation. After all, what I have said is known by everyone; what actions of mine have I to conceal? A downfall may be justly dreaded when we employ artifices or treachery. But what have I to fear? I, who cannot be taxed with anything but complaisance, who by my useful lessons do but follow up the Prince's natural inclination for jealousy. His soul seems to live upon suspicions; and so I do my very best to find him opportunities for his uneasiness, and to look out on all sides if anything has happened that may furnish a subject for a secret conversation. When I can go to him, with a piece of news that may give a deadly blow to his repose, then he loves me most: I can see him listen eagerly and swallow the poison, amd thank me for it too, as if I had brought him news of some victory which would make him happy and glorious for all his life. But my rival draws near, and so I leave you together; though I have renounced all hope of ever gaining your affection, yet it would pain me not a little to see you prefer him to me before my face; therefore I will avoid such a mortification[7] as much as I can.

EL. All judicious lovers should do the same.

SCENE II.—DON ALVAREZ, ELIZA.

ALV. At last we have received intelligence that the king of Navarre has this very day declared himself favourable to the Prince's love, and that a number of fresh troops will reinforce his army, ready to be employed in the service of her to whom his wishes aspire. As for me, I am surprised at their quick movements . . . but . . .

SCENE III—DON GARCIA, DON ALVAREZ, ELIZA.

GARC. What is the Princess doing?

EL. I think, my Lord, she is writing some letters; but I shall let her know that you are here.

---

[7] Don Lopez bears a distant resemblance to "honest Iago" in Othello, though Molière has only faintly shadowed forth what Shakespeare has worked out in so masterly a manner.

GARC. I will wait till she has done.

SCENE IV.—DON GARCIA (*Alone*).

Being on the point of seeing her, I feel my soul shaken by an unusual emotion; fear as well as excess of feeling makes me suddenly tremble. Take heed, Don Garcia, lest a blind caprice lead you to some precipice, and lest the great disorder of your mind cause you to yield a little too much to your senses. Consult reason, take her for your guide; see whether your suspicions are well founded; do not reject their voice, but yet take care not to believe them too readily, otherwise they might deceive you, and your first outburst might pass all bounds. Read carefully again this half of a letter. Ha, what would I, whose heart is full of agony, not give for the other half of it? But, after all, what do I say? This part suffices and is more than enough to convince me of my misfortune:

"*Though your rival* . .
you ought still . . .
It is in your power to . . .
the greatest obstacle . . .
I feel very grateful . . .
for rescuing me from the hands . . .
his love, his homage . . .
but his jealousy is . . .
Remove, therefore, from your love . . .
deserve the regards . . .
and when one endeavours . . .
do not persist . . .

Yes, my destiny is sufficiently explained by these words, which clearly show that she wrote what she felt; the imperfect meaning of this ominous letter does not require the other half to be clear to me. Let us, however, act gently at first; let us conceal our deep emotion from this faithless woman; let us employ against her the same arts she makes use of. Here she comes. Reason, be thou mistress of my soul, and for some time at least, keep me from giving way to my passion!

SCENE V.—DONNA ELVIRA, DON GARCIA.

ELV. I trust you will pardon me for letting you wait.

GARC. (*In a low voice and aside*). How well she dissembles.

ELV. We have just now heard that the King, your father, approves your designs, and consents that his son should restore us to our subjects. I am extremely rejoiced at this.

GARC. Yes, Madam, and my heart is rejoiced at it too; but . . .

ELV. The tyrant will doubtless find it difficult to defend himself against the thunderbolts which from all sides threaten him. I flatter myself that the same courage which was able to deliver me from the brutal rage of the usurper, to snatch me out of his hands, and place me safe within the walls of Astorga, will conquer the whole of Leon, and, by its noble efforts cause the head of the tyrant to fall.

GARC. A few days more will show if I am successful. But pray let us proceed to some other subject of conversation. If you do not consider me too bold, will you kindly tell me, Madam, to whom you have written since fate led us hither?

ELV. Why this question, and whence this anxiety?

GARC. Out of pure curiosity, Madam, that is all.

ELV. Curiosity is the daughter of jealousy.

GARC. No; it is not at all what you imagine; your commands have sufficiently cured that disease.

ELV. Without endeavouring further to discover what may be the reasons for your inquiry, I have written twice to the Countess Inez at Leon, and as often to the Marquis, Don Louis, at Burgos. Does this answer put your mind at rest?

GARC. Have you written to no one else, Madam?

ELV. No, certainly, and your questions astonish me.

GARC. Pray consider well, before you make such a statement, because people forget sometimes, and thus perjure themselves.

ELV. I cannot perjure myself in what I have stated.

GARC. You have, however, told a very great falsehood.

ELV. Prince!

GARC. Madam!

ELV. Heavens; what is the meaning of this! Speak! Have you lost your senses?

GARC. Yes, yes, I lost them, when to my misfortune I beheld you, and thus took the poison which kills me; when I thought to meet with some sincerity in those treacherous charms that bewitched me.

ELV. What treachery have you to complain of?

GARC. Oh! how double-faced she is! how well she knows to dissimulate! But all means for escape will fail you. Cast your eyes here, and recognize your writing.[8] Without having seen the other part of this letter, it is easy enough to discover for whom you employ this style.

ELV. And this is the cause of your perturbation of spirits?

GARC. Do you not blush on beholding this writing?

ELV. Innocence is not accustomed to blush.

GARC. Here indeed we see it oppressed. You disown this letter because it is not signed.

ELV. Why should I disown it, since I wrote it?[9]

GARC. It is something that you are frank enough to own your handwriting; but I will warrant that it was a note written to some indifferent person, or at least that the tender sentiments it contains were intended only for some lady friend or relative.

ELV. No, I wrote it to a lover, and, what is more, to one greatly beloved.

GARC. And can I, O perfidious woman . . . ?

ELV. Bridle, unworthy Prince, the excess of your base fury. Although you do not sway my heart, and I am accountable here to none but myself, yet for your sole punishment I will clear myself from the crime of which you so insolently accuse me. You shall be undeceived; do not doubt it. I have my defence at hand. You shall be fully enlightened; my innocence shall appear complete. You yourself shall be the judge in your own cause, and pronounce your own sentence.

---

[8] The lines, "Heavens! what is the meaning of this?" till "and recognize your writing," have been employed again by Molière in the *Misanthrope*, Act iv., Scene 3, (see vol. II). The misanthrope Alceste has also in his hand the written proofs of the faithlessness of the object of his love: but his suspicions are well founded, whilst those of Don Garcia are inspired only by jealousy.

[9] The words, "And this is the cause" until "since I wrote it," are, with a few slight alterations, found also in the *Misanthrope*, Act iv., Scene 3.

GARC. I cannot understand such mysterious talk.

ELV. You shall soon comprehend it to your cost. Eliza come hither!

SCENE VI.—DON GARCIA, DONNA ELVIRA, ELIZA.

EL. Madam.

ELV. (*to Don Garcia*). At least observe well whether I make use of any artifice to deceive you; whether by a single glance or by any warning gesture I seek to ward off this sudden blow. (*To Eliza*). Answer me quickly, where did you leave the letter I wrote just now?

EL. Madam, I confess I am to blame. This letter was by accident left on my table; but I have just been informed that Don Lopez, coming into my apartment, took, as he usually does, the liberty to pry everywhere, and found it. As he was unfolding it, Leonora wished to snatch it from him before he had read anything; and whilst she tried to do this, the letter in dispute was torn in two pieces, with one of which Don Lopez quickly went away, in spite of all she could do.

ELV. Have you the other half?

EL. Yes; here it is.

ELV. Give it to me. (*To Don Garcia*). We shall see who is to blame; join the two parts together, and then read it aloud. I wish to hear it.

GARC. "*To Don Garcia.*" Ha!

ELV. Go on! Are you thunderstruck at the first word?

GARC. (Reads). "*Though your rival, Prince, disturbs your mind, you ought still to fear yourself more than him. It is in your power to destroy now the greatest obstacle your passion has to encounter. I feel very grateful to Don Garcia for rescuing me from the hands of my bold ravishers; his love, his homage delights me much; but his jealousy is odious to me. Remove, therefore, from your love that foul blemish; deserve the regards that are bestowed upon it; and when one endeavours to make you happy, do not persist in remaining miserable.*"

ELV. Well, what do you say to this?

GARC. Ah! Madam, I say that on reading this I am quite confounded; that I see the extreme injustice of my complaints, and that no punishment can be severe enough for me.

ELV. Enough! Know that if I desired that you should read the letter, it was only to contradict everything I stated in it; to unsay a hundred times all that you read there in your favour. Farewell, Prince.

GARC. Alas, Madam! whither do you fly?

ELV. To a spot where you shall not be, over-jealous man.

GARC. Ah, Madam, excuse a lover who is wretched because, by a wonderful turn of fate, he has become guilty towards you, and who, though you are now very wroth with him, would have deserved greater blame if he had remained innocent. For, in short, can a heart be truly enamoured which does not dread as well as hope? And could you believe I loved you if this ominous letter had not alarmed me; if I had not trembled at the thunderbolt which I imagined had destroyed all my happiness? I leave it to yourself to judge if such an accident would not have caused any other lover to commit the same error; if I could disbelieve, alas, a proof which seemed to me so clear!

ELV. Yes, you might have done so; my feelings so clearly expressed ought to have prevented your suspicions. You had nothing to fear; if some others had had such a pledge they would have laughed to scorn the testimony of the whole world.

GARC. The less we deserve a happiness which has been promised us, the greater is the difficulty we feel in believing in it. A destiny too full of glory seems unstable, and renders us suspicious. As for me, who think myself so little deserving of your favours, I doubted the success of my rashness.[10] I thought that, finding yourself in a place under my command, you forced yourself to be somewhat kind to me; that, disguising to me your severity . . .

ELV. Do you think that I could stoop to so cowardly an action? Am I capable of feigning so disgracefully; of

---

10 Molière has with a few alterations placed this phrase beginning with "the less," and ending with "my rashness," in the mouth of *Tartuffe* in the play of the same name, Act iv., Sc. 5, (see Vol. II).

acting from motives of servile fear; of betraying my sentiments; and, because I am in your power, of concealing my contempt for you under a pretence of kindness? Could any consideration for my own reputation so little influence me? Can you think so, and dare to tell it me? Know that this heart cannot debase itself; that nothing under Heaven can compel it to act thus: if it has committed the great error of showing you some kindness, of which you were not worthy, know that in spite of your power, it will be able now to show the hatred it feels for you, to defy your rage, and convince you that it is not mean, nor ever will be so.

GARC.[11] Well, I cannot deny that I am guilty: but I beg pardon of your heavenly charms, I beg it for the sake of the most ardent love that two beautiful eyes ever kindled in a human soul. But if your wrath cannot be appeased; if my crime be beyond forgiveness; if you have no regard for the love that caused it, nor for my heart-felt repentance, then one propitious blow shall end my life, and free me from these unbearable torments. No, think not that having displeased you, I can live for one moment under your wrath. Even whilst we are speaking, my heart sinks under gnawing remorse; were a thousand vultures cruelly to wound it, they could not inflict greater pangs. Tell me, madam, if I may hope for pardon; if not, then this sword shall instantly, in your sight, by a well-directed thrust, pierce the heart of a miserable wretch; that heart, that irresolute heart, whose weakness has so deeply offended your excessive kindness, too happy if in death this just doom efface from your memory all remembrance of its crime, and cause you to think of my affection without dislike. This is the only favour my love begs of you.

ELV. Oh! too cruel Prince!

GARC. Speak, Madam.

ELV. Must I still preserve some kind feelings for you, and suffer myself to be affronted by so many indignities?

GARC. A heart that is in love can never offend, and finds excuses for whatever love may do.

[11] This scene beginning from "Well," until the end, has, with several alterations rendered necessary by change of metre, been treated by Molière in his *Amphitryon*, Act ii., Sc. 6, (see Vol. II.).

ELV. Love is no excuse for such outbursts.

GARC. Love communicates its ardour to all emotions, and the stronger it is, the more difficulty it finds . . .

ELV. No, speak to me no more of it; you deserve my hatred.

GARC. You hate me then?

ELV. I will at least endeavour to do so. But alas! I am afraid it will be in vain, and that all the wrath which your insults have kindled, will not carry my revenge so far.

GARC. Do not endeavour to punish me so severely, since I offer to kill myself to avenge you; pronounce but the sentence and I obey immediately.

ELV. One who cannot hate cannot wish anybody to die.

GARC. I cannot live unless you kindly pardon my rash errors; resolve either to punish or to forgive.

ELV. Alas! I have shown too clearly my resolution; do we not pardon a criminal when we tell him we cannot hate him?

GARC. Ah! this is too much. Suffer me, adorable Princess . . .

ELV. Forbear, I am angry with myself for my weakness.

GARC. (*Alone*). At length I am . . .

SCENE VII.—DON GARCIA, DON LOPEZ.

LOP. My Lord, I have to communicate to you a secret that may justly alarm your love.

GARC. Do not talk to me of secrets or alarms, whilst I am in such a blissful rapture. After what has just taken place, I ought not to listen to any suspicions. The unequalled kindness of a divine object ought to shut my ears against all such idle reports. Do not say anything more.

LOP. My Lord, I shall do as you wish; my only care in this business was for you. I thought that the secret I just discovered ought to be communicated with all diligence; but since it is your pleasure I should not mention it, I shall change the conversation, and inform you that every family in Leon threw off the mask, as soon as the report spread that the troops of Castile were approaching;

the lower classes especially show openly such an affection for their true King, that the tyrant trembles for fear.

GARC. Castile, however, shall not gain the victory without our making an attempt to share in the glory; our troops may also be able to terrify Mauregat. But what secret would you communicate to me? Let us hear it?

LOP. My Lord, I have nothing to say.[12]

GARC. Come, come, speak, I give you leave.

LOP. My Lord, your words have told me differently; and since my news may displease you, I shall know for the future how to remain silent.

GARC. Without further reply, I wish to know your secret.

LOP. Your commands must be obeyed; but, my Lord, duty forbids me to explain such a secret in this place. Let us go hence, and I shall communicate it to you; without taking anything lightly for granted, you yourself shall judge what you ought to think of it.

ACT III.

SCENE I.—DONNA ELVIRA, ELIZA.

ELV. What say you, Eliza, to this unaccountable weakness in the heart of a Princess? What do you say when you see me so quickly forego my desire for revenge, and, in spite of so much publicity, weakly and shamefully pardon so cruel an outrage.

EL. I say, Madam, that an insult from a man we love is doubtless very difficult to bear; but if there be none which makes us sooner angry, so there is none which we sooner pardon. If the man we love is guilty, and throws himself at our feet, he triumphs over the rash outbreak of the greatest anger; so much the more easily, Madam, if the offence comes from an excess of love. However great your displeasure may have been, I am not astonished to see it appeased; I know the power which, in spite of your threats, will always pardon such crimes.

ELV. But know, Eliza, however great the power of my love may be, I have blushed for the last time; if henceforth the Prince gives me fresh cause for anger, he must no

[12] Compare Iago's reticence in Shakespeare's *Othello* (iii. 3).

longer look for pardon. I swear, that in such a case, I will never more foster tender feelings for him: for in short, a mind with ever so little pride is greatly ashamed to go back from its word, and often struggles gallantly against its own inclinations; it becomes stubborn for honour's sake, and sacrifices everything to the noble pride of keeping its word. Though I have pardoned him now, do not consider this a precedent for the future. Whatever fortune has in store for me, I cannot think of giving my hand to the Prince of Navarre, until he has shown that he is completely cured of those gloomy fits which unsettle his reason, and has convinced me, who am the greatest sufferer by this disease, that he will never insult me again by a relapse.

EL. But how can the jealousy of a lover be an insult to us?

ELV. Is there one more deserving of our wrath? And since it is with the utmost difficulty we can resolve to confess our love; since the strict honour of our sex at all times strongly opposes such a confession, ought a lover to doubt our avowal, and should he not be punished? Is he not greatly to blame in disbelieving that which is never said but after a severe struggle with one's self?[13]

EL. As for me, I think that a little mistrust on such an occasion should not offend us; and that it is dangerous, Madam, for a lover to be absolutely persuaded that he is beloved. If . . .

ELV. Let us argue no more. Every person thinks differently. I am offended by such suspicions; and, in spite of myself, I am conscious of something which forebodes an open quarrel between the Prince and me, and which, notwithstanding his great qualities . . . . But Heavens! Don Silvio of Castile in this place!

SCENE II.—DONNA ELVIRA, DON ALPHONSO, *under the name of Don Silvio*, ELIZA.

ELV. Ah! my Lord, what chance has brought you here?

ALPH. I know, Madam, that my arrival must surprise

[13] The words "since it is" until "one's self" have been used by Molière with some slight alteration in the *Misanthrope*, Act iv., Scene 3, (see vol. II.)

you. To enter quietly this town, to which the access has become difficult through the orders of a rival, and to have avoided being seen by the soldiers, is an event you did not look for. But if, in coming here, I have surmounted some obstacles, the desire of seeing you is able to effect much greater miracles. My heart has felt but too severely the blows of merciless fate which kept me away from you; to allay the pangs which nearly kill me, I could not refuse myself some moments to behold in secret your inestimable person. I come, therefore, to tell you that I return thanks to Heaven, that you are rescued from the hands of an odious tyrant. But, in the midst of that happiness, I feel that I shall always be tortured with the thought that envious fate deprived me of the honour of performing such a noble deed, and has unjustly given to my rival the chance of venturing his life pleasantly to render you so great a service. Yes, Madam, my readiness to free you from your chains was undoubtedly equal to his; I should have gained the victory for you, if Heaven had not robbed me of that honour.

ELV. I know, my Lord, that you possess a heart capable of overcoming the greatest dangers; I doubt not but this generous zeal which incited you to espouse my quarrel, would have enabled you, as well as any one else, to overcome all base attempts; but even if you have not performed this noble deed—and you could have done it—I am already under sufficient obligations to the house of Castile. It is well known what a warm and faithful friend the Count, your father, was of the late King, and what he did for him. After having assisted him until he died, he gave my brother a shelter in his states; full twenty years he concealed him, in spite of the cowardly efforts to discover him, employed by barbarous and enraged enemies; and now to restore to his brow a crown, in all its splendour, you are marching in person against our usurpers. Are you not satisfied, and do not these generous endeavours place me under strong obligations to you? Would you, my Lord, obstinately persist in swaying my whole fate? Must I never receive even the slightest kindness unless from you? Ah! amidst these misfortunes, which seem to be my fate, suffer me to owe also something to another, and do not complain that another arm acquired some glory, when you were absent.

ALPH. Yes, Madam, I ought to cease complaining; you are quite right when you tell me so; we unjustly complain of one misfortune, when a much greater threatens to afflict us. This succour from a rival is a cruel mortification to me: but, alas! this is not the greatest of my misfortunes; the blow, the severe blow which crushes me, is to see that rival preferred to me. Yes, I but too plainly perceive that his greater reputation was the reason that his love was preferred to mine; that opportunity of serving you, the advantage he possessed of signalizing his prowess, that brillant exploit which he performed in saving you, was nothing but the mere effect of being happy enough to please you, the secret power of a wonderful astral influence which causes the object you love to become famed. Thus all my efforts will be in vain. I am leading an army against your haughty tyrants; but I fulfil this noble duty trembling, because I am sure that your wishes will not be for me, and that, if they are granted, fortune has in store the most glorious success for my happy rival. Ah! Madam, must I see myself hurled from that summit of glory I expected; and may I not know what crimes they accuse me of, and why I have deserved that dreadful downfall?

ELV. Before you ask me anything, consider what you ought to ask of my feelings. As for this coldness of mine, which seems to abash you, I leave it to you, my Lord, to answer for me; for, in short, you cannot be ignorant that some of your secrets have been told to me. I believe your mind to be too noble and too generous to desire me to do what is wrong. Say yourself if it would be just to make me reward faithlessness; whether you can, without the greatest injustice, offer me a heart already tendered to another; whether you are justified in complaining, and in blaming a refusal which would prevent you from staining your virtues with a crime? Yes, my Lord, it is a crime, for first love has so sacred a hold on a lofty mind, that it would rather lose greatness and abandon life itself, than incline to a second love.[14] I have that regard for you which

[14] The words "Yes my Lord" until "second love" are also, with some alterations, found in *The Blue Stockings*, Act iv. Scene 2, (see Vol. III).

is caused by an appreciation of your lofty courage, your magnanimous heart; but do not require of me more than I owe you, and maintain the honour of your first choice. In spite of your new love, consider what tender feelings the amiable Inez still retains for you; that she has constantly refused to be made happy for the sake of an ungrateful man; for such you are, my Lord! In her great love for you, how generously has she scorned the splendour of a diadem! Consider what attempts she has withstood for your sake, and restore to her heart what you owe it.

ALPH. Ah, Madam, do not present her merit to my eyes! Though I am an ungrateful man and abandon her, she is never out of my mind; if my heart could tell you what it feels for her, I fear it would be guilty towards you. Yes, that heart dares to pity Inez, and does not, without some hesitation follow the violent love which leads it on. I never flattered myself that you would reward my love without at the same time breathing some sighs for her; in the midst of these pleasant thoughts my memory still casts some sad looks towards my first love, reproaches itself with the effect of your divine charms, and mingles some remorse with what I wish most fervently. And since I must tell you all, I have done more than this. I have endeavoured to free myself from your sway, to break your chains, and to place my heart again under the innocent yoke of its first conqueror. But, after all my endeavours, my fidelity gives way, and I see only one remedy for the disease that kills me. Were I even to be forever wretched, I cannot forswear my love, or bear the terrible idea of seeing you in the arms of another; that same light, which permits me to behold your charms, will shine on my corpse, before this marriage takes place. I know that I betray an amiable Princess; but after all, Madam, is my heart guilty? Does the powerful influence which your beauty possesses leave the mind any liberty? Alas! I am much more to be pitied than she; for, by losing me, she loses only a faithless man. Such a sorrow can easily be soothed; but I, through an unparalleled misfortune, abandon an amiable lady, whilst I endure all the torments of a rejected love.

ELV. You have no torments but what you yourself create. for our heart is always in our own power. It may indeed sometimes show a little weakness; but, after all, reason sways our passions . . .

SCENE III.—DON GARCIA, DONNA ELVIRA, DON ALPHONSO, *under the name of Don Silvio.*

GARC. I perceive, Madam, that my coming is somewhat unseasonable, and disturbs your conversation. I must needs say I did not expect to find such good company here.

ELV. Don Silvio's appearance indeed surprised me very much; I no more expected him than you did.

GARC. Madam, since you say so, I do not believe you were forewarned of this visit; (*to Don Silvio*) but you, sir, ought at least to have honoured us with some notice of this rare happiness, so that we should not have been surprised, but enabled to pay you here those attentions which we would have liked to render you.

ALPH. My Lord, you are so busy with warlike preparations, that I should have been wrong had I interrupted you. The sublime thoughts of mighty conquerors can hardly stoop to the ordinary civilities of the world.

GARC. But those mighty conquerors, whose warlike preparations are thus praised, far from loving secrecy, prefer to have witnesses of what they do; their minds trained to glorious deeds from infancy, make them carry out all their plans openly; being always supported by lofty sentiments, they never stoop to disguise themselves. Do you not compromise your heroic merits in coming here secretly, and are you not afraid that people may look upon this action as unworthy of you?

ALPH. I know not whether any one will blame my conduct because I have made a visit here in secret; but I know, Prince, that I never courted obscurity in things which require light. Were I to undertake anything against you, you should have no cause to remark you were surprised. It would depend upon yourself to guard against it; I would take care to warn you beforehand. Meanwhile let us continue upon ordinary terms, and postpone the settlement of our quarrels until all other affairs are arranged. Let us suppress the outbursts of our rather excited passions, and not forget in whose presence we are both speaking.

ELV. (*To Don Garcia*). Prince, you are in the wrong; and his visit is such that you . . .

GARC. Ah! Madam, it is too much to espouse his quarrel You ought to dissemble a little better when you pretend that you were ignorant he was coming here. You defend him so warmly and so quickly, that it is no very convincing proof of his visit being unexpected.

ELV. Your suspicions concern me so little, that I should be very sorry to deny your accusation.

GARC. Why do you not go farther in your lofty pride, and, without hesitation, lay bare your whole heart? You are too prone to dissimulation. Do not unsay anything you once said. Be brief, be brief, lay aside all scruples; say that his passion has kindled yours, that his presence delights you so much . . .

ELV. And if I have a mind to love him, can you hinder me? Do you pretend to sway my heart, and have I to receive your commands whom I must love? Know that too much pride has deceived you, if you think you have any authority over me; my mind soars too high to conceal my feelings when I am asked to declare them. I will not tell you whether the Count is beloved; but I may inform you that I esteem him highly; his great merits, which I admire, deserve the love of a Princess better than you; his passion, the assiduity he displays, impress me very strongly; and if the stern decree of fate puts it out of my power to reward him with my hand, I can at least promise him never to become a prey to your love. Without keeping you any longer in slight suspense, I engage myself to act thus, and I will keep my word. I have opened my heart to you, as you desired it, and shown you my real feelings. Are you satisfied, and do you not think that, as you pressed me, I have sufficiently explained myself? Consider whether there remains anything else for me to do in order to clear up your suspicions. (*To Don Silvio*). In the meanwhile, if you persist in your resolution to please me, do not forget, Count, that I have need of your arm, and that whatever may be the outbreaks of temper of an eccentric man, you must do your utmost to punish our tyrants. In a word, do not listen to what he may say to you in his wrath, and in order to induce you so to act, remember that I have entreated you.

SCENE IV.—DON GARCIA, DON ALPHONSO.

GARC. Everything smiles upon you, and you proudly triumph over my confusion. It is pleasant to hear the glorious confession of that victory which you obtain over a rival; but it must greatly add to your joy to have that rival a witness to it. My pretensions, openly set aside, enhance all the more the triumph of your love. Enjoy this great happiness fully, but know that you have not yet gained your point; I have too just cause to be incensed, and many things may perhaps ere then come to pass. Despair, when it breaks out, goes a great way; everything is pardonable when one has been deceived. If the ungrateful woman, out of compliment to your love, has just now pledged her word never to be mine, my righteous indignation will discover the means of preventing her ever being yours.

ALPH. I do not trouble myself about your antagonism. We shall see who will be deceived in his expectations. Each by his valour will be able to defend the reputation of his love, or avenge his misfortune. But as between rivals the calmest mind may easily become irate, and as I am unwilling that such a conversation should exasperate either of us, I wish, Prince, you would put me in the way of leaving this place, so that the restraint I put upon myself may be ended.

GARC. No, no, do not fear that you will be compelled to violate the order you received. Whatever righteous wrath is kindled within me, and which no doubt delights you, Count, I know when it should break forth. This place is open to you; you can leave it, proud of the advantages you have gained. But once more I tell you that my head alone can put your conquest into your hands.

ALPH. When matters shall have reached that point, fortune and our arms will soon end our quarrel.

ACT IV.

SCENE I.—DONNA ELVIRA, DON ALVAREZ.

ELV. You can go back, Don Alvarez, but do not expect that you shall persuade me to forget this offence. The wound which my heart received is incurable; all endeavours to heal it make it but fester the more. Does the Prince think I shall listen to some simulated compliments? No, no, he has made me too angry; and his fruitless repentance, which led you hither, solicits a pardon which I will not grant.

ALV. Madam, he deserves your pity. Never was any offence expiated with more stinging remorse; if you were to see his grief, it would touch your heart, and you would pardon him. It is well known that the Prince is of an age at which we abandon ourselves to first impressions; that in fiery youth the passions hardly leave room for reflection. Don Lopez, deceived by false tidings, was the cause of his master's mistake. An idle report that the Count was coming, and that you had some understanding with those who admitted him within these walls, was indiscreetly bruited about. The Prince believed it; his love, deceived by a false alarm, has caused all this disturbance. But being now conscious of his error, he is well aware of your innocence; the dismissal of Don Lopez clearly proves how great his remorse is for the outburst of which he has been guilty.

ELV. Alas! He too readily believes me innocent; he is not yet quite sure of it. Tell him to weigh all things well, and not to make too much haste, for fear of being deceived.

ALV. Madam, he knows too well. . . .

ELV. I pray you, Don Alvarez, let us no longer continue a conversation which vexes me: it revives in me some sadness, at the very moment that a more important sorrow oppresses me. Yes, I have received unexpectedly the news of a very great misfortune; the report of the death of the Countess Inez has filled my heart with so much wretchedness, that there is no room for any other grief.

ALV. Madam, these tidings may not be true; but when

I return, I shall have to communicate to the Prince a cruel piece of news.

ELV. However great his sufferings may be, they fall short of what he deserves.

SCENE II.—DONNA ELVIRA, ELIZA.

EL. I waited, Madam until he was gone, to tell you something that will free you from your anxiety, since this very moment you can be informed what has become of Donna Inez. A certain person, whom I do not know, has sent one of his servants to ask an audience of you, in order to tell you all.

ELV. Eliza, I must see him; let him come quickly.

EL. He does not wish to be seen except by yourself; by this messenger he requests, Madam that his visit may take place without any one being present.

ELV. Well, we shall be alone, I will give orders about that, whilst you bring him here. How great is my impatience just now! Ye fates, shall these tidings be full of joy or grief?

SCENE III.—DON PEDRO, ELIZA.

EL. Where . . . .

PED. If you are looking for me, Madam, here I am.

EL. Where is your master . . . .

PED. He is hard by; shall I fetch him?

EL. Desire him to come; tell him that he is impatiently expected, and that no one shall see him. (*Alone*). I cannot unravel this mystery; all the precautions he takes . . . . But here he is already.

SCENE IV.—DONNA INEZ, *in man's dress*, ELIZA.

EL. My Lord, in order to wait for you, we have prepared . . . . But what do I see? Ah! Madam, my eyes . . . .

INEZ. Do not tell any one, Eliza, I am here; allow me to pass my sad days in peace. I pretended to kill myself. By this feigned death I got rid of all my tyrants; for this is the name my relatives deserve. Thus I have avoided a dreadful marriage; rather than have consented, I would really have killed myself. This dress, and the report of my death, will keep the secret of my fate from all, and secure me against that unjust persecution which may even follow me hither.

EL. My surprise might have betrayed you, if I had seen you in public; but go into this room and put an end to the sorrow of the Princess; her heart will be filled with joy when she shall behold you. You will find her there alone; she has taken care to see you by herself, and without any witnesses.

SCENE V.—DON ALVAREZ, ELIZA.

EL. Is this not Don Alvarez whom I see?

ALV. The Prince sends me to entreat you to use your utmost influence in his favour. His life is despaired of, unless he obtains by your means, fair Eliza, one moment's conversation with Donna Elvira; he is beside himself . . . but here he is.

SCENE VI.—DON GARCIA, DON ALVAREZ, ELIZA.

GARC. Alas, Eliza, feel for my great misfortune; take pity on a heart full of wretchedness, and given up to the bitterest sorrow.

EL. I should look upon your torments, my Lord, with other eyes than the Princess does; Heaven or our mood is the reason why we judge differently about everything. But, as she blames you, and fancies your jealousy to be a frightful monster, if I were in your place I should obey her wishes, and endeavour to conceal from her eyes what offends them. A lover undoubtedly acts wisely when he tries to suit his temper to ours; a hundred acts of politeness have less influence than this unison, which makes two hearts appear as if stirred by the same feelings. This similarity firmly unites them; for we love nothing so much as what resembles ourselves.

GARC. I know it, but alas! merciless fate opposes such a well intentioned plan; in spite of all my endeavours, it continually lays a snare for me, which my heart cannot avoid. It is not because the ungrateful woman, in the presence of my rival, avowed her love for him, and not for me; and that with such an excess of tenderness, that it is impossible I can ever forget her cruelty. But as too much ardour led me to believe erroneously that she had introduced him into this place, I should be very much annoyed if I left upon her mind the impression that she has any just cause of complaint against me. Yes, if I am abandoned, it shall be only through her faithlessness; for as I have come to beg her pardon for my impetuosity, she shall have no excuse for ingratitude.

EL. Give a little time for her resentment to cool, and do not see her again so soon, my Lord.

GARC. Ah! if you love me, induce her to see me; she must grant me that permission; I do not leave this spot until her cruel disdain at least . . . .

EL. Pray, my Lord, defer this purpose.

GARC. No; make no more idle excuses.

EL. (*Aside*). The Princess herself must find means to send him away, if she says but one word to him. (*To Don Garcia*). Stay here, my Lord, I shall go and speak to her.

GARC. Tell her that I instantly dismissed the person whose information was the cause of my offence, that Don Lopez shall never . . .

SCENE VII.—DON GARCIA, DON ALVAREZ.

GARC. (*Looking in at the door which Eliza left half open*). What do I see, righteous Heavens! Can I believe my eyes? Alas! they are, doubtless, but too faithful witnesses; this is the most terrible of all my great troubles! This fatal blow completely overwhelms me! When suspicions raged within me, it was Heaven itself, vaguely but ominously foretelling me this horrible disgrace.

ALV. What have you seen, my Lord, to disturb you?

GARC. I have seen what I can hardly conceive; the overthrow of all creation would less astonish me than this accident. It is all over with me . . . Fate . . . I cannot speak. [15]

ALV. My Lord, endeavour to be composed.

GARC. I have seen . . . Vengeance! O Heaven!

ALV. What sudden alarm . . . ?

---

[15] The words from "What have you seen" till "I cannot speak," are with some slight alterations, found in the *Misanthrope*, Act iv., Scene 2 (see Vol. II).

GARC. It will kill me, Don Alvarez, it is but too certain.

ALV. But, my Lord, what can . . .

GARC. Alas! Everything is undone. I am betrayed, I am murdered![16] A man, (can I say it and still live) a man in the arms of the faithless Elvira!

ALV. The Princess, my Lord, is so virtuous . . .

GARC. Ah, Don Alvarez, do not gainsay what I have seen. It is too much to defend her reputation, after my eyes have beheld so heinous an action.

ALV. Our passions, my Lord, often cause us to mistake a deception for a reality; to believe that a mind nourished by virtue can . . . .

GARC. Prithee leave me, Don Alvarez, a counsellor is in the way upon such an occasion; I will take counsel only of my wrath.

ALV. (*Aside*). It is better not to answer him when his mind is so upset.

GARC. Oh! how deeply am I wounded! But I shall see who it is, and punish with my own hand. . . . . But here she comes. Restrain thyself, O rage!

SCENE VIII.—DONNA ELVIRA, DON GARCIA, DON ALVAREZ.

ELV. Well, what do you want? However bold you may be, how can you hope for pardon, after the way you have behaved? Dare you again present yourself before me? And what can you say that will become me to hear?

GARC. That all the wickedness of this world is not to be compared to your perfidy; that neither fate, hell, nor Heaven in its wrath ever produced anything so wicked as you are.[17]

ELV. How is this? I expected you would excuse your outrage; but I find you use other words.

GARC. Yes, yes, other words. You did not think that, the door being by accident left half open, I should dis-

---

[16] The last sentences of Don Alvarez and Don Garcia are also found in the *Misanthrope*, Act iv., Scene 2 (see Vol. II).

[17] The above words of Don Garcia are also in the *Misanthrope*, Act iv., Scene 3 (see Vol. II).

cover the caitiff in your arms, and thus behold your shame, and my doom. Is it the happy lover who has returned, or some other rival to me unknown? O Heaven! grant me sufficient strength to bear such tortures. Now, blush, you have cause to do so; your treachery is laid bare. This is what the agitations of my mind prognosticated; it was not without cause that my love took alarm; my continual suspicions were hateful to you, but I was trying to discover the misfortune my eyes have beheld; in spite of all your care, and your skill in dissembling, my star foretold me what I had to fear. But do not imagine that I will bear unavenged the slight of being insulted! I know that we have no command over our inclinations; that love will everywhere spring up spontaneously; that there is no entering a heart by force, and that every soul is free to name its conqueror; therefore I should have no reason to complain, if you had spoken to me without dissembling; you would then have sounded the death-knell of my hope; but my heart could have blamed fortune alone. But to see my love encouraged by a deceitful avowal on your part, is so treacherous and perfidious an action, that it cannot meet with too great a punishment; I can allow my resentment to do anything. No, no, after such an outrage, hope for nothing. I am no longer myself, I am mad with rage.[18] Betrayed on all sides, placed in so sad a situation, my love must avenge itself to the utmost; I shall sacrifice everything here to my frenzy, and end my despair with my life.

ELV. I have listened to you patiently; can I, in my turn, speak to you freely?

GARC. And by what eloquent speeches, inspired by cunning. . . .

ELV. If you have still something to say, pray continue; I am ready to hear you. If not, I hope you will at least listen for a few minutes quietly to what I have to say.

GARC. Well, then, I am listening. Ye Heavens! what patience is mine!

---

[18] The whole of this speech, from "Now blush," until "mad with rage," has, with few alterations, been used in the *Misanthrope*, Act iv., Scene 3 (see Vol. II).

ELV. I restrain my indignation, and will without any passion reply to your discourse, so full of fury.

GARC. It is because you see . . .

ELV. I have listened to you as long as you pleased; pray do the like to me. I wonder at my destiny, and I believe there was never any thing under Heaven so marvellous, nothing more strange and incomprehensible, and nothing more opposed to reason. I have a lover, who incessantly does nothing else but persecute me; who, amidst all the expressions of his love, does not entertain for me any feelings of esteem; whose heart, on which my eyes have made an impression, does not do justice to the lofty rank granted to me by Heaven; who will not defend the innocence of my actions against the slightest semblance of false appearances. Yes, I see . . . (*Don Garcia shows some signs of impatience, and wishes to speak*). Above all, do not interrupt me. I see that my unhappiness is so great, that one who says he loves me, and who, even if the whole world were to attack my reputation, ought to claim to defend it against all, is he who is its greatest foe. In the midst of his love, he lets no opportunity pass of suspecting me; he not only suspects me, but breaks out into such violent fits of jealousy that love cannot suffer without being wounded. Far from acting like a lover who would rather die than offend her whom he loves, who gently complains and seeks respectfully to have explained what he thinks suspicious, he proceeds to extremities as soon as he doubts, and is full of rage, insults, and threats. However, this day I will shut my eyes to everything that makes him odious to me, and out of mere kindness afford him an opportunity of being reconciled, though he insulted me anew. This great rage with which you attacked me proceeds from what you accidentally saw; I should be wrong to deny what you have seen; I own you might have some reason to be disturbed at it.

GARC. And is it not . . .

ELV. Listen to me a little longer, and you shall know what I have resolved. It is necessary that our fates should be decided. You are now upon the brink of a great precipice; you will either fall over it, or save yourself, according to the resolution you shall take. If, notwithstanding what you have seen, Prince, you act towards me as you ought, and ask no other proof but that I tell you you are wrong; if you readily comply with my wishes and are willing to believe me innocent upon my word alone, and no longer yield to every suspicion, but blindly believe what my heart tells you; then this submission, this proof of esteem, shall cancel all your offences; I instantly retract what I said when excited by well-founded anger. And if hereafter I can choose for myself, without prejudicing what I owe to my birth, then my honour, being satisfied with the respect you so quickly show, promises to reward your love with my heart and my hand. But listen now to what I say. If you care so little for my offer as to refuse completely to abandon your jealous suspicions; if the assurance which my heart and birth give you do not suffice; if the mistrust that darkens your mind compels me, though innocent, to convince you, and to produce a clear proof of my offended virtue, I am ready to do so, and you shall be satisfied; but you must then renounce me at once, and for ever give up all pretensions to my hand. I swear by Him who rules the Heavens, that, whatever fate may have in store for us, I will rather die than be yours! I trust these two proposals may satisfy you; now choose which of the two pleases you.

GARC. Righteous Heaven! Was there ever anything more artful and treacherous? Could hellish malice produce any perfidy so black? Could it have invented a more severe and merciless way to embarrass a lover? Ah! ungrateful woman, you know well how to take advantage of my great weakness, even against myself, and to employ for your own purposes that excessive, astonishing, and fatal love which you inspired.[19] Because you have been taken by surprise, and cannot find an excuse, you cunningly offer to forgive me. You pretend to be good-natured, and invent some trick to divert the consequences of my vengeance; you wish to ward off the blow that threatens a wretch, by craftily entangling me with your offer. Yes, your artifices would fain avert an explanation

---

19 The phrase "Ah! ungrateful woman" until "inspired" is also found in the *Misanthrope*, Act iv., Scene 3 (see Vol. II).

which must condemn you; pretending to be completely innocent, you will give convincing proof of it only upon such conditions as you think and most fervently trust I will never accept; but you are mistaken if you think to surprise me. Yes, yes, I am resolved to see how you can defend yourself; by what miracle you can justify the horrible sight I beheld, and condemn my anger.

ELV. Consider that, by this choice, you engage yourself to abandon all pretensions to the heart of Donna Elvira.

GARC. Be it so! I consent to everything; besides, in my present condition, I have no longer any pretensions.

ELV. You will repent the wrath you have displayed.

GARC. No, no, your argument is a mere evasion; I ought rather to tell you that somebody else may perhaps soon repent. The wretch, whoever he may be, shall not be fortunate enough to save his life, if I wreak my vengeance.

ELV. Ha! This can no longer be borne; I am too angry foolishly to preserve longer my good nature. Let me abandon the wretch to his own devices, and, since he will undergo his doom, let him—Eliza! . . . (*To Don Garcia*). You compel me to act thus; but you shall see that this outrage will be the last.

SCENE IX.—DONNA ELVIRA, DON GARCIA, ELIZA, DON ALVAREZ.

ELV. (*To Eliza*). Desire my beloved to come forth . . Go, you understand me, say that I wish it.

GARC. And can I . . .

ELV. Patience, you will be satisfied.

EL. (*Aside, going out*). This is doubtless some new trick of our jealous lover.

ELV. Take care at least that this righteous indignation perseveres in its ardour to the end; above all, do not henceforth forget what price you have paid to see your suspicions removed.

SCENE X.—DONNA ELVIRA, DON GARCIA, DONNA INEZ, ELIZA, DON ALVAREZ.

ELV. (*To Don Garcia, showing him Donna Inez*).

Thanks to Heaven, behold the cause of the generous suspicions you showed. Look well on that face, and see if you do not at once recognize the features of Donna Inez.

GARC. O Heavens!

ELV. If the rage which fills your heart prevents you from using your eyes, you can ask others, and thus leave no room for doubt. It was necessary to pretend she was dead, so that she might escape from the tyrant who persecuted her: she disguised herself in this manner the better to profit by her pretended death. (*To Donna Inez*). You will pardon me, Madam, for having consented to betray your secrets and to frustrate your expectations; but I am exposed to Don Garcia's insolence; I am no longer free to do as I wish; my honour is a prey to his suspicions, and is every moment compelled to defend itself. This jealous man accidentally saw us embrace, and then he behaved most disgracefully. (*To Don Garcia*). Yes, behold the cause of your sudden rage, and the convincing witness of my disgrace. Now, like a thorough tyrant, enjoy the explanation you have provoked; but know that I shall never blot from my memory the heinous outrage done to my reputation. And if ever I forget my oath, may Heaven shower its severest chastisements upon my head; may a thunderbolt descend upon me if ever I resolve to listen to your love. Come, Madam, let us leave this spot, poisoned by the looks of a furious monster; let us quickly flee from his bitter attacks, let us avoid the consequences of his mad rage, and animated by just motives, let us only pray that we may soon be delivered from his hands.

INEZ. (*To Don Garcia*). My Lord, your unjust and violent suspicions have wronged virtue itself.

SCENE XI.—DON GARCIA, DON ALVAREZ.

GARC. What gleam of light clearly shows me my error, and, at the same time, involves my senses in such a profound horror that, dejected, I can see nothing but the dreadful object of a remorse that kills me! Ah! Don Alvarez, I perceive you were in the right; but hell breathed its poison into my soul; through a merciless fatality I am my worst enemy. What does it benefit me to love with the most ardent passion that an amorous heart ever displayed, if this love continually engenders suspicions which torment me, and thus renders itself hateful! I must, I must justly revenge by my death the outrage committed against her divine charms. What advice can I follow now? Alas! I have lost the only object which made life dear to me! As I relinquished all hope of ever being beloved by her, it is much easier to abandon life itself.

ALV. My Lord . . .

GARC. No, Don Alvarez, my death is necessary. No pains, no arguments shall turn me from it; yet my approaching end must do some signal service to the Princess. Animated by this noble desire, I will seek some glorious means of quitting life; perform some mighty deed worthy of my love, so that in expiring for her sake she may pity me, and say, it was excess of love that was my sole offence. Thus she shall see herself avenged! I must attempt a deed of daring, and with my own hand give to Mauregat that death he so justly deserves. My boldness will forestall the blow with which Castile openly threatens him. With my last breath, I shall have the pleasure of depriving my rival of performing such a glorious deed.

ALV. So great a service, my Lord, may perhaps obliterate all remembrance of your offence; but to risk . . .

GARC. Let me fulfil my duty, and strive to make my despair aid in this noble attempt.

ACT V.

SCENE I.—DON ALVAREZ, ELIZA.

ALV. No, never was anyone more astonished. He had just planned that lofty undertaking; inspired by despair, he was all anxiety to kill Mauregat; eager to show his courage, and to reap the advantage of this lawful deed; to endeavour to obtain his pardon, and prevent the mortification of seeing his rival share his glory. As he was leaving these walls, a too accurate report brought him the sad tidings, that the very rival whom he wished to forestall had already gained the honour he hoped to acquire; had anticipated him, in slaying the traitor, and urged the appearance of Don Alphonso, who will reap the fruits of Don

Silvio's prompt success, and come to fetch the Princess, his sister. It is publicly said and generally believed, that Don Alphonso intends to give the hand of his sister as a reward for the great services Don Silvio has rendered him, by clearing for him a way to the throne.

EL. Yes, Donna Elvira has heard this news, which has been confirmed by old Don Louis, who has sent her word that Leon is now awaiting her happy return and that of Don Alphonso, and that there, since fortune smiles upon her, she shall receive a husband from the hands of her brother. It is plain enough from these few words that Don Silvio will be her husband.

ALV. This blow to the Prince's heart . . .

EL. Will certainly be severely felt. I cannot help pitying his distress; yet, if I judge rightly, he is still dear to the heart he has offended; it did not appear to me that the Princess was well pleased when she heard of Don Silvio's success, and of the approaching arrival of her brother, or with the letter; but . . .

SCENE II.—DONNA ELVIRA, DONNA INEZ, ELIZA, DON ALVAREZ.

ELV. Don Alvarez, let the Prince come hither. (*Don Alvarez leaves*). Give me leave, Madam, to speak to him in your presence concerning this piece of news, which greatly surprises me; and do not accuse me of changing my mind too quickly, if I lose all my animosity against him. His unforeseen misfortune has extinguished it; he is unhappy enough without the addition of my hatred. Heaven, who treats him with so much rigour, has but too well executed the oaths I took. When my honour was outraged, I vowed openly never to be his; but as I see that fate is against him, I think I have treated his love with too great severity; the ill success that follows whatever he does for my sake, cancels his offence, and restores him my love. Yes, I have been too well avenged; the waywardness of his fate disarms my anger, and now, full of compassion, I am seeking to console an unhappy lover for his misfortunes. I believe his love well deserves the compassion I wish to show him.

INEZ. Madam, it would be wrong to blame the tender

sentiments you feel for him. What he has done for you . . . He comes; and his paleness shows how deeply he is affected by this surprising stroke of fate.

SCENE III.—DON GARCIA, DONNA ELVIRA, DONNA INEZ, ELIZA.

GARC. Madam, you must think me very bold in daring to come here to show you my hateful presence . . .

ELV. Prince, let us talk no more of my resentment; your fate has made a change in my heart. Its severity, and your wretched condition have extinguished my anger, and our peace is made. Yes, though you have deserved the misfortunes with which Heaven in its wrath has afflicted you; though your jealous suspicions have so ignominiously, so almost incredibly, sullied my fame, yet I must needs confess that I so far commiserate your misfortune, as to be somewhat displeased with our success. I hate the famous service Don Silvio has rendered us, because my heart must be sacrificed to reward it; I would, were it in my power, bring back the moments when destiny put only my oath in my way. But you know that it is the doom of such as we are, to be always the slaves of public interests; that Heaven has ordained that my brother, who disposes of my hand, is likewise my King. Yield, as I do, Prince, to that necessity which rank imposes upon those of lofty birth. If you are very unfortunate in your love, be comforted by the interest I take in you; and though you have been overwhelmed by fate, do not employ the power which your valour gives you in this place: it would, doubtless be unworthy of you to struggle against destiny; whilst it is in vain to oppose its decrees, a prompt submission shows a lofty courage. Do not therefore resist its orders; but open the gates of Astorga to my brother who is coming; allow my sad heart to yield to those rights which he is entitled to claim from me; perhaps that fatal duty, which I owe him against my will, may not go so far as you imagine.

GARC. Madam, you give me proofs of exquisite goodness in endeavouring to lighten the blow that is prepared for me, but without such pains you may let fall upon me all the wrath which your duty demands. In my present condition, I can say nothing. I have deserved the worst punishments which fate can inflict; and I know that, whatever evils I may suffer, I have deprived myself of the right to complain of them. Alas, amidst all my misfortunes, on what grounds can I be bold enough to utter any complaint against you? My love has rendered itself a thousand times odious, and has done nothing but outrage your glorious charms; when by a just and noble sacrifice, I was endeavouring to render some service to your family, fortune abandoned me, and made me taste the bitter grief of being forestalled by a rival. After this, Madam, I have nothing more to say. I deserve the blow which I expect; and I see it coming, without daring to call upon your heart to assist me. What remains for me in this extreme misfortune is to seek a remedy in myself, and, by a death which I long for, free my heart from all those tribulations. Yes, Don Alphonso will soon be here; already my rival has made his appearance; he seems to have hurried hither from Leon, to receive his reward for having killed the tyrant. Do not fear that I shall use my power within these walls to offer him any resistance. If you allowed it, there is no being on earth which I would not defy in order to keep you; but it is not for me, whom you detest, to expect such an honourable permission. No vain attempts of mine shall offer the smallest opposition to the execution of your just designs. No, Madam, your feelings are under no compulsion; you are perfectly free. I will open the gates of Astorga to the happy conqueror, and suffer the utmost severity of fate.

SCENE IV.—DONNA ELVIRA, DONNA INEZ, ELIZA.

ELV. Madam, do not ascribe all my afflictions to the interest which I take in his unhappy lot. You will do me but justice if you believe that you have a large share in my heart-felt grief; that I care more for friendship than for love. If I complain of any dire misfortune, it is because Heaven in its anger has borrowed from me those shafts which it hurls against you, and has made my looks guilty of kindling a passion which treats your kind heart unworthily.

INEZ. This is an accident caused, doubtless, by your looks,

for which you ought not to quarrel with Heaven. If the feeble charms which my countenance displays have exposed me to the misfortune of my lover abandoning me, Heaven could not better soften such a blow than by making use of you to captivate that heart. I ought not to blush for an inconstancy which indicates the difference between your attractions and mine. If this change makes me sigh, it is from foreseeing that it will be fatal to your love; amidst the sorrow caused by friendship, I am angry for your sake that my few attractions have failed to retain a heart whose devotion interferes so greatly with the love you feel for another.

ELV. Rather blame your silence, which, without reason, concealed the understanding between your hearts. If I had known this secret sooner, it might perhaps have spared us both some sad trouble; I might then coldly and justly have refused to listen to the sighs of a fickle lover, and perhaps have sent back whence they strayed . . .

INEZ. Madam, he is here.

ELV. You can remain without even looking at him. Do not go away, Madam, but stay, and, though you suffer, hear what I say to him.

INEZ. I consent, Madam; though I very well know that were another in my place, she would avoid being present at such a conversation.

ELV. If Heaven seconds my wishes, Madam, you shall have no cause to repine.

SCENE V.—DON ALPHONSO (*believed to be Don Silvio*), DONNA ELVIRA, DONNA INEZ.

ELV. Before you say a word, my Lord, I earnestly beg that you will deign to hear me for a moment. Fame has already informed us of the marvellous deeds you have performed. I wonder to see, as all do, how quickly and successfully you have changed our lot. I know very well that such an eminent service can never be sufficiently rewarded, and that nothing ought to be refused to you for that never-to-be-forgotten deed which replaces my brother on the throne of his ancestors. But whatever his grateful heart may offer you, make a generous use of your advantages, and do not employ your glorious action, my Lord, to make me bend under an imperious yoke; nor let your love—for you know who is the object of my passion—persist in triumphing over a well-founded refusal; let not my brother, to whom they are going to present me, begin his reign by an act of tyranny over his sister. Leon has other rewards which for the nonce, may do more honour to your lofty valour. A heart which you can obtain only by compulsion, would be too mean a reward for your courage. Can a man be ever really satisfied when, by coercion, he obtains what he loves? It is a melancholy advantage; a generous-minded lover refuses to be happy upon such conditions. He will not owe anything to that pressure which relatives think they have a right to employ; he is ever too fond of the maiden he loves, to suffer her to be sacrificed as a victim, even to himself. Not that my heart intends to grant to another what it refuses to you. No, my Lord, I promise you, and pledge you my word of honour, that no one shall ever obtain my hand, that a convent shall protect me against every other . . .

ALPH. Madam, I have listened long enough to your discourse, and might, by two words, have prevented it all, if you had given less credit to false tidings. I know that a common report, which is everywhere believed, attributes to me the glory of having killed the tyrant; but as we have been informed, the people alone, stirred up by Don Louis to do their duty, have performed this honourable and heroic act, which public rumour ascribed to me. The reason of these tidings was that Don Louis, the better to carry out his lofty purpose, spread a report that I and my soldiers had made ourselves masters of the town; by this news he so excited the people, that they hastened to kill the usurper. He has managed everything by his prudent zeal, and has just sent me notice of this by one of his servants. At the same time, a secret has been revealed to me which will astonish you as much as it surprised me. You expect a brother, and Leon its true master; Heaven now presents him before you. Yes, I am Don Alphonso; I was brought up and educated under the name of Prince of Castile; this clearly proves the sincere friendship that existed between Don Louis and the King, my father.

Don Louis has all the proofs of this secret, and will establish its truth to the whole world. But now my thoughts are taken up with other cares; I am clear how to act towards you; not that my passion is opposed to such a discovery, or that the brother in my heart quarrels with the lover. The revelation of this secret has, without the least murmur, changed my ardour into a love commanded by nature; the tie of relationship which unites us has so entirely freed me from the love which I entertained for you, that the highest favour I now long for is the sweet delights of my first chain, and the means of rendering to the adorable Inez that which her excessive goodness deserves.[20] But the uncertainty of her lot renders mine miserable; if what is reported be true, then it will be in vain for Leon to invite me, and for a throne to wait for me; for a crown could not make me happy. I only wished for its splendour in order to let me taste the joy of placing it on the head of that maiden for whom Heaven destined me, and by those means to repair, as far as I could, the wrong I have done to her extraordinary virtues. It is from you, Madam, I expect tidings as to what has become of her. Be pleased to communicate them, and by your words hasten my despair, or the happiness of my life.

ELV. Do not wonder if I delay answering you; for this news, my Lord, bewilders me. I will not take upon me to tell your loving heart, whether Donna Inez be dead or alive; but this gentleman here, who is one of her most intimate friends, will doubtless give you some information about her.

ALPH. (*Recognising Donna Inez*). Ah, Madam, in this dilemma I am happy to behold again your heavenly beauty. But with what eye can you look upon a fickle lover, whose crime . . .

INEZ. Ah! do not insult me, and venture to state that a heart, which I hold dear, could be inconstant. I cannot bear the thought, and the apology pains me. All the love you felt for the Princess could not offend me, because her great worth is a sufficient excuse. The love you bore

---

[20] Compare the manner in which Andrès, in *The Blunderer* (Act v., Scene 15), recognises his sister in Celia.

her is no proof of your guilt towards me. Learn that if you had been culpable, the lofty pride within me would have made you sue in vain to overcome my contempt, and that neither repentance nor commands could have induced me to forget such an insult.

ELV. Ah, dear brother,—allow me to call you by this gentle name,—you render your sister very happy! I love your choice, and bless fortune, which enables you to crown so pure a friendship! Of the two noble hearts I so tenderly love . . .

SCENE VI.—DON GARCIA, DONNA ELVIRA, DONNA INEZ, DON ALPHONSO, ELIZA.

GARC. For mercy's sake, Madam, hide from me your satisfaction, and let me die in the belief that a feeling of duty compels you. I know you can freely dispose of your hand; I do not intend to run counter to your wishes. I have proved this sufficiently, as well as my obedience to your commands. But I must confess that this levity surprises me, and shakes all my resolutions. Such a sight awakens a storm of passion which I fear I cannot command, though I would punish myself, if this could make me lose that profound respect I wish to preserve. Yes, you have ordered me to bear patiently my unfortunate love; your behest has so much influence over my heart, that I will rather die than disobey you. But still, the joy you display tries me too severely; the wisest man, upon such an occasion, can but ill answer for his conduct. Suppress it, I beseech you, for a few moments, and spare me, Madam, this cruel trial; however great your love for my rival may be, do not let me be a wretched witness of his felicity. This is the smallest favour I think a lover may ask, even when he is disliked as much as I am. I do not seek this favour for long, Madam; my departure will soon satisfy you. I go where sorrow shall consume my soul, and shall learn your marriage only by hearsay; I ought not to hasten to behold such a spectacle; for, without seeing it, it will kill me.

INEZ. Give me leave, my Lord, to blame you for complaining, because the Princess has deeply felt your misfortunes; this very joy at which you murmur, arises solely from the happiness that is in store for you. She rejoices in a success which has favoured your heart's desire, and has discovered that your rival is her brother. Yes, Don Alphonso, whose name has been so bruited about, is her brother; this great secret has just now been told to her.

ALPH. My heart, thank Heaven, after a long torture, has all that it can desire, and deprives you of nothing, my Lord. I am so much the happier, because I am able to forward your love.

GARC. Alas! my Lord, I am overwhelmed by your goodness, which condescends to respond to my dearest wishes. Heaven has averted the blow that I feared; any other man but myself would think himself happy. But the fortunate discovery of this favourable secret, proves me to be culpable towards her I adore; I have again succumbed to these wretched suspicions, against which I have been so often warned, and in vain; through them my love has become hateful, and I ought to despair of ever being happy. Yes, Donna Elvira has but too good reason to hate me; I know I am unworthy of pardon; and whatever success fortune may give me, death, death alone, is all that I can expect.

ELV. No, no, Prince, your submissive attitude brings more tender feelings into my heart; I feel that the oath I took is no longer binding on me; your complaints, your respect, your grief has moved me to compassion; I see an excess of love in all your actions, and your malady deserves to be pitied. Since Heaven is the cause of your faults, some indulgence ought to be allowed to them; in one word, jealous or not jealous, my King will have no compulsion to employ when he gives me to you.

GARC. Heaven! enable me to bear the excess of joy which this confession produces.

ALPH. I trust, my Lord, that after all our useless dissensions, this marriage may forever unite our hearts and kingdoms. But time presses, and Leon expects us; let us go therefore, and, by our presence and watchfulness give the last blow to the tyrant's party.

L'ÉCOLE DES MARIS.

COMÉDIE.

THE SCHOOL FOR HUSBANDS.

A COMEDY IN THREE ACTS.

(*THE ORIGINAL IN VERSE.*)

JUNE 24TH, 1661.

INTRODUCTORY NOTICE.

The School for Husbands was the first play in the title of which the word "School" was employed, to imply that, over and above the intention of amusing, the author designed to convey a special lesson to his hearers. Perhaps Molière wished not only that the general public should be prepared to find instructions and warnings for married men, but also that they who were wont to regard the theatre as injurious, or at best trivial, should know that he professed to educate, as well as to entertain. We must count the adoption of similar titles by Sheridan and others amongst the tributes, by imitation, to Molière's genius.

This comedy was played for the first time at Paris, on the 24th of June, 1661, and met with great success. On the 12th of July following it was acted at Vaux, the country seat of Fouquet, before the whole court, Monsieur, the brother of the King, and the Queen of England; and by them also was much approved. Some commentators say that Molière was partly inspired by a comedy of Lope de Vega, *La Discreta enamorada*, The Cunning Sweetheart; also by a remodelling of the same play by Moreto, *No puede ser guardar una muger*, One cannot guard a woman: but this has lately been disproved. It appears, however, that he borrowed the primary idea of his comedy from the *Adelphi* of Terence; and from a tale, the third of the third day, in the Decameron of Boccaccio, where a young woman uses her father-confessor as a go-between for herself and her lover. In the *Adelphi* there are two old men of dissimilar character, who give a different education to the children they bring up. One of them is a dotard, who, after having for sixty years been sullen, grumpy and avaricious, becomes suddenly lively, polite, and prodigal; this Molière had too much common sense to imitate.

The School for Husbands marks a distinct departure in the dramatist's literary progress. As a critic has well observed, it substitutes for situations produced by the mechanism of plot, characters which give rise to situations in accordance with the ordinary operations of human nature. Molière's method—the simple and only true one, and, consequently, the one which incontestably establishes the original talent of its employer—is this: At the beginning of a play, he introduces his principal personages: sets them talking; suffers them to betray their characters, as men and women do in every-day life,—expecting from his hearers that same discernment which he has himself displayed in detecting their peculiarities: imports the germ of a plot in some slight misunderstanding or equivocal act; and leaves all the rest to be effected by the action and reaction of the characters which he began by bringing out in bold relief. His plots are thus the plots of nature; and it is impossible that they should not be both interesting and instructive. That his comedies, thus composed, are besides amusing, results from the shrewdness with which he has selected and combined his characters, and the art with which he arranges the situations produced.

The character-comedies of Molière exhibit, more than any others, the force of his natural genius, and the comparative weakness of his artistic talent. In the exhibition and the evolution of character, he is supreme. In the unravelling of his plots and the *dénouement* of his situations, he is driven too willingly to the *deus ex machina.*

The School for Husbands was directed against one of the special and prominent defects of society in the age and country in which Molière lived. Domestic tyranny was not only rife, but it was manifested in one of its coarsest forms. Sganarelle, though twenty years younger than Ariste, and not quite forty years old, could not govern by moral force; he relied solely on bolts and bars. Physical restraint was the safeguard in which husbands and parents had the greatest confidence, not perceiving that the brain and the heart are always able to prevail against it. This truth Molière took upon himself to preach, and herein he surpasses all his rivals; in nothing more than in the artistic device by which he introduces the contrast of the wise and trustful Ariste, *raisonneur* as he is called in French, rewarded in the end by the triumph of his more humane mode of treatment. Molière probably expresses his own feelings by the mouth of Ariste: for *The School for Husbands* was performed on the 24th of June, 1661, and about eight months later, on the 20th of February, 1662, he married Armande Béjart, being then about double her age. As to Sganarelle in this play, he ceases to be a mere buffoon, as in some of Molière's farces, and becomes the personification of an idea or of a folly which has to be ridiculed.

Molière dedicated *The School for Husbands* to the Duke of Orleans, the King's only brother, in the following words:—

My Lord,

I here shew France things that are but little consistent. Nothing can be so great and superb as the name I place in front of this book; and nothing more mean than what it contains. Every one will think this a strange mixture; and some, to express its inequality, may say that it is like setting a crown of pearls and diamonds on an earthen statue, and making magnificent porticos and lofty triumphal arches to a mean cottage. But, my Lord, my excuse is, that in this case I had no choice to make, and that the honour I have of belonging to your Royal Highness,[1] absolutely obliged me to dedicate to you the first work that I myself published.[2] It is not a present I make you, it is a duty I discharge; and homages are never looked upon by the things they bring. I presumed, therefore, to dedicate a trifle to your Royal Highness, because I could not help it; but if I omit enlarging upon the glorious truths I might tell of you, it is through a just fear that those great ideas would make my offering the more inconsiderable. I have imposed silence on myself, meaning to wait for an opportunity better suited for introducing such fine things; all I intended in this epistle was to justify my action to France, and to have the glory of telling you yourself, my Lord, with all possible submission, that I am your Royal Highness' very humble, very obedient, and very faithful servant,

MOLIÈRE.

[1] Molière was the chief of the troupe of actors belonging to the Duke of Orleans, who had only lately married, and was not yet twenty-one years old.

[2] *Sganarelle* had been borrowed by Neufvillenaine; *The Pretentious Young Ladies* was only printed by Molière, because the copy of the play was stolen from him; *Don Garcia of Navarre* was not published till after his death, in 1682.

In the fourth volume of the "Select Comedies of M. de Molière, London, 1732," the translation of *The School for Husbands* is dedicated to the Right Honourable the Lady Harriot Campbell, in the following words:—

MADAM,

A *Comedy* which came abroad in its Native Language, under the Patronage of the *Duke* of ORLEANS, Brother to the *King* of FRANCE, attempts now to speak English, and begs the Honour of Your LADYSHIP'S Favour and Acceptance. That distinguishing good Sense, that nice Discernment, that refined Taste of Reading and Politeness for which Your LADYSHIP is so deservedly admir'd, must, I'm persuaded, make You esteem *Molière;* whose way of expression is easy and elegant, his Sentiments just and delicate, and his morals untainted: who constantly combats Vice and Folly with strong Reason and well turn'd Ridicule; in short, whose *Plays* are all instructive, and tend to some useful Purpose:—An Excellence sufficient to recommend them to your LADYSHIP.

As for this *Translation*, which endeavours to preserve the Spirit as well as Meaning of the Original, I shall only say, that if it can be so happy as to please Your LADYSHIP, all the Pains it cost me will be over-paid.

I beg Pardon for this Presumption, and am, with the greatest Respect that's possible, *Madam, Your Ladyship's Most Obedient and most Humble Servant,*

THE TRANSLATOR.

Sir Charles Sedley, well known through a history of a "frolick" which Pepys relates in his "Diary,"[3] wrote *The Mulberry Garden*, of which Langbaine, in his "An Account of the Dramatick Poets," states "I dare not say that the character of Sir John Everyoung and Sir Samuel Forecast are copies of Sganarelle and Ariste in Molière's *l'École des Maris;* but I may say, that there is some resemblance, though whoever understands both languages will readily and with justice give our English wit the preference; and Sir Charles is not to learn to copy Nature from the French." This comedy, which was played by his Majesty's servants at the Theatre Royal, 1688, is dedicated to the Duchess of Richmond and Lennox, a lady who has "'scap'd (prefaces) very well hitherto," but, says Sir Charles, "Madam, your time is come, and you must bear it patiently. All the favour I can show you is that of a good executioner, which is, not to prolong your pain." This play has two girls like Isabella, called Althea and Diana, two like Leonor, Victoria and Olivia, and four lovers, as well as a rather intricate plot. The Epilogue is amusing, and we give the beginning of it:—

Poets of all men have the hardest game,
Their best Endeavours can no Favours claim.
The Lawyer if o'erthrown, though by the Laws,
He quits himself, and lays it on your Cause.
The Soldier is esteem'd a Man of War,
And Honour gains, if he but bravely dare.
The grave Physician, if his Patient dye,
He shakes his head, and blames Mortality.
Only poor Poets their own faults must bear;
Therefore grave Judges be not too severe.

Flecknoe has also imitated several of the scenes of *The School for Husbands* in *The Damoiselles à la Mode*, which is a medley of several of Molière's plays (see Introductory Notice to *The Pretentious Young Ladies*).

James Miller has likewise followed, in *The Man of Taste* (Act i., Scene

[3] See Pepys' Diary, October 23, 1668.

2), (see Introductory Notice to *The Pretentious Young Ladies*), one scene of the first act of Molière's *The School for Husbands*.

Murphy, in *The School for Guardians*, has borrowed from three plays of Molière. The main plot is taken from *The School for Wives;* some incidents of the second act are taken from *The Blunderer* (see Introductory Notice to *The Blunderer*), but the scenes in which Oldcastle and Lovibond state their intention of marrying their wards, and the way in which one of the wards, Harriet, makes her love known to Belford is taken from *The School for Husbands*, though Leonor does not betray in the French comedy, as she does in the English, the confidence placed in her. The French Isabella acts like Harriet, but then she has a foolish and jealous guardian.

Wycherley in *The Country Wife*, probably acted in 1672 or 1673, and which is partly an imitation of Molière's *School for Wives*, has borrowed from *The School for Husbands*, the letter which Isabella writes to Valère (Act ii., Scene 8), and also the scene in which Isabella escapes disguised in her sister's clothes: but, of course, to give an additional zest to the English play, the author makes Pinchwife himself bring his wife to her lover, Horner. The scene hardly bears transcribing. He has also partly imitated in *The Gentleman Dancing-Master*, first performed in 1673, some scenes of *The School for Husbands*.

Otway, in *The Soldier's Fortune* (see Introductory Notice to *Sganarelle, or The Self-Deceived Husband*), has borrowed from Molière's *School for Husbands* that part of his play in which Lady Dunse makes her husband the agent for conveying a ring and a letter to her lover.

DRAMATIS PERSONÆ.

SGANARELLE,[4] } *brothers.*
ARISTE, }

VALÈRE, *lover to Isabella.*

ERGASTE, *servant to Valère.*

A MAGISTRATE.[5]

A NOTARY.

ISABELLA, } *sisters.*
LÉONOR, }

LISETTE, *maid to Isabella.*

Scene.—A PUBLIC PLACE IN PARIS.

---

[4] This part was played by Molière himself. In the inventory taken after Molière's death, and given by M. Soulié, we find: "A dress for *The School for Husbands*, consisting of breeches, doublet, cloak, collar, purse and girdle, all of a kind of brown coloured (*couleur de musc*) satin."

[5] The original has *un Commissaire*, who in Molière's time, appears to have been a kind of inferior magistrate under the authority of the *Lieutenant-général de la Police*. The *Commissaires de Police* were not established till 1699; and *The School for Husbands* was played for the first time in 1661.

THE SCHOOL FOR HUSBANDS.

(*L'ÉCOLE DES MARIS*).

ACT I.

SCENE I.— SGANARELLE, ARISTE.

SGAN. Pray, brother, let us talk less, and let each of us live as he likes. Though you have the advantage of me in years, and are old enough to be wise, yet I tell you that I mean to receive none of your reproofs; that my fancy is the only counsellor I shall follow, and that I am quite satisfied with my way of living.

AR. But every one condemns it.

SGAN. Yes, fools like yourself, brother.

AR. Thank you very much. It is a pleasant compliment.

SGAN. I should like to know, since one ought to hear everything, what these fine critics blame in me.

AR. That surly and austere temper which shuns all the charms of society, gives a whimsical appearance to all your actions, and makes everything peculiar in you, even your dress.

SGAN. I ought then to make myself a slave in fashion, and not to put on clothes for my own sake? Would you not, my dear elder brother—for, Heaven be thanked, so you are, to tell you plainly, by a matter of twenty years; and that is not worth the trouble of mentioning—would you not, I say, by your precious nonsense, persuade me to adopt the fashions of those young sparks[6] of yours? Oblige

[6] The original has *vos jeunes muguets*, literally "your young lilies of the valley," because in former times, according to some annotators, the courtiers wore natural or artificial lilies of the valley in their button-holes, and perfumed themselves with the essence of that flower. I think

me to wear those little hats which provide ventilation for their weak brains, and that flaxen hair, the vast curls whereof conceal the form of the human face;[7] those little doublets but just below the arms, and those big collars falling down to the navel; those sleeves which one sees at table trying all the sauces, and those petticoats called breeches; those tiny shoes, covered with ribbons, which make you look like feather-legged pigeons; and those large rolls wherein the legs are put every morning, as it were into the stocks, and in which we see these gallants straddle about with their legs as wide apart, as if they were the beams of a mill?[8] I should doubtless please you, bedizened in this way; I see that you wear the stupid gewgaws which it is the fashion to wear.

AR. We should always agree with the majority, and never cause ourselves to be stared at. Extremes shock,

---

that *muguet* is connected with the old French word *musguet*, smelling of musk. In Molière's time *muguet* had become rather antiquated; hence it was rightly placed in the mouth of Sganarelle, who likes to use such words and phrases. Rabelais employs it in the eighth chapter of *Gargantua*, *un tas de muguets*, and it has been translated by Sir Thomas Urquhart as "some fond wooers and wench-courters." The fashion of calling dandies after the name of perfumes is not rare in France. Thus Regnier speaks of them as *marjolets*, from *marjolaine*, sweet marjoram; and Agrippa d'Aubigné calls them *muscadins* (a word also connected with the old French *musguet*), which name was renewed at the beginning of the first French revolution, and bestowed on elegants, because they always smelled of musk.

[7] The fashion was in Molière's time to wear the hair, or wigs, very long, and if possible of a fair colour, which gave to the young fashionables, hence called *blondins*, an effeminate air. Sganarelle addresses Valère (Act ii. Scene 9), likewise as *Monsieur aux blonds cheveux*. In *The School for Wives* (Act ii. Scene 6), Arnolphe also tells Agnès not to listen to the nonsense of these *beaux blondins*. According to Juvenal (Satire VI.) Messalina put a fair wig on to disguise herself. Louis XIV. did not begin to wear a wig until 1673.

[8] The original has *marcher écarquillés ainsi que des volants*. Early commentators have generally stated that *volants* means here "the beams of a mill," but MM. Moland and E. Despois the last annotators of Molière, maintain that it stands for "shuttlecock," because the large rolls (*canons*), tied at the knee and wide at the bottom, bore a great resemblance to shuttlecocks turned upside down. I cannot see how this can suit the words *marcher écarquillés*, for the motion of the *canons* of gallants, walking or straddling about, is very unlike that produced by shuttlecocks beaten by battledores; I still think "beams of a mill" right, because, though the *canons* did not look like beams of a mill, the legs did, when in motion.

and a wise man should do with his clothes as with his speech; avoid too much affectation, and without being in too great a hurry, follow whatever change custom introduces. I do not think that we should act like those people who always exaggerate the fashion, and who are annoyed that another should go further than themselves in the extremes which they affect; but I maintain that it is wrong, for whatever reasons, obstinately to eschew what every one observes; that it would be better to be courted among the fools than to be the only wise person, in opposition to every one else.

SGAN. That smacks of the old man who, in order to impose upon the world, covers his grey hairs with a black wig.

AR. It is strange that you should be so careful always to fling my age in my face, and that I should continually find you blaming my dress as well as my cheerfulness. One would imagine that old age ought to think of nothing but death, since it is condemned to give up all enjoyment; and that it is not attended by enough ugliness of its own, but must needs be slovenly and crabbed.

SGAN. However that may be, I am resolved to stick to my way of dress. In spite of the fashion, I like my cap so that my head may be comfortably sheltered beneath it; a good long doublet buttoned close, as it should be,[9] which may keep the stomach warm, and promote a healthy digestion; a pair of breeches made exactly to fit my thighs; shoes, like those of our wise ancestors, in which my feet may not be tortured: and he who does not like the look of me may shut his eyes.

SCENE II.—LÉONOR, ISABELLA, LISETTE; ARISTE *and* SGANARELLE, *conversing in an under-tone, unperceived.*

LEO. (*To Isabella*). I take it all on myself, in case you are scolded.

LIS. (*To Isabella*). Always in one room, seeing no one?

---

[9] The young dandies in the beginning of the reign of Louis XIV., wore slashed doublets, very tight and short.

ISA. Such is his humour.

LEO. I pity you, sister.

LIS. (*To Léonor*). It is well for you, madam, that his brother is of quite another disposition; fate was very kind in making you fall into the hands of a rational person.

ISA. It is a wonder that he did not lock me up to-day, or take me with him.

LIS. I declare I would send him to the devil, with his Spanish ruff,[10] and . . .

SGAN. (*Against whom Lisette stumbles*). Where are you going, if I may ask?

LEO. We really do not know; I was urging my sister to talk a walk, and enjoy this pleasant and fine weather; but . . .

SGAN. (*To Léonor*). As for you, you may go wherever you please. (*To Lisette*). You can run off; there are two of you together. (*To Isabella*). But as for you, I forbid you—excuse me—to go out.

AR. Oh, brother! let them go and amuse themselves.

SGAN. I am your servant, brother.

AR. Youth will . . .

SGAN. Youth is foolish, and old age too, sometimes.

AR. Do you think there is any harm in her being with Léonor?

SGAN. Not so; but with me I think she is still better.

AR. But . . .

SGAN. But her conduct must be guided by me; in short, I know the interest I ought to take in it.

AR. Have I less in her sister's?

SGAN. By Heaven! each one argues and does as he likes. They are without relatives, and their father, our friend, entrusted them to us in his last hour, charging us both either to marry them, or, if we declined, to dispose of them hereafter. He gave us, in writing, the full authority of a father and a husband over them, from their infancy. You undertook to bring up that one; I charged

---

10 The Spanish ruff (*fraise*) was in fashion at the end of Henri IV.'s reign; in the reign of Louis XIII., and in the beginning of Louis XIV.'s, flat-lying collars, adorned with lace were worn, so that those who still stuck to the Spanish ruff in 1661, were considered very old-fashioned people.

myself with the care of this one. You govern yours at your pleasure. Leave me, I pray, to manage the other as I think best.

AR. It seems to me . . .

SGAN. It seems to me, and I say it openly, that is the right way to speak on such a subject. You let your ward go about gaily and stylishly; I am content. You let her have footmen and a maid; I agree. You let her gad about, love idleness, be freely courted by dandies; I am quite satisfied. But I intend that mine shall live according to my fancy, and not according to her own; that she shall be dressed in honest serge, and wear only black on holidays; that, shut up in the house, prudent in bearing, she shall apply herself entirely to domestic concerns, mend my linen in her leisure hours, or else knit stockings for amusement; that she shall close her ears to the talk of young sparks, and never go out without some one to watch her. In short, flesh is weak; I know what stories are going about. I have no mind to wear horns, if I can help it; and as her lot requires her to marry me, I mean to be as certain of her as I am of myself.

ISA. I believe you have no grounds for . . . .

SGAN. Hold your tongue, I shall teach you to go out without us!

LEO. What, sir . . . .

SGAN. Good Heavens, madam! without wasting any more words, I am not speaking to you, for you are too clever.

LEO Do you regret to see Isabella with us?

SGAN. Yes, since I must speak plainly; you spoil her for me. Your visits here only displease me, and you will oblige me by honouring us no more.

LEO. Do you wish that I shall likewise speak my thoughts plainly to you? I know not how she regards all this; but I know what effect mistrust would have on me. Though we are of the same father and mother, she is not much of my sister if your daily conduct produces any love in her.

LIS. Indeed, all these precautions are disgraceful. Are we in Turkey, that women must be shut up? There, they say, they are kept like slaves; this is why the Turks are accursed by God. Our honour, sir, is very weak indeed, if it must be perpetually watched. Do you think, after all, that these precautions are any bar to our designs? that when we take anything into our heads, the cleverest man would not be but a donkey to us? All that vigilance of yours is but a fool's notion; the best way of all, I assure you, is to trust us. He who torments us puts himself in extreme peril, for our honour must ever be its own protector. To take so much trouble in preventing us is almost to give us a desire to sin. If I were suspected by my husband, I should have a very good mind to justify his fears.

SGAN. (*to Ariste*). This, my fine teacher, is your training. And you endure it without being troubled?

AR. Brother, her words should only make you smile. There is some reason in what she says. Their sex loves to enjoy a little freedom; they are but ill-checked by so much austerity. Suspicious precautions, bolts and bars, make neither wives nor maids virtuous. It is honour which must hold them to their duty, not the severity which we display towards them. To tell you candidly, a woman who is discreet by compulsion only is not often to be met with. We pretend in vain to govern all her actions; I find that it is the heart we must win. For my part, whatever care might be taken, I would scarcely trust my honour in the hands of one who, in the desires which might assail her, required nothing but an opportunity of falling.

SGAN. That is all nonsense.

AR. Have it so; but still I maintain that we should instruct youth pleasantly, chide their faults with great tenderness, and not make them afraid of the name of virtue. Léonor's education has been based on these maxims. I have not made crimes of the smallest acts of liberty, I have always assented to her youthful wishes, and, thank Heaven, I never repented of it. I have allowed her to see good company, to go to amusements, balls, plays. These are things which, for my part, I think are calculated to form the minds of the young; the world is a school which, in my opinion, teaches them better how to live than any book. Does she like to spend money on clothes, linen, ribands—what then? I endeavour to gratify her wishes; these are pleasures which, when we are well-off, we may permit to the girls of our family. Her father's command requires her to marry me; but it is not my intention to tyrannize over her. I am quite aware that our years hardly suit, and I leave her complete liberty of choice.[11] If a safe income of four thousand crowns a-year, great affection and consideration for her, may, in her opinion, counterbalance in marriage the inequality of our age, she may take me for her husband; if not she may choose elsewhere. If she can be happier without me, I do not object; I prefer to see her with another husband rather than that her hand should be given to me against her will.

SGAN. Oh, how sweet he is! All sugar and honey!

AR. At all events, that is my disposition; and I thank Heaven for it. I would never lay down these strict rules which make children wish their parents dead.

SGAN. But the liberty acquired in youth is not so easily withdrawn later on; all those feelings will please you but little when you have to change her mode of life.

AR. And why change it?

SGAN. Why?

AR. Yes.

SGAN. I do not know.

AR. Is there anything in it that offends honour?

SGAN. Why, if you marry her, she may demand the same freedom which she enjoyed as a girl?

AR. Why not?

SGAN. And you so far agree with her as to let her have patches and ribbons?

AR. Doubtless.

SGAN. To let her gad about madly at every ball and public assembly?

AR. Yes, certainly.

SGAN. And the beaux will visit at your house?

AR. What then?

SGAN. Who will junket and give entertainments?

---

11 *The School for Husbands* was played for the first time, on the 24th of June, 1661, and Molière married Armande Béjart (see Prefatory Memoir), on the 20th of February, 1662, when he was forty, and she about twenty years old. It is therefore not unreasonable to suppose that the words he places in the mouth of Ariste are an expression of his own feelings.

AR. With all my heart.

SGAN. And your wife is to listen to their fine speeches?

AR. Exactly.

SGAN. And you will look on at these gallant visitors with a show of indifference?

AR. Of course.

SGAN. Go on, you old idiot. (*To Isabella*). Get indoors, and hear no more of this shameful doctrine.

SCENE III.—ARISTE, SGANARELLE, LÉONOR, LISETTE.

AR. I mean to trust to the faithfulness of my wife, and intend always to live as I have lived.

SGAN. How pleased I shall be to see him victimized!

AR. I cannot say what fate has in store for me; but as for you, I know that if you fail to be so, it is no fault of yours, for you are doing everything to bring it about.

SGAN. Laugh on, giggler! Oh, what a joke it is to see a railer of nearly sixty!

LÉO. I promise to preserve him against the fate you speak of, if he is to receive my vows at the altar. He may rest secure; but I can tell you I would pass my word for nothing if I were your wife.

LIS. We have a conscience for those who rely on us; but it is delightful, really, to cheat such folks as you.

SGAN. Hush, you cursed ill-bred tongue!

AR. Brother, you drew these silly words on yourself. Good bye. Alter your temper, and be warned that to shut up a wife is a bad plan. Your servant.

SGAN. I am not yours.

SCENE IV.—SGANARELLE, *alone*.

Oh, they are all well suited to one another! What an admirable family. A foolish old man with a worn-out body who plays the fop; a girl-mistress and a thorough coquette; impudent servants;—no, wisdom itself could not succeed, but would exhaust sense and reason, trying to amend a household like this. By such associations, Isabella might lose those principles of honour which she learned amongst us; to prevent it, I shall presently send her back again to my cabbages and turkeys.

SCENE V.—VALÈRE, SGANARELLE, ERGASTE.

VAL. (*Behind*). Ergaste, that is he, the Argus whom I hate, the stern guardian of her whom I adore.

SGAN. (*Thinking himself alone*). In short, is there not something wonderful in the corruption of manners now-a-days?

VAL. I should like to address him, if I can get a chance, and try to strike up an acquaintance with him.

SGAN. (*Thinking himself alone*). Instead of seeing that severity prevail which so admirably formed virtue in other days, uncontrolled and imperious youth here-about assumes . . . (*Valère bows to Sganarelle from a distance*).

VAL. He does not see that we bow to him.

ERG. Perhaps his blind eye is on this side. Let us cross to the right.

SGAN. I must go away from this place. Life in town only produces in me . . .

VAL. (*Gradually approaching*). I must try to get an introduction

SGAN. (*Hearing a noise*). Ha! I thought some one spoke . . . (*Thinking himself alone*). In the country, thank Heaven, the fashionable follies do not offend my eyes.

ERG. (*To Valère*). Speak to him.

SGAN. What is it? . . . my ears tingle . . . There, all the recreations of our girls are but . . . (*He perceives Valère bowing to him*). Do you bow to me?

ERG. (*To Valère*). Go up to him.

SGAN. (*Not attending to Valère*). Thither no coxcomb comes. (*Valère again bows to him*). What the deuce! . . . (*He turns and sees Ergaste bowing on the other side*). Another? What a great many bows!

VAL. Sir, my accosting you disturbs you, I fear?

SGAN. That may be.

VAL. But yet the honour of your acquaintance is so great a happiness, so exquisite a pleasure, that I had a great desire to pay my respects to you.

SGAN. Well.

VAL. And to come and assure you, without any deceit, that I am wholly at your service.

SGAN. I believe it.

VAL. I have the advantage of being one of your neighbours, for which I thank my lucky fate.

SGAN. That is all right.

VAL. But, sir. do you know the news going the round at Court, and thought to be reliable?

SGAN. What does it matter to me?

VAL. True; but we may sometimes be anxious to hear it? Shall you go and see the magnificent preparations for the birth of our Dauphin, sir?[12]

SGAN. If I feel inclined.

VAL. Confess that Paris affords us a hundred delightful pleasures which are not to be found elsewhere. The provinces are a desert in comparison. How do you pass your time?

SGAN. On my own business.

VAL. The mind demands relaxation, and occasionally gives way, by too close attention to serious occupations. What do you do in the evening before going to bed?

SGAN. What I please.

VAL. Doubtless no one could speak better. The answer is just, and it seems to be common sense to resolve never to do what does not please us. If I did not think you were too much occupied, I would drop in on you sometimes after supper.

SGAN. Your servant.

SCENE VI.—VALÈRE, ERGASTE.

VAL. What do you think of that eccentric fool?

ERG. His answers are abrupt and his reception is churlish.

VAL. Ah! I am in a rage.

ERG. What for?

VAL. Why am I in a rage? To see her I love in the power of a savage, a watchful dragon, whose severity will not permit her to enjoy a single moment of liberty.

ERG. That is just what is in your favour. Your love ought to expect a great deal from these circumstances.

---

[12] The Dauphin, the son of Louis XIV. was born at Fontainebleau, on the 1st of November, 1661; *The School for Husbands* was first acted on the 24th of June of the same year; hence Molière ventures to prophesy about the Dauphin's birth.

Know, for your encouragement, that a woman watched is half-won, and that the gloomy ill-temper of husbands and fathers has always promoted the affairs of the gallant. I intrigue very little; for that is not one of my accomplishments. I do not pretend to be a gallant; but I have served a score of such sportsmen, who often used to tell me that it was their greatest delight to meet with churlish husbands, who never come home without scolding,—downright brutes, who, without rhyme or reason, criticise the conduct of their wives in everything, and, proudly assuming the authority of a husband, quarrel with them before the eyes of their admirers. "One knows," they would say, "how to take advantage of this. The lady's indignation at this kind of outrage, on the one hand, and the considerate compassion of the lover, on the other, afford an opportunity for pushing matters far enough." In a word, the surliness of Isabella's guardian is a circumstance sufficiently favourable for you.

VAL. But I could never find one moment to speak to her in the four months that I have ardently loved her.

ERG. Love quickens people's wits, though it has little effect on yours. If I had been . . .

VAL. Why, what could you have done? For one never sees her without that brute; in the house there are neither maids nor men-servants whom I might influence to assist me by the alluring temptation of some reward.

ERG. Then she does not yet know that you love her?

VAL. It is a point on which I am not informed. Wherever the churl took this fair one, she always saw me like a shadow behind her; my looks daily tried to explain to her the violence of my love. My eyes have spoken much; but who can tell whether, after all, their language could be understood?

ERG. It is true that this language may sometimes prove obscure, if it have not writing or speech for its interpreter.

VAL. What am I to do to rid myself of this vast difficulty, and to learn whether the fair one has perceived that I love her? Tell me some means or other.

ERG. That is what we have to discover. Let us go in for a while—the better to think over it.

ACT II.

SCENE I.—ISABELLA, SGANARELLE.

SGAN. That will do; I know the house, and the person, simply from the description you have given me.

ISA. (*Aside*). Heaven, be propitious, and favour to-day the artful contrivance of an innocent love!

SGAN. Do you say they have told you that his name is Valère?

ISA. Yes.

SGAN. That will do; do not make yourself uneasy about it. Go inside, and leave me to act. I am going at once to talk to this young madcap.

ISA. (*As she goes in*). For a girl, I am planning a pretty bold scheme. But the unreasonable severity with which I am treated will be my excuse to every right mind.

SCENE II.—SGANARELLE, *alone*.

(*Knocks at the door of Valère's house*). Let us lose no time; here it is. Who's there? Why, I am dreaming! Hulloa, I say! hulloa somebody! hulloa! I do not wonder, after this information, that he came up to me just now so meekly. But I must make haste, and teach this foolish aspirant . . .

SCENE III.—VALÈRE, SGANARELLE, ERGASTE.

SGAN. (*To Ergaste, who has come out hastily*). A plague on the lubberly ox! Do you mean to knock me down—coming and sticking yourself in front of me like a post?

VAL. Sir, I regret . . .

SGAN. Ah! you are the man I want.

VAL. I, sir?

SGAN. You. Your name is Valère, is it not?

VAL. Yes.

SGAN. I am come to speak to you if you will allow me.

VAL. Can I have the happiness of rendering you any service?

SGAN. No; but I propose to do you a good turn. That is what brings me to your house.

VAL. To my house, sir!

SGAN. To your house. Need you be so much astonished?

VAL. I have good reason for it; I am delighted with the honour . . .

SGAN. Do not mention the honour, I beseech you.

VAL. Will you not come in?

SGAN. There is no need.

VAL. I pray you, enter.

SGAN. No, I will go no further.

VAL. As long as you stay there I cannot listen to you.

SGAN. I will not budge.

VAL. Well, I must yield. Quick, since this gentleman is resolved upon it, bring a chair.

SGAN. I am going to talk standing.

VAL. As if I could permit such a thing!

SGAN. What an intolerable delay!

VAL. Such incivility would be quite unpardonable.

SGAN. Nothing can be so rude as not to listen to people who wish to speak to us.

VAL. I obey you, then.

SGAN. You cannot do better. (*They make many compliments about putting on their hats*). So much ceremony is hardly necessary. Will you listen to me?

VAL. Undoubtedly, and most willingly.

SGAN. Tell me: do you know that I am guardian to a tolerably young and passably handsome girl who lives in this neighbourhood, and whose name is Isabella?

VAL. Yes.

SGAN. As you know it, I need not tell it to you. But do you know, likewise, that as I find her charming, I care for her otherwise than as a guardian, and that she is destined for the honour of being my wife?

VAL. No!

SGAN. I tell it you, then; and also that it is as well that your passion, if you please, should leave her in peace.

VAL. Who?—I, sir?

SGAN. Yes, you. Let us have no dissembling.

VAL. Who has told you that my heart is smitten by her?

SGAN. Those who are worthy of belief.

VAL. Be more explicit.

SGAN. She herself.

VAL. She!

SGAN. She. Is not that enough? Like a virtuous young girl, who has loved me from childhood, she told me all just now; moreover, she charged me to tell you, that, since she has everywhere been followed by you, her heart, which your pursuit greatly offends, has only too well understood the language of your eyes; that your secret desires are well known to her; and that to try more fully to explain a passion which is contrary to the affection she entertains for me, is to give yourself needless trouble.

VAL. She, you say, of her own accord, makes you . .

SGAN. Yes, makes me come to you and give you this frank and plain message; also, that, having observed the violent love wherewith your soul is smitten, she would earlier have let you know what she thinks about you if, perplexed as she was, she could have found anyone to send this message by; but that at length she was painfully compelled to make use of me, in order to assure you, as I have told you, that her affection is denied to all save me; that you have been ogling her long enough; and that, if you have ever so little brains, you will carry your passion somewhere else. Farewell, till our next meeting. That is what I had to tell you.

VAL. (*Aside*). Ergaste, what say you to such an adventure?

SGAN. (*Aside, retiring*). See how he is taken aback!

ERG. (*In a low tone to Valère*). For my part, I think that there is nothing in it to displease you; that a rather subtle mystery is concealed under it; in short, that this message is not sent by one who desires to see the love end which she inspires in you.

SGAN. (*Aside.*) He takes it as he ought.

VAL. (*In a low tone to Ergaste*). You think it a mystery . . .

ERG. Yes. . . . But he is looking at us; let us get out of his sight.

SCENE IV.—SGANARELLE, *alone.*

How his face showed his confusion! Doubtless he did not expect this message. Let me call Isabella; she is showing the fruits which education produces on the mind.

Virtue is all she cares for; and her heart is so deeply steeped in it, that she is offended if a man merely looks at her.

SCENE V.—ISABELLA, SGANARELLE.

ISA. (*Aside, as she enters*). I fear that my lover, full of his passion, has not understood my message rightly! Since I am so strictly guarded, I must risk one which shall make my meaning clearer.

SGAN. Here I am, returned again.

ISA. Well?

SGAN. Your words wrought their full purpose; I have done his business. He wanted to deny that his heart was touched; but when I told him I came from you, he stood immediately dumbfounded and confused; I do not believe he will come here any more.

ISA. Ah, what do you tell me? I much fear the contrary, and that he will still give us more trouble.

SGAN. And why do you fear this?

ISA. You had hardly left the house when, going to the window to take a breath of air, I saw a young man at yonder turning, who first came, most unexpectedly, to wish me good morning, on the part of this impertinent man, and then threw right into my chamber a box, enclosing a letter, sealed like a love-letter.[13] I meant at once to throw it after him; but he had already reached the end of the street. I feel very much annoyed at it.

SGAN. Just see his trickery and rascality!

ISA. It is my duty quickly to have this box and letter sent back to this detestable lover; for that purpose I need some one; for I dare not venture to ask yourself . . .

SGAN. On the contrary, darling, it shows me all the more your love and faithfulness; my heart joyfully accepts this task. You oblige me in this more than I can tell you.

ISA. Take it then.

---

[13] The original has *un poulet*, literally "a chicken," because love-letters were folded so as to represent a fowl, with two wings; this shape is now called *cocotte*, from *coq*, and, though no longer used to designate a billet-doux, is often employed in familiar phraseology, in speaking of a girl who does not lead a moral life.

SGAN. Well, let us see what he has dared to say to you.

ISA. Heavens! Take care not to open it!

SGAN. Why so?

ISA. Will you make him believe that it is I? A respectable girl ought always to refuse to read the letters a man sends her. The curiosity which she thus betrays shows a secret pleasure in listening to gallantries. I think it right that this letter should be peremptorily returned to Valère unopened, that he may the better learn this day the great contempt which my heart feels for him; so that his passion may from this time lose all hope, and never more attempt such a transgression.

SGAN. Of a truth she is right in this! Well, your virtue charms me, as well as your discretion. I see that my lessons have borne fruit in your mind; you show yourself worthy of being my wife.

ISA. Still I do not like to stand in the way of your wishes. The letter is in your hands, and you can open it.

SGAN. No, far from it. Your reasons are too good; I go to acquit myself of the task you impose upon me; I have likewise to say a few words quite near, and will then return hither to set you at rest.

SCENE VI.—SGANARELLE, *alone.*

How delighted I am to find her such a discreet girl! I have in my house a treasure of honour. To consider a loving look treason, to receive a love-letter as a supreme insult, and to have it carried back to the gallant by myself! I should like to know, seeing all this, if my brother's ward would have acted thus, on a similar occasion. Upon my word, girls are what you make them . . . Hulloa! (*Knocks at Valère's door*).

SCENE VII.—SGANARELLE, ERGASTE.

ERG. Who is there?

SGAN. Take this; and tell your master not to presume so far as to write letters again, and send them in gold boxes; say also that Isabella is mightily offended at it. See, it has not even been opened. He will perceive what regard she has for his passion, and what success he can expect in it.

SCENE VIII.—VALÈRE, ERGASTE.

VAL. What has that surly brute just given you?

ERG. This letter, sir, as well as this box, which he pretends that Isabella has received from you, and about which, he says, she is in a great rage. She returns it to you unopened. Read it quickly, and let us see if I am mistaken.

VAL. (*Reads*). "*This letter will no doubt surprise you; both the resolution to write to you and the means of conveying it to your hands may be thought very bold in me; but I am in such a condition, that I can no longer restrain myself. Well-founded repugnance to a marriage with which I am threatened in six days, makes me risk everything; and in the determination to free myself from it by whatever means, I thought I had rather choose you than despair. Yet do not think that you owe all to my evil fate; it is not the constraint in which I find myself that has given rise to the sentiments I entertain for you; but it hastens the avowal of them, and makes me transgress the decorum which the proprieties of my sex require. It depends on you alone to make me shortly your own; I wait only until you have declared your intentions to me before acquainting you with the resolution I have taken; but, above all remember that time presses, and that two hearts, which love each other, ought to understand even the slightest hint.*"

ERG. Well, sir, is not this contrivance original? For a young girl she is not so very ignorant. Would one have thought her capable of these love stratagems?

VAL. Ah, I consider her altogether adorable. This evidence of her wit and tenderness doubles my love for her, and strengthens the feelings with which her beauty inspires me . . .

ERG. Here comes the dupe; think what you will say to him.

SCENE IX.—SGANARELLE, VALÈRE, ERGASTE.

SGAN. (*Thinking himself alone*). Oh, thrice and four times blessed be the law which forbids extravagance in dress![14] No longer will the troubles of husbands be so great! women will now be checked in their demands. Oh, how delighted I am with the King for this proclamation![15] How I wish, for the peace of the same husbands, that he would forbid coquetry, as well as lace, and gold or silver embroidery. I have bought the law on purpose, so that Isabella may read it aloud; and, by and by, when she is at leisure, it shall be our entertainment after supper. (*Perceiving Valère*). Well, Mr. Sandy-hair,[16] would you like to send again love-letters in boxes of gold? You doubtless thought you had found some young flirt, eager for an intrigue, and melting before pretty speeches. You see how your presents are received! Believe me, you waste your powder and shot. Isabella is a discreet girl, she loves me and your love insults her. Aim at some one else, and be off!

VAL. Yes, yes; your merits, to which everyone yields, are too great an obstacle, sir. Though my passion be sincere, it is folly to contend with you for the love of Isabella.

SGAN. It is really folly.

VAL. Be sure I should not have yielded to the fascination of her charms, could I have foreseen that this wretched heart would find a rival so formidable as yourself.

SGAN. I believe it.

VAL. Now I know better than to hope; I yield to you, sir, and that too without a murmur.

SGAN. You do well.

VAL. Reason will have it so; for you shine with so many virtues, that I should be wrong to regard with an angry eye the tender sentiments which Isabella entertains for you.

SGAN. Of course.

---

[14] It is remarkable that Louis XIV., who was so extravagant himself in his buildings, dress, and general expenses published sixteen laws against luxury; the law Sganarelle speaks of was promulgated November 27th, 1660, against the use of ***guipures***, ***cannetilles***, ***paillettes***, etc., on men's dresses.

[15] The original has *décri* a proclamation which forbade the manufacturing, sale or wearing, of certain fabrics.

[16] See Note 7, page 264.

VAL. Yes, yes, I yield to you; but at least I pray you, —and it is the only favour, sir, begged by a wretched lover, of whose pangs this day you are the sole cause,— I pray you, I say, to assure Isabella that, if my heart has been burning with love for her these three months, that passion is spotless, and has never fostered a thought at which her honour could be offended.

SGAN. Ay.

VAL. That, relying solely on my heart's choice, my only design was to obtain her for my wife, if destiny had not opposed an obstacle to this pure flame in you, who captivated her heart.

SGAN. Very good.

VAL. That, whatever happens, she must not think that her charms can ever be forgotten; that to whatever decrees of Heaven I must submit, my fate is to love her to my last breath; and that, if anything checks my pursuit, it is the just respect I have for your merits.[17]

SGAN. That is wisely spoken; I shall go at once to repeat these words, which will not be disagreeable to her. But, if you will listen to me, try to act so as to drive this passion from your mind. Farewell.

ERG. (*To Valère*). The excellent dupe!

SCENE X.—SGANARELLE, *alone*.

I feel a great pity for this poor wretch, so full of affection. But it is unfortunate for him to have taken it into his head to try to storm a fortress which I have captured.

(*Sganarelle knocks at his door.*)

SCENE XI.—SGANARELLE, ISABELLA.

SGAN. Never did lover display so much grief for a love-letter returned unopened! At last he loses all hope, and retires. But he earnestly entreated me to tell you, that, at least, in loving you, he never fostered a thought at which your honour could be offended, and that, relying

[17] We are of course to read between the lines: "If there is anything which could strengthen my resolution to save her, it is the natural detestation which I feel for you."

solely on his heart's choice, his only desire was to obtain you for a wife, if destiny had not opposed an obstacle to his pure flame, through me, who captivated your heart; that, whatever happens, you must not think that your charms can ever be forgotten by him; that, to whatever decrees of Heaven he must submit, his fate is to love you to his last breath; and that if anything checks his pursuit, it is the just respect he has for my merits. These are his very words; and, far from blaming him, I think him a gentleman, and I pity him for loving you.

ISA. (*Aside*). His passion does not contradict my secret belief, and his looks have always assured me of its innocence.

SGAN. What do you say?

ISA. That it is hard that you should so greatly pity a man whom I hate like death; and that, if you loved me as much as you say, you would feel how he insults me by his addresses.

SGAN. But he did not know your inclinations; and, from the uprightness of his intentions, his love does not deserve . . .

ISA. Is it good intentions, I ask, to try and carry people off? Is it like a man of honour to form designs for marrying me by force, and taking me out of your hands? As if I were a girl to live after such a disgrace!

SGAN. How?

ISA. Yes, yes, I have been informed that this base lover speaks of carrying me off by force; for my part, I cannot tell by what secret means he has learned so early that you intend to marry me in eight days[18] at the latest, since it was only yesterday you told me so. But they say that he intends to be beforehand with you, and not let me unite my lot to yours.

SGAN. That is a bad case.

ISA. Oh, pardon me! He is eminently a gentleman, who only feels towards me . . .

SGAN. He is wrong; and this is past joking.

---

[18] In the letter which Isabella writes to Valère (see page 279), she speaks of a marriage with which she is threatened in six days. This is, I suppose, a pious fraud, to urge Valère to make haste, for here she mentions "eight days."

ISA. Yes, your good nature encourages his folly. If you had spoken sharply to him just now, he would have feared your rage and my resentment; for even since his letter was rejected, he mentioned this design which has shocked me. As I have been told, his love retains the belief that it is well received by me; that I dread to marry you, whatever people may think, and should be rejoiced to see myself away from you.

SGAN. He is mad!

ISA. Before you, he knows how to disguise; and his plan is to amuse you. Be sure the wretch makes sport of you by these fair speeches. I must confess that I am very unhappy. After all my pains to live honourably, and to repel the addresses of a vile seducer, I must be exposed to his vexatious and infamous designs against me!

SGAN. There, fear nothing.

ISA. For my part I tell you that if you do not strongly reprove such an impudent attempt, and do not find quickly means of ridding me of such bold persecutions, I will abandon all, and not suffer any longer the insults which I receive from him.

SGAN. Do not be so troubled, my little wife. There, I am going to find him, to give him a good blowing up.

ISA. Tell him at least plainly, so that it may be in vain for him to gainsay it, that I have been told of his intentions upon good authority; that, after this message, whatever he may undertake, I defy him to surprise me; and, lastly, that, without wasting any more sighs or time, he must know what are my feelings for you; that, if he wishes not to be the cause of some mischief, he should not require to have the same thing told twice over.

SGAN. I will tell him what is right.

ISA. But all this in such a way as to show him that I really speak seriously.

SGAN. There, I will forget nothing, I assure you.

ISA. I await your return impatiently. Pray, make as much haste as you can. I pine when I am a moment without seeing you.

SGAN. There, ducky, my heart's delight, I will return immediately.

SCENE XII.—SGANARELLE, *alone*.

Was there ever a girl more discreet and better behaved? Oh, how happy I am! and what a pleasure it is to find a woman just after my own heart! Yes, that is how our women ought to be, and not, like some I know, downright flirts, who allow themselves to be courted, and make their simple husbands to be pointed at all over Paris. (*Knocks at Valère's door*). Hulloa, my enterprising, fine gallant!

SCENE XIII.—VALÈRE, SGANARELLE, ERGASTE.

VAL. Sir, what brings you here again?

SGAN. Your follies.

VAL. How?

SGAN. You know well enough what I wish to speak to you about. To tell you plainly, I thought you had more sense. You have been making fun of me with your fine speeches, and secretly nourish silly expectations. Look you, I wished to treat you gently; but you will end by making me very angry. Are you not ashamed, considering who you are, to form such designs as you do? to intend to carry off a respectable girl, and interrupt a marriage on which her whole happiness depends?

VAL. Who told you this strange piece of news, sir?

SGAN. Do not let us dissimulate; I have it from Isabella, who sends you word by me, for the last time, that she has plainly enough shown you what her choice is; that her heart, entirely mine, is insulted by such a plan; that she would rather die than suffer such an outrage; and that you will cause a terrible uproar, unless you put an end to all this confusion.

VAL. If she really said what I have just heard, I confess that my passion has nothing more to expect. These expressions are plain enough to let me see that all is ended; I must respect the judgment she has passed.

SGAN. If . . . You doubt it then, and fancy all the complaints that I have made to you on her behalf are mere pretences! Do you wish that she herself should tell you her feelings? To set you right, I willingly consent to it. Follow me; you shall hear if I have added anything, and if her young heart hesitates between us two. (*Goes and knocks at his own door*).

SCENE XIV.—ISABELLA, SGANARELLE, VALÈRE, ERGASTE.

ISA. What! you bring Valère to me! What is your design? Are you taking his part against me? And do you wish, charmed by his rare merits, to compel me to love him, and endure his visits?

SGAN. No, my love; your affection is too dear to me for that; but he believes that my messages are untrue; he thinks that it is I who speak, and cunningly represent you as full of hatred for him, and of tenderness for me; I wish, therefore, from your own mouth, infallibly to cure him of a mistake which nourishes his love.

ISA. (*To Valère*). What! Is not my soul completely bared to your eyes, and can you still doubt whom I love?

VAL. Yes, all that this gentleman has told me on your behalf, Madam, might well surprise a man; I confess I doubted it. This final sentence, which decides the fate of my great love, moves my feelings so much that it can be no offence if I wish to have it repeated.

ISA. No, no, such a sentence should not surprise you. Sganarelle told you my very sentiments; I consider them to be sufficiently founded on justice, to make their full truth clear. Yes, I desire it to be known, and I ought to be believed, that fate here presents two objects to my eyes, who, inspiring me with different sentiments, agitate my heart. One by a just choice, in which my honour is involved, has all my esteem and love; and the other, in return for his affection, has all my anger and aversion. The presence of the one is pleasing and dear to me, and fills me with joy; but the sight of the other inspires me with secret emotions of hatred and horror. To see myself the wife of the one is all my desire; and rather than belong to the other, I would lose my life. But I have sufficiently declared my real sentiments; and languished too long under this severe torture. He whom I love must use diligence to make him whom I hate lose all hope, and deliver me by a happy marriage, from a suffering more terrible than death.

SGAN. Yes, darling, I intend to gratify your wish.

ISA. It is the only way to make me happy.

SGAN. You shall soon be so.

ISA. I know it is a shame for a young woman, so openly to declare her love.

SGAN. No, no.

ISA. But, seeing what my lot is, such liberty must be allowed me; I can, without blushing, make so tender a confession to him whom I already regard as a husband.

SGAN. Yes, my poor child, darling of my soul!

ISA. Let him think, then, how to prove his passion for me.

SGAN. Yes, here, kiss my hand.

ISA. Let him, without more sighing, hasten a marriage which is all I desire, and accept the assurance which I give him, never to listen to the vows of another. (*She pretends to embrace Sganarelle, and gives her hand to Valère to kiss.*[19]

SGAN. Oh, oh, my little pretty face, my poor little darling, you shall not pine long, I promise you. (*To Valère*). There, say no more. You see I do not make her speak; it is me alone she loves.

VAL. Well, Madam, well, this is sufficient explanation. I learn by your words what you urge me to do; I shall soon know how to rid your presence of him who so greatly offends you.

ISA. You could not give me greater pleasure. For, to be brief, the sight of him is intolerable. It is odious to me, and I detest it so much . . .

SGAN. Eh! Eh!

ISA. Do I offend you by speaking thus? Do I . . .

SGAN. Heavens, by no means! I do not say that. But in truth, I pity his condition; you show your aversion too openly.

ISA. I cannot show it too much on such an occasion.

VAL. Yes, you shall be satisfied; in three days your eyes shall no longer see the object which is odious to you.

ISA. That is right. Farewell.

SGAN. (*To Valère*); I pity your misfortune, but . . .

VAL. No, you will hear no complaint from me. The

19 This stage play is imitated by Congreve in *The Old Bachelor*, (Act iv., Scene 22) when Mrs. Fondlewife goes and hangs upon her husband's neck and kisses him; whilst Bellmour kisses her hand behind Fondlewife's back.

lady assuredly does us both justice, and I shall endeavour to satisfy her wishes. Farewell.

SGAN. Poor fellow! his grief is excessive. Stay, embrace me: I am her second self. (*Embraces Valère.*

SCENE XV.—ISABELLA, SGANARELLE.

SGAN. I think he is greatly to be pitied.

ISA. Not at all.

SGAN. For the rest, your love touches me to the quick, little darling, and I mean it shall have its reward. Eight days are too long for your impatience; to-morrow I will marry you, and will not invite . . .

ISA. To-morrow!

SGAN. You modestly pretend to shrink from it; but I well know the joy these words afford you; you wish it were already over.

ISA. But . . .

SGAN. Let us get everything ready for this marriage.

ISA. (*Aside*). Heaven! Inspire me with a plan to put it off!

ACT III.

SCENE I.—ISABELLA, *alone.*

Yes, death seems to me a hundred times less dreadful than this fatal marriage into which I am forced; all that I am doing to escape its horrors should excuse me in the eyes of those who blame me. Time presses; it is night; now, then, let me fearlessly entrust my fate to a lover's fidelity.

SCENE II.—SGANARELLE, ISABELLA.

SGAN. (*Speaking to those inside the house*). Here I am once more; to-morrow they are going, in my name . . .

ISA. O Heaven!

SGAN. Is it you, darling? Where are you going so late? You said when I left you that, being rather tired, you would shut yourself up in your room; you even begged that on my return I would let you be quiet till to-morrow morning. . . .

ISA. It is true; but . . .

SGAN. But what?

ISA. You see I am confused; I do not know how to tell you the reason.

SGAN. Why, whatever can it be?

ISA. A wonderful secret! It is my sister who now compels me to go out, and who, for a purpose for which I have greatly blamed her, has borrowed my room, in which I have shut her up.

SGAN. What?

ISA. Could it be believed? She is in love with that suitor whom we have discarded.

SGAN. With Valère?

ISA. Desperately! Her passion is so great that I can compare it with nothing; you may judge of its violence by her coming here alone, at this hour, to confide to me her love, and to tell me positively that she will die if she does not obtain the object of her desire; that, for more than a year, a secret intercourse has kept up the ardour of their love; and that they had even pledged themselves to marry each other when their passion was new.

SGAN. Oh, the wretched girl!

ISA. That, being informed of the despair into which I had plunged the man whom she loves to see, she came to beg me to allow her to prevent a departure which would break her heart; to meet this lover to-night under my name, in the little street on which my room looks, where counterfeiting my voice, she may utter certain tender feelings, and thereby tempt him to stay; in short, cleverly to secure for herself the regard which it is known he has for me.

SGAN. And do you think this . . .

ISA. I? I am enraged at it. "What," said I, "sister, are you mad? Do you not blush to indulge in such a love for one of those people who change every day? To forget your sex, and betray the trust put in you by the man whom Heaven has destined you to marry?"

SGAN. He deserves it richly; I am delighted by it.

ISA. Finally my vexation employed a hundred arguments to reprove such baseness in her, and enable me to refuse her request for to-night; but she became so importunate, shed so many tears, heaved so many sighs, said so

THE SCHOOL FOR HUSBANDS.

Act III sc 2.

often that I was driving her to despair if I refused to gratify her passion, that my heart was brought to consent in spite of me; and, to justify this night's intrigue, to which affection for my own sister made me assent, I was about to bring Lucretia to sleep with me, whose virtues you extol to me daily; but you surprised me by your speedy return.

SGAN. No, no, I will not have all this mystery at my house. As for my brother, I might agree to it; but they may be seen by some one in the street, and she whom I am to honour with my body must not only be modest and well-born; she must not even be suspected. Let us send the miserable girl away, and let her passion . . .

ISA. Ah, you would overwhelm her with confusion, and she might justly complain of my want of discretion. Since I must not countenance her design, at least wait till I send her away.

SGAN. Well, do so.

ISA. But above all, conceal yourself, I beg of you, and be content to see her depart without speaking one word to her.

SGAN. Yes, for your sake I will restrain my anger; but as soon as she is gone, I will go and find my brother without delay. I shall be delighted to run and tell him of this business.

ISA. I entreat you, then, not to mention my name. Good night; for I shall shut myself in at the same time.

SGAN. Till to-morrow, dear . . . How impatient I am to see my brother, and tell him of his plight! The good man has been victimized, with all his bombast![20] I would not have this undone for twenty crowns!

ISA. (*Within*). Yes, sister, I am sorry to incur your displeasure; but what you wish me to do is impossible. My honour, which is dear to me, would run too great a risk. Farewell, go home before it is too late.

---

[20] The original has *phébus*, which is often used for a swollen and pretentious style, because it is said that a work on the chase, written in the fourteenth century by Gaston, Count of Foix, in such a style, was called *Miroir de Phébus*. It is more probable that the word *phébus*, meaning showy language, is derived from the Greek φοῖβος, brilliant.

SGAN. There she goes, fretting finely, I warrant. Let me lock the door, for fear she should return.

ISA. (*Going out disguised*). Heaven! abandon me not in my resolve!

SGAN. Whither can she be going? Let me follow her.

ISA. (*Aside*). Night, at least, favours me in my distress.

SGAN. (*Aside*). To the gallant's house! What is her design?

SCENE III.—VALÈRE, ISABELLA, SGANARELLE

VAL. (*Coming out quickly*) Yes, yes; I will this night make some effort to speak to . . . Who is there?

ISA. (*To Valère*). No noise, Valère; I have forestalled you; I am Isabella.

SGAN. (*Aside*). You lie, minx; it is not she. She is too staunch to those laws of honour which you forsake; you are falsely assuming her name and voice.

ISA. (*To Valère*). But unless by the holy bonds of matrimony . . .

VAL. Yes; that is my only purpose; and here I make you a solemn promise that to-morrow I will go wherever you please to be married to you.

SGAN. (*Aside*). Poor deluded fool!

VAL. Enter with confidence. I now defy the power of your duped Argus; before he can tear you from my love, this arm shall stab him to the heart a thousand times.

SCENE IV.—SGANARELLE, *alone*.

Oh, I can assure you I do not want to take from you a shameless girl, so blinded by her passion. I am not jealous of your promise to her; if I am to be believed, you shall be her husband. Yes, let us surprise him with this bold creature. The memory of her father, who was justly respected, and the great interest I take in her sister, demand that an attempt, at least, should be made to restore her honour. Hulloa, there! (*Knocks at the door of a magistrate*).[21]

SCENE V.—SGANARELLE, A MAGISTRATE, A NOTARY, ATTENDANT *with a lantern*.

MAG. What is it?

---

[21] See page 261, note 5.

SGAN. Your servant, your worship. Your presence in official garb is necessary here. Follow me, please, with your lantern-bearer.

MAG. We were going . . .

SGAN. This is a very pressing business.

MAG. What is it?

SGAN. To go into that house and surprise two persons who must be joined in lawful matrimony. It is a girl with whom I am connected, and whom, under promise of marriage, a certain Valère has seduced and got into his house. She comes of a noble and virtuous family, but . . .

MAG. If that is the business, it was well you met us, since we have a notary here.

SGAN. Sir?

NOT. Yes, a notary royal.

MAG. And what is more, an honourable man.

SGAN. No need to add that. Come to this doorway; make no noise, but see that no one escapes. You shall be fully satisfied for your trouble, but be sure and do not let yourself be bribed.

MAG. What! do you think that an officer of justice . .

SGAN. What I said was not meant as a reflection on your position. I will bring my brother here at once; only let the lantern-bearer accompany me. (*Aside*). I am going to give this placable man a treat. Hulloa! (*Knocks at Ariste's door*).

SCENE VI.—ARISTE, SGANARELLE.

AR. Who knocks? Why, what do you want, brother?

SGAN. Come, my fine teacher, my superannuated buck; I shall have something pretty to show you.

AR. How?

SGAN. I bring you good news.

AR. What is it?

SGAN. Where is your Léonor, pray?

AR. Why this question? She is, as I think, at a friend's house at a ball.

SGAN. Eh! Oh yes! Follow me; you shall see to what ball Missy is gone.

AR. What do you mean?

SGAN. You have brought her up very well indeed. It is not good to be always finding fault; the mind is captivated by much tenderness; and suspicious precautions, bolts, and bars, make neither wives nor maids virtuous; we cause them to do evil by so much austerity; their sex demands a little freedom. Of a verity she has taken her fill of it, the artful girl; and with her, virtue has grown very complaisant.

AR. What is the drift of such a speech?

SGAN. Bravo, my elder brother! it is what you richly deserve; I would not for twenty pistoles that you should have missed this fruit of your silly maxims. Look what our lessons have produced in these two sisters: the one avoids the gallants, the other runs after them.

AR. If you will not make your riddle clearer . . .

SGAN. The riddle is that her ball is at Valère's; that I saw her go to him under cover of night, and that she is at this moment in his arms.

AR. Who?

SGAN. Léonor.

AR. A truce to jokes, I beg of you.

SGAN. I joke . . . He is excellent with his joking! Poor fellow! I tell you, and tell you again, that Valère has your Léonor in his house, and that they had pledged each other before he dreamed of running after Isabella.

AR. This story is so very improbable . . .

SGAN. He will not believe it, even when he sees it. I am getting angry; upon my word, old age is not good for much when brains are wanting!

(*Laying his finger on his forehead.*

AR. What! brother, you mean to . . .

SGAN. I mean nothing, upon my soul! Only follow me. Your mind shall be satisfied directly. You shall see whether I am deceiving you, and whether they have not pledged their troth for more than a year past.

AR. Is it likely she could thus have agreed to this engagement without telling me?—me! who in everything, from her infancy, ever displayed towards her a complete readiness to please, and who a hundred times protested I would never force her inclinations.

SGAN. Well, your own eyes shall judge of the matter. I

have already brought here a magistrate and a notary. We are concerned that the promised marriage shall at once restore to her the honour she has lost; for I do not suppose you are so mean-spirited as to wish to marry her with this stain upon her, unless you have still some arguments to raise you above all kinds of ridicule.

AR. For my part, I shall never be so weak as wish to possess a heart in spite of itself. But, after all, I cannot believe . . .

SGAN. What speeches you make! Come, this might go on for ever.

SCENE VII.—SGANARELLE, ARISTE, A MAGISTRATE, A NOTARY.

MAG. There is no need to use any compulsion here, gentlemen. If you wish to have them married, your anger may be appeased on the spot. Both are equally inclined to it; Valère has already given under his hand a statement that he considers her who is now with him as his wife.

AR. The girl . . .

MAG. Is within, and will not come out, unless you consent to gratify their desires.

SCENE VIII.—VALÈRE, A MAGISTRATE, A NOTARY, SGANARELLE, ARISTE.

VAL. (*At the window of his house*). No, gentlemen; no man shall enter here until your pleasure be known to me. You know who I am; I have done my duty in signing the statement, which they can show you. If you intend to approve of the marriage, you must also put your names to this agreement; if not, prepare to take my life before you shall rob me of the object of my love.

SGAN. No, we have no notion of separating you from her. (*Aside*). He has not yet been undeceived in the matter of Isabella. Let us make the most of his mistake.

AR. (*To Valère*). But is it Léonor?

SGAN. Hold your tongue!

AR. But . . .

SGAN. Be quiet!

AR. I want to know . . .

SGAN. Again! Will you hold your tongue, I say?

VAL. To be brief: whatever be the consequence, Isabella has my solemn promise; I also have hers; if you consider everything, I am not so bad a match that you should blame her.

AR. What he says is not . . .

SGAN. Be quiet! I have a reason for it. You shall know the mystery. (*To Valère*). Yes, without any more words, we both consent that you shall be the husband of her who is at present in your house.

MAG. The contract is drawn up in those very terms, and there is a blank for the name, as we have not seen her. Sign. The lady can set you all at ease by-and-by.

VAL. I agree to the arrangement.

SGAN. And so do I, with all my heart. (*Aside*). We will have a good laugh presently. (*Aloud*). There, brother, sign; yours the honour to sign first.

AR. But why all this mystery . . .

SGAN. The deuce! what hesitation. Sign, you simpleton.

AR. He talks of Isabella, and you of Léonor.

SGAN. Are you not agreed, brother, if it be she, to leave them to their mutual promises?

AR. Doubtless.

SGAN. Sign, then; I shall do the same.

AR. So be it. I understand nothing about it.

SGAN. You shall be enlightened.

MAG. We will soon return.

(*Exeunt Magistrate and Notary into Valère's house*).

SGAN. (*To Ariste*). Now, then, I will give you a cue to this intrigue. (*They retire to the back of the stage*).

SCENE IX.—LÉONOR, SGANARELLE, ARISTE, LISETTE.

LÉO. Ah, what a strange martyrdom! What bores all those young fools appear to me! I have stolen away from the ball, on account of them.

LIS. Each of them tried to make himself agreeable to you.

LÉO. And I never endured anything more intolerable. I should prefer the simplest conversation to all the babblings[22] of these say-nothings. They fancy that everything must give way before their flaxen wigs, and think they have said the cleverest witticism when they come up, with their silly chaffing tone, and rally you stupidly about the love of an old man. For my part, I value more highly the affection of such an old man than all the giddy raptures of a youthful brain. But do I not see . . .

SGAN. (*To Ariste*). Yes, so the matter stands. (*Perceiving Léonor*). Ah, there she is, and her maid with her.

AR. Léonor, without being angry, I have reason to complain. You know whether I have ever sought to restrain you, and whether I have not stated a hundred times that I left you full liberty to gratify your own wishes; yet your heart, regardless of my approval, has pledged its faith, as well as its love, without my knowledge. I do not repent of my indulgence; but your conduct certainly annoys me; it is a way of acting which the tender friendship I have borne you does not merit.

LEO. I know not why you speak to me thus; but believe me, I am as I have ever been; nothing can alter my esteem for you; love for any other man would seem to me a crime; if you will satisfy my wishes, a holy bond shall unite us to-morrow.

AR. On what foundation, then, have you, brother . . .

SGAN. What! Did you not come out of Valère's house? Have you not been declaring your passion this very day? And have you not been for a year past in love with him?

LEO. Who has been painting such pretty pictures of me? Who has been at the trouble of inventing such falsehoods?

SCENE X.—ISABELLA, VALÈRE, LÉONOR, ARISTE, SGANARELLE, MAGISTRATE, NOTARY, LISETTE, ERGASTE.

ISA. Sister, I ask you generously to pardon me, if, by the freedom I have taken, I have brought some scandal upon your name. The urgent pressure of a great necessity, suggested to me, some time ago, this disgraceful

[22] The original has *contes bleus*, literally "blue stories," because old tales, such as *The Four Sons of Aymon*, *Fortunatus*, *Valentine and Orson* were formerly sold, printed on coarse paper and with blue paper cover; a kind of popular, but not political, "blue-books."

stratagem. Your example condemns such an escapade; but fortune treated us differently. (*To Sganarelle*). As for you, sir, I will not excuse myself to you. I serve you much more than I wrong you. Heaven did not design us for one another. As I found I was unworthy of your love, and undeserving of a heart like yours, I vastly preferred to see myself in another's hands.

VAL. (*To Sganarelle*). For me, I esteem it my greatest glory and happiness to receive her, sir, from your hands.

AR. Brother, you must take this matter quietly. Your own conduct is the cause of this. I can see it is your unhappy lot that no one will pity you, though they know you have been made a fool of.

LIS. Upon my word, I am glad of this. This reward of his mistrust is a striking retribution.

LEO. I do not know whether the trick ought to be commended; but I am quite sure that I, at least, cannot blame it.

ERG. His star condemns him to be a cuckold; it is lucky for him he is only a retrospective one.

SGAN. (*Recovering from the stupor into which he had been plunged*). No, I cannot get the better of my astonishment. This faithlessness perplexes my understanding. I think that Satan in person could be no worse than such a jade! I could have sworn it was not in her. Unhappy he who trusts a woman after this! The best of them are always full of mischief; they were made to damn the whole world. I renounce the treacherous sex for ever, and give them to the devil with all my heart!

ERG. Well said.

AR. Let us all go to my house. Come, M. Valère, tomorrow we will try to appease his wrath.

LIS. (*To the audience*). As for you, if you know any churlish husbands, by all means send them to school with us.[23]

---

[23] This is the last time Molière directly addressed the audience at the end of one of his plays; in *Sganarelle* he did it for the first time.

LES FÂCHEUX.

COMÉDIE.

THE BORES.

A COMEDY IN THREE ACTS.

(*THE ORIGINAL IN VERSE.*)

AUGUST 17TH, 1661.

INTRODUCTORY NOTICE.

The Bores is a character-comedy; but the peculiarities taken as the text of the play, instead of being confined to one or two of the leading personages, are exhibited in different forms by a succession of characters, introduced one after the other in rapid course, and disappearing after the brief performance of their rôles. We do not find an evolution of natural situations, proceeding from the harmonious conduct of two or three individuals, but rather a disjointed series of tableaux—little more than a collection of monologues strung together on a weak thread of explanatory comments, enunciated by an unwilling listener.

The method is less artistic, if not less natural; less productive of situations, if capable of greater variety of illustrations. The circumstances under which Molière undertook to compose the play explain his resort to the weaker manner of analysis. The Superintendent-General of finance,[1] Nicolas Fouquet, desiring to entertain the King, Queen, and court at his mansion of Vaux-le-Vicomte, asked for a comedy at the hands of the Palais-Royal company, who had discovered the secret of pleasing the Grand Monarque. Molière had but a fortnight's notice; and he was expected, moreover, to accommodate his muse to various prescribed styles of entertainment.

Fouquet wanted a cue for a dance by Beauchamp, for a picture by Lebrun, for stage devices by Torelli. Molière was equal to the emergency. Never, perhaps, was a literary work written to order so worthy of being preserved for future generations. Not only were the intermediate ballets made sufficiently elastic to give scope for the ingenuity of the poet's auxiliaries, but the written scenes themselves were admirably contrived to display all the varied talent of his troupe.

The success of the piece on its first representation, which took place on the 17th of August, 1661, was unequivocal; and the King summoned the author before him in order personally to express his satisfaction. It is related that, the Marquis de Soyecourt passing by at the time, the King said to Molière, "There is an original character which you have not yet copied." The suggestion was enough. The result was that, at the next

[1] In Sir James Stephen's *Lectures on the History of France*, vol. ii. page 22, I find: "Still further to centralize the fiscal economy of France, Philippe le Bel created a new ministry. At the head of it he placed an officer of high rank, entitled the Superintendent-General of Finance, and, in subordination to him, he appointed other officers designated as Treasurers."

representation, Dorante the hunter, a new bore, took his place in the comedy.

Louis XIV. thought he had discovered in Molière a convenient mouthpiece for his dislikes. The selfish king was no lover of the nobility, and was short-sighted enough not to perceive that the author's attacks on the nobles paved the way for doubts on the divine right of kings themselves. Hence he protected Molière, and entrusted to him the care of writing plays for his entertainments; the public did not, however, see *The Bores* until the 4th of November of the same year; and then it met with great success.

The bore is ubiquitous, on the stage as in everyday life. Horace painted him in his famous passage commencing *Ibam forte via Sacrâ*, and the French satirist, Regnier, has depicted him in his eighth satire.

Molière had no doubt seen the Italian farce, "*Le Case svaliggiate ovvera gli Interrompimenti di Pantalone*," which appears to have directly provided him with the thread of his comedy. This is the gist of it. A girl, courted by Pantaloon, gives him a rendezvous in order to escape from his importunities; whilst a cunning knave sends across his path a medley of persons to delay his approach, and cause him to break his appointment. This delay, however, is about the only point of resemblance between the Italian play and the French comedy.

There are some passages in Scarron's *Epîtres chagrines* addressed to the Marshal d'Albret and M. d'Elbène, from which our author must have derived a certain amount of inspiration; for in these epistles the writer reviews the whole tribe of bores, in coarse but vigorous language.

Molière dedicated *The Bores* to Louis XIV. in the following words:

SIRE,

I am adding one scene to the Comedy, and a man who dedicates a book is a species of Bore insupportable enough. Your Majesty is better acquainted with this than any person in the kingdom: and this is not the first time that you have been exposed to the fury of Epistles Dedicatory. But though I follow the example of others, and put myself in the rank of those I have ridiculed; I dare, however, assure Your Majesty, that what I have done in this case is not so much to present You a book, as to have the opportunity of returning You thanks for the success of this Comedy. I owe, Sire, that success, which exceeded my expectations, not only to the glorious approbation with which Your Majesty honoured this piece at first, and which attracted so powerfully that of all the world; but also to the order, which You gave me, to add a *Bore*, of which Yourself had the goodness to give me the idea, and which was proved by every one to be the finest part of the work.[2] I must confess, Sire, I never did any thing with such ease and readiness, as that part, where I had Your Majesty's commands to work.

The pleasure I had in obeying them, was to me more than *Apollo* and all the *Muses;* and by this I conceive what I should be able to execute in a complete Comedy, were I inspired by the same commands. Those who are born in an elevated rank, may propose to themselves the honour of serving Your Majesty in great Employments; but, for my part, all the glory I can aspire to, is to amuse You.[3]

---

[2] See Prefatory Memoir, page xxviii. ?

[3] In spite of all that has been said about Molière's passionate fondness for his profession, I imagine he must now and then have felt some slight, or suffered from some want of consideration. Hence perhaps the above sentence. Compare with this Shakespeare's hundred and eleventh sonnet:

> "Oh! for my sake, do you with Fortune chide
> The guilty goddess of my harmful deeds,
> That did not better for my life provide
> Than public means which public manners breeds.
> Thence comes it that my name receives a brand;
> And almost thence my nature is subdu'd
> To what it works in, like the dyer's hand."

The ambition of my wishes is confined to this; and I think that, to contribute any thing to the diversion of her King, is, in some respects, not to be useless to France. Should I not succeed in this, it shall never be through want of zeal, or study; but only through a hapless destiny, which often accompanies the best intentions, and which, to a certainty, would be a most sensible affliction to SIRE, *Your* MAJESTY'S *most humble, most obedient, and most faithful Servant,*

MOLIÈRE.

In the eighth volume of the "Select Comedies of M. de Molière, London, 1732," the play of *The Bores* is dedicated, under the name of *The Impertinents*, to the Right Honourable the Lord Carteret,[4] in the following words:

MY LORD,

It is by Custom grown into a sort of Privilege for Writers, of whatsoever Class, to attack Persons of Rank and Merit by these kind of Addresses. We conceive a certain Charm in Great and Favourite Names, which sooths our Reader, and prepossesses him in our Favour: We deem ourselves of Consequence, according to the Distinction of our Patron; and come in for our Share in the Reputation he bears in the World. Hence it is, MY LORD, that Persons of the greatest Worth are most expos'd to these Insults.

For however usual and convenient this may be to a Writer, it must be confess'd, MY LORD, it may be some degree of Persecution to a *Patron;* Dedicators, as *Molière* observes, being a Species of *Impertinents*, troublesome enough. Yet the Translator of this Piece hopes he may be rank'd among the more tolerable ones, in presuming to inscribe to Your LORDSHIP the *Facheux* of *Molière* done into *English;* assuring himself that Your LORDSHIP will not think any thing this Author has writ unworthy of your Patronage; nor discourage even a weaker Attempt to make him more generally read and understood.

Your LORDSHIP is well known, as an absolute Master, and generous Patron of Polite Letters; of those Works especially which discover a Moral, as well as Genius; and by a delicate Raillery laugh men out of their Follies and Vices: could the Translator, therefore, of this Piece come anything near the Original, it were assured of your Acceptance. He will not dare to arrogate any thing to himself on this Head, before so good a Judge as Your LORDSHIP: He hopes, however, it will appear that, where he seems too superstitious a Follower of his Author, 'twas not because he could not have taken more Latitude, and have given more Spirit; but to answer what he thinks the most essential part of a Translator, to lead the less knowing to the Letter; and after better Acquaintance, Genius will bring them to the Spirit.

The Translator knows your LORDSHIP, and Himself too well to attempt Your Character, even though he should think this a proper occasion: The Scholar—the Genius—the Statesman—the Patriot—the Man of Honour and Humanity.——Were a Piece finish'd from these Out-lines, the whole World would agree in giving it Your LORDSHIP.

But that requires a Hand——the Person, who presents This, thinks it sufficient to be indulg'd the Honour of subscribing himself

My LORD, *Your Lordship's most devoted, most obedient, humble servant,*

THE TRANSLATOR.

Thomas Shadwell, whom Dryden flagellates in his *Mac-Flecknoe*, and in the second part of *Absalom and Achitophel*, and whom Pope mentions in his *Dunciad*, wrote *The Sullen Lovers, or the Impertinents*, which was first performed in 1668 at the Duke of York's Theatre, by their Majesties' Servants. This play is a working up of *The Bores* and *The Misanthrope*, with two scenes from *The Forced Marriage*, and a reminiscence from *The Love-Tiff*. It is dedicated to the "Thrice Noble, High and Puissant

[4] John, Lord Carteret, born 22d April, 1690, twice Lord-Lieutenant of Ireland, was Secretary of State and head of the Ministry from February, 1742, until November 23, 1744, became Earl Granville that same year, on the death of his mother; was president of the Council in 1751, and died in 1763.

Prince William, Duke, Marquis, and Earl of Newcastle," because all Men, who pretend either to Sword or Pen, ought " to shelter themselves under Your Grace's Protection." Another reason Shadwell gives for this dedication is in order "to rescue this (play) from the bloody Hands of the Criticks, who will not dare to use it roughly, when they see Your Grace s Name in the beginning." He also states, that " the first Hint I received was from the Report of a Play of Molière's of three Acts, called *Les Fascheux*, upon which I wrote a great part of this before I read that." He borrowed, after reading it, the first scene in the second act, and Molière's story of Piquet, which he translated into Backgammon, and says. " that he who makes a common practice of stealing other men's wit, would if he could with the same safety, steal anything else." Shadwell mentions, however, nothing of borrowing from *The Misanthrope* and *The Forced Marriage*. The preface was, besides political difference, the chief cause of the quarrel between Shadwell and Dryden; for in it the former defends Ben Jonson against the latter, and mentions that—" I have known some ot late so insolent to say that Ben Jonson wrote his best playes without wit, imagining that all the wit playes consisted in bringing two persons upon the stage to break jest, and to bob one another, which they call repartie." The original edition of *The Sullen Lovers* is partly in blank verse; but, in the first collected edition of Shadwell's works, published by his son in 1720, it is printed in prose. Stanford, " a morose, melancholy man, tormented beyond measure with the impertinence of people, and resolved to leave the world to be quit of them," is a combination of Alceste in *The Misanthrope*, and Éraste in *The Bores;* Lovel, " an airy young gentleman, friend to Stanford, one that is pleased with, and laughs at, the impertinents; and that which is the other s torment, is his recreation," is Philinte of *The Misanthrope;* Emilia and Carolina appear to be Célimène and Eliante; whilst Lady Vaine is an exaggerated Arsinoé of the same play. Sir Positive At-all, "a foolish knight that pretends to understand everything in the world, and will suffer no man to understand anything in his Company, so foolishly positive that he will never be convinced of an error, though never so gross," is a very good character, and an epitome of all the Bores into one.

The prologue of *The Sullen Lovers* begins thus :—

" How popular are Poets now-a-days !
Who can more Men at their first summons raise,
Than many a wealthy home-bred Gentleman,
By all his Interest in his Country can.
They raise their Friends ; but in one Day arise
'Gainst one poor Poet all these Enemies."

PREFACE.

Never was any Dramatic performance so hurried as this; and it is a thing, I believe, quite new, to have a comedy planned, finished, got up, and played in a fortnight. I do not say this to boast of an *impromptu*, or to pretend to any reputation on that account: but only to prevent certain people, who might object that I have not introduced here all the species of Bores who are to be found. I know that the number of them is great, both at the Court and in the City, and that, without episodes, I might have composed a comedy of five acts and still have had matter to spare. But in the little time allowed me, it was impossible to execute any great design, or to study much the choice of my characters, or the disposition of my subject. I therefore confined myself to touching only upon a small number of Bores; and I took those which first presented themselves to my mind, and which I thought the best fitted for amusing the august personages before whom this play was to appear; and, to unite all these things together speedily, I made use of the first plot I could find. It is not, at present, my intention to examine whether the whole might not have been better, and whether all those who were diverted with it laughed according to rule. The time may come when I may print my remarks upon the pieces I have written: and I do not despair letting the world see that, like a grand author, I can quote Aristotle and Horace. In expectation of this examination, which perhaps may never take place, I leave the decision of this affair to the multitude, and I look upon it as equally difficult to oppose a work which the public approves, as it is to defend one which it condemns.

There is no one who does not know for what time of rejoicing the piece was composed; and that *fete* made so much noise, that it is not necessary to speak of it[5] but it will not be amiss to say a word or two of the ornaments which have been mixed with the Comedy.

The design was also to give a ballet; and as there was only a small number of first-rate dancers, it was necessary to separate the *entrées*[6] of this ballet, and to interpolate them with the Acts of the Play, so that these intervals might give time to the same dancers to appear in different dresses; also to avoid breaking the thread of the piece by these interludes, it was deemed advisable to weave the ballet in the best manner one could into the subject, and make but one thing of it and the play. But as the time was exceedingly short, and the whole was not entirely regulated by the same person, there may be found, perhaps, some parts of the ballet which do not enter so naturally into the play as others do. Be that as it may, this is a medley new upon our stage; although one might find some authorities in antiquity: but as every one thought it agreeable, it may serve as a specimen for other things which may be concerted more at leisure.

Immediately upon the curtain rising, one of the actors, whom you may suppose to be myself, appeared on the stage in an ordinary dress, and addressing himself to the King, with the look of a man surprised, made excuses in great disorder, for being there alone, and wanting both time and actors to give his Majesty the diversion he seemed to expect; at the same time in the midst of twenty natural cascades, a large shell was disclosed, which every one saw: and the agreeable Naiad who appeared in it, advanced to the front of the stage, and with an heroic air pronounced the following verses which Mr. Pellison had made, and which served as a Prologue.

---

[5] *The Bores*, according to the Preface, planned, finished, got up, and played in a fortnight, was acted amidst other festivities, first at Vaux, the seat of Monsieur Fouquet, Superintendent of Finances, the 17th of August, 1661, in the presence of the King and the whole Court, with the exception of the Queen. Three weeks later Fouquet was arrested, and finally condemned to be shut up in prison, where he died in 1672. It was not till November, 1661, that *The Bores* was played in Paris.

[6] See Prefatory Memoir, page xxx., note 12.

PROLOGUE.

(*The Theatre represents a garden adorned with Termini and several fountains. A Naiad coming out of the water in a shell.*)

Mortals, from Grots profound I visit you,
Gallia's great Monarch in these Scenes to view;
Shall Earth's wide Circuit, or the wider Seas,
Produce some Novel Sight your Prince to please;
Speak He, or wish: to him nought can be hard,
Whom as a living Miracle you all regard.
Fertile in Miracles, his Reign demands
Wonders at universal Nature's Hands,
Sage, young, victorious, valiant, and august,
Mild as severe, and powerful as he's just,
His Passions, and his Foes alike to foil,
And noblest Pleasures join to noblest Toil;
His righteous Projects ne'er to misapply,
Hear and see all, and act incessantly:
He who can this, can all; he needs but dare,
And Heaven in nothing will refuse his Prayer.
Let Lewis but command, these Bounds shall move,
And trees grow vocal as Dodona's Grove.
Ye Nymphs and Demi-Gods, whose Presence fills
Their sacred Trunks, come forth; so Lewis wills;
To please him be our task; I lead the way,

Quit now your ancient Forms but for a Day,
With borrow'd Shape cheat the Spectator's Eye,
And to Theatric Art yourselves apply.

(*Several Dryads, accompanied by Fawns and Satyrs, come forth out of the Trees and Termini.*)

Hence Royal Cares, hence anxious Application,
(His fav'rite Work) to bless a happy Nation:
His lofty Mind permit him to unbend,
And to a short Diversion condescend;
The Morn shall see him with redoubled Force,
Resume the Burthen and pursue his Course,
Give Force to Laws, his Royal Bounties share,
Wisely prevent our Wishes with his Care.
Contending Lands to Union firm dispose,
And lose his own to fix the World's Repose.
But now, let all conspire to ease the Pressure
Of Royalty, by elegance of Pleasure.
Impertinents, avant; nor come in sight,
Unless to give him more supreme Delight.[7]

(*The Naiad brings with her, for the Play, one part of the Persons she has summoned to appear, whilst the rest begin a Dance to the sound of Hautboys, accompanied by Violins.*

[7] The Naiad was represented by Madeleine Béjart, even then good-looking, though she was more than forty years old. The verses are taken from the eighth volume of the "Select Comedies of M. de Molière in French and English, London, 1732," and as fulsome as they well can be. The English translation, which is not mine, fairly represents the official nonsense of the original.

DRAMATIS PERSONÆ.

ERASTE, *in love with Orphise.*

DAMIS, *guardian to Orphise.*

ALCIDOR, LISANDRE, ALCANDRE, ALCIPPE,	*bores.*	DORANTE, CARITIDÈS, ORMIN, FILINTE,

LA MONTAGNE, *servant to Éraste.*

L'ÉPINE, *servant to Damis.*

LA RIVIÈRE *and* TWO COMRADES.

ORPHISE, *in love with Éraste.*

ORANTE, } *female bores.*
CLIMÈNE, }

Scene.—PARIS.

---

[8] Molière himself played probably the parts of Lisandre the dancer, Alcandre the duellist, or Alcippe the gambler, and perhaps all three, with some slight changes in the dress. He also acted Caritidès the pedant, and Dorante the lover of the chase. In the inventory taken after Molière's death we find: "A dress for the Marquis of the *Fâcheux*, consisting in a pair of breeches very large, and fastened below with ribbands, (*rhingrave*), made of common silk, blue and gold-coloured stripes, with plenty of flesh-coloured and yellow trimmings, with Colbertine, a doublet of Colbertine cloth trimmed with flame-coloured ribbands, silk stockings and garters." The dress of Caritidès in the same play, "cloak and breeches of cloth, with picked trimmings, and a slashed doublet." Dorante's dress was probably "a hunting-coat, sword and belt; the above-mentioned hunting-coat ornamented with fine silver lace, also a pair of stag-hunting gloves, and a pair of long stockings (*bas a botter*) of yellow cloth." The original inventory, given by M. Soulié, has *toile Colbertine*, for "Colbertine cloth." I found this word in Webster's Dictionary described from *The Fop's Dictionary of* 1690 as "A lace resembling net-work, the fabric of Mons. Colbert, superintendent of the French king's manufactures." In Congreve's *The Way of the World*, Lady Wishfort, quarrelling with her woman Foible (Act v., Scene 1], says to her, among other insults: "Go, hang out an old Frisoneer gorget, with a yard of yellow colberteen again!"

THE BORES.

(*LES FÂCHEUX.*)

ACT I.

SCENE I.—ÉRASTE, LA MONTAGNE.

ER. Good Heavens! under what star am I born, to be perpetually worried by bores? It seems that fate throws them in my way everywhere; each day I discover some new specimen. But there is nothing to equal my bore of to-day. I thought I should never get rid of him; a hundred times I cursed the harmless desire, which seized me at dinner time, to see the play, where, thinking to amuse myself, I unhappily was sorely punished for my sins. I must tell you how it happened, for I cannot yet think about it coolly. I was on the stage,[9] in a mood to listen to the piece which I had heard praised by so many. The actors began; everyone kept silence; when with a good deal of noise and in a ridiculous manner, a man with large rolls entered abruptly, crying out "Hulloa, there, a seat directly!" and, disturbing the audience with his uproar, interrupted the play in its finest passage. Heavens! will Frenchmen, altho' so often corrected, never behave themselves like men of common-sense? Must we, in a public theatre, show ourselves with our worst faults, and so confirm, by our foolish outbursts what our neighbours everywhere say of us? Thus I spoke; and whilst I was

---

[9] It was the custom for young men of fashion to seat themselves upon the stage (see Vol. I., Prefatory Memoir, page 26, note 7). They often crowded it to such an extent, that it was difficult for the actors to move. This custom was abolished only in 1759, when the Count de Lauraguais paid the comedians a considerable sum of money, on the condition of not allowing any stranger upon the stage.

shrugging my shoulders, the actors attempted to continue their parts. But the man made a fresh disturbance in seating himself, and again crossing the stage with long strides, although he might have been quite comfortable at the wings, he planted his chair full in front, and, defying the audience by his broad back, hid the actors from three-fourths of the pit. A murmur arose, at which anyone else would have felt ashamed; but he, firm and resolute, took no notice of it, and would have remained just as he had placed himself, if, to my misfortune, he had not cast his eyes on me. "Ah, Marquis!" he said, taking a seat near me, "how dost thou do? Let me embrace thee." Immediately my face was covered with blushes that people should see I was acquainted with such a giddy fellow. I was but slightly known to him for all that: but so it is with these men, who assume an acquaintance on nothing, whose embraces we are obliged to endure when we meet them, and who are so familiar with us as to thou and thee us. He began by asking me a hundred frivolous questions, raising his voice higher than the actors. Everyone was cursing him; and in order to check him I said, "I should like to listen to the play." "Hast thou not seen it, Marquis? Oh, on my soul, I think it very funny, and I am no fool in these matters. I know the canons of perfection, and Corneille reads to me all that he writes." Thereupon he gave me a summary of the piece, informing me scene after scene of what was about to happen; and when we came to any lines which he knew by heart, he recited them aloud before the actor could say them. It was in vain for me to resist; he continued his recitations, and towards the end rose a good while before the rest. For these fashionable fellows, in order to behave gallantly, especially avoid listening to the conclusion. I thanked Heaven, and naturally thought that, with the comedy, my misery was ended. But as though this were too good to be expected, my gentleman fastened on me again, recounted his exploits, his uncommon virtues, spoke of his horses, of his love-affairs, of his influence at court, and heartily offered me his services. I politely bowed my thanks, all the time devising some way of escape. But he, seeing me eager to depart, said, "Let us leave; everyone is gone." And when we were outside, he prevented my going away, by saying, "Marquis, let us go to the Cours [10] to show my carriage. It is very well built, and more than one Duke and Peer has ordered a similar one from my coach-maker." I thanked him, and the better to get off, told him that I was about to give a little entertainment. "Ah, on my life, I shall join it, as one of your friends, and give the go-by to the Marshal, to whom I was engaged." "My banquet," I said, "is too slight for gentlemen of your rank." "Nay," he replied, "I am a man of no ceremony, and I go simply to have a chat with thee; I vow, I am tired of grand entertainments." "But if you are expected, you will give offence, if you stay away." "Thou art joking, Marquis! We all know each other; I pass my time with thee much more pleasantly." I was chiding myself, sad and perplexed at heart at the unlucky result of my excuse, and knew not what to do next to get rid of such a mortal annoyance, when a splendidly built coach, crowded with footmen before and behind, stopped in front of us with a great clatter; from which leaped forth a young man gorgeously dressed; and my bore and he, hastening to embrace each other, surprised the passers-by with their furious encounter. Whilst both were plunged in these fits of civilities, I quietly made my exit without a word; not before I had long groaned under such a martyrdom, cursing this bore whose obstinate persistence kept me from the appointment which had been made with me here.

LA M. These annoyances are mingled with the pleasures of life. All goes not, sir, exactly as we wish it. Heaven wills that here below everyone should meet bores; without that, men would be too happy.

ER. But of all my bores the greatest is Damis, guardian of her whom I adore, who dashes every hope she raises, and has brought it to pass that she dares not see me in his presence. I fear I have already passed the hour agreed on; it is in this walk that Orphise promised to be.

---

[10] The *Cours* is that part of the Champs-Elysées called *le Cours-la-Reine;* because Maria de Medici, the wife of Henry IV., had trees planted there. As the theatre finished about seven o'clock in the evening, it was not too late to show a carriage.

LA M. The time of an appointment has generally some latitude, and is not limited to a second.

ER. True; but I tremble; my great passion makes out of nothing a crime against her whom I love.

LA M. If this perfect love, which you manifest so well, makes out of nothing a great crime against her whom you love; the pure flame which her heart feels for you on the other hand converts all your crimes into nothing.

ER. But, in good earnest, do you believe that I am loved by her?

LA M. What! do you still doubt a love that has been tried?

ER. Ah, it is with difficulty that a heart that truly loves has complete confidence in such a matter. It fears to flatter itself; and, amidst its various cares, what it most wishes is what it least believes. But let us endeavour to discover the delightful creature.

LA M. Sir, your necktie is loosened in front.

ER. No matter.

LA M. Let me adjust it, if you please.

ER. Ugh, you are choking me, blockhead; let it be as it is.

LA M. Let me just comb . . .

ER. Was there ever such stupidity! You have almost taken off my ear with a tooth of the comb.[11]

LA M. Your rolls . . .

ER. Leave them; you are too particular.

LA M. They are quite rumpled.

ER. I wish them to be so.

LA M. At least allow me, as a special favour, to brush your hat, which is covered with dust.

ER. Brush, then, since it must be so.

LA M. Will you wear it like that?

ER. Good Heavens, make haste!

LA M. It would be a shame.

ER. (*After waiting*). That is enough.

LA M. Have a little patience.

---

[11] The servants had always a comb about them to arrange the wigs of their masters, whilst the latter thought it fashionable to comb and arrange their hair in public (see *The Pretentious Young Ladies*).

ER. He will be the death of me !

LA M. Where could you get all this dirt?

ER. Do you intend to keep that hat forever?

LA M. It is finished.

ER. Give it me, then.

LA M. (*Letting the hat fall*). Ah !

ER. There it is on the ground. I am not much the better for all your brushing ! Plague take you !

LA M. Let me give it a couple of rubs to take off . . .

ER. You shall not. The deuce take every servant who dogs your heels, who wearies his master, and does nothing but annoy him by wanting to set himself up as indispensable !

SCENE II.—ORPHISE, ALCIDOR, ÉRASTE, LA MONTAGNE. (*Orphise passes at the foot of the stage; Alcidor holds her hand.*)

ER. But do I not see Orphise? Yes, it is she who comes. Whither goeth she so fast, and what man is that who holds her hand? (*He bows to her as she passes, and she turns her head another way*).

SCENE III.—ÉRASTE, LA MONTAGNE.

ER. What! She sees me here before her, and she passes by, pretending not to know me! What can I think? What do you say? Speak if you will.

LA M. Sir, I say nothing, lest I bore you.

ER. And so indeed you do, if you say nothing to me whilst I suffer such a cruel martyrdom. Give me some answer; I am quite dejected. What am I to think? Say, what do you think of it? Tell me your opinion.

LA M. Sir, I desire to hold my tongue, and not to set up for being indispensable.

ER. Hang the impertinent fellow! Go and follow them; see what becomes of them, and do not quit them.

LA M. (*Returning*). Shall I follow at a distance?

ER. Yes.

LA M. (*Returning*). Without their seeing me, or letting it appear that I was sent after them?

ER. No, you will do much better to let them know that you follow them by my express orders.

LA M. (*Returning*). Shall I find you here?

ER. Plague take you. I declare you are the biggest bore in the world!

SCENE IV.—ÉRASTE, *alone*.

Ah, how anxious I feel; how I wish I had missed this fatal appointment! I thought I should find everything favourable; and, instead of that, my heart is tortured.

SCENE V.—LISANDRE, ÉRASTE.

LIS. I recognized you under these trees from a distance, dear Marquis; and I came to you at once. As one of my friends, I must sing you a certain air which I have made for a little Couranto,[12] which pleases all the connoisseurs at court, and to which more than a score have already written words. I have wealth, birth, a tolerable employment, and am of some consequence in France; but I would not have failed, for all I am worth, to compose this air which I am going to let you hear. (*He tries his voice*). La, la; hum, hum; listen attentively, I beg. (*He sings an air of a Couranto*). Is it not fine?

ER. Ah!

LIS. This close is pretty. (*He sings the close over again four or five times successively*). How do you like it?

ER. Very fine, indeed.

LIS. The steps which I have arranged are no less pleasing, and the figure in particular is wonderfully graceful. (*He sings the words, talks, and dances at the same time; and makes Eraste perform the lady's steps*). Stay, the genman crosses thus; then the lady crosses again: together: then they separate, and the lady comes there. Do you observe that little touch of a faint? This fleuret?[13] These coupés[14] running after the fair one. Back to back: face to face, pressing up close to her. (*After finishing*). What do you think of it, Marquis?

ER. All those steps are fine.

---

[12] See Vol. I., page 164, note 14.

[13] A fleuret was an old step in dancing formed of two half coupées and two steps on the point of the toes.

[14] A coupé is a movement in dancing, when one leg is a little bent, and raised from the ground, and with the other a motion is made forward.

LIS. For my part, I would not give a fig for your ballet-masters.

ER. Evidently.

LIS. And the steps then?

ER. Are wonderful in every particular.

LIS. Shall I teach you them, for friendship's sake?

ER. To tell the truth, just now I am somewhat disturbed . . .

LIS. Well, then, it shall be when you please. If I had those new words about me, we would read them together, and see which were the prettiest.

ER. Another time.

LIS. Farewell. My dearest Baptiste[15] has not seen my Couranto; I am going to look for him. We always agree about the tunes; I shall ask him to score it.

(*Exit, still singing.*

SCENE VI.—ÉRASTE, *alone.*

Heavens! must we be compelled daily to endure a hundred fools, because they are men of rank, and must we, in our politeness, demean ourselves so often to applaud, when they annoy us?

SCENE VII.—ÉRASTE, LA MONTAGNE.

LA M. Sir, Orphise is alone, and is coming this way.

ER. Ah, I feel myself greatly disturbed! I still love the cruel fair one, and my reason bids me hate her.

LA M. Sir, your reason knows not what it would be at, nor yet what power a mistress has over a man's heart. Whatever just cause we may have to be angry with a fair lady, she can set many things to rights by a single word.

ER. Alas, I must confess it; the sight of her inspires me with respect instead of with anger.

SCENE VIII.—ORPHISE, ÉRASTE, LA MONTAGNE.

ORPH. Your countenance seems to me anything but cheerful. Can it be my presence, Éraste, which annoys

---

[15] Jean Baptiste Lulli had been appointed, in the month of May of 1661, the same year that *The Bores* was first played, *Surintendant et Compositeur de la musique de la chambre du Roi.*

you? What is the matter? What is amiss? What makes you heave those sighs at my appearance?

ER. Alas! can you ask me, cruel one, what makes me so sad, and what will kill me? Is it not malicious to feign ignorance of what you have done to me? The gentleman whose conversation made you pass me just now . . .

ORPH. (*Laughing*). Does that disturb you?

ER. Do, cruel one, anew insult my misfortune. Certainly, it ill becomes you to jeer at my grief, and, by outraging my feelings, ungrateful woman, to take advantage of my weakness for you.

ORPH. I really must laugh, and declare that you are very silly to trouble yourself thus. The man of whom you speak, far from being able to please me, is a bore of whom I have succeeded in ridding myself; one of those troublesome and officious fools who will not suffer a lady to be anywhere alone, but come up at once, with soft speech, offering you a hand against which one rebels. I pretended to be going away, in order to hide my intention, and he gave me his hand as far as my coach. I soon got rid of him in that way, and returned by another gate to come to you.

ER. Orphise, can I believe what you say? And is your heart really true to me?

ORPH. You are most kind to speak thus, when I justify myself against your frivolous complaints. I am still wonderfully simple, and my foolish kindness . . .

ER. Ah! too severe beauty, do not be angry. Being under your sway, I will implicitly believe whatever you are kind enough to tell me. Deceive your hapless lover if you will; I shall respect you to the last gasp. Abuse my love, refuse me yours, show me another lover triumphant; yes, I will endure everything for your divine charms. I shall die, but even then I will not complain.

ORPH. As such sentiments rule your heart, I shall know, on my side . . .

SCENE IX.—ALCANDRE, ORPHISE, ÉRASTE, LA MONTAGNE.

ALC. (*To Orphise*). Marquis, one word. Madame, I pray you to pardon me, if I am indiscreet in venturing, before you, to speak with him privately. (*Exit Orphise.*

SCENE X.—ALCANDRE, ÉRASTE, LA MONTAGNE.

ALC. I have a difficulty, Marquis, in making my request; but a fellow has just insulted me, and I earnestly wish, not to be behind-hand with him, that you would at once go and carry him a challenge from me. You know that in a like case I should joyfully repay you in the same coin.

ER. (*After a brief silence*). I have no desire to boast, but I was a soldier before I was a courtier. I served fourteen years, and I think I may fairly refrain from such a step with propriety, not fearing that the refusal of my sword can be imputed to cowardice. A duel puts one in an awkward light, and our King is not the mere shadow of a monarch. He knows how to make the highest in the state obey him, and I think that he acts like a wise Prince. When he needs my service, I have courage enough to perform it; but I have none to displease him. His commands are a supreme law to me; seek some one else to disobey him. I speak to you, Viscount, with entire frankness; in every other matter I am at your service. Farewell.[16]

SCENE XI.—ÉRASTE, LA MONTAGNE.

ER. To the deuce with these bores, fifty times over! Where, now, has my beloved gone to?

LA M. I know not.

ER. Go and search everywhere till you find her. I shall await you in this walk.

BALLET TO ACT I.

First Entry.

Players at Mall, crying out "Ware!" compel Éraste to draw back. After the players at Mall have finished, Éraste returns to wait for Orphise.

---

16 During his long reign, Louis XIV. tried to put a stop to duelling; and, though he did not wholly succeed, he prevented the seconds from participating in the fight,—a custom very general before his rule, and to which Éraste alludes in saying that he does not "fear that the refusal of his (my) sword can be imputed to cowardice."

Second Entry.

Inquisitive folk advance, turning round him to see who he is, and cause him again to retire for a little while.

ACT II.

SCENE I.—ÉRASTE, *alone.*

Are the bores gone at last? I think they rain here on every side. The more I flee from them, the more I light on them; and to add to my uneasiness, I cannot find her whom I wish to find. The thunder and rain have soon passed over, and have not dispersed the fashionable company. Would to Heaven that those gifts which it showered upon us, had driven away all the people who weary me! The sun sinks fast; I am surprised that my servant has not yet returned.

SCENE II.—ALCIPPE, ÉRASTE.

ALC. Good day to you.

ER. (*Aside*). How now! Is my passion always to be turned aside?

ALC. Console me, Marquis, in respect of a wonderful game of piquet which I lost yesterday to a certain Saint-Bouvain, to whom I could have given fifteen points and the deal. It was a desperate blow, which has been too much for me since yesterday, and would make me wish all players at the deuce; a blow, I assure you, enough to make me hang myself in public.—I wanted only two tricks, whilst the other wanted a piquet. I dealt, he takes six, and asks for another deal. I, having a little of everything, refuse. I had the ace of clubs (fancy my bad luck!) the ace, king, knave, ten and eight of hearts, and as I wanted to make the point, threw away king and queen of diamonds, ten and queen of spades. I had five hearts in hand, and took up the queen, which just made me a high sequence of five. But my gentleman, to my extreme surprise, lays down on the table a sequence of six low diamonds, together with the ace. I had thrown away king and queen of the same colour. But as he wanted a piquet, I got the better of my fear, and was confident at least of making two tricks. Besides the seven diamonds he had four spades, and playing the smallest of them, put me in the predicament of not knowing which of my two aces to keep. I threw away, rightly as I thought, the ace of hearts; but he had discarded four clubs, and I found myself made *Capot* by a six of hearts, unable, from sheer vexation, to say a single word.[17] By Heaven, account to me for this frightful piece of luck. Could it be credited, without having seen it?[18]

ER. It is in play that luck is mostly seen.

ALC. 'Sdeath, you shall judge for yourself if I am wrong, and if it is without cause that this accident enrages me. For here are our two hands, which I carry about me on purpose. Stay, here is my hand, as I told you; and here . . .

ER. I understood everything from your description, and admit that you have a good cause to be enraged. But I must leave you on certain business. Farewell. But take comfort in your misfortune.

ALC. Who; I? I shall always have that luck on my mind; it is worse than a thunderbolt to me. I mean to

---

[17] In the seventeenth century, piquet was not played with thirty-two, but with thirty-six, cards; the sixes, which are now thrown away, remained then in the pack. Every player received twelve cards, and twelve remained on the table. He who had to play first could throw away seven or eight cards, the dealer four or five, and both might take fresh ones from those that were on the table. A trick counted only when taken with one of the court-cards, or a ten.

Saint-Bouvain, after having taken up his cards, had in hand six small diamonds with the ace, which counted 7, a sequence of six diamonds from the six to the knave counted 16, thus together 23, before he began to play. With his seven diamonds he made seven tricks, but only counted 3, for those made by the ace, knave, and ten; this gave him 26. Besides his seven diamonds he had four spades, most likely the ace, king, knave, and a little one, and a six of hearts; though he made all the tricks he only counted 3, which gave him 29. But as Alcippe had not made a single trick, he was *capot*, which gave Saint-Bouvain 40; this with the 29 he made before, brought the total up to 69. As the latter only wanted a *piquet*, that is 60,—which is when a player makes thirty in a game, to which an additional thirty are then added, Saint-Bouvain won the game. Alcippe does not, however, state what other cards he had in his hand at the moment the play began besides the ace of clubs and a high sequence of five hearts, as well as the eight of the same colour.

[18] Compare with Molière's description of the game of piquet Pope's poetical history of the game of Ombre in the third Canto of *The Rape of the Lock.*

shew it to all the world. (*He retires and on the point of returning, says meditatively*) A six of hearts! two points.

ER. Where in the world are we? Go where we will, we see nothing but fools.

SCENE III.—ÉRASTE, LA MONTAGNE.

ER. Hah! how long you have been, and how you have made me suffer.

LA M. Sir, I could not make greater haste.

ER. But at length do you bring me some news?

LA M. Doubtless; and by express command, from her you love, I have something to tell you.

ER. What? Already my heart yearns for the message. Speak!

LA M. Do you wish to know what it is?

ER. Yes; speak quickly.

LA M. Sir, pray wait. I have almost run myself out of breath.

ER. Do you find any pleasure in keeping me in suspense?

LA M. Since you wish to know at once the orders which I have received from this charming person, I will tell you . . . Upon my word, without boasting of my zeal, I went a great way to find the lady; and if . . .

ER. Hang your digressions!

LA M. Fie! you should somewhat moderate your passion; and Seneca . . .

ER. Seneca is a fool in your mouth, since he tells me nothing of all that concerns me. Tell me your message at once.

LA M. To satisfy you, Orphise . . . An insect has got among your hair.

ER. Let it alone.

LA M. This lovely one sends you word . . .

ER. What?

LA M. Guess.

ER. Are you aware that I am in no laughing mood?

LA M. Her message is, that you are to remain in this place, that in a short time you shall see her here, when she has got rid of some country-ladies, who greatly bore all people at court.

THE BORES.

Act II sc 4.

Er. Let us, then stay in the place she has selected. But since this message affords me some leisure, let me muse a little. (*Exit La Montagne*). I propose to write for her some verses to an air which I know she likes.

(*He walks up and down the stage in a reverie.*

SCENE IV.—ORANTE, CLIMÈNE, ÉRASTE (*at the side of the stage, unseen.*)

Or. Everyone will be of my opinion.

Cl. Do you think you will carry your point by obstinacy?

Or. I think my reasons better than yours.

Cl. I wish some one could hear both.

Or. I see a gentleman here who is not ignorant; he will be able to judge of our dispute. Marquis, a word, I beg of you. Allow us to ask you to decide in a quarrel between us two; we had a discussion arising from our different opinions, as to what may distinguish the most perfect lovers.

Er. That is a question difficult to settle; you had best look for a more skilful judge.

Or. No: you speak to no purpose. Your wit is much commended; and we know you. We know that everyone, with justice, gives you the character of a . . .

Er. Oh, I beseech you . . .

Or. In a word, you shall be our umpire, and you must spare us a couple of minutes.

Cl. (*To Orante*). Now you are retaining one who must condemn you: for, to be brief, if what I venture to hold be true, this gentleman will give the victory to my arguments.

Er. (*Aside*). Would that I could get hold of any rascal to invent something to get me off!

Or. (*To Climène*). For my part, I am too much assured of his sense to fear that he will decide against me. (*To Eraste*). Well, this great contest which rages between us is to know whether a lover should be jealous.

Cl. Or, the better to explain my opinion and yours, which ought to please most, a jealous man or one that is not so?

Or. For my part, I am clearly for the last.

CL. As for me, I stand up for the first.

OR. I believe that our heart must declare for him who best displays his respect.

CL. And I that, if our sentiments are to be shewn, it ought to be for him who makes his love most apparent.

OR. Yes; but we perceive the ardour of a lover much better through respect than through jealousy.

CL. It is my opinion that he who is attached to us, loves us the more that he shows himself jealous?

OR. Fie, Climène, do not call lovers those men whose love is like hatred, and who, instead of showing their respect and their ardour, give themselves no thought save how to become wearisome; whose minds, being ever prompted by some gloomy passion, seek to make a crime out of the slightest actions, are too blind to believe them innocent, and demand an explanation for a glance; who, if we seem a little sad, at once complain that their presence is the cause of it, and when the least joy sparkles in our eyes, will have their rivals to be at the bottom of it; who, in short, assuming a right because they are greatly in love, never speak to us save to pick a quarrel, dare to forbid anyone to approach us, and become the tyrants of their very conquerors. As for me, I want lovers to be respectful; their submission is a sure proof of our sway.

CL. Fie, do not call those men true lovers who are never violent in their passion; those lukewarm gallants, whose tranquil hearts already think everything quite sure, have no fear of losing us, and overweeningly suffer their love to slumber day by day, are on good terms with their rivals, and leave a free field for their perseverance. So sedate a love incites my anger; to be without jealousy is to love coldly. I would that a lover, in order to prove his flame, should have his mind shaken by eternal suspicions, and, by sudden outbursts, show clearly the value he sets upon her to whose hand he aspires. Then his restlessness is applauded; and, if he sometimes treats us a little roughly, the pleasure of seeing him, penitent at our feet, to excuse himself for the outbreak of which he has been guilty, his tears, his despair at having been capable of displeasing us, are a charm to soothe all our anger.

OR. If much violence is necessary to please you, I know

who would satisfy you; I am acquainted with several men in Paris who love well enough to beat their fair ones openly.

CL. If to please you, there must never be jealousy, I know several men just suited to you; lovers of such enduring mood that they would see you in the arms of thirty people without being concerned about it.

OR. And now you must, by your sentence, declare whose love appears to you preferable.

(*Orphise appears at the back of the stage, and sees Eraste between Orante and Climène*).

ER. Since I cannot avoid giving judgment, I mean to satisfy you both at once; and, in order, not to blame that which is pleasing in your eyes, the jealous man loves more, but the other loves wisely.

CL. The judgment is very judicious; but . . .

ER. It is enough. I have finished. After what I have said permit me to leave you.

SCENE V.—ORPHISE, ÉRASTE.

ER. (*Seeing Orphise, and going to meet her*). How long you have been, Madam, and how I suffer . . .

ORPH. Nay, nay, do not leave such a pleasant conversation. You are wrong to blame me for having arrived too late. (*Pointing to Orante and Climène, who have just left*). You had wherewithal to get on without me.

ER. Will you be angry with me without reason, and reproach me with what I am made to suffer? Oh, I beseech you, stay . . .

ORPH. Leave me, I beg, and hasten to rejoin your company.

SCENE VI.—ÉRASTE, *alone*.

Heaven! must bores of both sexes conspire this day to frustrate my dearest wishes? But let me follow her in spite of her resistance, and make my innocence clear in her eyes.

SCENE VII.—DORANTE, ÉRASTE.

DOR. Ah, Marquis, continually we find tedious people interrupting the course of our pleasures! You see me enraged on account of a splendid hunt, which a booby . . . It is a story I must relate to you.

ER. I am looking for some one, and cannot stay.

DOR. (*Retaining him*). Egad, I shall tell it you as we go along. We were a well selected company who met yesterday to hunt a stag; on purpose we went to sleep on the ground itself—that is, my dear sir, far away in the forest. As the chase is my greatest pleasure, I wished, to do the thing well, to go to the wood myself; we decided to concentrate our efforts upon a stag which every one said was seven years old.[19] But my own opinion was—though I did not stop to observe the marks—that it was only a stag of the second year.[20] We had separated, as was necessary, into different parties, and were hastily breakfasting on some new-laid eggs, when a regular country-gentleman, with a long sword, proudly mounted on his brood-mare, which he honoured with the name of his good mare, came up to pay us an awkward compliment, presenting to us at the same time, to increase our vexation, a great booby of a son, as stupid as his father. He styled himself a great sportsman, and begged that he might have the pleasure of accompanying us. Heaven preserve every sensible sportsman, when hunting, from a fellow who carries a dog's horn, which sounds when it ought not; from those gentry who, followed by ten mangy dogs, call them "my pack," and play the part of wonderful hunters. His request granted, and his knowledge commended, we all of us started the deer,[21] within thrice the length of the leash, tally-ho! the dogs were put on the track of the stag. I encouraged them, and blew a loud blast. My stag emerged from the wood, and crossed a pretty wide plain, the dogs after him, but in such good order that you could have covered them all with one cloak. He made for the forest. Then we slipped the old pack upon him; I quickly brought out my sorrel-horse. You have seen him?

19 The original expression is *cerf dix-corps;* this, according to the *dictionnaire de chasse*, is a seven years' old animal.

20 The technical term is: "a knobbler;" in French, *un cerf à sa seconde tête.*

21 The original has *frapper à nos brisées; brisées* means "blinks." According to Dr. Ash's Dictionary, 1775, "Blinks are the boughs or branches thrown in the way of a deer to stop its course."

ER. I think not.

DOR. Not seen him? The animal is as good as he is beautiful; I bought him some days ago from Gaveau.[22] I leave you to think whether that dealer, who has such a respect for me, would deceive me in such a matter; I am satisfied with the horse. He never indeed sold a better, or a better-shaped one. The head of a barb, with a clear star; the neck of a swan, slender, and very straight; no more shoulder than a hare; short-jointed, and full of vivacity in his motion. Such feet—by Heaven! such feet! —double-haunched: to tell you the truth, it was I alone who found the way to break him in. Gaveau's Little John never mounted him without trembling, though he did his best to look unconcerned. A back that beats any horse's for breadth; and legs! O ye Heavens![23] In short, he is a marvel; believe me, I have refused a hundred pistoles for him, with one of the horses destined for the King to boot. I then mounted, and was in high spirits to see some of the hounds coursing over the plain to get the better of the deer. I pressed on, and found myself in a by-thicket at the heels of the dogs, with none else but Drécar.[24] There for an hour our stag was at bay. Upon this, I cheered on the dogs, and made a terrible row. In short, no hunter was ever more delighted! I alone started him again; and all was going on swimmingly, when a young stag joined ours. Some of my dogs left the others. Marquis, I saw them. as you may suppose, follow with hesitation, and Finaut was at a loss. But he suddenly turned, which delighted me very much, and drew the dogs the right way, whilst I sounded horn and hallooed, "Finaut! Finaut!" I again with pleasure discovered the track of the deer by a mole-hill, and blew away at my leisure. A few dogs ran back to me, when, as ill-luck would have it, the young stag came over to our country bumpkin. My blunderer began blowing like mad, and bellowed aloud, "Tallyho! tallyho! tallyho!" All my

---

[22] A well-known horse- dealer in Molière's time.

[23] Compare the description of the horse given by the Dauphin in Shakespeare's Henry V., Act iii., Scene 6, and also that of the "round hoof'd, short jointed" jennet in the *Venus and Adonis* of the same author.

[24] A famous huntsman in Molière's time.

dogs left me, and made for my booby. I hastened there, and found the track again on the highroad. But, my dear fellow, I had scarcely cast my eyes on the ground, when I discovered it was the other animal, and was very much annoyed at it. It was in vain to point out to the country fellow the difference between the print of my stag's hoof and his. He still maintained, like an ignorant sportsman, that this was the pack's stag; and by this disagreement he gave the dogs time to get a great way off. I was in a rage, and, heartily cursing the fellow, I spurred my horse up hill and down dale, and brushed through boughs as thick as my arm. I brought back my dogs to my first scent, who set off, to my great joy, in search of our stag, as though he were in full view. They started him again; but, did ever such an accident happen? To tell you the truth, Marquis, it floored me. Our stag, newly started, passed our bumpkin, who, thinking to show what an admirable sportsman he was, shot him just in the forehead with a horse-pistol that he had brought with him, and cried out to me from a distance, "Ah! I've brought the beast down!" Good Heavens! did any one ever hear of pistols in stag-hunting? As for me, when I came to the spot, I found the whole affair so odd, that I put spurs to my horse in a rage, and returned home at a gallop, without saying a single word to that ignorant fool.

ER. You could not have done better; your prudence was admirable. That is how we must get rid of bores. Farewell.

DOR. When you like, we will go somewhere where we need not dread country-hunters.

ER. (*Alone*). Very well. I think I shall lose patience in the end. Let me make all haste, and try to excuse myself.

BALLET TO ACT II.

First Entry.

Bowlers stop Éraste to measure a distance about which there is a dispute. He gets clear of them with difficulty, and leaves them to dance a measure, composed of all the postures usual to that game.

Second Entry.

Little boys with slings enter and interrupt them, who are in their turn driven out by

Third Entry.

Cobblers, men and women, their fathers, and others, who are also driven out in their turn.

Fourth Entry.

A gardener, who dances alone, and then retires.

ACT III.

SCENE I.—ÉRASTE, LA MONTAGNE.

ER. It is true that on the one hand my efforts have succeeded; the object of my love is at length appeased. But on the other hand I am wearied, and the cruel stars have persecuted my passion with double fury. Yes, Damis, her guardian, the worst of bores, is again hostile to my tenderest desires, has forbidden me to see his lovely niece, and wishes to provide her to-morrow with another husband. Yet Orphise, in spite of his refusal, deigns to grant me this evening a favour; I have prevailed upon the fair one to suffer me to see her in her own house, in private. Love prefers above all secret favours; it finds a pleasure in the obstacle which it masters; the slightest conversation with the beloved beauty becomes, when it is forbidden, a supreme favour. I am going to the rendezvous; it is almost the hour; since I wish to be there rather before than after my time.

LA M. Shall I follow you?

ER. No. I fear least you should make me known to certain suspicious persons.

LA M. But . . .

ER. I do not desire it.

LA M. I must obey you. But at least, if at a distance . . .

ER. For the twentieth time will you hold your tongue? And will you never give up this practice of perpetually making yourself a troublesome servant?

SCENE II.—CARITIDÈS; ÉRASTE.

CAR. Sir, it is an unseasonable time to do myself the honour of waiting upon you; morning would be more fit for performing such a duty, but it is not very easy to meet you, for you are always asleep, or in town. At least your servants so assure me. I have chosen this opportunity to see you. And yet this is a great happiness with which fortune favours me, for a couple of moments later I should have missed you.

ER. Sir, do you desire something of me?

CAR. I acquit myself, sir, of what I owe you; and come to you . . . Excuse the boldness which inspires me, if . . .

ER. Without so much ceremony, what have you to say to me?

CAR. As the rank, wit, and generosity which every one extols in you . . .

ER. Yes, I am very much extolled. Never mind that, sir.

CAR. Sir, it is a vast difficulty when a man has to introduce himself; we should always be presented to the great by people who commend us in words, whose voice, being listened to, delivers with authority what may cause our slender merit to be known. In short, I could have wished that some persons well-informed could have told you, sir, what I am . . .

ER. I see sufficiently, sir, what you are. Your manner of accosting me makes that clear.

CAR. Yes, I am a man of learning charmed by your worth; not one of those learned men whose name ends simply in *us*. Nothing is so common as a name with a Latin termination. Those we dress in Greek have a much superior look; and in order to have one ending in *ès*, I call myself Mr. Caritidès.

ER. Caritidès be it. What have you to say?

CAR. I wish, sir, to read you a petition, which I venture to beg of you to present to the King, as your position enables you to do.

ER. Why, sir, you can present it yourself! . . .

CAR. It is true that the King grants that supreme favour;

but, from the very excess of his rare kindness, so many villainous petitions, sir, are presented that they choke the good ones; the hope I entertain is that mine should be presented when his Majesty is alone.

ER. Well, you can do it, and choose your own time.

CAR. Ah, sir, the door-keepers are such terrible fellows! They treat men of learning like snobbs and butts; I can never get beyond the guard-room. The ill-treatment I am compelled to suffer would make me withdraw from court for ever, if I had not conceived the certain hope that you will be my Mecænas with the King. Yes, your influence is to me a certain means . . .

ER. Well, then, give it me; I will present it.

CAR. Here it is. But at least, hear it read.

ER. No . . .

CAR. That you may be acquainted with it, sir, I beg.

"TO THE KING.

"*Sire,—Your most humble, most obedient, most faithful and most learned subject and servant, Caritidès, a Frenchman by birth, a Greek*[25] *by profession, having considered the great and notable abuses which are perpetrated in the inscriptions on the signs of houses, shops, taverns, bowling-alleys, and other places in your good city of Paris; inasmuch as certain ignorant composers of the said inscriptions subvert, by a barbarous, pernicious and hateful spelling, every kind of sense and reason, without any regard for etymology, analogy, energy or allegory whatsoever, to the great scandal of the republic of letters, and of the French nation, which is degraded and dishonoured, by the said abuses and gross faults, in the eyes of strangers, and notably of the Germans, curious readers and inspectors of the said inscriptions* . . ."[26]

ER. This petition is very long, and may very likely weary . . .

---

[25] The original has *Grec*, a Greek. Can Caritidès have wished to allude to the *græca fides?* *Grec* means also a cheat at cards, and is said to owe its name to a certain Apoulos, a knight of Greek origin, who was caught in the very act of cheating at play in the latter days of Louis XIV.'s reign, even in the palace of the *grand monarque*.

[26] This is an allusion either to the reputation of the Germans as great drinkers, or as learned decipherers of all kinds of inscriptions.

CAR. Ah, sir, not a word could be cut out.

ER. Finish quickly.

CAR. (Continuing). "*Humbly petitions your Majesty to constitute, for the good of his state and the glory of his realm, an office of controller, supervisor, corrector, reviser and restorer in general of the said inscriptions; and with this office to honour your suppliant, as well in consideration of his rare and eminent erudition, as of the great and signal services which he has rendered to the state and to your Majesty, by making the anagram of your said Majesty in French, Latin, Greek, Hebrew, Syriac, Chaldean, Arabic* . . .

ER. (*Interrupting him*). Very good. Give it me quickly and retire: it shall be seen by the King; the thing is as good as done.

CAR. Alas! sir, to show my petition is everything. If the King but see it, I am sure of my point; for as his justice is great in all things, he will never be able to refuse my prayer. For the rest, to raise y ur fame to the skies, give me your name and surname in writing, and I will make a poem, in which the first letters of your name shall appear at both ends of the lines, and in each half measure.

ER. Yes, you shall have it to-morrow, Mr. Caritidès. (*Alone*). Upon my word, such learned men are perfect asses. Another time I should have heartily laughed at his folly.

SCENE III.—ORMIN, ÉRASTE.

ORM. Though a matter of great consequence brings me here, I wished that man to leave before speaking to you.

ER. Very well. But make haste; for I wish to be gone.

ORM. I almost fancy that the man who has just left you has vastly annoyed you, sir, by his visit. He is a troublesome old man whose mind is not quite right, and for whom I have always some excuse ready to get rid of him. On the Mall,[27] in the Luxembourg,[28] and in the Tuileries he

---

[27] The Mall was a promenade in Paris, shaded by trees, near the Arsenal.

[28] The Luxembourg was in Molière's time the most fashionable promenade of Paris.

wearies people with his fancies; men like you should avoid the conversation of all those good-for-nothing pedants. For my part I have no fear of troubling you, since I am come, sir, to make your fortune.

ER. (*Aside*). This is some alchymist: one of those creatures who have nothing, and are always promising you ever so much riches. (*Aloud*). Have you discovered that blessed stone, sir, which alone can enrich all the kings of the earth?

ORM. Aha! what a funny idea! Heaven forbid, sir, that I should be one of those fools. I do not foster idle dreams; I bring you here sound words of advice which I would communicate, through you, to the King, and which I always carry about me, sealed up. None of those silly plans and vain chimeras which are dinned in the ears of our superintendents;[29] none of your beggarly schemes which rise to no more than twenty or thirty millions; but one which, at the lowest reckoning, will give the King a round four hundred millions yearly, with ease, without risk or suspicion, without oppressing the nation in any way. In short, it is a scheme for an inconceivable profit, which will be found feasible at the first explanation. Yes, if only through you I can be encouraged . . .

ER. Well, we will talk of it. I am rather in a hurry.

ORM. If you will promise to keep it secret, I will unfold to you this important scheme.

ER. No, no; I do not wish to know your secret.

ORM. Sir, I believe you are too discreet to divulge it, and I wish to communicate it to you frankly, in two words. I must see that none can hear us. (*After seeing that no one is listening, he approaches Eraste's ear*). This marvellous plan, of which I am the inventor, is . . .

ER. A little farther off, sir, for a certain reason.

ORM. You know, without any need of my telling you, the great profit which the King yearly receives from his seaports. Well, the plan of which no one has yet thought, and which is an easy matter, is to make all the coasts of France into famous ports. This would amount to vast sums; and if . . .

---

[29] This is an allusion to the giver of the feast, Mons. Fouquet, *surintendant des finances*. See also page 299, note 1.

ER. The scheme is good, and will greatly please the King. Farewell. We shall see each other again.

ORM. At all events assist me, for you are the first to whom I have spoken of it.

ER. Yes, yes.

ORM. If you would lend me a couple of pistoles, you could repay yourself out of the profits of the scheme . . .

ER. (*Gives money to Ormin*). Gladly. (*Alone*). Would to Heaven, that at such a price I could get rid of all who trouble me! How ill-timed their visit is! At last I think I may go. Will any one else come to detain me?

SCENE IV.—FILINTE, ÉRASTE.

FIL. Marquis, I have just heard strange tidings.

ER. What?

FIL. That some one has just now quarrelled with you.

ER. With me?

FIL. What is the use of dissimulation? I know on good authority that you have been called out; and, as your friend, I come, at all events, to offer you my services against all mankind.

ER. I am obliged to you; but believe me you do me . . .

FIL. You will not admit it; but you are going out without attendants. Stay in town, or go into the country, you shall go nowhere without my accompanying you.

ER. (*Aside*). Oh, I shall go mad.

FIL. Where is the use of hiding from me?

ER. I swear to you, Marquis, that you have been deceived.

FIL. It is no use denying it.

ER. May Heaven smite me, if any dispute . . .

FIL. Do you think I believe you?

ER. Good Heaven, I tell you without concealment that . . .

FIL. Do not think me such a dupe and simpleton.

ER. Will you oblige me?

FIL. No.

ER. Leave me, I pray.

FIL. Nothing of the sort, Marquis.

ER. An assignation to-night at a certain place . . .

FIL. I do not quit you. Wherever it be, I mean to follow you.

ER. On my soul, since you mean me to have a quarrel, I agree to it, to satisfy your zeal. I shall be with you, who put me in a rage, and of whom I cannot get rid by fair means.

FIL. That is a sorry way of receiving the service of a friend. But as I do you so ill an office, farewell. Finish what you have on hand without me.

ER. You will be my friend when you leave me. (*Alone*). But see what misfortunes happen to me! They will have made me miss the hour appointed.

SCENE V.—DAMIS, L'ÉPINE, ÉRASTE, LA RIVIÈRE, *and his Companions*.

DAM. (*Aside*). What! the rascal hopes to obtain her in spite of me! Ah! my just wrath shall know how to prevent him!

ER. (*Aside*). I see some one there at Orphise's door. What! must there always be some obstacle to the passion she sanctions!

DAM. (*To L'Epine*). Yes, I have discovered that my niece, in spite of my care, is to receive Éraste in her room to-night, alone.

LA R. (*To his companions*). What do I hear those people saying of our master? Let us approach softly, without betraying ourselves.

DAM. (*To L'Epine*). But before he has a chance of accomplishing his design, we must pierce his treacherous heart with a thousand blows. Go and fetch those whom I mentioned just now, and place them in ambush where I told you, so that at the name of Éraste they may be ready to avenge my honour, which his passion has the presumption to outrage; to break off the assignation which brings him here, and quench his guilty flame in his blood.

LA R. (*Attacking Damis with his companions*). Before your fury can destroy him, wretch! you shall have to deal with us!

ER. Though he would have killed me, honour urges me here to rescue the uncle of my mistress. (*To Damis*).

I am on your side, Sir. (*He draws his sword and attacks La Rivière and his companions, whom he puts to flight.*)

DAM. Heavens! By whose aid do I find myself saved from a certain death? To whom am I indebted for so rare a service?

ER. (*Returning*). In serving you, I have done but an act of justice.

DAM. Heavens. Can I believe my ears! Is this the hand of Éraste?

ER. Yes, yes, Sir, it is I. Too happy that my hand has rescued you: too unhappy in having deserved your hatred.

DAM. What! Éraste, whom I was resolved to have assassinated has just used his sword to defend me! Oh, this is too much; my heart is compelled to yield; whatever your love may have meditated to-night, this remarkable display of generosity ought to stifle all animosity. I blush for my crime, and blame my prejudice. My hatred has too long done you injustice! To show you openly I no longer entertain it, I unite you this very night to your love.

SCENE VI.—ORPHISE, DAMIS, ÉRASTE.

ORPH. (*Entering with a silver candlestick in her hand*). Sir, what has happened that such a terrible disturbance . . .

DAM. Niece, nothing but what is very agreeable, since, after having blamed, for a long time, your love for Éraste, I now give him to you for a husband. His arm has warded off the deadly thrust aimed at me; I desire that your hand reward him.

ORPH. I owe everything to you; if, therefore, it is to pay him your debt, I consent, as he has saved your life.

ER. My heart is so overwhelmed by this great miracle, that amidst this ecstasy, I doubt if I am awake.

DAM. Let us celebrate the happy lot that awaits you; and let our violins put us in a joyful mood. (*As the violins strike up, there is a knock at the door*).

ER. Who knocks so loud?

SCENE VII.—DAMIS, ORPHISE, ÉRASTE, L'ÉPINE.

L'EP. Sir, here are masks, with kits and tabors.

(*The masks enter, filling the stage*).

ER. What! Bores for ever? Hulloa, guards, here. Turn out these rascals for me.

BALLET TO ACT III.

First Entry.

Swiss guards, with halberds,[30] drive out all the troublesome masks, and then retire to make room for a dance of

Second Entry.

Four shepherds and a shepherdess, who, in the opinion of all who saw it, concluded the entertainment with much grace.

---

[30] The origin of the introduction of the Swiss Guards (mercenaries) in the service of the French and other foreign powers may be ascribed to the fact that Switzerland itself, being too poor to maintain soldiers in time of peace, allowed them to serve other nations on condition of coming back immediately to their own cantons in time of war or invasion.

It is particularly with France that Switzerland contracted treaties to furnish certain contingents in case of need. The first of these dates back as far as 1444 between the Dauphin, afterwards Charles VII., and the different cantons. This Act was renewed in 1453, and the number of soldiers to be furnished was fixed once for all, the minimum being 6,000, and the maximum 16,000. The Helvetians, who until 1515 had always been faithful to their engagements, turned traitors in that year against Francis I., who defeated them at Marignan. But the good feeling was soon afterwards re-established, and a new treaty, almost similar to the former, restored the harmony between the two nations.

Another document is extant, signed at Baden in 1553, by which the cantons bind themselves to furnish Henry II. with as many troops as he may want. It is particularly remarkable, inasmuch as it served as a basis for all subsequent ones until 1671. These conventions have not always been faithfully carried out, for the Swiss contracted engagements with other nations, notably with Spain, Naples, and Sardinia, and even with Portugal. At the commencement of the campaign of 1697, Louis XIV. had, notwithstanding all this, as many as 32,000 Swiss in his service, the highest number ever attained. The regulations for the foreign colonels and captains in their relations among themselves, and with the French Government, were not unlike those in force at present for the native soldiery in our Indian possessions. Towards the end of Louis XIV.'s reign the number decreased to 14,400, officers included; it rose in 1773 to 19,836, and during the wars of 1742–48, to 21,300. The ebb and flow of their numbers continued from that time until the Revolution of 1830, when they were finally abolished.

They received a much higher pay than the national troops, and had besides this many other advantages, one of them being that the officers had in the army the next grade higher than that which they occupied in their own regiments; for instance, the colonel of a Swiss regiment had the rank of a major-general, and retired on the pay of a lieutenant-general, &c. They enjoyed the same privileges, with some slight modifications, wherever they served elsewhere.

L'ÉCOLE DES FEMMES.

COMÉDIE.

THE SCHOOL FOR WIVES.

A COMEDY IN FIVE ACTS.

(*THE ORIGINAL IN VERSE.*)

DECEMBER 26TH, 1662.

INTRODUCTORY NOTICE.

The School for Wives, played for the first time in the theatre of the Palais-Royal, on the 26th of Dec. 1662, was the complement of *The School for Husbands*, which it succeeded at an interval of eighteen months, *The Bores* intervening. The one no doubt suggested the other. The central situations of the two have much in common: the arbitrary and jealous lover, to whom circumstances have given almost the authority of a husband; the simple ward, rescued from physical constraint by the unfettered cunning of love. In fact, there is not that contrast of character between the two plays, which the antithesis of their titles might lead us to expect. The text is not altered; we have merely another reading of the same text. Arnolphe is a more refined and rational Sganarelle; and if his fault is the same, and his catastrophe similar, we do not despise him and rejoice in his misfortune, as we were compelled to do with the tyrant of Isabella. His selfishness is, perhaps, equally great, but its exhibition does not render him so odious.

The reason of this is to be found in the display of his many eccentricities, his system of education, his cunning, his choice of foolish servants, his absurd whimsicalities, his pedantry, and, above all his perpetual restlessness. He hardly ever leaves the stage during the whole of the five acts of the play: he goes away, appears again, moves about, plots, scolds, loses his temper, recovers it, dogmatizes, entreats, and, after all, is punished by his very faults. His servants are more stupid than he wishes them to be, his ward more simple than he thought her; he has jeered at husbands who are deceived, and he himself is victimized; he wanted to abuse the confidence Horace placed in him, and becomes himself a dupe; he intended to sacrifice Agnès to his own happiness, and, at the end, becomes "The most unfortunate of mankind."

The troubles of Sganarelle and Arnolphe are the troubles of jealous husbands in every age, and it would be idle to heap up instances in the predecessors of Molière which may have contributed to form his conceptions. One of those that come nearest to the type before us is the story about a gentle knight of Hainault, in the forty-first of the *Nouvelles nouvelles du Roi Louis XI.*, reproduced by Scarron in his *Nouvelles tragi-comiques.*

Still more suggestive is Scarron's *la Précaution inutile*, partly based upon *The Jealous Man of Estremadura*, by Cervantes, in which there are several situations to which we must consider Molière to have been indebted for his first and second acts. The ingenuous self-confidence of Arnolphe, quaintly contrasting with his recurrent jealousies, finds an antetype in many an ancient Italian story. Straparola's fourth night of the *Piacevoli Notte* (*Agreeable Nights*) has suggested some hints for the third and fourth acts; the fifth is wholly original. Molière's own history also furnished him with his subject. We already mentioned in the Introductory Notice to *The School for Husbands* the supposed connection between Ariste and the author; the latter was now married, and did not find in marriage the happiness he hoped for. Without wishing to attribute to him all the ridiculous absurdities of Arnolphe, or to suppose that his wife was another Agnès, still we imagine that though he had scarcely been married a year, he felt already the necessity of watching over, and if possible, of guiding the steps of his youthful spouse. It seems to us that in many of the sayings of Arnolphe, there is to be found a feeling of bitterness and passion, rather out of place in the mouth of such a ridiculous personage, but which give clear indications of what was even then passing in the mind of our author. The words which Arnolphe uses when kneeling at the feet of Agnès show what tempestuous passions must have possessed Molière; and though it is often dangerous to identify a poet with his creation, still there must be always some part, however small, of the individuality of the originator in the character he produces.

As regards Agnès, whose name is the type of a simple, artless girl, her character develops as the plot of the comedy rolls on. In the first scene, she is an uneducated, ingenuous maiden; but she gradually changes under the influence of love, and becomes earnest, intelligent, and even logical.

This comedy was fiercely attacked by several, who accused it of being wanting in good taste, sound morality, rules of grammar, and, what was more dangerous, of undermining the principles of religion. The second scene of the third act, in which mention is made of "boiling cauldrons," of a soul as "white and spotless as a lily," but "as black as coal," when at fault; of "The Maxims of Marriage or the Duties of a Wife, together with her daily exercise," gave great offence, and were said to be like the phrases of the catechism or the confessional. A former patron of Molière, the Prince of Conti, who had become a mere devotee, wrote against it in his *Traité de la Comédie et des Spectacles*, and in later times, even such men as Fénelon, Jean Jacques Rousseau, and Geoffroy, a critic of the beginning of this century, have found much to blame in this comedy, whilst several literary men, Hazlitt amongst the English, and Honoré de Balzac amongst the French, consider this play as Molière's masterpiece.

This play was dedicated by Molière to the Duchess of Orleans,[1] in the following words:

MADAM,

I am the most perplexed man in the world when I have to dedicate a book, and I am so little cut out for the style of a dedication, that I do not know how to get through this. Another, in my place, would soon think of a hundred fine things to say of your ROYAL HIGHNESS, upon this title of *The School for Wives*, and upon the offering he made to you of it. But for my part, MADAM, I confess my weakness. I have not the talent of finding any relation between things which have so little con-

---

[1] Henrietta of England, daughter of Charles I., first wife of Monsieur, brother of Louis XIV., died at Saint Cloud, the 30th of June, 1670, twenty-six years old. Her funeral sermon, preached by Bossuet, remains a perennial monument of pulpit eloquence.

nection; whatever information my brother-authors every day give me in such cases, I do not see what your ROYAL HIGHNESS can have to do with the comedy I present to you.

Nobody indeed can be at a loss how to praise you. The matter, Madam, is but too obvious, and in whatever way we behold you, we meet with glory upon glory, and perfection upon perfection. You possess, MADAM, the perfection of rank and birth, which makes you respected by all the world. You possess the perfection of charms, both of the mind and body, which makes you admired by all who see you. You possess the perfection of soul, which, if any one dare to say so, makes you beloved by all who have the honour to come near you: I mean that charming gentleness, with which you temper the stateliness of the great titles you bear; that obliging goodness, that generous affability, which you shew to every body: and particularly these last, upon which I find plainly I one day shall not be able to be silent. But once more, Madam, I am ignorant of the manner how to bring in here such shining truths; and these are things, in my opinion, both of too vast an extent, and of too high a merit to be included in a dedication, and mixed with trifles. All things considered, Madam, I do not see what else I can do, beyond dedicating my comedy to you; and assuring you, with all possible respect, that I am, MADAM,

Your Royal Highness' most Humble, most Obedient, and most Obliged Servant,

MOLIÈRE.

Wycherley, in his *Country Wife*, acted probably in 1672 or 1673 and of which the subject is so indecent that it cannot even be mentioned at the present time, has borrowed from Molière's *School for Wives* the character of Agnès, whom he calls Mrs. Pinchwife; he has also partly imitated Arnolphe as Mr. Pinchwife, and followed the plot of the French play in all the scenes where those two characters are mentioned, and in some where Alithea and Horner appear. Voltaire, in his Essay on English Comedy, says of *The Country Wife*: "This piece, I admit is not a school for good morals and manners, but it is really a school for wit and sound *vis comica*." Garrick, in his *Country Girl*, acted in 1776, tried to make Wycherley's play more fit to appear on the English stage, but with little success. It is true he changed Mrs. Pinchwife into Miss Peggy: but he also destroyed the vigour of the original, and introduced some alterations in the ending taken chiefly from the last act of Molière's *School for Husbands*. Another alteration of Wycherley's play was a farce, in two acts, called *The Country Wife*, written by an actor, John Lee, and performed at Drury Lane in 1765, for his benefit. But deservedly it met with no success.

John Caryl, probably a Sussex man, and of the Roman Catholic persuasion, was secretary to Queen Mary, the wife of James the Second, and one who followed the fortunes of his abdicated master. For his attachment to this king he was rewarded by him, first, with the honour of knighthood, and afterwards with the honorary titles of Earl Caryl, Baron Dartford. How long he continued in the service of James is unknown; but he was in England in the reign of Queen Anne, and recommended the subject of Mr. Pope's *Rape of the Lock* to that author, who, on its publication addressed it to him. He was alive in 1717, and at that time must have been a very old man.[2] He wrote also a tragedy, *The English Princess, or the Death of Richard the Third*, 1667, and, a comedy, *Sir Salomon, or the Cautious Coxcomb*, which was not printed till 1671, but was certainly acted in the season of 1669-1670 at the latest. In May 1670, the king and the court being at Dover, they were extremely pleased with the performance of *Sir Salomon;* and as the French court at that time wore very short laced coats, the actor, Nokes, had one made still shorter, in which he acted Sir Arthur Addell; "the Duke of Monmouth

2 Baker's "Biographica Dramatica," 1812, vol. i., p. 91.

gave him his sword and belt from his side, and buckled it on himself, on purpose that he might ape the French,—his appearance was so ridiculous, that at his first entrance he put the King and Court in an excessive laughter; and the French were much chagrined to see themselves aped by such a buffoon as Sir Arthur."[3] All dramatic biographies are agreed that Caryl took his plot from Molière's *School for Wives*. We think that though several of the scenes are imitated from Molière, the plot in *Sir Salomon* is far more intricate. In the English play, old Sir Salomon Single, and in the French Arnolphe, bring up in strict seclusion a young girl, whom they afterwards intend to marry, and in both plays the old men are made the confidants of th: lovers, who afterwards really marry the innocent maidens; but in *The School for Wives* the characters of young Single, Mr. Barter, an Indy merchant, that of Timothy, the steward, Mr. Wary, and Mrs. Julia, are wanting, whilst no counterpart of either Chrysalde or Enrique from *The School for Wives* is to be found in *Sir Salomon*. Another personage not in the French comedy is Sir Arthur Addell, who is very well drawn; his way of wooing is at least original, and so are the following four lines with which he ends the first act:

"As sure, as Chick in Pouche, or . . . in Bosome
My flames are raging; and who dares oppose 'em?
They soon shall thaw her Heart, though ne'er so Icy;
Like Julius Caesar, *veni, vidi, vici.*"

The author, however, who ought to be the best judge of the sources from which he borrowed his play, admits his thefts in the epilogue to *Sir Salomon*,—an epilogue which we give below, and of which some of the points are not lost even at the present day.

Since stealing's grown a pretty thriving Trade,
Which many Rich, but few has guilty made:
To needy Poets why should you deny
The Privilege to steal, as well as lie?
Their Theft (alas) swells not the Nation's Debt,
Nor makes Wine dear, nor will Land-taxe beget.
Money they always wanted; Now they grow
No less in Fancy, than in Fortune, low;
And are compelled to rook, as Gamesters are,
That can hold out no longer on the square.
Faith, be good natur'd to this hungry Crew,
Who what they filch abroad, bring home to you.
But still exclude those men from all Relief,
Who steal themselves, yet boldly cry, Stop Thief:
Life taking Judges, these without remorse
Condemn all petty Thefts, and practice worse;
As if they robb'd by Patent, and alone
Had right to call each Foreign play their own.
What we have brought before you, was not meant
For a new Play, but a new Precedent;
For we with Modesty our theft avow,
(There is some conscience shown in stealing too)
And openly declare that if our Cheer
Does hit your Palates, you must thank Molière:
Molière, the famous Shakespeare of this Age,
Both when he writes, and when he treads the Stage.
I hope this Stranger's Praise gives no pretence
To charge us with a National Offence:
Since, were it in my power, I would advance
French Wit in England, English Arms in France.

[3] Geneste, 'Some Account of the English Stage," 10 vols., 1832, vol. i., p. 107.

Mrs. Cowley composed, with Caryl's *Sir Salomon* and Molière's *School for Wives* a comedy called *More Ways than One*, produced at Covent Garden Theatre in 1783, in which the only novelty appears to be the character of a rascally doctor, called Barkwell, and a lover, Bellair, who pretends to be dying in order to be near the object of his affection. Arabella, the Agnès of the French play; whilst the part of Sir Maxwell Mushroom is borrowed from Sir Positive in Shadwell's *Sullen Lovers*. The only thing remarkable in this comedy is the high-flown language of the dedication to the author's husband in India, of which we give the beginning—

Hence! Comic Scenes, to where rich Ganges laves
Hindostan's Golden shores with hallowed waves,
Where Palms gigantic rear their tufted heads,
And all colossal vegetation spreads,
Where rich Ananas court the Indian's eye,
And Groves of Citrons fan the feverish sky,
Where rattling Canes along the rivulets play,
And the Centennial Aloe conquers day,
In their deep Shades bid Lucidorus' smile
His heavy sense of distant hours beguile.

A collected edition of the works of Mrs. Cowley was published in 1813, in three volumes, with a preface, which is really a model of the longest and most Latinized words in the English language, with the smallest possible amount of sense.

Edward Ravenscroft (see Introductory Notice to the *Pretentious Young Ladies*), has, in *London Cuckolds*, acted at the Duke's Theatre, 1682, partly imitated *The School for Wives*, and given Arnolphe the name of Wiseacre, and Agnès that of Peggy; but the whole play is so filthy that nothing can be quoted from it. Until 1754 it was frequently represented on Lord Mayor's day, in contempt, as it were, of the City.

Isaac Bickerstaffe wrote *Love in the City* a comic opera, which was acted at Covent Garden in 1767, but did not meet with much success. The character of Priscilla, an unmanageable Creole girl, is partly taken from Agnès, and that of Barnacle from Chrysalde,—both from *The School for Wives*. Priscilla persuades her lover, young Walter Cockney, that her "love for the captain . . . . . was only a sham," and that if she "can manage it she will go off with him to Scotland to-night, where they say folks may be married in spite of anyone.' The characters of Wagg, the attorney, who disguises himself first as a Colonel, and afterwards as Captain Delany from "the county of Mayo," and of Spruce, who appears as a Lord, are partly borrowed from *The Pretentious Young Ladies*. The arguments of Wagg in Act iii., Scene 2, seem to owe their origin to Gros-René's speech in *Sganarelle or the Self-Deceived Husband*, whilst the whole scene appears to be taken from the sixth scene of the second act of Molière's *School for Wives*. This play, with the characters of Wagg, Spruce, and Miss Molly Cockney omitted, and cut down to two acts, was brought out as *The Romp*, and met with great success.

PREFACE.

A great many people at first hissed this comedy, but the laughers were for it, and all the ill that was said of it could not hinder its having a success with which I am very well satisfied. I know it is expected from me that I should give some preface in answer to the critics, and in justification of my work. Doubtless I am sufficiently indebted to all those who have given it their approbation, to think myself obliged to defend their judgment against that of others; but a great many of the things I should say on that head are already in a dissertation, which I have written in the form of a dialogue, with which as yet I do not know what I shall do. The idea of this dialogue, or, if you like it better, of this little comedy,[4] came into my head after the first two or three representations of my play. I mentioned this idea one evening at a house where I visited; and immediately a person of quality, whose wit is sufficiently known to the world,[5] and who does me the honour to call me his friend, liked the thought of it so well, that he not only begged me to put my hand to it, but likewise to put his own; and I was amazed that two days afterwards he

[4] This was *The School for Wives criticised*, played the 1st of June, 1663.

[5] The Abbé Dubuisson, who was called the *grand introducteur des ruelles*. (See page 154, note 25.)

showed me the whole thing done, in a manner which was indeed better written and more witty than I am able to do it. but which was too flattering for me, so that I was afraid that if I brought that work out in our theatre, I should presently be accused of having begged the praises which were therein bestowed upon me. Yet that hindered me, for some reason, from finishing what I had begun. But so many people daily urge me to write it, that I do not know what will be done; and this uncertainty is the reason I do not put in this preface, what will be seen in the Criticism, in case I resolve to let it appear—which, if it does, I say it again, it will only be to revenge the public for the squeamishness of some people. For my part, I think myself sufficiently revenged by the success of my Comedy, and I wish that all I shall hereafter write may receive the same treatment from them, provided it has the same good fortune elsewhere.

DRAMATIS PERSONÆ.

ARNOLPHE,[6] *alias* M. DE LA SOUCHE.
CHRYSALDE, *friend to Arnolphe.*
HORACE, *in love with Agnès.*
ENRIQUE, *brother-in-law of Chrysalde.*
ORONTE, *father to Horace and a great friend of Arnolphe.*
ALAIN, *a country fellow, servant to Arnolphe.*
A NOTARY.

AGNÈS, *a young innocent girl, brought up by Arnolphe.*
GEORGETTE, *a country-woman, servant to Arnolphe.*

Scene.—A SQUARE IN A TOWN.

---

[6] This part was played by Molière himself.

THE SCHOOL FOR WIVES.

(*L' ÉCOLE DES FEMMES.*)

ACT I.

SCENE I.—CHRYSALDE, ARNOLPHE.

CH. You have come to marry her, you say?

AR. Yes, I mean to settle the business to-morrow.

CH. We are here alone, and I think we can speak together without fear of being overheard. Do you wish me to open my heart to you like a friend? Your plan makes me tremble with fear for you. To take a wife is a rash step for you, whichever way you consider the matter.

AR. True, my friend. Possibly you find in your own home reasons why you should fear for me. I fancy that your own forehead shows that horns are everywhere the infallible accompaniment of marriage.

CH. These are accidents against which we cannot insure ourselves; it seems to me that the trouble people take about this is very ridiculous. But when I fear for you, it is on account of this raillery of which a hundred poor husbands have felt the sting. For you know that neither great nor small have been safe from your criticism; that your greatest pleasure, wherever you are, is to make a mighty outcry about secret intrigues . . .

AR. Exactly. Is there another city in the world where husbands are so patient as here? Do we not meet with them in every variety, and well provided with everything? One heaps up wealth, which his wife shares with those who are eager to make him a dupe; another, slightly more fortunate, but not less infamous, sees his wife receive presents day after day, and is not troubled in mind by any jealous twinge when she tells him that they are the rewards of virtue. One makes a great noise, which does him not the slightest good; another lets matters take their course in all meekness, and, seeing the gallant arrive at his house, very politely takes up his gloves and his cloak. One married woman cunningly pretends to make a confidant of her confiding husband, who slumbers securely under such a delusion, and pities the gallant for his pains, which, however, the latter does not throw away. Another married woman, to account for her extravagance, says that the money she spends has been won at play; and the silly husband, without considering at what play, thanks Heaven for her winnings. In short, we find subjects for satire everywhere, and may I, as a spectator, not laugh at them? Are not these fools . . .

CH. Yes; but he who laughs at another must beware, lest he in turn be laughed at himself. I hear what is said, and how some folks delight in retailing what goes on; but no one has seen me exult at reports, which are bruited about in the places I frequent. I am rather reserved in this respect; and, though I might condemn a certain toleration of these matters, and am resolved by no means to suffer quietly what some husbands endure, yet I have never affected to say so; for, after all, satire may fall upon ourselves, and we should never vow in such cases what we should or should not do. Thus, if by an overruling fate, some natural disgrace should ever happen to my brow, I am almost sure, after the way in which I have acted, that people would be content to laugh at it in their sleeve; and possibly, in addition, I may reap this advantage, that a few good fellows will say "What a pity!" But with you, my dear friend, it is otherwise. I tell you again you are running a plaguy risk. As your tongue has always persistently bantered husbands accused of being tolerant; as you have shown yourself like a demon let loose upon them, you must walk straight for fear of being made a laughing-stock; and, if it happens that they get the least pretext, take care they do not publish your disgrace at the public market-cross, and . . .

AR. Good Heaven, friend, do not trouble yourself. He will be a clever man who catches me in this way. I know all the cunning tricks and subtle devices which women use to deceive us, and how one is fooled by their dexterity, and I have taken precaution against this mischance. She whom I am marrying possesses all the innocence which may protect my forehead from evil influence.

CH. Why, what do you imagine? That a silly girl, to be brief . . .

AR. To marry a silly girl is not to become silly myself. I believe, as a good Christian, that your better half is very wise; but a clever wife is ominous, and I know what some people have to pay for choosing theirs with too much talent. What, I go and saddle myself with an intellectual woman, who talks of nothing but of her assembly and *ruelle*;[7] who writes tender things in prose and in verse, and is visited by Marquises and wits, whilst, as "Mrs. So-and-so's husband," I should be like a saint, whom no one calls upon! No, no, I will have none of your lofty minds. A woman who writes knows more than she ought to do. I intend that my wife shall not even be clever enough to know what a rhyme is. If one plays at *corbillon* with her, and asks her in her turn "What is put into the basket," I will have her answer, "A cream tart."[8] In a word, let her be very ignorant; and to tell you the plain truth, it is enough for her that she can say her prayers, love me, sew and spin.

CH. A stupid wife, then, is your fancy?

AR. So much so that I should prefer a very stupid and ugly woman to a very beautiful one with a great deal of wit.

CH. Wit and beauty . . .

AR. Virtue is quite enough.

CH. But how can you expect, after all, that a mere simpleton can ever know what it is to be virtuous? Besides, to my mind, it must be very wearisome for a man to have a stupid creature perpetually with him. Do you think you act rightly, and that, by reliance on your plan,

---

7 See page 154, note 24.

8 In France there was, and may be still, a kind of round game which consists in replying with a word ending in *on* to the question, *Que met on dans mon corbillon?*—(what is put into my little basket?) The supposed answer of Agnès, "A cream tart," though it does not rhyme with *corbillon*, may come natural enough, because the *corbillon* was a kind of basket in which pastry-cooks took home pastry to their customers.

a man's brow is saved from danger? A woman of sense may fail in her duty; but she must at least do so knowingly; a stupid woman may at any time fail in hers, without desiring or thinking of it.

AR. To this fine argument, this deep discourse, I reply as Pantagruel did to Panurge: Urge me to marry any other woman than a stupid one; preach and lecture till Whitsuntide, you shall be amazed to find, when you have done, that you have not persuaded me in the very slightest.[9]

CH. I do not want to say another word.

AR. Every man has his own way. With my wife, as in everything, I mean to follow my fashion. I think I am rich enough to take a partner who shall owe all to me, and whose humble station and complete dependence cannot reproach me either with her poverty or her birth. A sweet and staid look made me love Agnès, amongst other children, when she was only four. It came into my mind to ask her from her mother, who was very poor; the good country-woman, learning my wish, was delighted to rid herself of the charge. I had her brought up, according to my own notions, in a little solitary convent; that is to say, directing them what means to adopt in order to make her as idiotic as possible. Thank Heaven, success has crowned my efforts; and I am very thankful to say, I have found her so innocent that I have blessed Heaven for having done what I wished, in giving me a wife according to my desire. Then I brought her away; and as my house is continually open to a hundred different people, and as we must be on our guard against everything, I have kept her in another house where no one comes to see me; and where her good disposition cannot be spoiled, as she meets none but people as simple as herself. You will say, "Wherefore this long story?" It is to let you see the

---

[9] In the fifth chapter of the third book of Rabelais' *Pantagruel: How Pantagruel altogether abhorreth the debtors and borrowers*, we find: "I understand you very well, quoth Pantagruel, and take you to be very good at topics, and thoroughly affectioned to your own cause. But preach it up and patrocinate it, prattle on it, and defend it as much as you will, even from hence to the next Whitsuntide, if you please so to do, yet in the end will you be astonished to find how you shall have gained no ground at all upon me, nor persuaded me . . . never so little."

care I have taken. To crown all, and as you are a trusty friend, I ask you to sup with her to-night. I wish you would examine her a little, and see if I am to be condemned for my choice.

CH. With all my heart.

AR. You can judge of her looks and her innocence when you converse with her.

CH. As to that, what you have told me cannot . . .

AR. What I have told you falls even short of the truth: I admire her simplicity on all occasions; sometimes she says things at which I split my sides with laughing. The other day—would you believe it?—she was uneasy, and came to ask me, with unexampled innocence, if children came through the ears.

CH. I greatly rejoice, Mr. Arnolphe . . .

AR. What! will you always call me by that name?

CH. Ah, it comes to my lips in spite of me; I never remember Mr. de la Souche. Who on earth has put it into your head to change your name at forty-two years of age, and give yourself a title from a rotten old tree on your farm?

AR. Besides that the house is known by that name, la Souche pleases my ear better than Arnolphe.[10]

CH. What a pity to give up the genuine name of one's fathers, and take one based on chimeras! Most people have an itching that way, and, without including you in the comparison, I knew a country-fellow called Gros-Pierre, who, having no other property but a rood of land, had a muddy ditch made all around it, and took the high-sounding name of M. de l'Isle.[11]

AR. You might dispense with such examples. But, at all events, de la Souche is the name I bear. I have a reason for it, I like it; and to call me otherwise is to annoy me.

---

[10] Arnulphus was in the middle ages considered the patron saint of deceived husbands; this belief was not wholly forgotten in the seventeenth century: hence the dislike of Arnolphe to his name.

[11] Some contemporaries of Molière imagined he alluded to Thomas Corneille, or to Charles Sorel, the author of *Francion*, who, it is said, had both adopted the name of M. de l'Isle.—As Mr. Big Peter (*Gros-Pierre*) had made of his rood of land a kind of island, he thought he had a right to call himself after an isle.

CH. Most people find it hard to fall in with it; I even yet see letters addressed . . .

AR. I endure it easily from those who are not informed; but you . . .

CH. Be it so; we will make no difficulty about that; I will take care to accustom my lips to call you nothing else than M. de la Souche.

AR. Farewell. I am going to knock here, to wish them good morning, and simply to say that I have come back.

CH. (*Aside*). Upon my word, I think he is a perfect fool.

AR. (*Alone*). He is a little touched on certain points. Strange, to see how each man is passionately fond of his own opinion. (*Knocks at his door*). Hulloa!

SCENE II.—ARNOLPHE, ALAIN, GEORGETTE, *within.*

AL. Who knocks?

AR. Open the door! (*Aside*). I think they will be very glad to see me after ten days' absence.

AL. Who is there?

AR. I.

AL. Georgette!

GEO. Well!

AL. Open the door there!

GEO. Go, and do it yourself!

AL. You go and do it!

GEO. Indeed, I shall not go.

AL. No more shall I.

AR. Fine compliments, while I am left without. Hulloa! Here, please.

GEO. Who knocks?

AR. Your master.

GEO. Alain!

AL. What!

GEO. It is the master. Open the door quickly.

AL. Open it yourself.

GEO. I am blowing the fire.

AL. I am taking care that the sparrow does not go out, for fear of the cat.

AR. Whoever of you two does not open the door shall have no food for four days. Ah!

GEO. Why do you come when I was running?

AL. Why should you more than I? A pretty trick indeed!

GEO. Stand out of the way.

AL. Stand out of the way yourself.

GEO. I wish to open the door.

AL. And so do I.

GEO. You shall not.

AL. No more shall you.

GEO. Nor you.

AR. I need have patience here.

AL. (*Entering*). There; it is I, master.

GEO. (*Entering*). Your servant; it is I.

AL. If it were not out of respect for master here, I . . .

AR. (*Receiving a push from Alain*). Hang it!

AL. Pardon me.

AR. Look at the lout!

AL. It was she also, master . . .

AR. Hold your tongues, both of you. Just answer me and let us have no more fooling. Well, Alain, how is every one here?

AL. Master, we . . . (*Arnolphe takes off Alain's hat*). Master, we . . . (*Arnolphe takes it off again.*) Thank Heaven, we . . .

AR. (*Taking off the hat a third time and flinging it on the ground*). Who taught you, impertinent fool, to speak to me with your hat on your head?

AL. You are right; I am wrong.

AR. (*To Al.*). Ask Agnès to come down.

SCENE III.—ARNOLPHE, GEORGETTE.

AR. Was she sad after I went away?

GEO. Sad? No.

AR. No?

GEO. Yes, yes.

AR. Why, then?

GEO. May I die on the spot, but she expected to see you return every minute; and we never heard a horse, an ass, or a mule pass by without her thinking it was you.

SCENE IV.—ARNOLPHE, AGNÈS, ALAIN, GEORGETTE.

AR. Work in hand? That is a good sign. Well, Agnès, I have returned. Are you glad of it?

AG. Yes, sir, Heaven be thanked.

AR. I too am glad to see you again. You have always been well? I see you have.

AG. Except for the fleas, which troubled me in the night.

AR. Ah, you shall soon have some one to drive them away.

AG. I shall be pleased with that.

AR. I can easily imagine it. What are you doing there?

AG. I am making myself some caps. Your night-shirts and caps are finished.

AR. Ah, that is all right. Well, go up stairs. Do not tire yourself. I will soon return, and talk to you of important matters.

SCENE V.—ARNOLPHE, *alone.*

Heroines of the day, learned ladies, who spout tender and fine sentiments, I defy in a breath all your verses, your novels, your letters, your love-letters, your entire science, to be worth as much as this virtuous and modest ignorance. We must not be dazzled by riches; and so long as honour is . . .

SCENE VI.—HORACE, ARNOLPHE.

AR. What do I see? Is it . . . Yes. I am mistaken. But no. No; it is himself. Hor . . .

HOR. Mr. Arn . . .

AR. Horace.

HOR. Arnolphe.

AR. Ah! what joy indeed! And how long have you been here?

HOR. Nine days.

AR. Really.

HOR. I went straight to your house, but in vain.

AR. I was in the country

HOR. Yes, you had been gone ten days.

AR. Oh, how these children spring up in a few years! I am amazed to see him so tall, after having known him no higher than that.

HOR. You see how it is.

AR. But tell me how is Oronte, your father, my good and dear friend, whom I esteem and revere? What is he doing? What is he saying? Is he still hearty? He knows I am interested in all that affects him; we have not seen one another these four years, nor, what is more, written to each other, I think.

HOR. Mr. Arnolphe, he is still more cheerful than ourselves; I had a letter from him for you. But he has since informed me in another letter, that he is coming here, though as yet I do not know the reason for it. Can you tell me which of your townsmen has returned with abundance of wealth earned during a fourteen years' residence in America?

AR. No. Have you not heard his name?

HOR. Enrique.

AR. No.

HOR. My father speaks of him and his return, as though he should be well known to me; he writes that they are about to set out together, on an affair of consequence, of which his letter says nothing. (*Gives Oronte's letter to Arnolphe*).

AR. I shall assuredly be very glad to see him, and shall do my best to entertain him. (*After reading the letter*). Friends do not need to send such polite letters, and all these compliments are unnecessary. Even if he had not taken the trouble to write one word, you might have freely disposed of all I have.

HOR. I am a man who takes people at their word; and I have present need of a hundred pistoles.

AR. Upon my word, you oblige me by using me thus. I rejoice that I have them with me. Keep the purse too.

HOR. I must . . . .

AR. Drop this ceremony. Well, how do you like this town so far?

HOR. Its inhabitants are numerous, its buildings splendid, and I should think that its amusements are wonderful.

AR. Everyone has his own pleasures, after his own fashion; but for those whom we christen our gallants, they have in this town just what pleases them, for the women are born flirts. Dark and fair are amiably disposed, and the husbands also are the most kind in the world. It is a pleasure fit for a King; to me it is a mere comedy to see the pranks I do. Perhaps you have already smitten some one. Have you had no adventure yet? Men of your figure can do more than men who have money, and you are cut out to make a cuckold.

HOR. Not to deceive you as to the simple truth, I have had a certain-love passage in these parts, and friendship compels me to tell you of it.

AR. (*Aside*). Good. Here is another queer story to set down in my pocket-book.

HOR. But pray, let these things be secret.

AR. Oh!

HOR. You know that in these matters a secret divulged destroys our expectations. I will then frankly confess to you that my heart has been smitten in this place by a certain fair maid. My little attentions were at once so successful that I obtained a pleasant introduction to her; not to boast too much, nor to do her an injustice, affairs go very well with me.

AR. (*Laughing*). Ha! ha! And she is . . .

HOR. (*Pointing to the house of Agnès*). A young creature living in yonder house, of which you can see the red walls from this. Simple, of a truth, through the matchless folly of a man who hides her from all the world; but who, amidst the ignorance in which he would enslave her, discloses charms that throw one into raptures, as well as a thoroughly engaging manner, and something indescribably tender, against which no heart is proof. But perhaps you have seen this young star of love, adorned by so many charms. Agnès is her name.

AR. (*Aside*). Oh, I shall burst with rage!

HOR. As for the man, I think his name is De la Zousse, or Souche; I did not much concern myself about the name. He is rich, by what they told me, but not one of the wisest of men; they say he is a ridiculous fellow. Do you not know him?

AR. (*Aside*). It is a bitter pill I have to swallow!

HOR. Why, you do not speak a word.

AR. Oh yes . . . I know him.

HOR. He is a fool, is he not?

AR. Ugh!

HOR. What do you say? Ugh!—that means yes? Jealous, I suppose, ridiculously so? Stupid? I see he is just as they told me. To be brief, the lovely Agnès has succeeded in enslaving me. She is a pretty jewel, to tell you honestly; it would be a sin if such a rare beauty were left in the power of this eccentric fellow. For me, all my efforts, all my dearest wishes, are to make her mine in spite of this jealous wretch; and the money which I so freely borrow of you, was only to bring this laudable enterprise to a conclusion. You know better than I, that, whatever we undertake, money is the master-key to all great plans, and that this sweet metal, which distracts so many, promotes our triumphs, in love as in war. You seem vexed? Can it be that you disapprove of my design?

AR. No; but I was thinking . . .

HOR. This conversation wearies you? Farewell. I will soon pay you a visit to return thanks.

AR. (*Thinking himself alone*). What! must it . . .

HOR. (*Returning*). Once again, pray be discreet; do not go and spread my secret abroad.

AR. (*Thinking himself alone*). I feel within my soul . .

HOR. (*Returning again*). And above all to my father, who would perhaps get enraged, if he knew of it.

AR. (*Expecting Horace to return again*). Oh! . . .

SCENE VII.—ARNOLPHE, *alone*.

Oh, what I have endured during this conversation! Never was trouble of mind equal to mine! With what rashness and extreme haste did he come to tell me of this affair! Though my second name keeps him at fault, did ever any blunderer run on so furiously? But, having endured so much, I ought to have refrained until I had learned that which I have reason to fear, to have drawn out his foolish chattering to the end, and ascertained their secret understanding completely. Let me try to overtake him; I fancy he is not far-off. Let me worm from him the whole mystery. I tremble for the misfortune which may befal me; for we often seek more than we wish to find.

ACT II.

SCENE I.—ARNOLPHE, *alone.*

It is no doubt well, when I think of it, that I have lost my way, and failed to find him; for after all, I should not have been able entirely to conceal from his eyes the overwhelming pang of my heart. The grief that preys upon me would have broken forth, and I do not wish him to know what he is at present ignorant of. But I am not the man to put up with this, and leave a free field for this young spark to pursue his design. I am resolved to check his progress, and learn, without delay, how far they understand each other. My honour is specially involved in this. I regard her already as my wife. She cannot have made a slip without covering me with shame; and whatever she does will be placed to my account. Fatal absence! Unfortunate voyage! (*Knocks at his door.*

SCENE II.—ARNOLPHE, ALAIN, GEORGETTE.

AL. Ah, master, this time . . .

AR. Peace. Come here, both of you. That way, that way. Come along, come, I tell you.

GEO. Ah, you frighten me; all my blood runs cold.

AR. Is it thus you have obeyed me in my absence? You have both combined to betray me!

GEO. (*Falling at Arnolphe's feet*). Oh master, do not eat me, I implore you.

AL. (*Aside*). I am sure some mad dog has bitten him.

AR. (*Aside*). Ugh, I cannot speak, I am so filled with rage. I am choking, and should like to throw off my clothes . . . (*To Alain and Georgette*). You cursed scoundrels, you have permitted a man to come . . . (*To Alain, who tries to escape*). You would run away, would you! You must this instant . . . (*To Georgette*). If you move . . . Now I wish you to tell me . . . (*To Alain*). Hi! . . . Yes, I wish you both . . . (*Alain and Georgette rise, and again try to escape*) . . . Whoever of you moves, upon my word, I shall knock him down. How came that man into my house? Now speak. Make haste, quick, directly, instantly, no thinking! Will you speak?

BOTH. Oh, oh!

GEO. (*Falling at his knees*). My heart fails me!

AL. (*Falling at his knees*). I am dying.

ARN. (*Aside*). I perspire all over. Let me take a breath. I must fan myself, and walk about. Could I believe, when I saw Horace as a little boy, that he would grow up for this? Heaven, how I suffer! I think it would be better that I should gently draw from Agnès' own mouth an account of what touches me so. Let me try to moderate my anger. Patience, my heart; softly, softly. (*To Alain and Georgette*). Rise, go in, and bid Agnès come to me . . . Stay, her surprise would be less. They will go and tell her how uneasy I am. I will go myself and bring her out. (*To Alain and Georgette*). Wait for me here.

SCENE III.—ALAIN, GEORGETTE.

GEO. Heavens, how terrible he is! His looks made me afraid—horribly afraid. Never did I see a more hideous Christian.

AL. This gentleman has vexed him; I told you so.

GEO. But what on earth is the reason that he so strictly makes us keep our mistress in the house? Why does he wish to hide her from all the world, and cannot bear to see any one approach her?

AL. Because that makes him jealous.

GEO. But how has he got such a fancy into his head?

AL. Because . . . because he is jealous.

GEO. Yes; but wherefore is he so? and why this anger?

AL. Because jealousy . . . understand me, Georgette, jealousy is a thing . . . a thing . . . which makes people uneasy . . . and which drives folk all round the house. I am going to give you an example, so that you may understand the thing better. Tell me, is it not true that, when you have your broth in your hand, and some hungry person comes up to eat it, you would be in a rage, and be ready to beat him?

GEO. Yes, I understand that.

AL. It is just the same. Woman is in fact the broth of man; and when a man sees other folks sometimes, trying to dip their fingers in his broth, he soon displays extreme anger at it.

GEO. Yes; but why does not every one do the same? Why do we see some who appear to be pleased when their wives are with handsome fine gentlemen?

AL. Because every one has not the greedy love which will give nothing away.

GEO. If I am not blind, I see him returning.

AL. Your eyes are good; it is he.

GEO. See how vexed he is.

AL. That is because he is in trouble.

SCENE IV.—ARNOLPHE, ALAIN, GEORGETTE.

AR. (*Aside*). A certain Greek told the Emperor Augustus, as an axiom as useful as it was true, that when any accident puts us in a rage, we should, first of all, repeat the alphabet; so that in the interval our anger may abate, and we may do nothing that we ought not to do.[12] I have followed his advice in the matter of Agnès; and I have brought her here designedly, under pretence of taking a walk, so that the suspicions of my disordered mind may cunningly lead her to the topic, and, by sounding her heart, gently find out the truth.

SCENE V.—ARNOLPHE, AGNÈS, ALAIN, GEORGETTE.

AR. Come, Agnès. (*To Alain and Georgette*). Get you in.

SCENE VI.—ARNOLPHE, AGNÈS.

AR. This is a nice walk.

AG. Very nice.

AR. What a fine day.

AG. Very fine.

AR. What news?

AG. The kitten is dead.

AR. Pity! But what then? We are all mortal, and

---

[12] The story is in Plutarch, and is told of Athenodorus from Tarsus and Augustus; only the stoic philosopher advised the Roman emperor never to undertake anything until he had said twenty-four letters to himself. The emperor was so grateful for this advice that he kept Athenodorus another year, and at last dismissed him with a rich reward, quoting a line from Simonides, imitated by Horace in the second ode of the third book: There is a certain reward even for silence.

every one is for himself. Did it rain when I was in the country?

AG. No.

AR. Were you not wearied?

AG. I am never wearied.

AR. What did you do then, these nine or ten days?

AG. Six shirts, I think, and six nightcaps also.

AR. (*After musing*). The world, dear Agnès, is a strange place. Observe the scandal, and how everybody gossips. Some of the neighbours have told me that an unknown young man came to the house in my absence; that you permitted him to see and talk to you. But I did not believe these slandering tongues, and I offered to bet that it was false . . .

AG. Oh, Heaven, do not bet; you would assuredly lose.

AR. What! It is true that a man . . .

AG. Quite true. I declare to you that he was scarcely ever out of the house.

AR. (*Aside*). This confession, so candidly made, at least assures me of her simplicity. (*Aloud*). But I think, Agnès, if my memory is clear, that I forbade you to see any one.

AG. Yes; but you do not know why I saw him; you would doubtless have done as much.

AR. Possibly; but tell me then how it was.

AG. It is very wonderful, and hard to believe. I was on the balcony, working in the open air, when I saw a handsome young man passing close to me under the trees, who, seeing me look at him, immediately bowed very respectfully. I, not to be rude, made him a curtsey. Suddenly he made another bow; I quickly made another curtsey; and when he repeated it for the third time, I answered it directly with a third curtsey. He went on, returned, went past again, and each time made me another bow. And I, who was looking earnestly at all these acts of politeness, returned him as many curtseys; so that if night had not fallen just then, I should have kept on continually in that way; not wishing to yield, and have the vexation of his thinking me less civil than himself.

AR. Very good.

AG. Next day, being at the door, an old woman accosted me, and said to me something like this; "My child, may good Heaven bless you, and keep you long in all your beauty. It did not make you such a lovely creature to abuse its gifts; you must know that you have wounded a heart which to-day is driven to complain."

AR. (*Aside*). Oh, tool of Satan! damnable wretch!

AG. "Have I wounded any one?" I answered, quite astonished. "Yes," she said, "wounded; you have indeed wounded a gentleman. It is him you saw yesterday from the balcony." "Alas!" said I, "what could have been the cause? Did I, without thinking, let anything fall on him?" "No," replied she; "it was your eyes which gave the fatal blow; from their glances came all his injury." "Alas! good Heaven," said I, "I am more than ever surprised. Do my eyes contain something bad, that they can give it to other people?" "Yes," cried she, "your eyes, my girl, have a poison to hurt withal, of which you know nothing. In a word, the poor fellow pines away; and if," continued the charitable old woman, "your cruelty refuses him assistance, it is likely he shall be carried to his grave in a couple of days." "Bless me!" said I, "I would be very sorry for that; but what assistance does he require of me?" "My child," said she, "he requests only the happiness of seeing and conversing with you. Your eyes alone can prevent his ruin, and cure the disease they have caused." "Oh! gladly," said I; "and, since it is so, he may come to see me here as often as he likes."

AR. (*Aside*). O cursed witch! poisoner of souls! may hell reward your charitable tricks!

AG. That is how he came to see me, and got cured. Now tell me, frankly, if I was not right? And could I, after all, have the conscience to let him die for lack of aid?—I, who feel so much pity for suffering people, and cannot see a chicken die without weeping!

AR. (*Aside*). All this comes only from an innocent soul; I blame my imprudent absence for it, which left this kindliness of heart without a protector, exposed to the wiles of artful seducers. I fear that the rascal, in his bold passion, has carried the matter somewhat beyond a joke.

AG. What ails you? I think you are a little angry. Was there anything wrong in what I have told you?

AR. No. But tell me what followed, and how the young man behaved during his visits.

AG. Alas! if you but knew how delighted he was; how he got rid of his illness as soon as I saw him, the present he made me of a lovely casket, and the money which Alain and Georgette have had from him, you would no doubt love him, and say, as we say . . .

AR. Yes. But what did he do when he was alone with you?

AG. He swore that he loved me with an unequalled passion, and said the prettiest words possible, things that nothing ever can equal, the sweetness of which charms me whenever I hear him speak, and moves I know not what within me.

AR. (*Aside*). Oh! sad inquiry into a fatal mystery, in which the inquirer alone suffers all the pain. (*Aloud*). Besides all these speeches, all these pretty compliments, did he not also bestow a few caresses on you?

AG. Oh, so many! He took my hands and my arms, and was never tired of kissing them.

AR. Agnès, did he take nothing else from you? (*Seeing her confused*). Ugh!

AG. Why, he . . .

AR. What?

AG. Took . . .

AR. Ugh!

AG. The . . .

AR. Well?

AG. I dare not tell you; you will perhaps be angry with me.

AR. No.

AG. Yes, but you will.

AR. Good Heavens! no.

AG. Swear on your word.

AR. On my word, then.

AG. He took my . . . You will be in a passion.

AR. No.

AG. Yes.

AR. No, no, no, no! What the devil is this mystery? What did he take from you?

AG. He . . .

AR. (*Aside*). I am suffering the torments of the damned.

AG. He took away from me the ribbon you gave me. To tell you the truth, I could not prevent him.

AR. (*Drawing his breath*). Oh! let the ribbon go. But I want to know if he did nothing to you but kiss your arms.

AG. Why! do people do other things?

AR. Not at all. But, to cure the disorder which he said had seized him, did he not ask you for any other remedy?

AG. No. You may judge that I would have granted him anything to do him good, if he had asked for it.

AR. (*Aside*). By the kindness of Heaven, I am cheaply out of it! May I be blessed if I fall into such a mistake again! (*Aloud*). Pooh! That is the result of your innocence, Agnès. I shall say no more about it. What is done is done. I know that, by flattering you, the gallant only wishes to deceive you, and to laugh at you afterwards.

AG. Oh, no! He told me so more than a score of times.

AR. Ah! you do not know that he is not to be believed. But, now, learn that to accept caskets, and to listen to the nonsense of these handsome fops,[13] to allow them languidly to kiss your hands and charm your heart, is a mortal sin, and one of the greatest that can be committed.

AG. A sin, do you say? And why, pray?

AR. Why? The reason is the absolute law that Heaven is incensed by such doings.

AG. Incensed! But why should it be incensed? Ah, it is so sweet and agreeable! How strange is the joy one feels from all this; up to this time I was ignorant of these things.

AR. Yes, all these tender passages, these pretty speeches and sweet caresses, are a great pleasure; but they must be enjoyed in an honest manner, and their sin should be taken away by marriage.

---

[13] The original has *beaux blondins*. See page 264, note 7.

AG. Is it no longer a sin when one is married?

AR. No.

AG. Then please marry me quickly.

AR. If you wish it, I wish it also; I have returned hither for the purpose of marrying you.

AG. Is that possible?

AR. Yes.

AG. How happy you will make me!

AR. Yes, I have no doubt that marriage will please you.

AG. Then we two shall . . . .

AR. Nothing is more certain.

AG. How I shall caress you, if this comes to pass.

AR. Ha! And I shall do the same to you.

AG. I can never tell when people are jesting. Do you speak seriously?

AR. Yes, you might see that I do.

AG. We are to be married?

AR. Yes.

AG. But when?

AR. This very evening.

AG. (*Laughing*). This very evening?

AR. This very evening. Does that make you laugh?

AG. Yes.

AR. To see you happy is my desire.

AG. Oh, how greatly I am obliged to you, and what satisfaction I shall have with him!

AR. With whom?

AG. With . . . . him there . . . .

AR. Him there! I am not speaking of him there. You are a little quick in selecting a husband. In a word, it is some one else whom I have ready for you. And as for that gentleman, I require, by your leave (though the illness of which he accuses you should be the death of him), that henceforth you break off all intercourse with him; that, when he comes to the house, you will, by way of compliment, just shut the door in his face; throw a stone out of the window at him when he knocks, and oblige him in good earnest never to appear again. Do you hear me, Agnès? I shall observe your behaviour, concealed in a recess.

AG. Oh dear, he is so handsome! He is . . . .

AR. Ha! How you are talking!

AG. I shall not have the heart . . . .

AR. No more chatter. Go up stairs

AG. But surely! Will you . . . .

AR. Enough. I am master; I command; do you go and obey.

ACT III.

SCENE I.—ARNOLPHE, AGNÈS, ALAIN, GEORGETTE.

AR. Yes, all has gone well; my joy is extreme. You have obeyed my orders to perfection, and brought the fair seducer[14] to utter confusion. See what it is to have a wise counsellor. Your innocence, Agnès, had been betrayed; look what you had been brought to, before you had been aware of it. You were treading, deprived of my warnings, right-down the broad path to hell and perdition. The way of all these young fops is but too well known. They have their fine rolls, plenty of ribbons and plumes, big wigs, good teeth, a smooth address; but I tell you they have the cloven foot beneath; and they are very devils, whose corrupt appetites try to prey upon the honour of women. This time, however, thanks to the care that has been taken, you have escaped with your virtue. The style in which I saw you throw that stone at him, which has dashed the hopes of all his plans, still more determines me not to delay the marriage for which I told you to prepare. But, before all, it is well I should speak a few words with you which may be salutary. (*To Georgette and Alain*). Bring out a chair in the open air. As for you, if you ever . . .

GEO. We shall take care to remember all your instructions, that other gentleman imposed on us, but . . .

AL. If he ever gets in here, may I never drink another drop. Besides he is a fool. He gave us two gold crowns the other day, which were under weight.[15]

AR. Well, get what I ordered for supper; and as to the

---

[14] The original has *blondin séducteur*. See page 264, and note 7.

[15] The clipping of coin was very common at that time. The golden crown was then worth five livres four sous, and would be now of the value of ten francs and a-half.

contract I spoke of, let one of you fetch the notary who lives at the corner of the market-place.

SCENE II.—ARNOLPHE, AGNÈS.

AR. (*Seated*). Agnès, put your work down, and listen to me. Raise your head a little, and turn your face round. (*Putting his finger on his forehead*). There, look at me here while I speak, and take good note of even the smallest word. I am going to wed you, Agnès; you ought to bless your stars a hundred times a day, to think of your former low estate, and at the same time, to wonder at my goodness in raising you from a poor country girl to the honourable rank of a citizen's wife; to enjoy the bed and the embraces of a man who has shunned all such trammels, and whose heart has refused to a score of women, well fitted to please, the honour which he intends to confer on you. You must always keep in mind, I say, how insignificant you would be without this glorious alliance, in order that the picture may teach you the better to merit the condition in which I shall place you, and make you always know yourself, so that I may never repent of what I am doing. Marriage, Agnès, is no joke. The position of a wife calls for strict duties; I do not mean to exalt you to that condition, in order that you may be free and take your ease. Your sex is formed for dependence. Omnipotence goes with the beard. Though there are two halves in the connection, yet these two halves are by no means equal. The one half is supreme, the other subordinate: the one is all submission to the other which rules; the obedience which the well disciplined soldier shows to his leader, the servant to his master, a child to his parent, the lowest monk to his superior, is far below the docility, obedience, humility, and profound respect due from the wife to her husband, her chief, her lord, and her master. When he looks at her gravely, her duty is at once to lower her eyes, never daring to look him in the face, until he chooses to favour her with a tender glance. Our women now-a-days do not understand this; but do not be spoiled by the example of others. Take care not to imitate those miserable flirts whose pranks are talked of all over the city; and do not let the evil one tempt you, that is, do not listen to any young coxcomb. Remember, Agnès, that, in making you part of my self, I give my honour into your hands, which honour is fragile, and easily damaged; that it will not do to trifle in such a matter, and that there are boiling cauldrons in hell, into which wives who live wickedly are thrown for evermore. I am not telling you a parcel of stories; you ought to let these lessons sink into your heart. If you practice them sincerely, and take care not to flirt, your soul will ever be white and spotless as a lily; but if you stain your honour, it will become as black as coal. You will seem hideous to all, and one day you will become the devil's own property, and boil in hell to all eternity—from which may the goodness of Heaven defend you! Make a curtsey. As a novice in a convent ought to know her duties by heart, so it ought to be on getting married: here in my pocket I have an important document which will teach you the duty of a wife. I do not know the author, but it is some good soul or other; and I desire that this shall be your only study. (*Rises*). Stay. Let me see if you can read it fairly.

AG. (*Reads*). "*The Maxims of Marriage; or the Duties of a Wife; together with her Daily Exercise.*

"*First Maxim.*

"She who is honourably wed should remember, notwithstanding the fashion now-a-days, that the man who marries does not take a wife for anyone but himself."

AR. I shall explain what that means, but at present let us only read.

AG. (*Continues*)—

"*Second Maxim.*

"She ought not to bedeck herself more than her husband likes. The care of her beauty concerns him alone; and if others think her plain, that must go for nothing.

"*Third Maxim.*

"Far from her be the study of ogling, washes, paints, pomatums, and the thousand preparations for a good complexion. These are ever fatal poisons to honour; and the pains bestowed to look beautiful are seldom taken for a husband.

"*Fourth Maxim.*

"When she goes out, she should conceal the glances of her eyes beneath her hood, as honour requires; for in order to please her husband rightly, she should please none else.

"*Fifth Maxim.*

"It is fit that she receive none but those who visit her husband. The gallants that have no business but with the wife, are not agreeable to the husband.

"*Sixth Maxim.*

"She must firmly refuse presents from men, for in these days nothing is given for nothing.

"*Seventh Maxim.*

"Amongst her furniture, however she dislikes it, there must be neither writing-desk, ink, paper, nor pens. According to all good rules everything written in the house should be written by the husband.

"*Eighth Maxim.*

"Those disorderly meetings, called social gatherings, ever corrupt the minds of women. It is good policy to forbid them; for there they conspire against the poor husbands.

"*Ninth Maxim.*

"Every woman who wishes to preserve her honour should abstain from gambling as a plague; for play is very seductive, and often drives a woman to put down her last stake.

"*Tenth Maxim.*

"She must not venture on public promenades nor picnics; for wise men are of opinion that it is always the husband who pays for such treats.

"*Eleventh Maxim* . . ."

AR. You shall finish it by yourself; and, by and by, I

shall explain these things to you properly, word for word. I bethink myself of an engagement. I have but one word to say, and I shall not stay long. Go in again, and take special care of this volume. If the notary comes, let him wait for me a short time.

SCENE III.—ARNOLPHE, *alone.*

I cannot do better than make her my wife. I shall be able to mould her as I please; she is like a bit of wax in my hands, and I can give her what shape I like. She was near being wiled away from me in my absence through her excess of simplicity; but, to say the truth, it is better that a wife should err on that side. The cure for these faults is easy; every simple person is docile; and if she is led out of the right way, a couple of words will instantly bring her back again. But a clever woman is quite another sort of animal. Our lot depends only on her judgment; nought can divert her from what she is set on, and our teaching in such a case is futile. Her wit avails her to ridicule our maxims, often to turn her vices into virtues, and to find means to cheat the ablest, so as to compass her own ends. We labour in vain to parry the blow; a clever woman is a devil at intrigue, and when her whim has mutely passed sentence on our honour, we must knock under. Many good fellows could tell as much. But my blundering friend shall have no cause to laugh; he has reaped the harvest of his gossip. This is the general fault of Frenchmen. When they have a love adventure, secrecy bores them, and silly vanity has so many charms for them, that they would rather hang themselves than hold their tongues. Ah! women are an easy prey to Satan when they go and choose such addle-pates! And when . . . But here he is . . . I must dissemble, and find out how he has been mortified.

SCENE IV.—HORACE, ARNOLPHE.

HOR. I am come from your house. Fate seems resolved that I shall never meet you there. But I shall go so often that some time or other . . .

AR. Bah, for goodness sake, do not let us begin these idle compliments. Nothing vexes me like ceremony; and, if I could have my way, it should be abolished. It is a wretched custom, and most people foolishly waste two-thirds of their time on it. Let us put on our hat, without more ado. (*Puts on his hat*). Well, how about your love affair? May I know, Mr. Horace, how it goes? I was diverted for a while by some business that came into my head; but since then I have been thinking of it. I admire the rapidity of your commencement, and am interested in the issue.

HOR. Indeed, since I confided in you, my love has been unfortunate.

AR. Ay! How so?

HOR. Cruel fate has brought her governor back from the country.

AR. What bad luck!

HOR. Moreover, to my great sorrow, he has discovered what has passed in private between us.

AR. How the deuce could he discover this affair so soon?

HOR. I do not know; but it certainly is so. I meant, at the usual hour, to pay a short visit to my young charmer, when, with altered voice and looks, her two servants barred my entrance, and somewhat rudely shut the door in my face, saying "Begone, you bring us into trouble!"

AR. The door in your face!

HOR. In my face.

AR. That was rather hard.

HOR. I wished to speak to them through the door; but to all I said their only answer was, "You shan't come in; master has forbidden it."

AR. Did they not open the door then?

HOR. No. And Agnès from the window made me more certain as to her master's return, by bidding me begone in a very angry tone, and flinging a stone at me into the bargain.

AR. What, a stone?

HOR. Not a small one either; that was how she rewarded my visit with her own hands.

AR. The devil! These are no trifles. Your affair seems to me in a bad way.

HOR. True, I am in a quandary through this unlucky return.

AR. Really I am sorry for you; I declare I am.

HOR. This fellow mars all.

AR. Yes; but that is nothing. You will find a way to recover yourself.

HOR. I must try by some device to baffle the strict watch of this jealous fellow.

AR. That will be easy: after all the girl loves you.

HOR. Doubtless.

AR. You will compass your end.

HOR. I hope so.

AR. The stone has put you out, but you cannot wonder at it.

HOR. True; and I understood in a moment that my rival was there, and that he was directing all without being seen. But what surprised me, and will surprise you, is another incident I am going to tell you of; a bold stroke of this lovely girl, which one could not have expected from her simplicity. Love, it must be allowed, is an able master; he teaches us to be what we never were before; a complete change in our manners is often the work of a moment under his tuition. He breaks through the impediments in our nature, and his sudden feats have the air of miracles. In an instant he makes the miser liberal, a coward brave, a churl polite. He renders the dullest soul fit for anything, and gives wit to the most simple. Yes, this last miracle is surprising in Agnès; for, blurting out these very words: "Begone, I am resolved never to receive your visits. I know all you would say, and *there* is my answer!"—this stone, or pebble, at which you are surprised, fell at my feet, with a letter. I greatly admire this note, chiming in with the significance of her words, and the casting of the stone. Are you not surprised by such an action as this? Does not love know how to sharpen the understanding? And can it be denied that his ardent flames have marvellous effects on the heart? What say you of the trick, and of the letter? Ah, do you not admire her cunning contrivance? Is it not amusing to see what a part my jealous rival has played in all this game? Say . . .

AR. Ay, very amusing.

HOR. Laugh at it, then. (*Arnolphe forces a laugh.* This

fellow, garrisoned against my passion, who shuts himself up in his house, and seems provided with stones, as though I were preparing to enter by storm, who, in his ridiculous terror, encourages all his household to drive me away, is tricked before his very eyes by her whom he would keep in the utmost ignorance! For my part, I confess that, although his return throws my love affair into disorder, I think all this so exceedingly comical, that I cannot forbear laughing at it whenever it comes into my head. It seems to me that you do not laugh at it half enough.

AR. (*With a forced laugh*). I beg pardon; I laugh at it as much as I can.

HOR. But I must shew you her letter, for friendship's sake. Her hand knew how to set down all that her heart felt; but in such touching terms, so kind, so innocently tender, so ingenuous—in a word, just as an unaffected nature confesses its first attack of love.

AR. (*Softly*). This is the use you make of writing, you hussey. It was against my wish you ever learned it.

HOR. (Reads). "*I wish to write to you, but I am at a loss how to begin. I have some thoughts which I should like you to know; but I do not know how to tell them to you, and I mistrust my own words. As I begin to feel that I have been always kept in ignorance, I fear to say something which is not right, and to express more than I ought. In fact I do not know what you have done to me; but I feel that I am desperately vexed at what I am made to do against you, that it will be the hardest thing in the world for me to do without you, and that I should be very glad to be with you. Perhaps it is wrong to say that, but the truth is I cannot help saying it, and I wish it could be brought about without harm. I am assured that all young men are deceivers, that they must not be listened to, and that all you told me was but to deceive me; but I assure you I have not yet come to believe that of you, and I am so touched by your words that I could not believe them false. Tell me frankly if they be: for, to be brief, as I am without an evil thought, you would be extremely wicked to deceive me, and I think I should die of vexation at such a thing.*"

AR. (*Aside*). Ah, the cat!

HOR. What is wrong?

AR. Wrong? Nothing! I was only coughing.

HOR. Have you ever heard a more tender expression? In spite of the cursed endeavours of unreasonable power, could you imagine a more genuine nature? Is it not beyond doubt a terrible crime villainously to mar such an admirable spirit, to try to stifle this bright soul in ignorance and stupidity? Love has begun to tear away the veil, and if, thanks to some lucky star, I can deal, as I hope, with this sheer animal, this wretch, this hang-dog, this scoundrel, this brute . . .

AR. Good-bye.

HOR. Why are you in such a hurry?

AR. It just occurs to me that I have a pressing engagement.

HOR. But do you not know anyone, for you live close by, who could get access to this house? I am open with you, and it is the usual thing for friends to help each other in these cases. I have no one there now except people who watch me; maid and man, as I just experienced, would not cease their rudeness and listen to me, do what I would. I had for some time in my interest an old woman of remarkable shrewdness; in fact more than human. She served me well in the beginning; but the poor woman died four days ago. Can you not devise some plan for me?

AR. No, really. You will easily find some one without me.

HOR. Good-by then. You see what confidence I put in you.

SCENE V.—ARNOLPHE, *alone.*

How I am obliged to suffer before him! How hard it is to conceal my gnawing pain! What! Such ready wit in a simpleton? The traitress has pretended to be so to my face, or the devil has breathed this cunning into her heart. But now that cursed letter is the death of me. I see that the rascal has corrupted her mind, and has established himself there in my stead. This is despair and deadly anguish for me. I suffer doubly by being robbed of her heart, for love as well as honour is injured by it. It drives me mad to find my place usurped, and I am enraged to see my prudence defeated. I know that to punish her guilty passion I have only to leave her to her evil fate, and that I shall be revenged on her by herself; but it is very vexatious to lose what we love. Good Heaven! after employing so much philosophy in my choice, why am I to be so terribly bewitched by her charms? She has neither relatives, friends, nor money; she abuses my care, my kindness, my tenderness; and yet I love her to distraction, even after this base trick! Fool, have you no shame? Ah, I cannot contain myself; I am mad; I could punch my head a thousand times over. I shall go in for a little; but only to see what she looks like after so vile a deed. Oh Heaven, grant that my brow may escape dishonour; or rather, if it is decreed that I must endure it, at least grant me, under such misfortunes, that fortitude with which few are endowed.

ACT IV.

SCENE I.—ARNOLPHE, *alone*.

I declare I cannot rest anywhere; my mind is troubled by a thousand cares, thinking how to contrive, both in-doors and out, so as to frustrate the attempts of this coxcomb. With what assurance the traitress stood the sight of me! She is not a whit moved by all that she has done, and though she has brought me within an inch of the grave, one could swear, to look at her, that she had no hand in it. The more composed she looked when I saw her, the more I was enraged, and those ardent transports which inflamed my heart seemed to redouble my great love for her. I was provoked, angry, incensed against her, and yet I never saw her look so lovely. Her eyes never seemed to me so bright; never before did they inspire me with such vehement desires; I feel that it will be the death of me, if my evil destiny should bring upon me this disgrace. What! I have brought her up with so much tenderness and forethought; I have had her with me from her infancy; I have indulged in the fondest hopes about her; my heart trusted to her growing charms; I have fondled her as my own for thirteen years, as I imagined,

—all for a young fool, with whom she is in love, to come and carry her off before my face, and that when she is already half married to me! No, by Heaven—no, by Heaven, my foolish young friend; you will be a cunning fellow to overturn my scheme, for, upon my word, all your hopes will be in vain, and you shall find no reason for laughing at me!

SCENE II.—A NOTARY, ARNOLPHE.

NOT. Ah, there he is. Good-day. Here I am, ready to draw up the contract which you wish.

AR. (*Not seeing or hearing him*). How is it to be done?

NOT. It must be in the usual form.

AR. (*Thinking himself alone*). I shall take the greatest possible care.

NOT. I shall do nothing contrary to your interests.

AR. (*Not seeing him*). I must guard against all surprise.

NOT. It is enough that your affairs are placed in my hands. For fear of deception, you must not sign the contract before receiving the portion.

AR. (*Thinking himself alone*). I fear, if I let anything get abroad, that this business will become town talk.

NOT. Well, it is easy to avoid this publicity, and your contract can be drawn up privately.

AR. (*Thinking himself alone*). But how shall I manage it with her?

NOT. The jointure should be proportionate to the fortune she brings you.

AR. (*Not seeing him*). I love her, and that love is my great difficulty.

NOT. In that case the wife may have so much the more.

AR. (*Thinking himself alone*). How can I act towards her in such a case?

NOT. The regular way is that the husband that is to be settles on the wife that is to be a third of her marriage portion as a jointure; but this rule goes for nothing, and you may do a great deal more if you have a mind to it.

AR. If . . . (*Seeing him*).

NOT. As for the *préciput*,[16] that is a question for both sides. I say the husband can settle on his wife what he thinks proper.

AR. Eh?

NOT. He can benefit her, when he loves her much, and wishes to do her a favour, and that by way of jointure, or settlement as it is called, which is lost upon her death; either without reversion, going from her to her heirs, or by statute, as people have a mind, or by actual deed of gift in form, which may be made either single or mutual. Why do you shrug your shoulders? Am I talking like a fool, or do I not understand contracts? Who can teach me? No one, I imagine. Do I not know that when people are married, they have a joint right to all moveables, moneys, fixtures, and acquisitions, unless they resign it by act of renunciation? Do I not know that a third part of the portion of the wife that is to be becomes common, in order . . .

AR. Yes, verily, you know all this; but who has said one word to you about it?

NOT. You, who seem to take me for a fool, shrugging your shoulders, and making faces at me.

AR. Hang the man and his beastly face! Good day: that's the way to get rid of you.

NOT. Was I not brought here to draw up a contract?

AR. Yes, I sent for you. But the business is put off; I shall send for you again when the time is fixed. What a devil of a fellow he is with his jabbering!

NOT. (*Alone*). I think he is mad, and I believe I am right.

SCENE III.—A NOTARY, ALAIN, GEORGETTE.

NOT. Did you not come to fetch me to your master?

AL. Yes.

NOT. I do not know what you think; but go and tell him from me that he is a downright fool.

GEO. We will not fail.

---

[16] *Préciput* is an advantage stipulated by the marriage-contract, in favour of the survivor, and which is taken from the joint fund before the property is divided.

SCENE IV.—ARNOLPHE, ALAIN, GEORGETTE.

GEO. Sir . . .

AR. Come here! You are my faithful, my good, my real friends; I have news for you.

AL. The notary . . .

AR. Never mind; some other day for that. A foul plot is contrived against my honour. What a disgrace it would be for you, my children, if your master's honour were taken away! After that, you would not dare to be seen anywhere; for whoever saw you would point at you. So, since the affair concerns you as well as me, you must take care that this spark may not in any way . . .

GEO. You have tanght us our lesson just now.

AR. But take care not to listen to his fine speeches.

AL. Oh, certainly . . .

GEO. We know how to deny him.

AR. Suppose he should come now, wheedling: "Alain my good fellow cheer my drooping spirits by a little help."

AL. You are a fool.

AR. You are right! (*To Georgette*). "Georgette, my darling, you look so sweet-tempered and so kind!"

GEO. You are a lout.

AR. You are right (*To Alain*). "What harm do you find in an honest and perfectly virtuous scheme?"

AL. You are a rogue.

AR. Capital! (*To Georgette*). "I shall surely die if you do not take pity on my sufferings."

GEO. You are a brazen-faced blockhead.

AR. First-rate! (*To Alain*). "I am not one who expects something for nothing; I can remember those who serve me. Here, Alain, is a trifle in advance, to have a drink with; and, Georgette, here is wherewith to buy you a petticoat. (*Both hold out their hands and take the money*). This is only an earnest of what I intend to do for you; I ask no other favour but that you will let me see your pretty mistress."

GEO. (*Pushing him*). Try your games elsewhere.

AR. That was good.

AL. (*Pushing him*). Get out of this.

AR. Very good!

GEO. (*Pushing him*). Immediately!

AR. Good! Hulloa, that is enough.

GEO. Am I not doing right?

AL. Is this how you would have us act?

AR. Yes, capital; except for the money, which you must not take.

GEO. We did not think of that.

AL. Shall we begin again now?

AR. No. It is enough. Go in, both of you.

AL. You need only say so.

AR. No, I tell you; go in when I desire you. You may keep the money. Go. I shall soon be with you again; keep your eyes open, and second my efforts.

SCENE V.—ARNOLPHE, *alone*.

I will get the cobbler, who lives at the corner of the street, to be my spy, and tell me everything. I mean to keep her always indoors, watch her constantly . . . and banish in particular all sellers of ribbons, tire-women, hair-dressers, kerchief-makers, glove-sellers, dealers in left-off apparel, and all those folks who make it their business clandestinely to bring people together who are in love. In fact, I have seen the world, and understand its tricks. My spark must be very cunning, if a love-letter or message gets in here.

SCENE VI.—HORACE, ARNOLPHE.

HOR. How lucky I am to meet you here? I had a narrow escape just now, I can assure you. As I left you, I unexpectedly saw Agnès alone on her balcony, breathing the fresh air from the neighbouring trees. After giving me a sign, she contrived to come down into the garden and open the door. But we were scarcely into her room before she heard her jealous gentleman upon the stairs; and all she could do in such a case was to lock me into a large wardrobe. He entered the room at once. I did not see him, but I heard him walking up and down at a great rate, without saying a word, but sighing desperately at intervals, and occasionally thumping the table, striking a little frisky dog, and madly throwing about whatever came in his way. In his rage he broke the very vases with which the beauty had adorned her mantel-piece; doubtless the tricks she played must have come to the ears of this cuckold in embryo. At last, having in a score of ways vented his passion on things that could not help themselves, my restless jealous gentleman left the room without saying what disturbed him, and I left my wardrobe. We would not stay long together, for fear of my rival; it would have been too great a risk. But late tonight I am to enter her room without making a noise. I am to announce myself by three hems, and then the window is to be opened; whereby, with a ladder, and the help of Agnès, my love will try to gain me admittance. I tell you this as my only friend. Joy is increased by imparting it; and should we taste perfect bliss a hundred times over, it would not satisfy us unless it were known to some one. I believe you will sympathize in my success. Good-bye. I am going to make the needful preparations.

SCENE VII.—ARNOLPHE, *alone.*

What, will the star which is bent on driving me to despair allow me no time to breathe? Am I to see, through their mutual understanding, my watchful care and my wisdom defeated one after another? Must I, in my mature age, become the dupe of a simple girl and a scatter-brained young fellow? For twenty years, like a discreet philosopher, I have been musing on the wretched fate of married men, and have carefully informed myself of the accidents which plunge the most prudent into misfortune. Profiting in my own mind by the disgrace of others, and having a wish to marry, I sought how to secure my forehead from attack, and prevent its being matched with those of other men. For this noble end, I thought I had put in practice all that human policy could invent; but, as though it were decreed by fate that no man here below should be exempt from it, after all my experience and the knowledge I have been able to glean of such matters, after more than twenty years of meditation, so as to guide myself with all precaution, I have avoided the tracks of so many husbands to find myself after all involved in the same disgrace! Ah, cursed fate, you shall yet be a liar! I am still possessor of the loved one; if her heart be stolen by this obnoxious fop, I shall at least take care that he does not seize anything else. This night, which they have chosen for their pretty plan, shall not be spent so agreeably as they anticipate. It is some pleasure to me, amidst all this, to know that he has warned me of the snare he is laying, and that this blunderer, who would be my ruin, makes a confidant of his own rival.

SCENE VIII.—CHRYSALDE, ARNOLPHE.

CH. Well, shall we take our supper before our walk?

AR. No, I fast to-night.

CH. Whence this fancy?

AR. Pray excuse me; there is something that hinders me.

CH. Is not your intended marriage to take place?

AR. You take too much trouble about other people's affairs.

CH. Oh ho, so snappish? What ails you? Have you encountered any little mishap in your love, my friend? By your face I could almost swear you have.

AR. Whatever happens, I shall at least have the advantage of being unlike some folks, who meekly suffer the visits of gallants.

CH. It is an odd thing that, with so much intelligence, you always get so frightened at these matters; that you set your whole happiness on this, and imagine no other kind of honour in the world. To be a miser, a brute, a rogue, wicked and cowardly, is nothing in your mind compared with this stain; and however a man may have lived, he is a man of honour if he is not a cuckold. After all, why do you imagine that our glory depends on such an accident, and that a virtuous mind must reproach itself for the evil which it cannot prevent? Tell me, why do you hold that a man in taking a wife deserves praise or blame for the choice he makes, and why do you form a frightful bugbear out of the offence caused by her want of fidelity? Be persuaded that a man of honour may have a less serious notion of cuckoldom; that as none is secure from strokes of chance, this accident ought to be a matter of indifference; and that all the evil, whatever the world may say, is in the mode of receiving it. To behave well under these difficulties, as in all else, a man must shun extremes; not ape those over-simple folks who are proud of such affairs, and are ever inviting the gallants of their wives, praising them everywhere, and crying them up, displaying their sympathy with them, coming to all their entertainments and all their meetings, and making everyone wonder at their having the assurance to show their faces there. This way of acting is no doubt highly culpable; but the other extreme is no less to be condemned. If I do not approve of such as are the friends of their wives' gallants; no more do I approve of your violent men whose indiscreet resentment, full of rage and fury, draws the eyes of all the world on them by its noise, and who seem, from their outbreaks, unwilling that any one should be ignorant of what is wrong with them. There is a mean between these extremes, where a wise man stops in such a case. When we know how to take it, there is no reason to blush for the worst a woman can do to us. In short, say what you will, cuckolding may easily be made to seem less terrible; and, as I told you before, all your dexterity lies in being able to turn the best side outwards.

AR. After this fine harangue, all the brotherhood owes your worship thanks; any one who hears you speak will be delighted to enrol himself.

CH. I do not say that; for that is what I have found fault with. But as fortune gives us a wife, I say that we should act as we do when we gamble with dice, when, if you do not get what you want, you must be shrewd and good-tempered, to amend your luck by good management.[17]

AR. That is, sleep and eat well, and persuade yourself that it is all nothing.

CH. You think to make a joke of it; but, to be candid, I know a hundred things in the world more to be dreaded,

---

17 This is from Terence's *Adelphi*, Act iv., Scene 8, where he says: Life is like a game where dice are employed. If we do not get the chance we need, the science of the player ought to correct fate. It may perhaps not be unnecessary to hint that the whole of Chrysalde's speeches are meant ironically, and are an imitation of the ancient *fabliaux* and of Rabelais.

and which I should think a much greater misfortune, than the accident you are so grievously afraid of. Do you think that, in choosing between the two alternatives, I should not prefer to be what you say, rather than see myself married to one of those good creatures whose ill-humour makes a quarrel out of nothing—those dragons of virtue, those respectable she-devils, ever piquing themselves on their wise conduct, who, because they do not do us a trifling wrong, take on themselves to behave haughtily, and, because they are faithful to us, expect that we should bear everything from them? Once more, my friend, know that cuckoldom is just what we make of it, that on some accounts it is even to be desired, and that it has its pleasures like other things.

AR. If you are of a mind to be satisfied with it, I am not disposed to try it myself; and rather than submit to such a thing . . .

CH. Bless me! do not swear, lest you should be forsworn. If fate has willed it, your precautions are useless; and your advice will not be taken in the matter.

AR. I!—I a cuckold!

CH. You are in a bad way. A thousand folks are so—I mean no offence—who, for bearing, courage, fortune and family, would scorn comparison with you.

AR. And I, on my side, will not draw comparisons with them. But, let me tell you, this pleasantry annoys me. Let us have done with it, if you please.

CH. You are in a passion. We shall know the cause. Good-bye; but remember, whatever your honour prompts you to do in this business, to swear you will never be what we have talked of is half-way towards being it.

AR. And I swear it again! I am going this instant to find a good remedy against such an accident.

SCENE IX.—ARNOLPHE, ALAIN, GEORGETTE.

AR. My friends, now is the time that I beg your assistance. I am touched by your affection; but it must be well proved on this occasion; and if you serve me in this, as I am sure you will, you may count on your reward. The man you wot of (but not a word!) seeks, as I understand, to trick me this very night, and enter, by a ladder, into Agnès' room. But we three must lay a trap for him. I would have each of you take a good cudgel, and, when he shall be nearly on the top round of the ladder (for I shall open the window at the proper time), both of you shall fall on the rascal for me, so that his back may be sure to remember it, in order that he may learn never to come here again. Yet do it without naming me in any way, or making it appear that I am behind. Would you have the courage to execute my resentment?

AL. If the thrashing is all, sir, rely on us. You shall see, when I beat, if I am a slow coach.

GEO. Though my arm may not look so strong, it shall play its part in the drubbing.

AR. Get you in, then; and, above all, mind you do not chatter. (*Alone*). This is a useful lesson for my neighbours; if all the husbands in town were to receive their wives' gallants in this fashion, the number of cuckolds would not be so great.

ACT V.

SCENE I.—ARNOLPHE, ALAIN, GEORGETTE.

AR. Wretches! what have you done by your violence?

AL. We have obeyed you, sir.

AR. It is of no use trying to defend yourselves by such an excuse. My orders were to beat him, not to murder him. I told you to discharge your blows on his back, and not on his head.[18] Good Heavens! into what a plight my fate has now thrown me! And what course can I take, as the man is dead? Go into the house, and be sure to say nothing of the harmless order that I gave you. (*Alone*). It will be daylight presently, and I shall go and consider how to bear myself under this misfortune. Alas! what will become of me? And what will Horace's father say when he shall suddenly hear of this affair?

---

18 This is imitated by Otway in *The Soldier's Fortune* (Act iv., Scene the last), when Lady Dunce and Sir Jolly Jumble accuse Sir Davy Dunce of having ordered Beaugard to be killed, and Sir Davy answers; "As I hope to be saved, neighbour, I only bargained with 'em to bastinado him in a way, or so, as one Friend might do to another; but do you say that he is dead?"

SCENE II.—ARNOLPHE, HORACE.

HOR. (*Aside*). I must go and make out who it is.

AR. (*Thinking himself alone*). Could one ever have foreseen . . . (*Running against Horace*). Who is there, pray?

HOR. Is it you, Mr. Arnolphe?

AR. Yes; but who are you?

HOR. Horace. I was going to your house to beg a favour. You are out very early.

AR. (*To himself aside*). Wonderful! Is it magic? Is it a vision?

HOR. To tell the truth, I was in a great difficulty; I thank Heaven's great goodness that at the nick of time I thus meet you. Let me tell you that everything has succeeded, much better even than I could have predicted, and by an accident which might have spoiled all. I do not know how our appointment could possibly have been suspected; but just as I was reaching the window, I unluckily saw some persons, who, unceremoniously raising their hand against me, made me miss my footing, and fall to the ground, which, at the expense of a bruise, saved me from a score of blows. These people, of whom, I fancy, my jealous rival was one, attributed my fall to their blows, and as the pain compelled me to lie for some time motionless, they honestly thought they had killed me, and were greatly alarmed. I heard all their noise in profound silence. Each, accusing the other of the violence, and complaining of their ill fortune, came softly, without a light, to feel if I were dead. You may imagine that I contrived, in the darkness of night, to assume the appearance of a real corpse. They went away in great terror; and as I was thinking how I should make my escape, the young Agnès, frightened by my pretended death, came to me in great concern. For the talking of those people had reached her ears from the very first, and, being unobserved during all this commotion, she easily escaped from the house. But finding me unhurt, she displayed a transport which it would be difficult to describe. What more need I say? The lovely girl obeyed the promptings of her affection, would not return to her room, and committed her fate to my honour. You may judge, from this instance of innocence, to what she is exposed by the mad intolerance of a fool, and what frightful risks she might have run, if I were a man to hold her less dear than I do. But too pure a passion fills my soul; I would rather die than wrong her. I see in her charms worthy of a better fate, and nought but death shall part us. I foresee the rage my father will be in. But we must find an opportunity to appease his anger. I cannot help being transported by charms so delightful; and, in short, we must in this life be satisfied with our lot. What I wish you to do, as a confidential friend, is to let me place this beauty under your care; and that, in the interest of my love, you will conceal her in your house for at least a day or two. For, besides that I must conceal her flight from every one, to prevent any successful pursuit of her, you know that a young girl, especially such a beautiful one, would be strongly suspected in the company of a young man; and as I have trusted the whole secret of my passion to you, being assured of your prudence, so to you only, as a generous friend, can I confide this beloved treasure.

AR. Be assured I am entirely at your service.

HOR. You will really do me so great a favour?

AR. Very willingly, I tell you; I am delighted at the opportunity of serving you. I thank Heaven for putting it in my way; I never did anything with so much pleasure.

HOR. How much I am obliged to you for all your kindness! I feared a difficulty on your part; but you know the world, and your wisdom can excuse the ardour of youth. One of my servants is with her at the corner of this street.

AR. But how shall we manage, for day begins to break? If I take her here, I may be seen; and if you come to my house the servants will talk. To take a safe course you must bring her to me in a darker place. That alley of mine is convenient; I shall wait for her there.

HOR. It is quite right to use these precautions. I shall only place her in your hands, and return at once to my lodgings, without more ado.

AR. (*Alone*). Ah, fortune! This propitious accident

Desenne p.t Nargeot sc.t

THE SCHOOL FOR WIVES.

makes amends for all the mischief which your caprice has done! (*He muffles himself up in his cloak*).

SCENE III.—AGNÈS, HORACE, ARNOLPHE.

AR. (*To Agnès*). Do not be uneasy at the place I am taking you to. I conduct you to a safe abode. It would ruin all for you to lodge with me. Go in at this door, and follow where you are led. (*Arnolphe takes her hand, without being recognised by her*).

AG. (*To Horace*). Why do you leave me?

HOR. Dear Agnès, it must be so.

AG. Remember, then, I pray you to return soon.

HOR. My love urges me sufficiently for that.

AG. I feel no joy but when I see you.

HOR. Away from you I also am sad.

AG. Alas, if that were so, you would stay here.

HOR. What! Can you doubt my excessive love?

AG. No; you do not love me as much as I love you! Ah! he is pulling me too hard! (*Arnolphe pulls her away*).

HOR. It is because it is dangerous, dear Agnès, for us to be seen together here; this true friend, whose hand draws you away, acts with the prudent zeal that inspires him on our behalf.

AG. But to follow a stranger . . .

HOR. Fear nothing. In such hands you cannot but be safe.

AG. I would rather be in Horace's; and I should . . (*To Arnolphe, who still drags her away*). Stay a little.

HOR. Farewell. The day drives me away.

AG. When shall I see you, then?

HOR. Very soon, you may be sure.

AG. How weary I shall be till I do!

HOR. (*Going*). Thank Heaven, my happiness is no longer in suspense; now I can sleep securely.

SCENE IV.—ARNOLPHE, AGNÈS.

AR. (*Concealed by his cloak, and disguising his voice*). Come; it is not there you are going to lodge. I have provided a room for you elsewhere, and intend to place you where you will be safe enough. (*Discovering himself*). Do you know me?

AG. Ah!

AR. My face frightens you now, hussey; it is a disappointment to you to see me here. I interrupt your love and its pretty contrivances. (*Agnès looks for Horace*). Do not imagine you can call your lover to your aid with those eyes of yours; he is too far off to give you any assistance. So, so! young as you are, you can play such pranks. Your simplicity, that seemed so extraordinary, asks if infants came through the ear; yet you manage to make an assignation by night, and to slink out silently in order to follow your gallant? Gad, how coaxing your tongue was with him! You must have been at a good school. Who the deuce has taught you so much all on a sudden? You are no longer afraid, then, to meet ghosts; this gallant has given you courage in the night time. Ah, baggage, to arrive at such a pitch of deceit! To form such a plot in spite of all my kindness! Little serpent that I have warmed in my bosom, and that, as soon as it feels it is alive, tries ungratefully to injure him that cherished it!

AG. Why do you scold me?

AR. Of a truth, I do wrong!

AG. I am not conscious of harm in all that I have done.

AR. To run after a gallant is not, then, an infamous thing?

AG. He is one who says he wishes to marry me. I followed your directions; you have taught me that we ought to marry in order to avoid sin.

AR. Yes; but I meant to take you to wife myself; I think I gave you to understand it clearly enough.

AG. You did. But, to be frank with you, he is more to my taste for a husband than you. With you, marriage is a trouble and a pain, and your descriptions give a terrible picture of it; but there—he makes it seem so full of joy that I long to marry.

AR. Oh, traitress, that is because you love him!

AG. Yes, I love him.

AR. And you have the impudence to tell me so!

AG. Why, if it is true, should I not say so?

AR. Ought you to love him, minx?

AG. Alas! can I help it? He alone is the cause of it; I was not thinking of it when it came about.

AR. But you ought to have driven away that amorous desire.

AG. How can we drive away what gives us pleasure?

AR. And did you not know that it would displease me?

AG. I? Not at all. What harm can it do you?

AR. True. I ought to rejoice at it. You do not love me then after all?

AG. You?

AR. Yes.

AG. Alack! no.

AR. How! No?

AG. Would you have me tell a fib?

AR. Why not love me, Madam Impudence?

AG. Heaven! you ought not to blame me. Why did you not make yourself loved, as he has done? I did not prevent you, I fancy.

AR. I tried all I could; but all my pains were to no purpose.

AG. Of a truth then he knows more about it than you; for he had no difficulty in making himself loved.

AR. (*Aside*). See how the jade reasons and retorts! Plague! could one of your witty ladies say more about it? Ah, I was a dolt; or else, on my honour, a fool of a girl knows more than the wisest man. (*To Agnes*). Since you are so good at reasoning, Madam Chop-logic, should I have maintained you so long for his benefit?

AG. No. He will pay you back, even to the last farthing.[19]

AR. (*Aside*). She hits on words that double my vexation. (*Aloud*). With all his ability, hussey, will he discharge me the obligations that you owe me?

AG. I do not owe you so much as you may think.

AR. Was the care of bringing you up nothing?

AG. Verily, you have been at great pains there, and have caused me to be finely taught throughout. Do you

---

[19] In the original *jusqu' au dernier doub'e*. A *double* was a small coin, worth two *deniers*, of which twelve made one *sou*; twenty *sous* made a *livre*, and eleven *livres* a golden *louis*.

think I flatter myself so far as not to know in my own mind that I am an ignoramus? I am ashamed of myself, and at my age, I do not wish to pass any longer for a fool, if I can help it.

AR. You shrink from ignorance, and would learn something of your spark, at any cost.

AG. To be sure. It is from him I know what I do know; I fancy I owe him much more than you.

AR. Really, what prevents me from revenging this saucy talk with a cuff? I am enraged at the sight of her provoking coldness: and to beat her would be a satisfaction to me.

AG. Ah, you can do that if you choose.

AR. (*Aside*). That speech and that look disarm my fury, and bring back the tenderness to my heart which effaces all her guilt. How strange it is to be in love! To think that men should be subject to such weakness for these traitresses! Everyone knows their imperfection. They are extravagant and indiscreet. Their mind is wicked and their understanding weak. There is nought weaker, more imbecile, more faithless; and, in spite of all, everything in the world is done for the sake of these bipeds. (*To Agnès*). Well, let us make peace. Listen, little wretch, I forgive all, and restore you to my affection. Learn thus how much I love you; and, seeing me so good, love me in return.

AG. With all my heart I should like to please you, if it were in my power.

AR. Poor little darling, you can if you will. Just listen to this sigh of love. See this dying look, behold my person, and forsake this young coxcomb and the love he inspires. He must have thrown some spell over you, and you will be a hundred times happier with me. Your desire is to be finely dressed and frolicsome; then I swear you shall ever be so; I will fondle you night and day, I will hug you, kiss you, devour you; you shall do everything you have a mind to. I do not enter into particulars; and that is saying everything. (*Aside*). To what length will my passion go? (*Aloud*). In short, nothing can equal my love. What proof would you have me give you, ungrateful girl? Would you have me weep? Shall I beat myself? Shall I tear out one half of my hair? Shall I kill myself? Yes, say so if you will. I am quite ready, cruel creature, to convince you of my love.

AG. Stay. All you say does not touch my heart. Horace could do more with a couple of words.

AR. Ah, this is too great an insult, and provokes my anger too far. I will pursue my design, you intractable brute, and will pack you out of the town forthwith. You reject my addresses and drive me to extremities: but the innermost cell of a convent shall avenge me of all.[20]

SCENE V.—ARNOLPHE, AGNÈS, ALAIN.

AL. I do not know how it is, master, but it seems to me that Agnès and the corpse have run away together.

AR. She is here. Go and shut her up in my room. (*Aside*). Horace will not come here to see her. Besides, it is only for half an hour. (*To Alain*). Go and get a carriage, for I mean to find her a safe dwelling. Shut yourselves safely in, and, above all, do not take your eyes off her. (*Alone*). Perhaps when her mind is buried in solitude, she will be disabused of this passion.

SCENE VI.—HORACE, ARNOLPHE.

HOR. Oh, I come here, plunged in grief. Heaven, Mr. Arnolphe, has decreed my ill fortune! By a fatal stroke of extreme justice, I am to be torn away from the beauty whom I love. My father arrived this very evening. I found him alighting close by. In a word the reason of his coming, with which, as I said, I was unacquainted, is, that he has made a match for me, without a word of warning; he has arrived here to celebrate the nuptials. Feel for my anxiety, and judge if a more cruel disappointment could happen to me. That Enrique, whom I asked you about yesterday, is the source of all my trouble. He has come with my father to complete my ruin; it is for his

20 Molière probably puts in the mouth of Arnolphe the doubts and fears that beset himself after a few months of his marriage with Armande Béjart, who was about half his age. This comedy was written in the summer of 1662, and was performed on the 26th of December, whilst Molière was married on the 20th of February of the same year. (See Introductory Notice to this play, page 339.)

only daughter that I am destined. I thought I should have swooned when they first spoke of it; not caring to hear more, as my father spoke of paying you a visit, I hurried here before him, my mind full of consternation. I pray you be sure not to let him know anything of my engagement, which might incense him; and try, since he has confidence in you, to dissuade him from this other match.

AR. Ay, to be sure!

HOR. Advise him to delay; and thus, like a friend, help me in my passion.

AR. No fear!

HOR. All my hope is in you.

AR. It could not be better placed.

HOR. I look on you as my real father. Tell him that my age . . . Ah, I see him coming! Hear the arguments I can supply you with.

SCENE VII.—ENRIQUE, ORONTE, CHRYSALDE, HORACE, ARNOLPHE.

(*Horace and Arnolphe retire to the back of the stage and whisper together*).

EN. (*To Chrysalde*). As soon as I saw you, before anyone could tell me, I should have known you. I recognise in your face the features of your lovely sister, whom marriage made mine in former days. Happy should I have been if cruel fate had permitted me to bring back that faithful wife, to enjoy with me the great delight of seeing once more, after our continual misfortunes, all her former friends. But since the irresistible power of destiny has for ever deprived us of her dear presence, let us try to submit, and to be content with the only fruit of love which remains to me. It concerns you nearly; without your consent I should do wrong in wishing to dispose of this pledge. The choice of the son of Oronte is honourable in itself; but you must be pleased with this choice as well as I.

CH. It would argue a poor opinion of my judgment to doubt my approbation of so reasonable a choice.

AR. (*Aside to Horace*). Ay, I will serve you finely!

HOR. Beware, once more . . .

AR. Have no uneasiness. (*Leaves Horace, and goes up to embrace Oronte*).

OR. Ah, this is indeed a tender embrace.

AR. How delighted I am to see you!

OR. I am come here . . .

AR. I know what brings you, without your telling me.

OR. You have already heard?

AR. Yes.

OR. So much the better.

AR. Your son is opposed to this match; his heart being pre-engaged, he looks on it as a misfortune. He has even prayed me to dissuade you from it; for my part, all the advice I can give you is, to exert a father's authority, and not allow the marriage to be delayed. Young people should be managed with a high hand; we do them harm by being indulgent.

HOR. (*Aside*). Oh, the traitor!

CH. If it is repugnant to him, I think we ought not to force him. I think my brother will be of my mind.

AR. What? Will he let himself be ruled by his son? Would you have a father so weak as to be unable to make his son obey him? It would be fine indeed to see him at his time of life receiving orders from one who ought to receive them from him. No, no, he is my intimate friend, and his honour is my own. His word is passed, and he must keep it. Let him now display his firmness, and control his son's affections.

OR. You speak well; in this match I will answer for my son's obedience.

CH. (*To Arnolphe*). I am indeed surprised at the great eagerness which you shew for this marriage, and cannot guess what is your motive . . .

AR. I know what I am about, and speak sensibly.

OR. Yes, yes, Mr. Arnolphe; he is . . .

CH. That name annoys him. He is Monsieur de la Souche, as you were told before.

OR. It makes no difference.

HOR. (*Aside*). What do I hear?

AR. (*Turning to Horace*). Ay, that is the mystery; you can judge as to what it behooved me to do.

HOR. (*Aside*). What a scrape . . .

SCENE VIII.—ENRIQUE, ORONTE, CHRYSALDE, HORACE, ARNOLPHE, GEORGETTE.

GEO. Sir, if you do not come, we shall scarcely be able to hold Agnès; she is trying all she can to get away; I fear she will throw herself out of the window.

AR. Bring her to me, for I mean to take her away. (*To Horace*). Do not be disturbed. Continual good fortune makes a man proud. Every dog has his day, as the proverb says.

HOR. (*Aside*). Good Heaven, what misfortune can equal mine? Was ever a man in such a mess as this?

AR. (*To Oronte*). Hasten the day of the ceremony I am bent on it, and invite myself beforehand.

OR. That is just my intention.

SCENE IX.—AGNÈS, ORONTE, ENRIQUE, ARNOLPHE, HORACE, CHRYSALDE, ALAIN, GEORGETTE.

AR. (*To Agnès*). Come hither, my beauty, whom they cannot hold, and who rebels. Here is your gallant, to whom, to make amends, you may make a sweet and humble curtesy. (*To Horace*). Farewell. The issue rather thwarts your desires; but all lovers are not fortunate.

AG. Horace, will you let me be carried off in this manner?

HOR. I scarcely know where I am, my sorrow is so great.

AR. Come along, chatterbox.

AG. I shall stay here.

OR. Tell us the meaning of this mystery. We are all staring at each other without being able to understand it.

AR. I shall inform you at a more convenient time. Till then, good-bye.

OR. Where are you going? You do not speak to us as you should.

AR. I have advised you to complete the marriage, let Horace grumble as much as he likes.

OR. Ay; but to complete it, have you not heard—if they have told you all—that the lady concerned in this affair is in your house?—that she is the daughter of Enrique and of the lovely Angelica, who were privately married? Now, what was at the bottom of your talk just now?

CH. I too was astonished at his proceedings.

AR. What?

CH. My sister had a daughter by a secret marriage, whose existence was concealed from the whole family.

OR. And in order that nothing might be discovered, she was put out to nurse in the country by her husband, under a feigned name.

CH. At that time, fortune being against him, he was compelled to quit his native land.

OR. To encounter a thousand various dangers in far-distant countries, and beyond many seas.

CH. Where his industry has acquired what in his own land he lost through roguery and envy.

OR. And when he returned to France, the first thing he did was to seek out her to whom he had confided the care of his daughter.

CH. This country-woman frankly told him that she had committed her to your keeping from the age of four.

OR. And that she did it because she received money from you, and was very poor.

CH. Oronte, transported with joy, has even brought this woman hither.

OR. In short, you shall see her here directly to clear up this mystery to every one.

CH. (*To Arnolphe*). I can almost imagine what is the cause of your grief; but fortune is kind to you. If it seems so good to you not to be a cuckold, your only course is not to marry.

AR. (*Going away full of rage, and unable to speak*). Ugh! ugh! ugh!

SCENE LAST. — ENRIQUE, ORONTE, CHRYSALDE, AGNÈS, HORACE.

OR. Why does he run away without saying a word?

HOR. Ah, father, you shall know the whole of this surprising mystery. Accident has done here what your wisdom intended. I had engaged myself to this beauty in the sweet bonds of mutual love; it is she, in a word, whom you come to seek, and for whose sake I was about to grieve you by my refusal.

EN. I was sure of it as soon as I saw her; my heart has yearned for her ever since. Ah, daughter, I am overcome by such tender transports!

CH. I could be so, brother, just as well as you. But this is hardly the place for it. Let us go inside, and clear up these mysteries. Let us shew our friend some return for his great pains, and thank Heaven, which orders all for the best.

LA CRITIQUE DE L'ÉCOLE DES FEMMES.

COMÉDIE.

THE SCHOOL FOR WIVES CRITICISED.

A COMEDY IN ONE ACT.

(*THE ORIGINAL IN PROSE.*)

JUNE 1ST, 1663.

INTRODUCTORY NOTICE.

The School for Wives criticised was first brought out at the theatre of the Palais Royal, on the 1st of June, 1663. It can scarcely be called a play, for it is entirely destitute of action. It is simply a reported conversation of "friends in council;" but we cannot be surprised that it had a temporary success on the stage. It was acted as a pendant to *The School for Wives*, and the two were played together, with much profit to the company, thirty-two consecutive times. Molière, in the Preface to *The School for Wives*, mentions that the idea of writing *The School for Wives criticised* was suggested to him by a person of quality, who, it is said, was the Abbé Dubuisson, *the grand introducteur des ruelles* or, in other words, the Master of the Ceremonies to the *Précieuses*. Our author had also just been inscribed on the list of pensions which Louis XIV. allowed to eminent literary men, for a sum of a thousand *livres*.

The happy idea of self-criticism adopted by Molière in this piece has been caught at by many subsequent French writers. Thus we find *la Critique du Légataire*, by Regnard; *la, Critique du Philosophe marié* by Destouches; *le Procès de la Femme juge et partie*, by Montfleury. But in none of these is the subject so ably treated as by Molière, who did not scruple to attack the different cabals leagued against him. Climène is an example of those ladies "whose ears are more chaste than all the rest of their body," and is a preliminary study for Philaminte of the *Femmes Savantes*. The Marquis represents the "noble patron," who judges of a play before he has seen it, who is a critic by virtue of his rank, but not of his knowledge; Lysidas is the envious pedant, who "damns with faint praise," who wishes everything measured according to the rules of Cocker's arithmetic, who employs the little knowledge with which Heaven has afflicted him to hide his own mediocrity, and who afterwards will be farther developed in the *Femme Savantes* as Trissotin and Vadius. Dorante, the man of sense, is also more fully shown in the Clitandre of the same play.

A few days after the play was produced, it was reported that Lysidas was meant for Boursault, the ridiculous Marquis for the Duke de La Feuillade, whilst it was said that the Abbé d'Aubignac was also laughed at; but as Molière himself states in *The School for Wives criticised*:—"All the ridiculous delineations which are drawn on the stage should be looked on by everyone without annoyance. They are public mirrors in which we must never pretend to see ourselves."

Boursault believed, or affected to believe, that Molière intended to pourtray him, and hence replied in the *Portrait du Peintre* which was performed at the hôtel de Bourgogne. Tradition mentions that the Duke de la Feuillade took other means to avenge himself. He one day met Molière in one of the galleries of the Palace of Versailles. Pretending to be very polite and courteous, he ran towards him smiling, and whilst embracing him, and rubbing all the while the actor's face against the metal-worked buttons of his coat, he shouted out, "Cream-tart, Molière! Cream-tart!" It is said that Louis XIV. banished the Duke from the Court for some time for this offence, and that he ordered Molière to take anew vengeance upon his enemies. There can be no doubt about the order, for Molière states so expressly in *The Impromptu of Versailles*.

The School for Wives criticised may be taken as Molière's general reply to his critics; for it deals as much with the points of good and bad criticism as with the special features of *The School for Wives*. Indeed, the defence raised, through the mouth of Dorante, of certain passages of the latter play which had been roughly handled by the poet's contemporaries, are perhaps the weakest parts of *The School for Wives criticised;* whereas the generalities which deal with the art and practice of criticism are exceptionally shrewd and pungent.

The School for Wives met with a flattering reception, in the sense that the public were greatly divided as to its merits, and carried on the discussion of it with much warmth, and even bitterness. The play was town-talk for many days; and in this sequel, Molière no doubt reflected the principal arguments of his friends and of his opponents. If he reflected them aright, he did well to preserve them in this form, side by side; for Dorante, Urania, and their dissembling ally Eliza, have infinitely the best of the discussion, whether we regard them as champions of Molière only, or as vindicators of the highest principle of dramatic criticism in general. Perhaps the "School for Critics" would better describe the most valuable half of the piece.

Molière dedicated *The School for Wives criticised* to the Queen-mother[1] in the following words:—

MADAM,—I very well know that your Majesty has no need of our dedications, and that those pretended duties of which people elegantly tell you they acquit themselves, are marks of respect with which, to speak the truth, you could very willingly dispense. But yet I have the boldness to dedicate to you *The School for Wives criticised;* and I could not omit this opportunity of testifying to your Majesty my joy upon that happy recovery, which restores to us the greatest and best Princess in the world, and which promises us in you long years of vigorous health. As everyone regards things from his own point of view, I rejoice in this general satisfaction, that I may again be able to have the honour of diverting your Majesty. You, Madam, who so well prove that true devotion is not opposed to innocent diversions; who, from your lofty thoughts and important occupations, descend so kindly to the pleasure of our performances, and who do not disdain to smile with the same mouth with which you pray to God so devoutly, I flatter my mind, I say, with the expectation of this glory; I await that moment with the utmost impatience; and, when I shall enjoy that happiness, it will be the greatest satisfaction in the world to,—MADAM, *your Majesty's most humble, most obedient, and most obliged servant,*

MOLIÈRE.

Thomas Brown, of Shipnal, in Yorkshire, so well known for his free

---

[1] Anne of Austria, eldest daughter of Philip III., King of Spain, wife of Louis XIII., and mother of Louis XIV., was born in 1602, and died the 20th of January, 1666, sixty-four years old. She did not long survive the "happy recovery" Molière congratulates her upon.

and easy writings, wrote an imitation of *The School for Wives criticised*, which he calls, "*The Stage-Beaux toss'd in a Blanket, or Hypocrisie à la mode;* Expos'd in a true picture of Jerry . . . a pretending scourge to the English Stage, A Comedy with a Prologue on Occasional Conformity; being a full Explanation of the Poussin Doctor's book; and an Epilogue on the Reformers. Spoken at the Theatre-Royal in Drury Lane, with the motto, 'Simulant Curios et Bacchanalia vivunt,—Juv.' London, Printed and Sold by J. Nott, near Stationer's Hall, 1704." This piece consists of three acts, while the French has only one. It is a satire against Jeremy Collier, on account of his *Short View of the Immorality and Prophaneness of the English Stage*, and was never acted. It was severely chastised and answered in sermons and pamphlets; amongst others, in "*Serious Reflections on the Scandalous Abuse and Effects of the Stage*, in a Sermon preached at Bristol, Jany. 7th, 1704–5, by A. Bedford," at the end of which is printed "a copy of the Presentation of the Grand Jury to Mayor, Aldermen, and Justices of the Peace, asking them to forbid the Acting of Plays," and praising them "for having endeavoured to suppress Musick-houses, and other Lewd and Disorderly Houses, Tipling, or Idle walking on the Lord's Day;" also in *A Representation of the Impiety and Immorality of the English Stage*, 1704, A. Bedford; in *A Second Advertisement concerning the Profaneness of the Playhouse;* and in *The Evil and Danger of Stage Plays in almost 2000 instances taken from the plays of the two last years*, by A. Bedford, 1706. Again, in *A Serious Remonstrance in behalf of the Christian Religion against the horrid Blasphemies and Impieties which are still used in the English Play-House, etc., from almost 7000 instances, taken out of the Plays of the present Century*, 1719, by A. Bedford; and finally, in *The Absolute unlawfulness of the Stage Entertainment fully demonstrated*, by W. Law, A. M., 1726. *The Stage-Beaux* is dedicated to Christopher Rich, patentee of the Theatre Royal, in a humorous epistle, in which Themistocles, Milton, and even Collier himself are mentioned as friends of the Drama, and in which it is stated that "the stage exposes Knaves and Fools, Misers, Prodigals, Affectation, Hypocrisie, etc., and that has provoked some to be its zealous Foes, under the pretended Name of Sanctity and Religion." The Prologue, spoken by, "one dress'd one-half like a Noncon Parson, and the other like an Orthodox Divine," opens thus:—

"My Dress is Odd, but yet 'tis Alamode,
Invented to unite Mammon with God.
This Side is Real, and full of Native Spite;
This I put on to get some Money by't.
This Side is fill'd with Sanctify'd Grimace;
This is more Debonair in hopes of Place.
This Obstinate against Religious Forms;
This, brib'd by Gain, occasionally conforms.
Occasional conforming is our Darling,
Which, if y'Attaque, you set us All a Snarling."

The character in Brown's play which is not in the French comedy is Sir Jerry Witwind, a pert, talkative, half-witted coxcomb, an arrant hypocrite, and a most immoral man,—a rather free imitation of Tartuffe, whose very words he sometimes employs, and whose worst actions he exaggerates at the end of the third act. The two last acts of the *Stage Beaux* are chiefly occupied with attacks on Collier, some of which are very amusing; but the first act contains a very fair imitation of a few scenes of *The School for Wives criticised.*

Wycherley has also borrowed from *The School for Wives criticised* a scene of his *Plain-Dealer*, which, as a whole, is partly taken from Molière's *Misanthrope.* In the part thus imitated he tries to defend *The Country Wife*, and boldly states that "a lady may call her own modesty in question by publicly cavilling with the poets;" but Olivia's defence of the play is as bad as *The Country Wife* itself. She reminds us of a certain French wit, of the last century, called Duclos, who one day stated in the presence of some ladies that respectable women might hear any story without being shocked; and then he went on relating some, which were bad enough, and was going to tell some which were even worse, when one of the ladies present stopped him by saying "Monsieur Duclos, you really believe us to be more respectable than we are."

DRAMATIS PERSONÆ.

THE MARQUIS.

DORANTE, *or* THE CHEVALIER.

LYSIDAS, *a poet.*

GALOPIN, *a lackey.*

URANIA.

ELIZA.[2]

CLIMÈNE.

Scene.—PARIS, IN THE HOUSE OF URANIA.

---

[2] Eliza is the first part created by Molière's wife, who had only been married about fifteen months. Our author always wrote for his wife parts in which sharp sayings, caustic wit, and a certain amount of coquetry are to be found. Madam Molière begins as Eliza, and ends as Célimène, in *The Misanthrope.*

THE SCHOOL FOR WIVES CRITICISED.

(*LA CRITIQUE DE L' ÉCOLE DES FEMMES.*)

SCENE I.—URANIA, ÉLIZA.

UR. What! cousin, has no one been to visit you?

EL. Not a soul.

UR. I am really astonished that we have both of us been alone the whole day.

EL. It astonishes me, too; for it is by no means usual; and your house, thank Heaven! is the ordinary resort of all the loungers at Court.

UR. The afternoon, to be candid, seems very tedious to me.

EL. And I have found it very short.

UR. That, cousin, is because witty people love solitude.

EL. Oh! I am not one of those witty people. You know I have no pretensions to that.

UR. For my part, I confess I like company.

EL. So do I, but I like it select; and the number of stupid visits we have to endure is, amongst others, the reason why I often take pleasure in being alone.

UR. It is an over-refinement, not to be able to bear any but select people.

EL. And it is too indiscriminate a complaisance to bear all sorts of people with indifference.

UR. I relish those who are sensible, and amuse myself with those who talk nonsense.

EL. In truth, those who talk nonsense do not proceed far without wearying you; and most of those folks are no longer amusing after the second visit. But, talking of your nonsensical people, will you not rid me of your troublesome Marquis? Do you mean always to leave him on my hands, and do you think that I can hold out for ever against his everlasting quips?[3]

UR. It is the language of fashion, and they make merry over it at Court.

EL. So much the worse for those who do, and who rack their brains all day long to talk such an obscure jargon. A fine thing, to introduce into the conversation of the Louvre their stale *double entendres,* raked together from the kennels of the markets and of the Place Maubert![4] A pretty style of jesting for courtiers, and for a man to display his wit by coming up to you, and saying, "Madame, you are in the Place Royale; every one sees you three leagues from Paris, for every one is pleased to see you;" because Bonneuil is a village three leagues off![5] Is it not very gallant and very witty? And ought they not to be proud for having hit upon such pretty puns?

UR. At the same time, they do not say this as a piece of wit; for most of those who affect this language know themselves that it is ridiculous.

EL. Worse still, to be at such pains to talk nonsense,

---

[3] The original has *turlupinades.* Turlupins were certain heretics, in the thirteenth and fourteenth centuries, condemned by the Roman Catholic Church; hence the name, after some time, was given to any bad joker. There was an actor at the hôtel de Bourgogne, Henri Legrand, who died in 1634, and was a famous *turlupin.* After the performance of *The School for Wives Criticised*, the Marquises affected the name of *turlupins.*

[4] The language of the markets, *halles*, is not very choice, something like "Billingsgate." The Place Maubert is a square in Paris, at the foot of the Montagne St. Geneviève, in the thickly populated neighbourhood of the quartier Mouffetard. Various origins are adduced for its name but the most feasible seems to me this one. In the fourteenth century, a celebrated German professor of Philosophy settled in Paris, and met in a short time with such a great success that no building could be found large enough to contain his audience. He therefore delivered his lectures in the open air. His name was maître Albert Groot, (Albertus Magnus) hence the contraction Maubert for maître Albert. After this and until very lately, in fact until the improvements inaugurated by the Empire took a corner of it away to make room for the Boulevard St. Germain, it was a rendezvous for mountebanks, bear-leaders, and fire-eaters, a sort of fair as is now the Place de la Bastille, hence the allusion to the *double entendres.*

[5] There is a pun in the original which cannot be translated: *chacun vous voit de bon œil* means "every one is pleased to see you," but *Bonneuil* is also a village three leagues from Paris.

and to be sorry jokers on purpose! I think them less excusable for this; and if I were their judge, I know well to what I would condemn all these gentry, the punsters.

UR. A truce to this subject, which seems to excite you; let us talk of Dorante, who, methinks, is long in coming to the supper we are to take together.

EL. Perhaps he has forgotten it, and . . .

SCENE II.—URANIA, ELIZA, GALOPIN.

GAL. Madam, Climène has come to see you.

UR. Oh! bless me, here is a visit!

EL. You complained of being alone; so Heaven punishes you for it.

UR. Quick! go and tell her I am not at home.

GAL. She has already been told that you are in.

UR. Who is the fool that told her?

GAL. I, madam.

UR. Deuce take the little rascal! I shall teach you to give answers on your own behalf!

GAL. I go and tell her, madam, that you do not wish to be at home.

UR. Stay, you stupid! As the mischief is done, let her come up.

GAL. She is still talking to a man in the street.

UR. Ah! cousin, how annoying this visit is just now!

EL. True; the lady is naturally rather troublesome. I always disliked her much; and, though she is a lady of rank, she is the most stupid creature that ever pretended to sense.

UR. The term is rather strong.

EL. Come, come; she richly deserves it, and more too, if justice were done her. Is there any one that better deserves to go by the name of a *précieuse*[6] than she, to use the word in its worst sense?

UR. She disclaims the epithet, at all events.

EL. So she does. She disclaims the epithet, but not the thing; for she is finical from head to foot, and the most formal creature in the world. Her whole body appears to be out of joint, and the motions of her hips, her shoulders

---

[6] See *The Pretentious Young Ladies*.

and her head seem to go like a piece of clock-work. She always assumes a languishing and silly tone, grimaces to make her mouth appear small, and rolls her eyes to make them seem large.

UR. Softly, pray. If she should happen to overhear . . .

EL. No, no; she is not coming up yet. I shall never forget that evening when she was anxious to see Damon, on account of his reputation, and of the books he had published. You know the man, and his natural indolence in keeping up a conversation. She had invited him to supper as a wit, and never did he appear such a fool amidst half-a-dozen people for whom she had meant him to be a treat, and who stared at him with all their might, as if he ought not to be made like other men. They all thought he was there to entertain the company with witty sayings; that every word from his mouth was to be something extraordinary; that he ought to deliver an impromptu repartee on everything that was said, and not even to ask for a glass of wine without uttering a witticism. But he took them in by his silence; and the lady was as ill pleased with him as I was with her.

UR. Be quiet! I will go and receive her at the door.

EL. One word more.—I wish she was married to the Marquis we spoke of. What a fine match it would be, between a *précieuse* and a *turlupin!*

UR. Will you be quiet! Here she comes.

SCENE III.—CLIMÈNE, URANIA, ELIZA, GALOPIN.

UR. How long you have been . . .

CL. Oh! for Heaven's sake, my dear, make them bring me a chair immediately!

UR. (*To Galopin*). An arm-chair here, quick!

CL. Oh, good Heaven!

UR. What can be the matter?

CL. I can bear it no longer.

UR. What ails you?

CL. I am going to faint.

UR. Have you got the vapours?

CL. No.

UR. Shall I unlace you?

CL. O lord! no,—Oh!

UR. What is your ailment, then? When did it seize you?

CL. Above three hours ago; and I brought it from the Palais Royal.[7]

UR. How?

CL. I have just seen, as a punishment for my sins, that villainous rhapsody *The School for Wives*. I feel still a twinge from the fainting-fit which it gave me; I believe I shall not be myself again for a fortnight.

EL. Just see how our ailments arise without our suspecting it!

UR. I do not know what stuff my cousin and I are made of; but we were at the same play the day before yesterday, and we both came away well and hearty.

CL. What! have you seen it?

UR. Yes, and listened to every word.

CL. And did you not almost go into convulsions, my dear?

UR. I am not so delicate, thank Heaven! For my part, I fancy that this comedy would be more likely to cure folks, than to make them sick.

CL. Oh, good Heaven! What are you saying? Can such a proposition be advanced by any one who has the smallest stock of common sense? Do you think that everyone can, with impunity, insult reason, as you do? And is there in very truth a mind so hungry for a joke as to relish the silly things with which this play is seasoned? I confess, for my part, I could not find the least wit in the whole of it. *Children through the ear* was, to my thinking, in execrable taste;[8] the *cream tart*[9] turned me sick; and I thought I must have vomited when I heard *broth*[10] mentioned.

EL. Heavens! most elegantly spoken! I was inclined to think the piece good; but the lady's eloquence is so persuasive, and gives such an agreeable turn to things, that I must be of her opinion in spite of myself.

---

[7] Molière's troop was then playing at the Palais Royal.

[8] See page 351, Act i., Scene 2. [9] See page 352, Act i., Scene 1.

[10] See page 353, Act ii., Scene 3.

UR. For my part, I am not so easily moved. To be candid, I look on this play as one of the most diverting which the author has produced.

CL. Oh! I pity you for talking so. I cannot let you display so much bluntness of perception. Can a virtuous person find anything pleasant in a piece that keeps her modesty in continual alarm, and sullies the imagination at every turn?

EL. What a nice way of speaking! What a terrible hand you are at criticism, madam; and how I pity poor Molière in having you for an enemy!

CL. Believe me, dear, correct your judgment in good earnest; for the sake of your honour, do not openly say that this comedy has pleased you.

UR. I cannot think what you found in it to shock your modesty.

CL. Good lack! all of it. I do maintain it for a fact that a gentlewoman cannot see it without confusion; so much impropriety and nastiness did I find in it.

UR. You must have a special discernment for impropriety. I own I could see none.

CL. It is undoubtedly because you would not see it; for in short, all its impropriety, thank Heaven! is plain enough. It has not the least cloak to hide it; and the boldest eyes are shocked by its nakedness.

EL. Oh!

CL. Ah! ah! ah!

UR. Yet once more, if you please, point out to me some of the improprieties you speak of.

CL. Alas! is it necessary to point them out?

UR. Yes. I ask of you but one passage that shocked you very much.

CL. Do you wish any other than the scene with that Agnès, when she tells what Horace took from her?

UR. What do you find improper in that?

CL. Ah!

UR. Please.

CL. Fie!

UR. But . . .

CL. I have nothing more to say to you.

UR. For my part, I see no harm in it.

CL. So much the worse for you.

UR. So much the better, I think. I look at things as they are shown to me, and do not turn them round to look at what should not be seen.

CL. But a woman's modesty . . .

UR. A woman's modesty does not consist in grimacing. It ill becomes us to be over-wise. Affectation of this kind is worse than anything; and I see nothing more ridiculous than that delicate honour which takes everything amiss, gives a bad meaning to the most innocent words, and is startled at shadows. Believe me, those who make so much ado are not esteemed the most honest women. On the contrary, their mysterious severity and affected grimaces provoke public animadversions upon the actions of their own lives. The world is only too glad to discover anything to carp at. To give you a proof, there were some ladies at this comedy the other day, in a box opposite to ours, who, by their affected gestures throughout the piece, by averting their heads and hiding[11] their faces, gave rise to a hundred impertinent remarks upon their behaviour, which would never have been uttered but for that; one of the footmen even cried out aloud that their ears were more chaste than all the rest of their bodies.

CL. In short, we ought to be blind throughout this play, and pretend not to see anything in it.

UR. We ought not to see what is not there.

CL. Do not tell me. I maintain that the improprieties are glaring.

UR. And I remain still of a different mind.

CL. What! Is not modesty plainly shocked by Agnès in the passage we are speaking about?

UR. No, truly. She does not say a word which is indelicate in itself; and if you will understand something else, it is you who create the impropriety, and not she, for she only speaks of the ribbon that was taken from her.

CL. Oh yes, the ribbon! But that *the*, when she checks herself, is not put there for nothing. Odd ideas are suggested by this *the*. That *the* is tremendously scandalous.

---

[11] There are no nouns in the French language for "averting." and "hiding:" Molière coins here *détournement* and *cachement*, but these words have not been adopted.

Say what you will, you cannot defend the coarseness of this *the*.

El. True, cousin, I am with this lady against that *the*. That *the* is excessively coarse; you are wrong to defend that *the*.

Cl. Its obscenity is unbearable.

El. What word do you use, Madam?

Cl. Obscenity, Madam.

El. Oh, good gracious! obscenity. I do not know the meaning of the word; but I think it very nice![12]

Cl. There! You see how your own relation takes my part.

Ur. Ah! she is a chatter-box, who does not speak as she thinks. Do not trust her much, if you will take my advice.

El. Oh! you wicked creature, to try to make this lady suspect me. Just think what would become of me, if she were to believe what you say. Could I be so unfortunate, Madam, as to have you think this of me?

Cl. No, no. I do not mind her words, and I believe that you are more sincere than she says.

El. Oh, you are quite right, Madam; and you do me justice when you believe that I think you the most engaging person in the world; that I enter into all your sentiments, and am charmed with every expression that comes from your lips.

Cl. Indeed, I speak without affectation.

El. We can see that, Madam, quite well; and everything about you is natural. Your words, the tone of your voice, your gait, your actions, and your dress, have an indescribable air of fashion about them, which is quite enchanting. I study you with my eyes and ears; and I am so full of you that I strive to ape you and imitate you in everything.

Cl. You are bantering me, Madam.

El. Pardon me, Madam. Who could banter you?

Cl. I am not a good model, Madam.

El. Oh, yes, Madam.

---

[12] *Obscénité* was then in French a new word; it was employed for the first time by the translators of the Bible, called *traducteurs de Mons*.

CL. You flatter me, Madam.

EL. Not at all, Madam.

CL. Spare me, I beg you, Madam.

EL. I do spare you, Madam, and I say not half of what I think, Madam.

CL. Ah, good Heavens! let us stop it, I beseech you. You throw me into a dreadful confusion. (*To Urania*). There, you see we are both against you, and obstinacy so ill becomes clever people . . .

SCENE IV.—THE MARQUIS, CLIMÈNE, URANIA, ELIZA, GALOPIN.

GAL. (*At the door*). Stop sir, please?

MAR. Do you not know me, fellow?

GAL. Ay, I know you; but you shall not come in.

MAR. What a noise you are making, little lackey.

GAL. It is not fair to wish to get in where you are not wanted.

MAR. I wish to see your mistress.

GAL. She is not at home, I tell you.

MAR. Why, she is in her room there!

GAL. That may be; she is there, but she is not at home.

UR. What is the matter?

MAR. Your lackey, Madam, is playing the fool.

GAL. Madam, I am telling him you are not at home, and he will insist on coming in.

UR. And why did you tell this gentleman that I am not at home?

GAL. You scolded me the other day for telling him you were at home.

UR. The insolent fellow! Pray, sir, do not attend to what he says. He is a little stupid creature, who takes you for some one else.

MAR. I saw as much, Madam; and, had it not been out of respect for you, I should have taught him to distinguish people of quality.

EL. My cousin is much obliged to you for this deference.

UR. (*To Galopin*). Bring a chair there, impertinent.

GAL. Is there not one there?

UR. Bring it nearer! (*Galopin pushes it rudely and exit*).

SCENE V.—THE MARQUIS, CLIMÈNE, URANIA, ELIZA.

MAR. Your little lackey, madam, has a special contempt for me.

EL. He would certainly be much to blame.

MAR. It is possibly because I pay interest on my ill looks. Ha, ha, ha! (*laughing*).

EL. Age will make him know people of fashion better.

MAR. Of what were you speaking, ladies, when I interrupted you?

UR. Of the comedy, *The School for Wives.*

MAR. I have just come from it.

CL. Well, sir, pray how do you like it?

MAR. It is altogether silly.

CL. Oh, I am so delighted to hear you say so!

MAR. The most wretched piece imaginable. What the deuce! I could hardly get a seat. I thought I should have been crushed to death at the door, and I was never so trampled upon. Pray see what a state my rolls and ribbons are in!

EL. That certainly speaks volumes against *The School for Wives*, and you justly condemn it

MAR. Never, I think, was such a wretched play composed.

UR. Ah, here is Dorante, whom we were expecting.

SCENE VI.—DORANTE, THE MARQUIS, CLIMÈNE, ELIZA, URANIA.

DOR. Pray do not move, and do not break off your conversation. You are on a subject which, for four days, has been the common talk of Paris; and never was anything more amusing than to hear the various judgments that are passed upon it. For, indeed, I have heard this play condemed by some for the very things that others most praise.

UR. The Marquis speaks very ill of it.

MAR. It is true. I think it detestable, detestable, egad! to the last degree detestable; what you may call detestable!

DOR. And I, dear Marquis, think the judgment detestable.

MAR. How, Chevalier, do you mean to vindicate this play?

DOR. Yes, I do mean to vindicate it.

MAR. Egad, I warrant it to be detestable.

DOR. That guarantee would not be accepted in the city.[13] But Marquis, for what reason, pray, is this comedy as you describe it?

MAR. Why detestable?

DOR. Ay.

MAR. It is detestable—because it is detestable.

DOR. After that, there is not a word to be said; the cause is ended. But still, instruct us, and tell us its faults.

MAR. How can I? I did not so much as give myself the trouble to listen to it. But yet I assure you I never saw anything so wretched, as I hope to be saved; and Dorilas, who sat opposite to me, was of my mind.

DOR. The authority is weighty, and you are well backed.

MAR. You have only to mark the continual bursts of laughter from the pit. I wish no more to prove its utter worthlessness.

DOR. You are then, Marquis, one of those grand gentlemen who will not allow the pit to have common sense, and who would be vexed to join in their laugh, though it were at the best thing conceivable? The other day, I saw one of our friends on the stage, who made himself ridiculous by this. He heard the piece out with the most gloomy seriousness imaginable; and whatever tickled others made him frown. At every burst of laughter he shrugged his shoulders and cast a look of pity on the pit; occasionally, too, he glanced contemptuously at them, saying in an audible voice, "Laugh away, pit, laugh away!"[14] Our friend's annoyance was a second comedy. He acted bravely before the whole house, and everyone agreed that he could not have played his part better. Pray, note, Marquis, and your friends as well, that com-

[13] The original has *la caution n'est pas bourgeoise*, a saying which owes its origin to the ancient custom of giving a certain number of the chief-citizens of a town as hostages to a conqueror; hence it came to mean "a security as good as that of any well known townsman." Molière uses the same term in *The Pretentious Young Ladies*, when Mascarille says: "I shall . . . expect very good security that they do me no mischief."

[14] The name of this fine gentleman has come down to us; he was called Plapisson, and used the words which Dorante mentions, at the representation of *The School for Wives*.

mon sense has no fixed place at a theatre; that the difference between half a louis and fifteen sous[15] makes none whatever in the matter of good taste; that whether we sit or stand, we may pass a bad judgment; and that, in short, speaking generally, I would place considerable reliance on the applause of the pit, because, amongst those who go there, many are capable of judging the piece according to rule, whilst others judge it as they ought, allowing themselves to be guided by circumstances, having neither a blind prejudice, nor an affected complaisance, nor a ridiculous refinement.

MAR. So, sir, you are a defender of the pit! Egad, I am glad of it; I shall not fail to let them know that you are one of their friends. Ha, ha, ha, ha, ha!

DOR. Laugh as much as you like. I am for good sense, and I cannot bear the brain-bubbles of our Mascarille-Marquises.[16] It drives me mad to see people make themselves ridiculous, in spite of their rank; folks who always decide, and talk boldly of everything without knowledge: who will shout with pleasure at the bad parts of a comedy, and never applaud those which are good; who, when they see a picture, or go to a concert, blame and praise all by rule of contraries; who pick up artistic shibboleths wherever they can, get them by heart, and never fail to twist and misplace them. Zounds, gentlemen, hold your peace. Since Heaven has not blessed you with the knowledge of one single thing, do not make yourselves laughing-stocks to those who hear you; and remember, that, if you never open your mouths, you may perhaps be taken for clever men.

MAR. Egad, sir, you are carrying this . . .

DOR. Why, Marquis, I am not speaking to you. I am addressing a round dozen of those gentry who disgrace courtiers by their nonsensical manners, and make people believe we are all alike. For my part, I shall disclaim it as much as I can. I shall fall foul of them whenever we meet, until they grow wise at last.

MAR. Now tell me, sir, do you think Lysander has wit?

---

15 See Prefatory Memoir, page 26., note 7.

16 See *The Pretentious Young Ladies*, page 130.

DOR. Yes, doubtless, and a good deal of it.

UR. That is what no one can deny.

MAR. Ask him what he thinks of *The School for Wives.* You shall see he will tell you he does not like it.

DOR. Upon my word, there are plenty who are spoiled by too much wit, who see things imperfectly, because the light is too strong, and who would even be very sorry to be of other people's opinion, so that they may have the glory of passing judgment themselves.[17]

UR. It is true. Our friend is doubtless one of those people. He must be first in his opinion, and would have others wait respectfully for his decision. All applause which precedes his own is an outrage on his enlightenment, which he avenges openly by taking the other side. He expects people to consult him in all questions of wit: and I am sure that if the author had shown him his play before he let the public see it, he would have thought it the finest in the world.

MAR. And what do you say of the Marchioness Araminta, who declares *The School for Wives* everywhere dreadful, and says she never could endure the improprieties of which it is full?

DOR. I say that this is of a piece with the character she assumes, and that some folks make themselves ridiculous by affecting too much honour. Witty, no doubt, she is, but she has followed the bad example of those who, being in the decline of life, wish to replace by some means or other what they have lost, and fancy that grimaces of fastidious prudery will serve instead of youth and beauty. The lady in question carries it farther than any one; her scrupulous ingenuity finds obscenity where no one would ever have seen it. I hear that these scruples go the length of disfiguring our language; and that there are scarcely any words in it of which our lady's severity will not dock either head or tail, on account of the immodest syllables she finds in them.[18]

---

17 Compare, in Vol. II., in *The Misanthrope* (Act ii. Scene 5), the description of Damis by Célimène.

18 This idea is also developed by Molière in *The Countess of Escarbagnas* (Scene 19), and in *The Blue Stockings* (Act iii. Scene 2). Both these plays will be found in the third volume.

UR. What a wag you are, Chevalier !

MAR. So, Chevalier, you think to defend your play by satirizing those who condemn it?

DOR. By no means; but I think that this lady is scandalized without reason . . .

EL. Gently, Chevalier; there may be other ladies of the same mind.

DOR. I know, at all events, that you are not; and that when you saw this play . . .

EL. True, but I have changed my opinion, and this lady (*pointing to Climène*) supports her by such convincing reasons, that she has won me over to her side.

DOR. (*To Climène*). Oh! Madam, I beg your pardon; and if you will, I shall for your sake unsay all that I have said.

CL. I will not have it for my sake, but for reason's sake: for indeed this piece, if you look at it properly, is quite indefensible, and I cannot imagine . . .

UR. Ah, here is Mr. Lysidas, the author. He comes just in time for this discussion. Mr. Lysidas, take a chair, and sit down here.

SCENE VII.—LYSIDAS, CLIMÈNE, URANIA, ELIZA, DORANTE, THE MARQUIS.

LYS. Madam, I am rather late; but I was obliged to read my piece at the house of the Marchioness, of whom I spoke to you; the praise bestowed on it kept me an hour longer than I anticipated.

EL. Praise has a great charm to delay an author.

UR. Sit down, then, Mr. Lysidas; we shall read your play after supper.

LYS. All who were there are coming to the first representation, and have promised to do their duty as they ought.

UR. I believe it. But pray, once more, please to sit down. We are engaged on a subject which I shall be glad we should pursue.

LYS. I trust, Madam, that you will also take a box for that day.

UR. We shall see. Pray let us go on with our conversation.

LYS. I warn you, Madam, that they are nearly all taken.

UR. That is capital. Now I was wanting you when you came, and every one here was against me.

EL. (*To Urania, and pointing to Dorante*). He was on your side at first, but now (*pointing to Climène*) that he knows that Climène is at the head of the opposite party, I fancy you may just look for other aid.

CL. No, no; I would not have him neglect your cousin, and I will allow his wit to be on the side of his heart.

DOR. With this permission, Madam, I shall make bold to defend myself.

UR. But first let us know somewhat of Lysidas' mind.

LYS. Upon what, Madam?

UR. On the subject of *The School for Wives.*

LYS. Ah—h!

DOR. What do you think of it?

LYS. I have nothing to say on that head. You know that, amongst us authors, we must speak of each other's works with great circumspection.

DOR. But still, between ourselves, what do you think of this play?

LYS. I, Sir?

UR. Tell us your candid opinion.

LYS. I think it very fine.

DOR. Really?

LYS. Really. Why not? Is it not indeed the finest conceivable?

DOR. Hum, hum; you are a wicked fellow, Mr. Lysidas. You do not speak as you think.

LYS. Pardon me.

DOR. Oh dear, I know you. Do not dissemble.

LYS. I, Sir?

DOR. I see clearly that you praise the piece only through politeness, and that, at the bottom of your heart, you agree with the many who think it bad.

LYS. Ha, ha, ha!

DOR. Come, confess that this comedy is a wretched thing.

LYS. True, it is not admired by connoisseurs.

MAR. Upon my word, Chevalier, you have got it! You are paid for your raillery. Ha, ha, ha!

DOR. Laugh away, dear Marquis, laugh away.

MAR. You see we have the learned on our side.

DOR. It is true. ' Lysidas' judgment is worth consideration. But he will excuse me if I do not yield for all that; and since I have presumed to defend myself against this lady's opinion (*pointing to Climène*), he will not take it amiss if I oppose his.

EL. What! when you see this lady, the Marquis, and Mr. Lysidas against you, dare you still resist? Fie, what bad manners!

CL. For my part, what confounds me is that sensible people can take it into their heads to defend the stupidities of this piece.

MAR. Egad, Madam, it is wretched from beginning to end.

DOR. That is soon said, Marquis. There is nothing more easy than to cut the matter short in that way; and I do not see anything that can stand against the sovereignty of your decisions.

MAR. Gad, all the other actors who went to see it spoke all the ill they could of it.

DOR. Oh! I will not say another word. You are right, Marquis. Since the other actors speak ill of it, we must certainly believe them. They are all discerning gentlemen, and speak disinterestedly. There is no more to be said. I give in.

CL. Give in or not, I am sure you will never persuade me to endure the immodesties of this play, any more than the rude satires on woman which are to be found in it.

UR. For my part, I shall be careful not to be offended, and to take nothing to myself that is said in it. Satire of this kind is aimed directly at habits, and only hits individuals by rebound. Let us not apply to ourselves the points of general censure; let us profit by the lesson, if possible, without assuming that we are spoken against. All the ridiculous delineations which are drawn on the stage should be looked on by every one without annoyance. They are public mirrors, in which we must never pretend to see ourselves. To bruit it about that we are offended at being hit, is to state openly that we are at fault.

CL. As for me, I do not speak of these things for any part I may have in them; I think I live in such a manner before the world as not to fear being looked for in a picture of ill-behaved women.

EL. Certainly, Madam, we will never look for you there. Your conduct is sufficiently well known, and these are things that no one thinks of discussing.

UR. (*To Climène*). Madam, I said nothing that could apply to you; my words, like the satire of a comedy, are confined to generalities.

CL. I do not doubt it, Madam. But let us no longer dwell on this episode. I do not know how you take the insults cast upon our sex in a certain part of the play; for my part, I own I am in a terrible passion to hear this impertinent author call us *bipeds.*[19]

UR. Do you not see that it is a ridiculous character he makes to speak so?

DOR. And besides, Madam, do you not know that the reproaches of lovers never offend; that it is pretty much the same with furious, as with mawkish lovers; and that on such occasions the strangest words, and worse than strange, are often taken as marks of affection by the very persons who receive them?

EL. Say what you will, I cannot digest that, any more than the *broth* and *cream tart*, of which this lady was just speaking.

MAR. Oh! Upon my word, yes; *cream tart!* That is what I was saying; *cream tart!* How I thank you, Madam, for reminding me of *cream tart!* Are there apples enough in Normandy[20] for *cream tart? Cream tart*, egad, *cream tart!*

DOR. Well, what do you mean with your *cream tart?*

MAR. 'Sdeath! *Cream tart,* Chevalier!

DOR. But what?

MAR. *Cream tart!*

DOR. Let us have your reasons.

MAR. *Cream tart!*

---

[19] See *The School for Wives*, Act v., Scene 4.

[20] Normandy is especially an apple-growing country; hence the allusion to the custom of throwing cooked or raw apples at the actors who displease the public.

UR. But I think you should explain your meaning.

MAR. *Cream tart*, Madam!

UR. What do you find there to object to?

MAR. I? Nothing!—*Cream tart!*

UR. Oh! I give it up.

EL. My lord goes the right way to work, and gives it you nicely. But I wish Mr. Lysidas would finish, and give them a touch or two in his fashion.

LYS. It is not my wont to find fault. I am very indulgent to the works of other people. But, indeed, without any offence to the friendship which the Chevalier bears to the author, it must be owned that comedies of this kind are not genuine comedies, and that there is a vast difference between these trifles and the beauty of serious pieces. Yet, every one gives into it nowadays; nothing else is run after; we find lamentable solitude at great productions, whilst these stupid plays have all Paris after them. My heart, I own, bleeds at it sometimes; it is a scandal to all France.

CL. It is true that people's taste is strangely corrupted in this matter, and that the age is getting very low.[21]

EL. Oh, that is exquisite again—*getting very low*. Did you invent that, Madam?

CL. Ay!

EL. I thought so.

DOR. So you think, Lysidas, that all the wit and beauty are to be found in serious poems, and that comic pieces are trifles which deserve no praise?

UR. I certainly do not think so. Tragedy no doubt is very fine when it is well written; but comedy has also its charms, and I believe that one is no less difficult than the other.

DOR. Assuredly, Madam; and as to the difficulty, if you should rather set it on the side of comedy, perhaps you would not be far wrong.. Indeed, I think that it is much easier to soar with grand sentiments, to brave fortune in verse, to arraign destiny and reproach the Gods, than to broach ridicule in a fit manner, and to make the

---

[21] The original has *s'encanailler*, a word which had only lately been coined by the Marchioness de Maulny, one of the *précieuses*.

faults of all mankind seem pleasant on the stage. When you paint heroes you can do as you like. These are fancy portraits, in which we do not look for a resemblance; you have only to follow your soaring imagination, which often neglects the true in order to attain the marvellous. But when you paint men, you must paint after nature. We expect resemblance in these portraits; you have done nothing, if you do not make us recognise the people of your day. In a word, in serious pieces, it suffices, to escape blame, to speak good sense, and to write well. But this is not enough in comedy. You must be merry; and it is a difficult undertaking to make gentle folks laugh.

CL. I think I am one of the gentle folks; and yet I did not find cause for laughter in all I saw.

MAR. Upon my word, no more did I!

DOR. Oh, you, Marquis—I am not astonished. That was because you found no puns in it.

LYS. Faith, sir, what we find there is not much better; all the jokes in this comedy are to my mind a little insipid.

DOR. The Court did not think so.

LYS. Ah, sir, the Court?

DOR. Pray, finish, Mr. Lysidas. I see you mean to say that the Court is no judge in these matters; and this is the usual refuge of you gentlemen authors, in the scant success of your own works, to accuse the injustice of the age, and the want of discernment of the courtiers. Be assured, Mr. Lysidas, that courtiers have as good eyes as other people; that folks who wear Venice lace and feathers may be as acute as those who wear a bob-wig and a little all-round cravat; that the grand test of all your plays is the judgment of the Court; that you must study its taste, in order to find the art of success; that there is no place where decisions are so just; and that, not to speak of all the learned men to be found there, a style of wit is created amongst them, by sheer natural common sense and the intercourse of people of fashion, which, beyond question, judges more delicately of things than all the rusty learning of pedants.[22]

---

[22] Compare Dryden's *Defence of the Epilogue*, in which he states :—

UR. It is true that, however little you remain there, you have plenty of things daily passing before your eyes to give you a habit of recognising them; and especially, as to what concerns good or bad raillery.

DOR. The Court, I grant you, has a few ridiculous people; and I am, as you may see, the first to banter them. But, upon my word, there is a great number, too, amongst professional wits; if we ridicule some Marquises, I fancy there is much more reason to ridicule authors. It would be amusing to put them on the stage, with their learned antics and ridiculous refinements; their vicious custom of killing folks in their plays, their greed of praise, their scantiness of thought, their traffic of reputation, their cliques, offensive and defensive, as well as their wars of wit, and combats in prose and verse.

LYS. Molière is very happy, sir, in having so warm a defender. But, to come to facts, the question is whether this piece is good; I engage to shew in it a hundred manifest faults.

UR. It is strange in you gentlemen poets that you always condemn the pieces which every one runs after, and speak well only of those which no one goes to see. You display an unconquerable hatred for the one, and an inconceivable tenderness for the others.

DOR. That is because it is generous to side with the unfortunate.

UR. But, pray, Mr. Lysidas, point us out some of those faults, which I could not detect.

LYS. Those who are versed in Aristotle and Horace, Madam, see at once that this comedy sins against all the rules of Art.

UR. I confess that I am not familiar with those gentlemen, and that I do not know the rules of Art.

DOR. You are a most amusing set with your rules of Art, with which you embarrass the ignorant, and deafen us perpetually. To hear you talk, one would suppose that

---

"Whence is it that our conversation is so much refined? I must freely, and without flattery, ascribe it to the court; and in it, particularly to the king, whose example gives a law to it." Sir Walter Scott, in a note on these words, remarks, "this passage, though complimentary to Charles, contains much sober truth."

those rules of Art were the greatest mysteries in the world; and yet they are but a few simple observations which good sense has made upon that which may impair the pleasure taken in that kind of poems; and the same good sense which in former days made these observations makes them every day easily, without resorting to Horace and Aristotle. I should like to know whether the great rule of all rules is not to please; and whether a play which attains this has not followed a good method? Can the whole public be mistaken in these matters, and cannot everyone judge what pleases him?

UR. I have observed one thing in these gentlemen; and that is, that those who speak most of rules, and who know them better than others, write comedies which no one admires.

DOR. Which shews, Madam, how little notice we should take of their troublesome objections. For, in short, if pieces according to rule do not please, and those do please which are not according to rule, then the rules must, of necessity, have been badly made. So let us laugh at the sophistry with which they would trammel the public taste, and let us judge a comedy only by the effect which it produces upon ourselves. Let us give ourselves up honestly to whatever stirs us deeply, and never hunt for arguments to mar our pleasure.

UR. For my part, when I see a play, I look only whether the points strike me; and when I am well entertained, I do not ask whether I have been wrong, and whether the rules of Aristotle would forbid me to laugh.

DOR. It is just as if a man were to taste a capital sauce, and wished to know whether it were good according to the recipe in the cookery-book.

UR. Very true; and I wonder at the critical refinements of certain people about things in which we should think for ourselves.

DOR. You are right, madam, in thinking all these mysterious critical refinements very odd. For really, if they are to subsist, we are reduced to discrediting ourselves. Our very senses must be slaves in everything; and, even in eating and drinking, we must no longer dare to find anything good, without permission from the committee of Taste.

Lys. So, sir, your only reason is that *The School for Wives* has pleased you; you care not whether it be according to rule, provided . . .

Dor. Gently, Mr. Lysidas; I do not grant you that. I certainly say that the great art is to please; and that, as this comedy has pleased those for whom it was written, I think that is enough, and that we need not care about anything else. But, at the same time, I maintain that it does not sin against any of the rules to which you allude. I have read them, thank Heaven! as well as other men, and I could easily prove that perhaps we have not on the stage a more regular play than this.

El. Courage, Mr. Lysidas; we are undone if you give way.

Lys. What, sir! when the protasis, the epitasis, the peripetia . . .

Dor. Nay, Mr. Lysidas, you overwhelm us with your fine words. Pray, do not seem so learned. Humanize your discourse a little, and speak intelligibly. Do you fancy a Greek word gives more weight to your arguments? And do you not think that it would look as well to say, "the exposition of the subject," as the "protasis;" the "progress of the plot," as the "epitasis; the "crowning incident," as the "peripetia?"

Lys. These are terms of art that we are allowed to make use of. But as these words offend your ears. I shall explain myself in another way; and I ask you to give me a plain answer to three or four things which I have to say. Can a piece be endured which sins against the very description of a play? For, after all, the name of a dramatic poem comes from a Greek word which signifies to act, in order to shew that the nature of the poem consists in action. But, in this comedy, there are no actions; it is made up of narratives by Agnès, or by Horace.

Mar. Ha! ha! Chevalier.

Cl. Ingeniously said. Now we come to the point.

Lys. Can anything be less witty, or, rather, more low, than some of the words at which every one laughs; above all, *children through the ear?*

CL. Capital!

EL. Oh!

LYS. Is not the scene of the servant-man and maid, indoors, of tedious length, and absolutely contemptible?[23]

MAR True.

CL. Assuredly.

EL. He is right.

LYS. Does not Arnolphe give his money too readily to Horace? And, as he is the ridiculous character of the piece, ought he to be made to do the action of a gentleman?

MAR. Good! The observation is good again.

CL. Admirable!

EL. Marvellous!

LYS. Are not the sermon and maxims ridiculous, offending against the respect due to religion?[24]

MAR. Well said!

CL. Spoken as it ought to be!

EL. Nothing could be better!

LYS. And this Monsieur de la Souche, to be brief, who is supposed to be a sensible man, and who appears so grave in many passages, does he not descend to something too comical and too exaggerated in the fifth act, when he declares the vehemence of his love for Agnès, with that wild rolling of his eyes, those ridiculous sighs, those silly tears, which set every one laughing?

MAR. Wonderful, egad!

CL. Miraculous!

EL. Long live Mr. Lysidas!

LYS. I pass over a hundred thousand other things, for fear of being tedious.

MAR. Upon my word, Chevalier, you are in for it!

DOR. We shall see.

MAR. You have met your man.

DOR. Perhaps so.

MAR. Answer, answer, answer, answer.

DOR. Willingly. It is . . .

MAR. Answer, I beg you.

---

[23] See *The School for Wives*, Act i., scene 2, page 369.

[24] See *The School for Wives*, Act iii., Scene 2, page 354.

DOR. Allow me then. If . . .

MAR. 'Gad, I defy you to answer.

DOR. Yes. If you talk perpetually.

CL. Pray let us hear his reasons.

DOR. First, it is not true to say that the whole piece consists only of narratives. There is a good deal of action in it, passing on the stage; the narratives are themselves actions, according to the constitution of the piece, inasmuch as these narratives are all naturally told to the person concerned, who, by these means, is every moment thrown into a confusion which delights the audience, and who, at each fresh tiding, takes all the measures he can to ward off the misfortune which he dreads.

UR. For my part, I think the beauty of the subject of *The School for Wives* consists in this continual confidence; and what seems to me diverting enough is, that a sensible man who is warned of everything by an innocent creature whom he loves, and by a marplot, who is his rival, cannot, for all that, escape his fate.

MAR. Nonsense! nonsense!

CL. A weak answer.

EL. Pitiful reasons.

DOR. As to the *children through the ear*, it has no jest in it except as regards Arnolphe; the author did not insert it as a jest, but only as a characteristic of the man, and the better to depict his craze; since he repeats a vulgar, stupid saying of Agnès as the finest thing in the world, and one which has given him inconceivable pleasure.

MAR. Wretchedly answered.

CL. That will not satisfy us.

EL. It is saying nothing.

DOR. As to the money which he gives so liberally, besides that the letter of his best friend is a sufficient surety for him, it is by no means incompatible for a man to be ridiculous in some things and worthy in others. And as to the scene between Alain and Georgette, in the house, which some think long and insipid, it is certainly not without its reasons; and just as Arnolphe is victimized during his journey by the pure innocence of his mistress, so, on his return, he is kept a long time at his own door by the innocence of his servants, just that he may be punished throughout by the very things whereby he thought to make his precautions good.

MAR. These reasons are good-for-nothing.

CL. All this is not worth a jot.

EL. It is pitiful.

DOR. As to the moral discourse, which you call a sermon, it is a fact that truly religious people who heard it saw nothing that shocked what you mentioned; and doubtless those words, "hell," and "boiling cauldrons" are sufficiently justified by the extravagance of Arnolphe, and by the innocence of her to whom he speaks. As for the amorous transports of the fifth act, which you blame as too exaggerated and burlesqued, I should like to know whether this is not a satire on lovers, and whether sober people, and even the most staid, on such occasions, do not do things . . .

MAR. Upon my word, Chevalier, you had better hold your tongue.

DOR. Very well. In short, if we were to look at ourselves when we are much in love . . .

MAR. I will not so much as listen to you.

DOR. Hear me, pray. In the violence of our passion . .

MAR. Tol, lol, lol, lol, de rol, tol, lol, lol, lol, de rol. (*Humming*).

DOR What?

MAR. Tol, lol, lol, lol, lol, de rol, tol, lol, lol, de rol.

DOR. I am not aware . . .

MAR. Tol, lol, lol, lol, de rol, tol, lol, lol, lol, de rol.

UR. I think that . . .

MAR. Tol, lol, lol, la, la, la, la, la, la, la, la, la, la.

UR. There are many funny things in our discussion. I fancy a little comedy might be made out of them, and that it would not be a bad wind-up to *The School for Wives*.

DOR. You are right.

MAR. Egad, Chevalier, you would play a part in it not at all to your advantage.

DOR. True, Marquis.

CL For my part, I wish it could be done, if they could give the whole thing just as it has happened.

EL. And I would gladly furnish them with my part.

LYS. I think I should not refuse them mine.

UR. As every one is satisfied, Chevalier, write out our discussion, and give it to Molière, whom you know, to work into a play.

CL. He would not care for it, I am sure; it would be no panegyric upon him.

UR. No, no, I know his mood; he does not mind if people criticise his pieces, so that they come to see them.

DOR. Ay. But what ending can we find to this plot? For there can be neither marriage nor recognition, and I do not see how we can finish the discussion.

UR. We must think of some incident for that.

SCENE LAST.—CLIMÈNE, URANIA, ELIZA, DORANTE, MARQUIS, LYSIDAS, GALOPIN.

GAL. Madam, supper is ready.

DOR. Ah! This is just what we wanted for an ending and we can find nothing more natural. They shall dispute hard and fast on both sides, as we have done, without any one giving way; a boy shall come and say "supper is ready;" every one shall rise and go to supper.

UR. The comedy cannot end better; we shall do well to stop here.

L'IMPROMPTU DE VERSAILLES.

COMÉDIE.

THE IMPROMPTU OF VERSAILLES.

A COMEDY IN ONE ACT.

(*THE ORIGINAL IN PROSE.*)

OCT. 14TH, 1663.

INTRODUCTORY NOTICE.

IN the delightful *Impromptu de Versailles*, which was performed for the first time at Versailles, during some part of the month of October, 1663,[1] Molière hits round freely and pleasantly at all the world, himself included; but the principal object which he had in its conception was to retaliate upon his critics, and, in particular, upon his rivals of the hôtel de Bourgogne. *The School for Wives criticised* had, by its keen satire, exasperated that part of Parisian society which had been loudest in its cavils at Molière's genius and success; and they who had felt the directness of his blows thirsted for revenge. The rival company, eager to pay their satirist in his own coin, and anticipating a run upon a play which should hold the poet up to ridicule, commissioned a young and unknown writer, Edme Boursault,[2] to supply them with a new comedy, and the result was *The Painter's Portrait*, in which *The School for Wives* is one of the staple subjects of ridicule. This piece, which was not represented until the last week in October, was well attended, and still more applauded; but its merits were not such as to bring lasting fame to its author. There can, however, be no doubt that Molière was hit by it rather harder than would appear from the dignified manner in which he rejoins—or rather declines to rejoin—to it in the *Impromptu*. It has been said that Molière and his company were sent for by the King to Versailles, and that Louis commanded his favourite comic dramatist to reply to the attack of his critics,[3] for which purpose he placed the Court theatre at his disposal. Molière found the task a difficult one, having only a few days in which to execute the commission; but he cannot be held to have done anything unworthy of his fame in the bright and

---

[1] According to Taschereau's *Histoire de la vie et des ouvrages de Molière*, Vol. I., page 82, and which precedes the works of our author, edited by the same gentleman, in 1858, in six volumes, Molière and his troupe did not go to Versailles before the 16th of October, and remained there until the 23d; hence *The Impromptu* could not have been performed on the 14th of that month, as is generally stated. In looking, however, at the second volume of Molière's works, edited by the same Mons. Taschereau, I find, page 353, on the title-page of the *Impromptu de Versailles*, "*Représentée . . . le 14 Octobre 1663.*" The edition, published by M. Lemerre, and which is a faithful reprint of the original editions of 1666 and 1682, gives the same date; so does Jal in his *Dictionnaire*, and he even mentions that the King gave two thousand livres to Molière and his troupe for this representation. M. Moland mentions the 24th of October 1663.

[2] Edme Boursault (1638-1701) was a dramatic author of moderate talents, but whose kind and frank character gained him many friends. *Le Mercure Galant*, *Esope a la ville*, and *Esope a la cour*, are considered his best plays.

[3] See page 448, note 6.

sparkling *Impromptu.* It satisfied the King; and as a reply to Boursault's play, was acted on the 4th of November at the Theatre of the Palais-Royal, and subsequently for three weeks, with considerable effect in bringing Molière's rivals back to their senses. I strongly suspect that between the performance at Court and that before the public, Molière enhanced and deepened some of his remarks against Boursault, and that the latter, Montfleury and De Villiers, did the same with the plays they wrote, attacking Molière. In any case, our author did not think *The Impromptu of Versailles* of sufficiently enduring interest to merit printing and it was not until after his death that his friend La Grange gave it to the world.

It must have astonished the Court to see, on the rising of the curtain Molière and his troupe not disguised, but in their every day apparel, with their ordinary countenances, all quarrelling among themselves, grumbling at the manager and author, preparing for a rehearsal, and behaving as if there was no public before them, and, above all, such a courtly public as was to be found in the Salle des Comédies at Versailles. But the fiction that the King was not present, and should not come for a couple of hours, saved appearances.

It is to be regretted that Molière in *The Impromptu* gave way to personalities,—a habit in which dramatic authors were formerly inclined to indulge too freely in every country, and which the improved good taste of the public has now generally banished from the stage.

The Impromptu was attempted to be answered by Montfleury, junior, in *l'Impromptu de l'hôtel de Condé,* and by De Villiers in *la Vengeance des Marquis;* both these plays were acted at the hôtel de Bourgogne, but are now deservedly forgotten. The actors of the hôtel du Marais (see Prefatory Memoir,) tried to remain neutral, and played a comedy by Chevalier, called *les Amours de Calotin,* in which both parties, the troupe of Molière and that of the hôtel de Bourgogne, are faintly criticized. Two dissertations about *The School for Wives,* in the form of dialogues, were also printed, but not acted; the one was called *Le Panégyrique de l'Ecole des femmes, ou Conversation comique sur les Oeuvres de M. de Molière,* by Robinet; the other, which probably concludes in favour of Molière, bore the title of *La Guerre comique, ou la Défense de l'Ecole des Femmes,* and was written by de la Croix. In "*Le Panégyrique de l'Ecole des Femmes,* published in Paris by *Jean Guignard, le fils, en la grande salle du Palais, à l'image de St. Jean,* 1664, the author makes an Englishman (Lysandre) give his opinion upon *The School for Wives.* Upon being asked whether he had seen the piece, he answers that if business had not taken him to Paris, he would have come expressly in order to see it, as it had made a great noise already in England. Says he in reply to a question as regards the feeling upon it in his own country. "Two reasons prevent it being to the taste of every one, the first that it is a languishing comedy, and that as you are aware, the English only like pure tragedy; the second, that the master of this school is morose and peevish, and wishes to make husbands the reverse of what they are in England, at which our ladies are not altogether pleased." A friend of his, a Frenchman, replies to this:—"You are right, the husbands there are altogether good, I know it by experience. I have seen some here, who have really surprised me by their goodness. Far from being jealous of their wives, they like those who pay them attentions, and you can do them no greater favour than flatter their better halves."

As in *The Impromptu of Versailles,* Molière's actors appear, not in their dramatic, but in their own, characters, it behooves us to say something of them here. In the Prefatory Memoir we have stated the names of those actors who were members of the Illustre Théâtre, as well as those who left with Molière for the provinces, and those who returned to Paris with him. We shall now briefly give a few details about the actors of the troupe of Molière in 1663. Only two of them, Messrs. Duparc and Debrie, are not mentioned in the list of Dramatis Personæ of *The Impromptu;* later on, Hubert, Baron, Beauval and his wife, and Marie de l'Estang became members of his company.

Brécourt, whose real name was Guillaume Marcoureau, was a member of Molière's troupe only from June 1662 until Easter 1664; before that time he had been an actor at the Théâtre du Marais, and, after a quarrel with Molière, left him for the hôtel de Bourgogne. His life was full of accidents. Having killed a coachman, he was obliged to fly to Holland; took service there under the Prince of Orange; but having failed in his attempt to carry off one of his countrymen whom the French ministry wished to get hold of, and whom Brécourt had promised to deliver into their hands, he came back to Paris, received his pardon, and returned to the stage. He once, in presence of Louis XIV., and after a severe struggle, killed a wild boar with a sword. As a dramatic author, he possesses some, though not great, merit. One of his pieces, *The Ghost of Molière*, written after Molière's death, and in his praise, is dedicated to the Duke d'Enghien, formerly a great enemy of Molière; it was played at the hôtel de Bourgogne; and was, for a long time, printed at the end of Molière's works. Brécourt died March 28th, 1685, from his having broken a blood-vessel, whilst playing before the Court in his own comedy *Timon.*

Charles Varlet, known as de la Grange, was one of the best actors of Molière's troupe, and the very words' our author uses in addressing him (see page 453, prove this. He was the official orator of the company, delivered all the customary speeches, and announced the new plays at the closing or opening of the theatre. Together with Vinot, he published in 1682 the first collected edition of Molière's works, in which appeared for the first time, *Don Garcia of Navarre*, *The Impromptu of Versailles*, *Don Juan Mélicerte*, *The Magnificent Lovers*, *The Countess of Escarbagnas*, and *The Hypochondriac.* He died on the first of March, 1692, and left behind him a manuscript book, in quarto, which is even now carefully kept in an iron chest by the *Comédie francaise*, and has for its title: *Extrait des receptes et des affaires de la Comédie depuis pasques de l'année* 1659, *apartenant au sr. de la Grange, l'un des comédiens du Roy.*"

Du Croisy, whose real name was Philbert Gassot, was a very able actor, who played the part of Tartuffe. After Molière's death, he withdrew from the stage, and went to live at Conflans-Sainte-Honorine, in the neighbourhood of Paris, where he died in 1695.

La Thorillière, whose real name was Lenoir, had been a captain in an infantry regiment, and *maréchal de camp.* Smitten by a theatrical mania, he asked and obtained permission from Louis XIV., to resign, and to adopt the stage as a profession. He was of lofty stature, and is said to have played kings and peasants very well, for, in Molière's time, these two parts were played by the same actor. A tragedy of his, *Marc Antoine et Cléopâtre*, which was never printed, had some success in its time. He died in 1680.

Louis Béjart, surnamed L'Eguisé, the sharp one, one of the early actors in Molière's troupe, was a younger brother of Madeleine and Geneviève Béjart, and appears to have acted servants' parts. He became lame in trying to separate two of his friends who wished to fight a duel. He was pensioned off in 1670, and died in 1678.

Madame Duparc was the wife of Berthelot, otherwise called Duparc, with the cognomen of Gros-René, because he was very stout. Both husband and wife had joined Molière's troop at Lyons in 1653, and remained with him, except for one year, when they were with the troupe of the Marais. Madame Duparc played the princesses in tragedies, and was so very handsome, that she attracted, and scandal says, responded to, the attentions of some of the most celebrated poets of the day. In 1667, three years after the death of her husband, she went to the hôtel de Bourgogne, and there acted Andromaque in Racine's tragedy of that name. Report states that she was rather stiff and ceremonious: hence, in answer to Molière's remarks in the *Impromptu* (see page 352), she replies "that no one in the world" is less so than she. She died in 1668, only twenty-five years old.

Madame Madeleine Béjart's life has been already described in the Prefatory Memoir; to which we refer the reader.

Madame Debrie, the wife of Edme Villequin Debrie, played inferior parts in Molière's troupe. The stage gossip of the times, at no period a very sound authority, pretends that she had been beloved by Molière. She was a very good and handsome actress, and acted, amongst others, the parts of Isabella in *The School for Husbands*, of Agnès in *The School for Wives*, and of Éliante in *The Misanthrope*. She retained her youthful appearance to an advanced age, and died in 1706.

Madame Molière was the wife of our celebrated author. In the Prefatory Memoir, I have already given some details of her marriage, and of the way in which she is said to have behaved to her husband. Her great charm appears to have been in her voice, which, according to all accounts, was both musical and pre-eminently feminine. The author of the *Entretiens galants* says: "Of this she is herself so well aware, that she has a different tone of voice for every different part she plays:" hence she was an excellent actress. It has been generally said that Molière describes his wife in *The Citizen who apes the Nobleman* (see Vol. III. Act iii. Sc. 9) in the following words: "Her eyes are not large, but they are full of fire, the most brilliant, the most piercing, the most moving, imaginable. Her mouth is large; but it possesses attractions unseen in other mouths. She is not tall; but she is easy and elegant. She affects a careless air in her speech and carriage, but there is grace in all, and her manners have an inexpressible charm that appeals to every heart. Her wit is most refined and delicate; her conversation delightful; and if she be capricious beyond compare,—why, everything is becoming in a beauty, and we bear everything from a beauty."

If we are to believe the gossip of the time, as repeated but not substantiated by many of Molière's biographers, Madame Molière must have been a very depraved woman, who chose her lovers amongst the most elegant courtiers, such as the Duke de Lauzun, the Abbé de Richelieu, Count du Guiche, and several others. These accusations are really backed by very little proof; but that Molière was jealous is only too well ascertained. According to a libellous booklet, published fifteen years after Molière's death, and called: *La Femeuse comédienne, ou Histoire de la Guérin, auparavant femme et veuve de Molière*,[4] which is a store-house of the scandal from behind the wings, and has been a repository for all

[4] This book was published in 1688 at Frankfort, by Frans Rottemberg.

the attacks made against Molière or his wife,—our author was one day walking with his friend Chapelle in his garden at Auteuil, "who perceiving him to be more than usually out of sorts, pressed him several times to tell him the reason." Molière, who was somewhat ashamed to have so little fortitude under so common a misfortune, avoided replying as long as he could; but, as he was just then in one of those moods when the heart is full, so well known to persons in love, he yielded to the desire of unbosoming himself, and confessed frankly to his friend that the cause of his dejection was the manner in which he was compelled to treat his wife. Chapelle, who thought Molière above that sort of thing, rallied him, because a man who could so well depict the foibles of others gave way to the very one he was constantly attacking; adding, that the most absurd thing of all was to continue loving a woman who responds in no way to the tenderness lavished upon her! "As for me," he continued, "I own that if I were so unfortunate as to find myself in such a case, and if I had a strong suspicion that the person in question granted her favours to others, I should feel so much scorn for her that it would infallibly cure me of my passion. Moreover, you have a satisfaction which you could not have were she a mistress; for vengeance, which generally succeeds to love in a heart that has been wronged, may indemnify you for all that your wife makes you suffer; since you have only to shut her up, and that will be a sure means of setting your mind at rest." Molière, who had listened to his friend pretty quietly, here interrupted him to inquire whether he had ever been in love? "Yes," replied Chapelle, "I have been so, as a sensible man should be; but I should never have fretted at a course which my honour required I should pursue; and I blush to find you so uneasy." "I see you have never yet been really in love," answered Molière; "you have taken the semblance of love for love itself. I will not quote you a great many examples showing the potency of this passion; I will merely describe to you faithfully my own condition, that you may comprehend how little one is master of oneself, when once the passion has assumed that ascendency of which temperament is usually the cause. In answer to your remark upon my perfect knowledge of the human heart, judging by those delineations of character which I daily put forth, I agree that I studied myself to the utmost, in order the more thoroughly to know its weakness; but if my knowledge has taught me that peril is to be shunned, my experience has but too truly proved to me that it is impossible to avoid it; I learn this every day in my own case. I am by nature gifted with a great propensity to tenderness . . . , I wished that the innocence of my choice should be a guarantee for my happiness. I took my wife, so to say, from her cradle. I brought her up with a care which was the cause of the rumours you have no doubt heard. I imagined that force of habit would inspire her with feelings, which time could not destroy. I have omitted nothing which might tend to win them. As she was very young when I married her, I did not perceive her bad tendencies; and I believed myself a little less unfortunate than the generality of those who enter into similar engagements. Marriage, therefore, did not slacken my attentions; but I discovered in her so much indifference, that I began to perceive that all my precaution had been useless, and that what she felt towards me was far removed from what I could have desired to form my happiness. I reproached myself with feeling a delicacy which seemed to me ridiculous in a husband. I attributed to her mood what was in fact her want of affection for me. But I had only too many opportunities to convince me of my error; and the foolish passion she displayed shortly after for the Count de Guiche was too notorious for me to remain long in this apparent tranquillity. As soon as I heard of it, I spared no pains to conquer my own feelings, as I felt it impossible to change hers. I summoned all my strength of mind to this end. I called to my aid everything that might tend to console me. I considered her as one whose sole merit was her innocence; and who, because she was unfaithful, retained none. I resolved from that time to live with her as a man of honour should who has a coquettish wife, and who believes, notwithstanding what is generally said, that his good name is not dependent upon his wife's ill behaviour. Yet I had the mortification to see that a woman without beauty, and one who owes the small amount of wit she possesses to the education which I had given her, could destroy, in a single moment, all my philosophy. Her presence makes me forget my resolutions; and the very first word she says to me in her own defence leaves me so convinced that my suspicions were unfounded, that I ask her pardon for having been so credulous. Yet my indulgence has not changed her. I have therefore determined to live with her as if she were not my wife; but if you knew what I suffer, you would pity me. My passion has reached such a height, that it actually takes her part against myself; and when I reflect how impossible it is to overcome what I feel for her, I, at the same time, tell myself that perhaps she has equal difficulty in suppressing her inclination for coquetry: thus finding myself more ready to pity than to blame her. No doubt, you will tell me that a man must be mad to love in such a manner; but, in my opinion, there is only one sort of love, and those who have never had such delicate feelings have never truly loved. Every earthly thing is associated with her in my heart; my mind is so full of her, that I can do nothing in her absence to divert my thoughts. When I behold her, a thrill of emotion and transport, which can be experienced but not expressed, deprives me of composure. I have no eyes left for her defects: I see only all that renders her so irresistible. Is not this the height of infatuation? And do you not wonder to find that what sense I have left serves but to make me perceive my weakness, without the power of conquering it?" "I confess, indeed," answered his friend, "that you are more to be pitied than I could have believed; but we must hope all from time. Meanwhile, do not relax your efforts; they will produce their effect when you least expect it. For my part, I shall not cease my prayers that your wishes may speedily be crowned." He thereupon withdrew; leaving Molière, who remained for some time lost in thought on the means of relieving his distress of mind."

Four years after Molière's death his widow married another comedian, François Guérin du Tricher or d'Estriché, who appears not to have possessed the intellectual qualities of her first husband, but to have had other charms which captivated the fair widow, if we can believe an epigram written at the time of her marriage, in which it is said that Mad. Molière had little love for her first husband, who was all mind, but much for her second, who was all body. She died the 30th of November, 1700, about fifty-eight years old.

Madame Du Croisy, whose maiden name was Marie Claveau, was an actress of very little talent. Her daughter was Madame Poisson, (see Prefatory Memoir).

Madame Hervé, whose real name was Géneviève Béjart, was an elder sister of Madame Molière, and took the name of Madame Hervé, after her mother. She was twice married. Of her talents as an actress, very little is known. As to her acquaintance with Molière, we have given a suggestion of Soulié in the Prefatory Memoir. She died at the end of June 1675.

I have said above that the *Impromptu* was first represented before Louis XIV., hence its name of *Impromptu de Versailles.* It may be interesting to know how the actors and actresses were treated when at court. They each received an extra pay of six livres, all their expenses were paid, and even carriages were provided. If they had to go out of town the troupe had one thousand crowns per month, and each actor and actress two crowns per day for their expenses, as well as free lodgings. In summer, as well as in winter, each had three logs (*pièces*) of wood, one bottle of wine, one loaf, and, when at the Louvre, two wax candles; when at Saint Germain, one large candle weighing two pounds; they also had every day, when they played at the King's, a lunch, which cost twenty-five crowns. This is what M. Chappuzeau states in his *Théâtre Francais*, but the picture appears a little over-drawn, though it may have been true during the beginning of the reign of Louis XIV. But later on, if we consult the *régistres de la Comédie francaise*, we find that no carriages nor extras were provided, and that often the indemnity which was allowed, did not cover the expenses.

DRAMATIS PERSONÆ.

MOLIÈRE, *a ridiculous Marquis.*
BRÉCOURT, *a man of Quality.*
LA GRANGE, *a ridiculous Marquis.*
DU CROISY, *a poet.*
LA THORILLIÈRE, *a fidgetty Marquis.*
BÉJART, *a busybody.*
FOUR BUSYBODIES.

Mademoiselle DUPARC,[5] *a ceremonious Marchioness.*
Mademoiselle BÉJART, *a prude.*
Mademoiselle DEBRIE, *a sage coquette.*
Mademoiselle MOLIÈRE, *a satirical wit.*
Mademoiselle DU CROISY, *a whining plague.*
Mademoiselle HERVÉ, *a conceited chambermaid.*

Scene.—VERSAILLES, IN THE KING'S ANTECHAMBER.

---

5 For the use of "Mademoiselle" instead of "Madame," see Prefatory Memoir.

THE IMPROMPTU OF VERSAILLES.

(*L'IMPROMPTU DE VERSAILLES.*)

SCENE I.—MOLIÈRE, BRÉCOURT, LA GRANGE, DU CROISY, MAD. DUPARC, MAD. BÉJART, MAD. DEBRIE, MAD. MOLIÈRE, MAD. DU CROISY, MAD. HERVÉ.

MOL. (*Alone, speaking to his fellow-actors behind the scenes*). Come, ladies and gentlemen, is this delay meant for a joke? Are you never coming here? Plague take the people! I say, Brécourt!

BRÉ. (*Behind*). What?

MOL. La Grange!

LA GR. (*Behind*). What is it?

MOL. Du Croisy!

DU C. (*Behind*). Who calls?

MOL. Mademoiselle Duparc!

MAD. DUP. (*Behind*). Well?

MOL. Mademoiselle Béjart!

MAD. BÉJ. (*Behind*). What is the matter?

MOL. Mademoiselle Debrie!

MAD. DEB. (*Behind*). What do you want?

MOL. Mademoiselle Du Croisy!

MAD. DU C. (*Behind*). Whatever is it?

MOL. Mademoiselle Hervé!

MAD. HER. (*Behind*). I am coming.

MOL. I think I shall go mad with these people. Listen to me! (*Enter Brécourt, La Grange, Du Croisy*). Deuce take me! gentlemen, will you drive me out of my wits today?

BRÉ. What would you have us do? We do not know our parts, and you will drive *us* out of our wits, if you force us to play in this style.

MOL. Oh, what an awkward team to drive are actors! (*Enter Mesdemoiselles Béjart, Duparc, Debrie, Molière, Du Croisy, and Hervé*).

MAD. BÉJ. Well, here we are. What do you mean to do?

MAD. DUP. What is your idea?

MAD. DEB. What is to be done?

MOL. Pray, let us take our positions; and, since we are ready dressed, and the King will not come for a couple of hours, let us employ the time in rehearsing our piece, and see how we are to play our parts.

LA. GR. How are we to play what we do not know?

MAD. DUP As for me, I declare that I do not remember a word of my part.

MAD. DEB. I am sure I shall have to be prompted from beginning to end.

MAD. BÉJ. And I just mean to hold mine in my hand.

MAD. MOL. So do I.

MAD. HER. For my part, I have not much to say.

MAD. DU C. Nor I either; but, for all that, I would not promise not to make a slip.

DU C. I would give ten pistoles to be out of it.

BRÉ. I would stand a score of good blows with a whip to be the same, I assure you.

MOL. You are all just disgusted at having parts that do not please you. What would you do if you were in my place, I should like to know.

MAD. BÉJ. Who, you? You are not to be pitied; for having written the piece, you need not be afraid of tripping.

MOL. And have I nothing to fear but want of memory? Do you reckon the anxiety as to our success, which is entirely my own concern, nothing? And do you think it a trifle to provide something comic for such an assembly as this; to undertake to excite laughter in those who command our respect, and who only laugh when they choose? Must not any author tremble when he comes to such a test? Would it not be natural for me to say that I would give everything in the world to be quit of it?

MAD. BÉJ. If that makes you tremble, you should have been more careful, and not have undertaken what you have done in eight days

MOL. How could I refuse the command of a King?

MAD. BÉJ. How? By a respectful excuse, based on the impossibility of the thing in the short time that was allowed you. Anyone else in your place would have thought more of his reputation, and would have taken care not to expose himself, as you are doing. What will you do, pray, if the thing fails? Think what advantage all your enemies will take of it.

MAD. DEB. Ay, to be sure! You ought to have respectfully excused yourself to the King, or required more time.

MOL. Oh! Mademoiselle, Kings like nothing better than a ready obedience, and are not at all pleased to meet with obstacles. Things are not acceptable, save at the moment when they desire them; to try to delay their amusement is to take away all the charm. They want pleasures that do not keep them waiting; and those that are least prepared are always the most agreeable to them. We ought never to think of ourselves in what they desire of us; our only business is to please them; and, when they command us, it is our part to respond quickly to their wish. We had better do amiss what they require of us, than not do it soon enough; if we have the shame of not succeeding, we always have the credit of having speedily obeyed their commands. But now, pray, let us set about our rehearsal.

MAD. BÉJ. What would you have us do, if we do not know our parts?

MOL. I tell you, you shall know them; even if you do not quite know them, can you not fill in out of your own heads, as it is in prose, and you know your subject?

MAD. BÉJ. Thank you for nothing! Prose is worse than verse.

MAD. MOL. Shall I tell you what it is? You ought to write a comedy in which you could act all alone.

MOL. Be quiet, wife. What a dunce you are!

MAD. MOL. Thanks, dear husband. That just shows

how strangely marriage alters people. You would not have said that to me eighteen months ago.

MOL. Pray be quiet.

MAD. MOL. It is an odd thing that a trifling ceremony deprives us of all our good qualities, and that a husband and a lover regard the same woman with such different eyes.

MOL. Here is a sermon!

MAD. MOL. Upon my word, if I were to write a comedy, that should be my subject; I would justify women in many things of which they are accused, and I would make husbands afraid of the contrast between their abrupt manners and the civility of lovers.

MOL. Well, let it pass. We cannot chatter now; we have something else to do.

MAD. BÉJ. But, since you were ordered to work on the subject of the criticism that is passed on you,[6] why not write that comedy of actors[7] that you have talked about so long? It was a ready-made notion, and would have come quite pat; the more so, as, having undertaken to delineate you, they gave you an opportunity to delineate them; it might have been called their portrait, far more justly than all their productions can be called yours. For, to try to mimic a comedian in a comic part is not to describe himself, but only after him the characters he represents, and making use of the same touches, and the same hues which he is obliged to employ in the various ridiculous characters that he draws from nature. But to mimic an actor in serious parts is to describe him by faults which are entirely his own, since characters of this kind do not carry either the gestures or ridiculous tones by which the actor is recognised.

MOL. It is true; but I have my reasons for not doing it; between ourselves, I did not think it would be worth the trouble; and, besides, I should want more time to work out the idea. As their days for acting are the same

---

[6] See Introductory Notice, page 435.

[7] See *The School for Wives criticised*, where Dorante throws out this idea: "It would be amusing to put them (the actors) on the stage, with their learned antics and ridiculous refinements," &c.

as our own,[8] I have hardly seen them three or four times since we have been in Paris; I have caught nothing of their style of delivery, but what was at once apparent to the eye; I should have to study them more, to make my portraits very like them.[9]

MAD. DUP. I must say I have recognised some of them in your imitations.

MAD. DEB. I never heard this talked of.

MOL. I had the idea once in my head, but I dismissed it as a trifle, a jest, which might have raised a laugh.

MAD. DEB. Give me a specimen, as you have given it to others.

MOL. We have no time now.

MAD. DEB. Just a word or two!

MOL. I thought of a comedy in which there should have been a poet, whose part I would have taken myself, coming to offer a piece to a strolling company fresh from the provinces. "Have you actors and actresses," he was to say, "capable of doing justice to a play? For my play is a play . . . " "Oh, sir," the comedians were to answer, "we have ladies and gentlemen who have passed muster wherever we have been." "And who plays the Kings amongst you?" "There is an actor who sometimes undertakes it." "Who? That well-made young man? Surely you jest. You want a King who is very fat, and as big as four men. A king, by Jove, well stuffed out. A king of vast circumference, who could fill a throne handsomely.[10] Only fancy a well-made king! There is one great fault to begin with; but let me hear him recite a dozen lines." Then the actor should repeat for example, some lines of the king in Nicomède: [11]

---

[8] By "their," is meant the comedians of the hôtel de Bourgogne, who, as well as Molière's troupe, played on Tuesdays, Fridays and Sundays.

[9] A clever side hit at the rival comedians who had been satirizing our poet, and who had no better opportunity of studying Molière, than he of studying them.

[10] An allusion to Montfleury, an actor of the hôtel de Bourgogne who was very stout, and of whom one of his contemporaries said: "He is so fat, that it takes several days to give him a sound beating."

[11] *Nicomède* is a tragedy of Corneille. These lines are said by Prusias, and the passage is Act ii., Scene I.

"I say, Araspus, he has too well served me,
Has raised my power . . ."

and so on, in the most natural manner he could. Then the poet:—"What? Call you that reciting? You are joking. You should say things with an emphasis. Listen to me." (*He imitates Montfleury, a comedian of the hotel de Bourgogne*).

"I say, Araspus," &c.

"Do you see this attitude? Observe that well. There, lay the proper stress on the last line; that is what elicits approbation, and makes the public applaud you." "But, sir," the actor was to answer, "methinks a King who is conversing alone with the captain of his guards talks a little more mildly, and hardly uses this demoniacal tone." "You do not understand it. Go and speak in your way, and see if you get an atom of applause." "Ah, let us hear a scene between a lover and his mistress." On which an actor and actress should have played a scene together —that of Camilla and Curiatius:—[12]

"Dost go, dear soul, and does this fatal honour
So charm thee at the cost of all our bliss?
Ah! now too well I see, etc . . . ."

—like the other, as naturally as they could. And the poet would break out: "You are joking; that is good for nothing. This is how you ought to recite it:" (*Imitating Mad. de Beauchateau, an actress of the hotel de Bourgogne*).

"Dost go, dear soul, &c.
"Nay, but I know the better, etc.[13] . .

"See how natural and impassioned this is. Admire the smiling face she maintains in the deepest affliction."

[12] Personages from *Les Horaces*, a tragedy by P. Corneille.

[13] Madeleine de Bouget, the wife of Beauchâteau, the actor, a very handsome and clever actress, played the princesses in tragedy, as well as the *ingénues* in comedy. She died at Versailles, on the 6th of January, 1683. The first two lines, "Dost go," are from *les Horaces* (Act ii., Scene 5); the third is the answer of Curiatius, to whom Camilla replies in a speech beginning with, "Nay, but I know thee better." Molière probably imitated the actor Beauchâteau as Curiatius.

There, that was my idea; and my poet should have run through all the actors in the same manner.

MAD. DEB. I like the notion; and I recognised some of them by the very first lines. Do go on.

MOL. (*Imitating Beauchateau in some lines from Cid.*[14])

"Pierced to the centre of my heart," &c.

And do you know this man in *Sertorius's* Pompey? (*Imitating Hauteroche, a comedian of the hotel de Bourgogne*)[15]

"The enmity which either faction sways
Engenders here no honour," &c.

MAD. DEB. I think I know him a little.

MOL. And this one? (*Imitating de Villiers, another comedian of the hotel de Bourgogne*[16])

"My lord, Polybius is dead," &c.[17]

MAD. DEB. Yes, I know who he is; but I fancy there are some amongst them whom you would find it hard to mimic.

MOL. Good Heavens! there is not one that cannot be had somewhere, if I had studied them well.[18] But you make me lose precious time. Pray, let us think of ourselves, and not amuse ourselves any longer with talking. (*To La Grange*). Take care how you act the part of Marquis with me.

MAD. MOL. Marquises again?

MOL. Yes, Marquises again. What the deuce would you have me hit on for a character acceptable to the audience? The Marquis in these days is the funny

---

[14] *The Cid and Sertorius* were two tragedies by P. Corneille.

[15] Noel de Breton, sieur de Hauteroche, born in Paris 1617, was of very good family, and became a comedian against their wish. After many adventures he came to Paris, where he played, first at the théâtre du Marais, and afterwards at the hôtel du Bourgogne, chiefly the confidants of the tragic heroes. Hauteroche was of lofty stature, and remarkably lean; he was also an author, and died 1707, at the age of ninety years.

[16] De Villiers answered Molière in *la Vengeance des Marquis*.

[17] This is taken from the third scene of the fifth act of *Œdipe*, a tragedy by Corneille, but it ought to be "King Polybius is dead."

[18] The only actor of the hôtel de Bourgogne whom Molière does not imitate is Floridor, who was really excellent.

character in a comedy; and as, in all the old comedies, there was always a clownish servant to make the spectators laugh, so now, in all our pieces, there must be always a ridiculous Marquis to divert the company.

MAD. BÉJ. It is true, that cannot be left out.

MOL. As to you, Mademoiselle . . .

MAD. DUP. Nay, as to me, I shall act wretchedly; I do not know why you have given me this ceremonious part.

MOL. Good Heavens! Mademoiselle, that is what you said when you had your part in *The School for Wives criticised;*[19] yet you acquitted yourself admirably, and everyone agreed that it could not be better done. Believe me, this will be the same; you will play it better than you think.

MAD. DUP. How can that be? There is no one in the world less ceremonious than I.

MOL. True; and that is how you prove yourself to be an excellent actress, representing well a character which is opposed to your mood. Try then, all of you, to catch the spirit of your parts aright, and to imagine that you are what you represent. (*To Du Croisy*). You play a poet, and you ought to be taken up with your part; to mark the pedantic air which is maintained amidst the converse of the fashionable world; that sententious voice and precision of pronunciation, dwelling on every syllable, and not letting a letter drop from the strictest spelling. (*To Brécourt*). As for you, you play a courtier, as you have already done in *The School for Wives criticised;* that is, you must assume a sedate air, and a natural tone of voice, and gesticulate as little as possible. (*To La Grange*). As for you, I have nothing to say to you. (*To Mademoiselle Béjart*). You represent one of those women who, provided they are not making love, think everything else is permitted to them; who are always proudly entrenched in their prudery, looking up and down on everyone, holding all the good qualities that others possess as nothing in comparison with a miserable honour which no one cares

---

19 Madame Duparc played the part of Climène in *The School for Wives criticised.*

about. Keep this character always before your eyes, that you may show all its tricks. (*To Mademoiselle Debrie*). As for you, you play one of those women who think they are the most virtuous persons in the world, so long as they save appearances; who believe that the sin lies only in the scandal; who would quietly carry on their intrigues in the style of an honourable attachment, and call those friends whom others call lovers. (*To Mademoiselle Molière*). You play the same character as in *The School for Wives criticised*, and I have nothing more to say to you than to Mademoiselle Duparc. (*To Mademoiselle Du Croisy*). As for you, you represent one of those people who are sweetly charitable to every one, who always give a passing sting with their tongues, and who would be very sorry if they let their neighbours be well spoken of. I believe you will not acquit yourself badly in this part. (*To Mademoiselle Hervé*). For you, you are the maid of the *précieuse*, who is always putting her spoke into the conversation, and picks up all her mistress' expressions, as well as she can. I tell you all your characters, that you may impress them strongly on your minds. Let us now begin to rehearse, and see how it will do. Oh, here comes a bore. This is all we wanted!

SCENE II.—LA THORILLIÈRE, MOLIÈRE, BRÉCOURT, LA GRANGE, DU CROISY, MAD. DUPARC, MAD. BÉJART, MAD. DEBRIE, MAD. MOLIÈRE, MAD. DU CROISY, MAD. HERVÉ.

LA THOR. Good day, Molière.

MOL. Sir, your servant. (*Aside*). Plague take the man.

LA THOR. How goes it?

MOL. Very well. What can I do for you? (*To the actresses*). Ladies, do not . . .

LA THOR. I come from a place where I have been praising you up.

MOL. I am obliged to you. (*Aside*). The devil take you! (*To the actors*). Pray take care . . .

LA THOR. You play a new piece to-night?

MOL. Yes, sir. (*To the actresses*). Do not forget . . .

LA THOR. The King got you to do it?

MOL. Yes, sir. (*To the actors*). Pray remember . . .

LA THOR. What do you call it?

MOL. Yes, sir.

LA THOR. I ask what you call it?

MOL. Oh! Upon my word I do not know. (*To the actresses*). You must, if you please . . .

LA THOR. How are you going to be dressed?

MOL. As you see. (*To the actors*). I beg you . . .

LA THOR. When do you begin?

MOL. When the King comes. (*Aside*). The deuce take him and his questions.

LA THOR. When do you think he will come?

MOL. May the quinsy choke me if I know, sir!

LA THOR. Do you not know . . .

MOL. Look here, sir; I am the most ignorant man in the world. I swear I know nothing of anything about what you may ask. (*Aside*). I am going mad. This wretch comes cross-examining me in his cool way, never dreaming that I may have other things to attend to.

LA THOR. Ladies, your servant.

MOL. Ah good! now he is on the other side.

LA THOR. (*To Mademoiselle Du Croisy*). You are as handsome as a little angel. Do you both play to-day? (*Looking at Mademoiselle Hervé*).

MAD. DU C. Yes, sir.

LA THOR. Without you, the comedy would not be worth much.[20]

MOL. (*Whispering to the actresses*). Can you not send that man about his business?

MAD. DEB. Sir, we have a rehearsal on.

LA THOR. Oh, Zounds, I shall not prevent you; you have only to go on.

MAD. DEB. But . . .

LA THOR. Nay, nay, I should be sorry to trouble any one. Do what you have to do without scruple.

MAD. DEB. Yes; but . . .

LA THOR. I assure you, I am a man of no ceremony; and you can rehearse what you like.

---

[20] This compliment is addressed to Mesdemoiselles Du Croisy and Hervé, two of the weakest actresses in Molière's troupe.

MOL. Sir, these ladies hesitate to tell you that they would much prefer that no one should be present during this rehearsal.

LA THOR. But why? You have nothing to fear from me.

MOL. Sir, it is their custom; you will be the better pleased when the thing takes you by surprise.

LA THOR. Then I shall go and tell them you are ready.

MOL. By no means, sir; do not be in a hurry, pray.

SCENE III.—MOLIÈRE, BRÉCOURT, LA GRANGE, DU CROISY, MAD. DUPARC, MAD. BÉJART, MAD. DEBRIE, MAD. MOLIÈRE, MAD. DU CROISY, MAD. HERVÉ.

MOL. Oh dear, this world is full of impertinent people! But now come, let us begin. In the first place, then, imagine that the scene is in the King's antechamber; for it is a place where plenty of amusing things go on every day. It is easy to introduce there whomsoever we please; and reasons can even be found to explain the appearance of the ladies whom I bring in. The comedy opens with the meeting of two Marquises. (*To La Grange*). Be sure and do not forget to come from that side, as I told you, with what they call a distinguished air, combing your wig, and humming a tune between your teeth. La, la, la, la, la, la, la! Just move aside, the rest of you; for a couple of Marquises require room, and they are not the sort of persons to be satisfied with a small space. (*To La Grange*). Now then, speak.

LA GR. "Good day, Marquis."

MOL. Oh dear! That is not the way in which Marquises talk. It must be a little higher. Most of these gentlemen affect a special tone to distinguish themselves from the vulgar. "Good day, Marquis." Try again.

LA GR. "Good day, Marquis."

MOL. "Ah, Marquis, your most obedient."

LA GR. "What are you doing there?"

MOL. "'Sdeath, you may see. I am waiting until all these persons have cleared away from the door, that I may show my face there."

LA GR. "Zounds! what a crowd! I do not care to go and push myself through, I had rather wait till the last."

MOL. "There is a score there who have no chance of getting in, but they take good care to press forward, and occupy all the approaches to the door."

LA GR. "Let us call out our names to the door-keeper, so that he may summon us."

MOL. "That may do for you; but I do not wish Molière to take me off."

LA GR. "Yet I think, Marquis, that it is you he takes off in *The School for Wives criticised.*"

MOL. "Me? Most mighty potentate! it is your very self."

LA GR. "Ah! upon my word, you are kind, to fit me with your own character."

MOL. "Death, you are amusing, to give me what belongs to yourself."

LA GR. (*Laughing*). "Ah, ha! How entertaining!"

MOL. (*Laughing*). "Ah, ha! How comical!"

LA GR. "What! you mean to maintain that it is not you who are exhibited in the Marquis of *The School for Wives criticised?*"

MOL. "Just so; it is I. 'Detestable; egad! detestable! Cream tart!' Oh, it is I, it is I, assuredly it is I!"

LA GR. "Yes, it is you. You need not jest; and we shall lay a wager, if you like, and see which of us is right."

MOL. "Well then, what will you bet?"

LA GR. "I bet a hundred pistoles that it is you."

MOL. "And I bet a hundred it is you."

LA GR. "Money down!"

MOL. "Money down! Ninety on Amyntas, and ten cash."

LA GR. "Content!"

MOL. "Done, then.

LA GR. "Your money runs a great risk."

MOL. "Yours is in danger."

LA GR. "Who shall be umpire?"

MOL. "Here is a gentleman who shall decide. Chevalier!"

BRÉ. "What is it?"

MOL. Good. Here is the other who assumes the tone

of a Marquis. Did I not tell you that you were playing a part in which you had to speak naturally?

BRÉ. So you did.

MOL. Now then. "Chevalier . . ."

BRÉ. "What is it?"

MOL. "Just decide betwixt us on a wager we have made."

BRÉ. "What wager?"

MOL. "We cannot agree who is the Marquis in Molière's *School for Wives criticised.* He bets that it is I, and I bet that it is he."

BRÉ. "Well, I decide that it is neither the one nor the other. You are fools, both of you, to wish that these caps should fit; this is just what I heard Molière complaining of the other day, when he was talking to some people who charged him with the same thing. He said that nothing annoyed him so much as to be accused of animadverting upon anyone in the portraits he drew; that his design is to paint manners without striking at individuals, and that all the characters whom he introduces are imaginary—phantoms, so to speak, which he clothes according to his fancy in order to please his audience; that he would be much vexed to have hit any one through them; and that if aught could sicken him of writing comedies, it would be the resemblances that people always insisted on finding, and on which his enemies maliciously tried to fix attention, in order to do him an injury with certain persons of whom he had never thought. And, indeed, I think he is right; for why, pray, should you apply all his actions and words, and seek to draw him into quarrels by publicly declaring that he is showing up so-and-so, when the facts are such as will fit a hundred people? As the business of comedy is to represent in a general way all the faults of men, and especially of the men of our day, it is impossible for Moliére to create any character not to be met with in the world; and if he must be accused of thinking of everyone in whom are to be found the faults which he delineates he must, of course, give up writing comedies."[21]

---

[21] This is an intentional and very forcible self-defence upon the part of the author, to which the nature of the comedy lends itself admirably. No

MOL. "Upon my word, Chevalier, you wish to justify Molière, and spare our friend here."

LA GR. "Not at all. It is you he spares; and we shall find another umpire."

MOL. "So be it. But tell me, Chevalier, do you not think that Molière is exhausted by this time, and that he will find no more subjects for . . . ?"

BRÉ. "No more subjects? Ah, dear Marquis, we shall always go on providing him with plenty; and we are scarcely taking the course to grow wise, for all that he can do or say."

MOL. Stay. You must be more emphatic with this passage. Just listen to me for a moment.[22] "And that he will find no more subjects for . . .—No more subjects? Ah, dear Marquis, we shall always go on providing him with plenty, and we are scarcely taking the course to grow wise, for all that he can do or say. Do you imagine that he has exhausted in his comedies all the follies of men; and without leaving the Court, are there not a score of characters which he has not yet touched upon? For instance, has he not those who profess the greatest friendship possible, and who, when they turn their backs, think it a piece of gallantry to tear each other to pieces? Has he not those unmitigated sycophants, those vapid flatterers, who never give a pinch of salt with their praises, and whose flatteries have a sickly sweetness which nauseate those who hear them? Has he not the craven courtiers of favourites, the treacherous worshippers of fortune, who praise you in prosperity, and run you down in adversity? Has he not those who are always discontented with the Court, those useless hangers-on, those troublesome, officious creatures, those people who can count up no services except importunities, and who expect to be rewarded for having laid a ten years' siege to the King? Has he not

doubt Molière had much ado to keep himself out of an endless series of personal quarrels with those whom his satire affected; and though one object of *The School for Wives criticised* was to lay stress on the general meaning of his delineations, its immediate effect was, doubtless, to aggravate the annoyance of his lay-figures. The *Impromptu* could not fail to allay these grievances, and to conciliate the author's contemporaries.

[22] This is very skilful; Molière now takes up his own argument in his proper person, thus challenging the closer attention of his audience.

those who fawn on all the world alike, who hand their civilities from left to right, who run after all whom they see, with the same salutations, and the same professions of friendship? 'Sir, your most obedient. Sir, I am entirely at your service. Consider me wholly yours, dear sir. Reckon me, sir, as the warmest of your friends. Sir, I am enchanted to embrace you. Ah! sir, I did not see you. Oblige me by making use of me; be assured I am wholly yours. You are the one man in the world whom I most esteem. There is no one whom I honour like you. I entreat you to believe it. I beg of you not to doubt it. Your servant. Your humble slave.' Oh, Marquis, Marquis, Molière will always have more subjects than he needs; and all that he has aimed at as yet is but a trifle to the treasure which is within his reach." That is something of the style in which it should be played.

BRÉ. It is sufficient.

MOL. Go on.

BRÉ. "Here are Climène and Eliza."

MOL. (*To Mesdemoiselles Duparc and Molière*). Hereupon you two are to come up. (*To Mademoiselle Duparc*). Be sure, you, to attitudinize well, and observe a good many formalities. That will constrain you a little; but it cannot be helped. One must sometimes do violence to oneself.

MAD. MOL. "Madam, I easily recognized you a long way off, and perceived from your bearing that it could be no other than you."

MAD DUP. "You see, I have come to wait for a man with whom I have a little matter of business."

MAD. MOL. "That is just my case."

MOL. Ladies, these boxes will serve you for arm-chairs.

MAD. DUP. "Come, Madam, I beg you to be seated."

MAD. MOL. "After you, Madam."

MOL. Good. After these little dumb shows, let each take a seat, and speak sitting, whilst the Marquises must sometimes get up and sometimes sit down again, in accordance with their natural restlessness. "'Sdeath, Chevalier, you ought to physic your rolls."

BRÉ. "How so?"

MOL. "They look ill.'

BRÉ. "I salute your punstership."

MAD. MOL. "Heavens, Madam, I do think your complexion dazzling white, and your lips of a marvellous flame-colour."

MAD. DUP. "Ah! what is that you say, Madam? Do not look at me; I am frightfully ugly to-day."

MAD. MOL. "Do, Madam, just raise your hood."

MAD. DUP. "Fie! I am frightful, I tell you, and shock even myself."

MAD. MOL. "You are so lovely."

MAD. DUP. "No, no."

MAD. MOL. "Show yourself."

MAD. DUP. "Oh, pray do not."

MAD. MOL. "Please do."

MAD. DUP. "Heavens, no!"

MAD. MOL. "Yes, do."

MAD. DUP. "How troublesome you are!"

MAD. MOL. "Just for an instant."

MAD. DUP. "Ah!"

MAD. MOL. "You positively shall show yourself. We cannot do without seeing you."

MAD. DUP. "Good gracious, what an odd creature you are! What you wish you wish so desperately."

MAD. MOL. "Ah, Madam, I am sure you need not dread the broad daylight. How wicked people are to say that you use any paint! I shall certainly be able to contradict them now."

MAD. DUP. "Lackaday, I do not so much as know what you mean by using paint! But where are those ladies going?"

MAD. DEB. "Permit us, ladies, to give you in passing the most agreeable news conceivable. Here is Mr. Lysidas, who has just told us that some one has made a play against Molière, which the grand company are going to act."

MOL. "It is true, they wished to read it to me. A certain Br . . . Brou . . . Brossaut has written it."

DU CR. "Sir, it is advertised under the name of Boursault; but, to let you into the secret, many people have contributed to this piece, and one is disposed to form pretty high expectations of it. Since all authors and actors look on Molière as their greatest enemy, we all unite against him to do him an ill turn. Each of us has added a stroke to his portrait; but we have taken good care not to put our names to it. It would have been too much honour for him to succumb, before the eyes of the world, to the efforts of a combined Parnassus; and so, to make his discomfiture more ignominious, we thought of picking out on purpose an author without repute."

MAD. DUP. "For my part, I confess that I am greatly rejoiced at it."

MOL. "And so am I. Gad, the mocker shall be mocked; upon my word, he shall have a rap over the knuckles."

MAD. DUP. "That will teach him to satirize everybody. What! This impertinent fellow will have it that women have no wit. He condemns all our lofty modes of expression, and makes out that we are always speaking in a humdrum way."

MAD. DEB. "Speech matters nothing; but he blames all our intimacies, however harmless they may be; and according to him, it is criminal to possess merit."

MAD. DU C. "It is unbearable. Women can do nothing henceforth. Why cannot he let our husbands be at peace, without opening their eyes and making them notice things of which they never thought?"

MAD. BÉJ. "All this is a trifle; but he satirizes even virtuous women; the wicked buffoon styles them 'respectable she-devils.'"[23]

MAD. MOL. "He is an impertinent wretch. He deserves all he gets."

DU CR. "This play, Madam, must needs be supported: and the comedians of the hôtel . . ."

MAD. DUP. "Oh, let them have no fear. I will lay my life on the success of this piece."

MAD. MOL. "You are right, Madam. Too many people are interested in thinking it good. You may judge whether all those who believe themselves to have been satirized by Molière will not take the opportunity of avenging themselves on him by applauding this comedy."

---

[23] See *The School for Wives*, Act iv., Scene 8.

BRÉ. (*Ironically*). "No doubt; and for my part I can answer for a dozen Marquises, six *précieuses*, a score of coquettes, and thirty victimized husbands, who will not fail to applaud."

MAD MOL. "Exactly so. Why should he go and offend all these people, and especially the victimized husbands, who are the best people in the world?"[24]

MOL. "Gad, I have been told that they will have a rub both at him and at all his plays, in fine style, and that actors and authors, from great to small, are deucedly savage against him."

MAD. MOL. "That just serves him right. Why does he write wicked pieces that all Paris goes to see, and in which he paints people so well, that everybody knows himself? Why does he not make plays like those of Mr. Lysidas? He would have no one against him, and all the authors would speak well of him. It is true that such plays do not draw large audiences; but, on the other hand, they are always well written; nobody writes against them, and all who see them are desperately anxious to think them fine."

DU CR. "It is true that I have the advantage of making no enemies, and that all my works are approved of by the learned."[25]

MAD. MOL. "You are justified in being satisfied with yourself. That is worth more than all the applause of the public, and than all the money that Molière's pieces may draw. What does it matter to you whether people come to see your plays, so long as they are praised by your professional friends?"

LA GR. "But when will *The Painter's Portrait* be acted?"

DU CR. "I do not know; but I intend to appear in the front seat, and cry, This is something like a play!"

MOL. Gad, and I too."

LA GR. "And so do I, as I hope to be saved."

---

[24] One of the commentators of Molière says that the proof that our author was not jealous is to be found in the words he puts into his wife's mouth. I imagine Mad. Molière spoke ironically.

[25] On page 460 Molière, in answer to Mad. Debrie's remarks, replies for Lysidas, here it is Du Croisy; this seems a contradiction.

MAD. DUP. "For my part, I shall show myself there, as I ought; and I will answer for a round of applause which shall drown all adverse opinion. It is really the least we can do, to assist with our approbation the avenger of our cause."

MAD. MOL. "Well said!"

MAD. DEB. "That is what we must all do."

MAD. BÉJ. "Assuredly."

MAD. DU C. "Undoubtedly."

MAD. HER. "No quarter to this mimic."

MOL. "Upon my word, Chevalier, your Molière must hide his head."

BRÉ. "Who? He? I promise you, Marquis, that he intends to take a seat upon the stage, and laugh with the rest at the portrait they have drawn of him."[26]

MOL "Gad, then, he will laugh on the wrong side of his face."

BRÉ. "Come, come; perchance he will find more cause for laughter than you think. I was shown the play; and as everything amusing in it was exactly taken from Molière, the pleasure which this will afford, will not be likely to offend him; for, as to the parts where they set themselves to blacken him, I am very much mistaken if this is applauded by any one. And as for all the people whom they have tried to set against him, of whom, it is said, he had drawn too faithful likenesses, not only is it in bad taste, but I never saw anything more ridiculous, or worse done; I never yet thought that it was a reproach to a dramatic author to depict men too well."

LA GR. "The actors told me they expected a rejoinder from him, and that . . ."

BRÉ. "A rejoinder? Verily, I should think him a great fool if he took the trouble to reply to their invectives. Every one knows well enough from what motives they must be acting; and the best answer which he can make them is a comedy which will succeed like all the others. This is the true plan of being avenged on them;

---

[26] De Villiers, in the *Vengeance des Marquis*, mentions that Molière took one day a seat on the stage of the hôtel de Bourgogne to listen to Boursalt's *Painter's Portrait*.

and judging from what I know of their disposition, I am sure that a new play, which will take their audiences from them, will annoy them much more than all the satires which could be written against them individually."

MOL. "But, Chevalier . . . ?"

MAD. BÉJ. Let me interrupt the rehearsal for a moment. (*To Molière*). May I make a suggestion? If I had been you, I should have treated the thing in another way. Every one expects a vigorous rejoinder from you; and, after the way in which they tell me you have been treated in this comedy, you were justified in saying anything against the actors; and you ought not to spare one of them.

MOL. I am annoyed to hear you speak thus. This is just the way with you ladies. You would have me fire up against them, and follow their example by rushing into invectives and insults. A great deal of honour I should get from it, and a vast deal of vexation I should bring them! Are they not quite prepared for that kind of thing? And, when they were discussing whether they should play *The Painter's Portrait*, for fear of a rejoinder, did not some of them say: "Let him abuse us as much as he likes, so long as we get money?"—Is not that the mark of a soul very sensitive to shame; and should I not be well avenged by giving them what they greatly long to receive?

MAD. DEB. They complained strongly of three or four words you said of them in *The School for Wives criticised*, and *The Pretentious Young Ladies*.

MOL. It is true that these three or four words are very offensive; and they have great reason to quote them. Come, come, it is not that. The greatest harm I have done them is that I have been fortunate enough to please a little more than they would have liked; their whole conduct since we came to Paris has too clearly shown what pricks them. But let them do what they will, all their efforts cannot disturb me. They criticise my plays, so much the better; and Heaven forbid that I should ever do aught that pleased them! It would be a bad business for me.

MAD. DEB. Still there is not much pleasure in seeing one's works pulled to pieces

MOL. What does it matter to me? Have I not got from my comedy all that I wished, since it had the good fortune to please those lofty personages whom I specially aim at pleasing? Have I not cause to be content with my lot, and are not all their censures a little too late? Does that affect me now, pray? When they attack a piece which has been successful, do they not attack the judgment of those who praised it, rather than the skill of him who wrote it?

MAD. DEB. Upon my word, I should have had a hit at that little scribe, who is rash enough to write against people who do not trouble their heads about him.

MOL. How silly you are. A fine subject for diversion monsieur Boursault would be! I should like to know how he could be tricked out to make him amusing; and whether, if he were ridiculed on the stage, he would be fortunate enough to make any one laugh. It would be too much honour for him, to be represented, before an august assembly. He would ask nothing better; and he attacks me wantonly in order to make himself known in any way. He is a man who has nothing to lose, and the actors have let him loose on me only in order to engage me in a foolish quarrel, and turn me aside, by this dodge, from other works which I have on hand; and yet you are simple enough to fall into the trap. But I shall make a public declaration on this point. I do not mean to make any reply to all their criticisms and counter-criticisms. Let them say all the evil they can of my pieces; I am quite willing. Let them take our leavings, and turn them inside out like a coat, to bring them on their own stage, and try to profit by any pleasant thing they find in them, and by a little of my good fortune; I give them leave; they have need of it, and I shall be happy to contribute to their necessities, provided they will be satisfied with what I can decently grant them. Courtesy must have its limits; and there are some things which can make neither spectators laugh, nor him of whom they are spoken. I gladly leave to them my works, my figure, my attitudes, my words, the tone of my voice, and my style of recitation, to make and say whatever they will of them, if they can snatch some profit from them. I have nothing to say against all this, and shall be delighted if this can please people; but whilst I give them all this, they must do me the favour to leave me the remainder, and not to touch on things of the nature of those upon which, I hear, they attack me in their comedies.[27] This I shall politely request of the honourable gentleman who undertakes to write for them; and this is all the answer they shall have from me.

MAD. BÉJ. But, in a word . . .

MOL. But, in a word, you will drive me mad. Let us say no more of this. We amuse ourselves by talking when we ought to be rehearsing our comedy. Where were we? I do not remember.

MAD. DEB. You were at the very place . . .

MOL. Good Heavens, what noise do I hear? Surely the King is come! I can plainly see we shall have no time to get through it. That is what comes of our gossipping. Oh, well, you must do the best you can with the rest.

MAD. BÉJ. On my word, I am in such a fright, I shall never be able to play my part unless I rehearse it all.

MOL. What! You will not be able to play your part.

MAD. BÉJ. No.

MAD. DUP. Nor I mine.

MAD. DEB. No more shall I.

MAD. MOL. Nor I.

MAD. HER. Nor I.

MAD. DU C. Nor I.

MOL. What on earth do you mean to do? Are you all mocking me.

SCENE IV.—BÉJART, LA THORILLIÈRE, MOLIÈRE, BRÉCOURT, LA GRANGE, DU CROISY, MAD. DUPARC, MAD. BÈJART, MAD. DEBRIE, MAD. MOLIÈRE, MAD. DU CROISY, MAD. HERVÉ.

BÉJ. Gentlemen, I come to inform you that the King has arrived, and waits for you to begin.

MOL. Ah, sir, you see me in a terrible strait. I am distracted as I speak to you. These ladies are frightened, and say they must rehearse their parts before commencing.

[27] Most likely Boursault's *le Portrait du Pointre*, Montfleury's *Impromptu de l'hotel de Condé*, and De Villier's *la Vengeance des Marquis*, contained some personal attacks, either against Molière, his wife, or his friends, which were suppressed when those plays were printed.

We beg the favour of another moment. The King is kind, and he knows well that the piece has been done hurriedly.

SCENE V.—LA THORILLIÈRE, MOLIÈRE, BRÉCOURT, LA GRANGE, DU CROISY, MAD. DUPARC, MAD. BÉJART, MAD. DEBRIE, MAD. MOLIÈRE, MAD. DU CROISY, MAD. HERVÉ.

MOL. Oh, pray try and recover yourselves. Take courage, I entreat you.

MAD. DUP. You must go and excuse yourself.

MOL. How can I excuse myself?

SCENE VI.—A BUSYBODY, LA THORILLIÈRE, MOLIÈRE, BRÉCOURT, LA GRANGE, DU CROISY, MAD. DUPARC, MAD. BÉJART, MAD. DEBRIE, MAD. MOLIÈRE, MAD. DU CROISY, MAD. HERVÉ.

1 BUSY. Gentlemen, begin.

MOL. At once, sir. I believe I shall go out of my mind over this precious business . . .

SCENE VII.—A SECOND BUSYBODY, LA THORILLIÈRE, MOLIÈRE, BRÉCOURT, LA GRANGE, DU CROISY, MAD. DUPARC, MAD. BÉJART, MAD. DEBRIE, MAD. MOLIÈRE, MAD. DU CROISY, MAD. HERVÉ.

2 BUSY. Gentlemen, begin!

MOL. In a moment, sir. (*To his fellow-actors*). What, would you have me affronted . . .

SCENE VIII.—A THIRD BUSYBODY, LA THORILLIÈRE, MOLIÈRE, BRÉCOURT, LA GRANGE, DU CROISY, MAD. DUPARC, MAD. BÉJART, MAD. DEBRIE, MAD. MOLIÈRE, MAD. DU CROISY, MAD. HERVÉ.

3 BUSY. Gentlemen, begin!

MOL. Yes, sir, that is what we are about to do. How officious these gentry are, coming and bidding us begin, when the King did not order them!

SCENE IX.—A FOURTH BUSYBODY, LA THORILLIÈRE, MOLIÈRE, BRÉCOURT, LA GRANGE, DU CROISY, MAD. DUPARC, MAD. BÉJART, MAD. DEBRIE, MAD. MOLIÈRE, MAD. DU CROISY, MAD. HERVÉ.

4 BUSY. Gentlemen, begin!

MOL. It is done sir. (*To his fellow-actors*). What! must I be covered with confusion . . .

SCENE X.—BÉJART, LA THORILLIÈRE, MOLIÈRE, BRÉCOURT, LA GRANGE, DU CROISY, MAD. DUPARC, MAD. BÉJART, MAD. DEBRIE, MAD. MOLIÈRE, MAD. DU CROISY, MAD. HERVÉ.

MOL. Sir, you come to bid us begin, but . . .

BEJ. No, gentlemen, I come to say that the King has heard of the trouble you are in, and that, in the kindness which distinguishes him, he defers your new comedy to another time, and will be satisfied to-day with the first you can give him.

MOL. Oh, sir, you give me new life. The King bestows on us the greatest possible favour in giving us time for that which he desired; we shall all go and thank him for the extreme goodness which he displays towards us.[28]

---

[28] A flattery to the Grand Monarque, heightened by what had previously been said by Molière of the impatience of Kings to taste the pleasures on which they have set their minds. (Scene I, *ad init.*).

LE MARIAGE FORCÉ.

COMÉDIE.

THE FORCED MARRIAGE.

COMEDY IN ONE ACT.

(*THE ORIGINAL IN PROSE.*)

JAN. 29TH, 1664.

INTRODUCTORY NOTICE.

The Forced Marriage is described as a *Comédie-ballet,* and was due to the request made to Molière by Louis XIV., for an entertainment in the manner of *The Bores,* in which a genuine comedy should be combined with a ballet, and wherein the Court itself might figure upon the stage. Even Louis did not disdain to show himself amongst his courtiers on special occasions of this kind, submitting himself to the direction of the dancing-masters, who held no contemptible position at the Court of the *Grand Monarque.* Molière had recently received from the royal grace a pension of a thousand livres, and he thus had more than one inducement to do his best for the young King's pleasure. It was on the 29th of January, 1664, in the drawing-room of the Queen-mother, at the Louvre, that *The Forced Marriage* was first produced. Louis, then in his twenty-sixth year, figured as one of the gipsies in the ballet. The play had three acts, with entries, and, as the King danced in it, was called the *Ballet du Roi.*

The Comedy-ballet was subsequently brought out at the Palais-Royal, at great expense, and had a run of thirteen days. But Molière had separated the comedy from the ballet, and reduced the former from three acts to one. For the singing magician and the demons who frightened Sganarelle into trying to get out of his marriage engagement, the poet substituted the twelfth scene, introducing Alcidas, who is called Lycante in the ballet.

The comedy supplies us with yet another of those senile gallants whom the poet delights to paint; though in one of his preceding comedies, *The School for Husbands,* the deceived gallant, Sganarelle, is twenty years younger than the wise Ariste, who is not betrayed. The comic element in *The Forced Marriage* springs, not only from the incongruity of the amorous old suitor and the coquettish young girl, but also from the fact that the butt of the piece discovers his mistake before marriage, into which he is nevertheless forced with the full knowledge of the fate that is awaiting him. The idea, at all events up to the eve of the catastrophe, had been worked out by Rabelais, whom Molière follows with considerable closeness. In the ninth chapter of the third book of the older writer's work, "Panurge asketh counsel of Pantagruel whether he should marry, yea or nay?" and whether, if married, he will be able to escape *"la disgrace dont on ne plant personne."* Pantagruel (the Geronimo of the play) gives his advice in the same complaisant manner as Sganarelle's crony,—"Then do not marry;" "Then marry, in the name of God."

What Coleridge says of this chapter of Rabelais may well be applied to the first scene of Molière's play:—"Pantagruel (Geronimo) stands for the reason, as contradistinguished from the understanding and choice, that is, from Panurge (Sganarelle); and the humour consists in the latter asking advice of the former, on a subject in which the reason can only give the inevitable conclusion, the syllogistic *ergo*, from the premises provided by the understanding itself, which puts each case so as of necessity to predetermine the verdict thereon. This chapter, independently of the allegory, is an exquisite satire on the spirit in which people commonly ask advice."

But Rabelais himself was not the first to adopt this illustration of wavering advice; for we find similar scenes in Poggio, and in the *Itinerarium Paradisi* of Raulin, a preacher of the beginning of the fifteenth century, in his sermon *De Viduitate*.

The two philosophers are not quite original creations, Marphurius being no other than the Ephectic and Pyrrhonian sage Trouillogan, whom Rabelais delineates in the thirty-fifth and thirty-sixth chapters of the third book of *Pantagruel*. It has been often said that the scenes between Sganarelle and the two philosophers are too farcical, and only induce laughter. But Molière never acted more courageously than in writing those scenes; for he openly attacked the Aristotelian philosophy, so strongly defended by the University of Paris, which intended to get confirmed a sentence of the parliament of Paris, of the 4th of September 1624, by which all those who attacked the Aristotelian doctrines were condemned to death. Besides this, the above-mentioned scenes are connected with several philosophical observations, to be found in *The Pretentious Young Ladies*, and in *The Blue Stockings* (see Vol. III). Trissotin and Vadius, in the latter play, belong to the same race as the illustrious Pancrace and Marphurius.

According to some commentators of Molière, an adventure of the Count de Grammont, when on the point of leaving England, has given to our author the chief idea of his piece. This Count, being banished from the court of Louis XIV., went to that of Charles II., and there became engaged to Miss Hamilton, a grand-daughter of the Duke of Ormond. Being suddenly recalled to France, he forgot his engagement and left at once. But the two brothers of the young lady immediately started after him, came up with him at Dover, and asked him "if he had not forgotten anything in London?" His answer was, "Pardon me, gentlemen, I have forgotten to marry your sister." He returned with them married Miss Hamilton, and went back with her to France.

Tradition states that the original of the over-polite Alcidas was a certain Marquis de la Trousse, killed at the siege of Tortosa in 1648, and who was so polite that he always used compliments when fighting a duel, and expressed his great sorrow whilst killing his opponent.

In the seventh volume of "Select Comedies of M. de Molière," published in London, 1732, this play is dedicated to the Right Honourable the Lady Harvey, in the following words:

MADAM,

You will not, I hope, be frighted at the sight of a Dedication with Your Name before it, when I promise Your LADYSHIP, that I am not going to give You the Pain of reading Your own Character: tho' at the same time, I must assure You, that it is with great reluctance I relinquish so fair an Opportunity of describing everything that is lovely, desirable, and praiseworthy, and forbear setting before the Beauties of the present Age a charming Pattern, which the greatest and best of them might be proud to copy. But for fear I should be unable to resist the Temptation, if I think any longer of Lady HARVEY, I'll conclude this Address, with desiring Your LADYSHIP's Acceptance of one of MOLIÈRE's Comedies, which has both Wit and Humour in the *Original*. . . I hope, too, they are not quite lost in the *Translation*.

Only give me leave to add, that I am, MADAM, your Ladyship's most obedient and most humble servant, THE TRANSLATOR.

Ravenscroft has imitated part of this play in his *Scaramouch a Philosopher, Harlequin a School-Boy, Bravo, Merchant and Magician*, acted at the Theatre Royal, 1677. This Comedy is a medley of three of Molière's plays, *The Forced Marriage*, *The Citizen who apes the Nobleman*, and *The Tricks of Scapin*. This, with a Harlequin, borrowed from an Italian farce, who jumps about as in a pantomime, but speaks, forms the whole play. It appears not to have had much success. The actors were dilatory in getting it up, and the theatre in Dorset Garden forestalled them by bringing out a translation of Molière's *Tricks of Scapin*. This is what the Prologue says:

Very unfortunate this play has bin,
A slippery trick was played us by Scapin,
Whilst here our actors made a long delay,
When some were idle, others run away,
The City House comes out with half our Play.

The English dramatist ends:

Let both French and Italians share the fame,
But if't be bad, let them too bear the blame.

Mrs. Centlivre, who was then Mrs. Carroll, has in her *Love's Contrivance, or Le Médecin malgré lui*, acted at Drury Lane, June 4, 1703, borrowed nearly everything from Molière's *Forced Marriage*, and from *The Physician in spite of Himself*, (see Vol. ii.), with a reminiscence *of Sganarelle*. She impudently states in the Preface—' Some scenes, I confess, are partly taken from Molière, and I dare be bold to say it has not suffered in the translation. . . . The French have that light airiness in their Temper, that the least Glimpse of Wit sets them a-laughing, when t'would not make us so much as smile; so that where I found the stile too poor, I endeavoured to give it a Turn." In the Prologue she says, however—

So feverish is the Humour of the Town
It surfeits of a Play ere three Days run.
At Locket's, Brown's, and at Pontack's[1] enquire,
What modish Kick-shaws the nice Beaus desire,
What famed Ragouts, what new-invented Sallad
Has best pretensions to regale the Palate.
Il we present you with a Medley here,
A hodge-podge Dish, served up in China Ware,
We hope 'twill please, 'cause like your Bills of Fare.

Sganarelle is called, in the English comedy, Sir Toby Doubtful, and Geronimo, Octavio. The only new, and perhaps original, thing in *Love's Contrivance* is Bellmie's former servant, Martin, hiding a letter in an orange, and pretending to sell fruit, and the trick being discovered by Self-will, father to Lucinda, the heroine of the play.

Another imitation, *An Hour before Marriage*, was written by an Irish gentleman, and brought out at Covent Garden, January 25, 1772, with a prologue by Colman. The piece was very unfavourably received, and

[1] Three noted restaurants of that time. The last one is mentioned in Sir Walter Scott's "Fortunes of Nigel."

not allowed to be finished. Why, it is difficult to say, for it is a very good comedy in two acts. The character of Sir Andrew Melville is drawn cleverly, and the nice way in which, on meeting Elwood, he claims first the long-established friendship, the early and close intimacy "that has subsisted between us from our very childhood," but denies this friendship when he finds out that Elwood is poor, is well and originally delineated Very forcibly also is Miss Melville's (Dorimène) brother boasting of his ancient descent, which is not in the French play. The eighth scene of Molière's play is likewise well imitated by Mr. Tardy, the lawyer, and Stanley; whilst the 15th and 16th scenes are thrown into one in the English version, the characters of Alcantor and Alcidas having been combined in the personage of Sir Andrew Melville.

The Irish Widow is another imitation of Molière's *Forced Marriage*, written by David Garrick. The character of Widow Brady is skilfully drawn; it is she who, dressed in the uniform of a lieutenant, frightens poor Whittle; whilst in the French play, it is Alcidas, Dorimène's brother, and not Dorimène herself, who compels Sganarelle either to fight or to marry.

Some scenes of Molière's play are also borrowed in *Love without Interest*, or *The Man too hard for the Master*. The author of this piece is unknown; but the dedication is subscribed, Penkethman, and is directed to six lords, six knights, and twenty-four esquires; yet, notwithstanding this splendid patronage, it met with very little success on its appearance at the Theatre Royal.[2]

Shadwell, in *The Sullen Lovers* (see Introductory Notice to *The Bores*), has also partly imitated the fourth and sixth scenes of *The Forced Marriage*.

[2] Baker, Reed, and Jones, "Biographica Dramatica," 1812, ii., p. 391.

DRAMATIS PERSONÆ.

SGANARELLE.

GERONIMO.

ALCANTOR, *father to Dorimène.*

ALCIDAS, *brother to Dorimène.*

LYCASTE, *in love with Dorimène.*

PANCRACE, *an Aristotelian Philosopher.*

MARPHURIUS, *a Pyrrhonian Philosopher.*

DORIMÈNE, *a young coquette betrothed to Sganarelle.*

TWO GIPSIES.

The Scene is in a Public Place.

[3] Molière played the part of Sganarelle. According to the inventory taken after his death, and given by M. Eud. Soulié, in his *Recherches sur Molière*, we find "a dress for *The Forced Marriage*, composed of breeches and cloak of olive-colour, lined with green, adorned with violet and plate buttons, and a satin skirt with deep yellow-coloured flowers, with the same kind of buttons, and a belt."

THE FORCED MARRIAGE.

(*LE MARIAGE FORCÉ.*)

SCENE I.—SGANARELLE, GERONIMO.

SGAN. (*Speaking behind the scenes as he enters*). I shall be back in a moment. Take good care of the house, and let everything go on quite regularly. If any one brings me money, come for me quickly at Mr. Geronimo's; and if any one comes to ask for any, tell him I am out, and shall not be back to-day.

SCENE II.—SGANARELLE, GERONIMO.

GER. (*Having heard the last words of Sganarelle*). That is a very prudent order.

SGAN. Ah! Geronimo, well met. I was going to your house to look for you.

GER. And why, pray?

SGAN. To tell you of something I have in my mind, and ask your advice about it.

GER. Very willingly. I am glad we have met; we can speak here at our ease.

SGAN. Pray, be covered then. The business is about something of importance which has been proposed to me. It is well to do nothing without the advice of one's friends.

GER. I am obliged to you for having chosen me. You have only to tell me what it is.

SGAN. But, first of all, I must implore you not to flatter me, but to tell me your opinion candidly.

GER. Since you wish it, I will.

SGAN. I know nothing worse than a friend who does not speak frankly.

GER. You are right.

SGAN. Now-a-days, we meet few sincere friends.

GER. That is true.

SGAN. Promise me, then, Geronimo, to speak with all frankness.

GER. I promise.

SGAN. Swear on your word.

GER. Ay, on the word of a friend. Now, do tell me your business.

SGAN. I wish to have your opinion whether I shall do well to marry.

GER. Who? You?

SGAN. Yes, I myself. What is your advice on the subject?

GER. First of all, I beg you to tell me one thing.

SGAN. What is that?

GER. How old do you think you may be now?

SGAN. I?

GER. Yes.

SGAN. Why, really I do not know; but I am in very good health.

GER. What! Do you not know your age, within a year or two?

SGAN. No. Who thinks about his age?

GER. Hem! Just tell me, please, how old you were when we first became acquainted?

SGAN. Oh, I was only twenty then.

GER. How long were we together at Rome?

SGAN. Eight years.

GER. How long did you stay in England?

SGAN. Seven years.

GER. And in Holland, where you went next?

SGAN. Five years and a-half.

GER. How long is it since you returned?

SGAN. I came back in "fifty-two."

GER. From "fifty-two" to "sixty-four"[4] makes twelve

[4] It must not be forgotten that *The Forced Marriage* was played in 1664; hence Geronimo counts to "sixty-four."

years, I think. Five years in Holland makes seventeen; seven years in England make twenty-four; eight years for our stay in Rome make thirty-two; and twenty—your age when we became acquainted—make just fifty-two years. So, Sganarelle, according to your own confession, you are in about your fifty-second or fifty-third year.

SGAN. Who? I? It cannot be.

GER. By Jove, the reckoning is exact; and so I must tell you candidly, and as a friend, as you made me promise, that marriage is hardly in your line. It is a thing about which young people ought to think seriously before they engage in it; but persons at your time of life ought not to think of it at all. If, as some say, marriage is the greatest of all follies, I know of nothing more ridiculous than to commit this folly at a season when we ought to be most prudent. To be brief, I shall tell you my idea in a few words. I advise you not to dream of marrying; I should think you the silliest man in the world if, after remaining free up to this time, you were to go and burden yourself now with the heaviest of all chains.

SGAN. And I tell you in return, that I am resolved to marry; and that I shall not be silly in marrying the girl I am after.

GER. Oh! that is another thing. You never told me that.

SGAN. I like the girl; I love her with all my heart.

GER. You love her with all your heart?

SGAN. Undoubtedly; and I have asked her of her father.

GER. You have asked her?

SGAN. Yes. The marriage is to take place this evening; and I have plighted my troth.

GER. Oh! marry then. I have not another word to say.

SGAN. Am I to abandon my design? Do you imagine, Geronimo, that I am no longer fit to think of a wife? Do not talk of what my age may be; but let us look at things as they are. Is there a man of thirty that looks fresher or more active than I? Have I not the use of my limbs as much as ever? Do I look as if I needed a carriage or chair to get about in? Are not all my teeth in excellent condition? (*Showing his teeth*). Do I not eat heartily four times a-day, and is any man's stomach stronger than mine? (*Coughing*). Hem, hem, hem! What say you?

GER. You are right; I was mistaken. Pray, marry; you cannot do better.

SGAN. I used to fight shy of it; but now I have strong reasons in its favour. Besides the pleasure I shall have in possessing a wife to fondle me, and to coddle me when I am tired; besides this pleasure, I consider that, by remaining as I am, I suffer the race of the Sganarelles to become extinct; whilst, by marrying, I may see myself reproduced, and shall have the joy of seeing children sprung from me, little images as like me as two peas, who will be always playing about the house, calling me their papa when I come back from town, and talking nonsense to me in the pleasantest manner possible. Oh, I can fancy I am already in the midst of them; and that I see half-a-dozen round about me.[5]

GER. Nothing could be nicer than that; and I advise you to marry as quickly as possible.

SGAN. Seriously? You advise it?

GER. Assuredly. You could not do better.

SGAN. I am indeed delighted that you give me this advice as a true friend.

GER. And pray, who is the lady whom you are going to marry?

SGAN. Dorimène.

GER. Young Dorimène, that gay, well-dressed girl?

SGAN. Yes.

GER. Alcantor's daughter?

SGAN. The very same.

GER. And the sister of Alcidas, who presumes to carry a sword?

SGAN. That is the girl.

GER. My goodness!

---

[5] Molière has evidently been influenced in writing this scene by the ninth chapter of the third book of Rabelais' *Pantagruel*, and by a passage from a Sermon on Widowhood by Jean Raulin, in the *Itinerarium Paradisi*, Paris, 1524, which has been elegantly rendered, under the name of Fredegonde, in *Bon Gautier's Ballads*.

SGAN. What have you to say to it?

GER. A good match. Make haste and get married.

SGAN. Have I not made an excellent choice?

GER. No doubt of it. Ah, you will be well matched! Lose no time about it.

SGAN. I am overjoyed to hear you say so. I thank you for your advice, and I invite you to come to-night to my wedding.

GER. I shall be sure to be there; I shall come masked, the better to honour the occasion.[6]

SGAN. Good day.

GER. (*Aside*). Young Dorimène, Alcantor's daughter, to Sganarelle, who is only fifty-three.[7] Oh! what a fine match! what a fine match! (*He repeats this over and over again, as he goes away*).

SCENE III.—SGANARELLE, *alone*.

This marriage ought to be a happy one; for it pleases every one. All laugh to whom I mention it. I declare I am the happiest of men!

SCENE IV.—DORIMÈNE, SGANARELLE.

DOR. (*Speaking to a page, who holds up her train*). Mind, youngster, hold up my train properly, and do not be playing your tricks.

SGAN. (*Aside, seeing Dorimène*). Here comes my mistress. Ah, how pleasing she is! What an air, what a figure! Who could see her without wishing to marry her? (*Going up to her*). Where are you going, pretty darling, my dear wife that is to be?

DOR. I am going to make a few purchases.

SGAN. Well, my dear, both of us are going to be happy now. You will no longer have a right to refuse me any-

---

[6] *The Forced Marriage* was originally a Comedy-ballet, and most likely Geronimo said "he should come masked" to announce a masquerade of young people in honour of the wedding of Sganarelle, but possibly Molière left it afterwards with an ironical meaning, as if Geronimo wanted to hide his laughter at Sganarelle's ridiculous marriage.

[7] On page 478 Geronimo says, "Sganarelle, you are in about your fifty-second or fifty-third year," giving to the latter "the benefit of a doubt," but at the end of this scene he states frankly, when Sganarelle has left, that the latter is fifty-three years old.

thing; and I can do with you just as I please, without any one being shocked. You will be mine from head to foot, and I shall be master of everything, of your little sparkling eyes, your little roguish nose, your tempting lips, your lovely ears, your pretty little chin, your little round breasts, your . . . In short, your whole person will be mine, to do what I like with, and I shall be entitled to fondle you as I choose. Are you not glad of this marriage, my lovely pet?

DOR. Immensely glad, I assure you. For, indeed, my father's severity has kept me hitherto in the most grievous subjection. I have been raging, I do not know how long, at the scanty liberty he allows me; I have wished a hundred times that he would get me a husband, so that I might quickly escape from the durance in which I have been kept by him, and be able to do as I pleased. Thank Heaven, you luckily came in the way; I mean henceforth to give myself up to pleasure, and make up finely for the time I have lost. As you are a well-bred man, and know the world, I think we shall get on wonderfully well together, and that you will not be one of those bothering husbands who wish their wives to live like owls.[8] I confess that would not suit me! Solitude drives me mad. I like gambling, visiting, assemblies, entertainments, promenades; in fact, all kinds of pleasure. You must be overjoyed to have a wife like me. We shall never have a difference; I shall not constrain your actions, and I hope that you will not constrain mine. For my part, I think we ought to be mutually complaisant, and not be married only to annoy each other. In a word, we shall live, when we get married, like two people who know the world. No jealous suspicions shall trouble our heads; it will suffice for you to be assured of my fidelity, as I shall be persuaded of yours. But what is the matter? A change has come over you.

SGAN. I am taken with a sudden pain in my head.

DOR. That is a malady which attacks many people in

---

[8] The original has *loup-garou*, were-wolf, a warlock, who, in the form of a wolf, roamed about devouring men, and whose hide was said to be bullet-proof. It is curious that the French and Germans have a wolf to frighten timorous people, and the English a bugbear.

these days; but our marriage will remove all that. Good-bye. I long to have a proper dress, that I may quickly throw these rags aside. I am going now to finish the purchase of all the things which I want; and I shall send in the bills to you.

SCENE V.—GERONIMO, SGANARELLE.

GER. Ah! Sganarelle, I am glad to find you here. I have met with a goldsmith who, having heard that you were in search of a handsome diamond ring to make a present to your bride, entreated me to recommend him to you, and to tell you that he has one to sell, the finest in the world.

SGAN. God bless me! there is no hurry for that.

GER. How? What does that mean? Where is the ardour you displayed just now?

SGAN. Within the last few moments, I have had some slight scruples as to marriage. Before going farther I wish to sift this matter to the bottom, and to have interpreted to me a dream which I had last night, and which just recurred to me.[9] You know that dreams are like mirrors, which sometimes show all that is to happen to us. I dreamt I was in a ship, on a rough sea, and that . . .

GER. Sganarelle, I have a little business on hand, which will not let me stay to hear you. I do not understand dreams; and, as to arguments upon marriage, you have for neighbours a couple of scholars, of philosophers, who are just the men to tell you all that can be said on the subject. As they belong to different sects, you can compare their several opinions upon it. For my part, I adhere to what I said just now, and am your servant.

SGAN. (*Alone*). He is right. I must consult these men in my present uncertainty.

SCENE VI.—PANCRACE, SGANARELLE.

PAN. (*Speaking to somebody within, and not seeing Sganarelle*). Go, you are an impertinent fellow, my friend, a man ignorant of all method and order, who ought to be expelled the Republic of letters.

---

[9] This is also an intimation of Rabelais' *Panurge*, Book III., Chapters 13 and 14.

SGAN. Ah! capital, here is one of them in the nick of time.

PAN. (*As before, and not seeing Sganarelle*). Yes, I shall maintain it on strong grounds, I will prove it you out of Aristotle, the philosopher of philosophers, that you are *ignorans*, *ignorantissimus*, *ignorantificans*, and *ignorantificatus*, in all imaginable cases and moods.

SGAN. He has fallen out with somebody. (*To Pancrace*). Sir!

PAN. (*As before, and not seeing Sganarelle*). You presume to argue, and do not know the very elements of reasoning.

SGAN. His passion prevents his seeing me. (*To Pancrace*). Sir!

PAN. (*As before, and not seeing Sganarelle*). It is a proposition condemned in all the regions of philosophy.

SGAN. (*Aside*). He must have been mightily vexed. (*To Pancrace*). I say . . .

PAN. (*As before, and not seeing Sganarelle*). *Toto cœlo, toto via aberras.*[10]

SGAN. I kiss your hands, Master Doctor!

PAN. At your service.

SGAN. May I . . .

PAN. (*Turning round again*). Do you know what you have perpetrated? A syllogism *in Balordo!*[11]

SGAN. I . . .

PAN. (*As before*). The major is foolish, the minor trivial, and the conclusion ridiculous.

SGAN. I . . .

PAN. (*As before*). I would rather die than admit what you say; and I shall maintain my opinion to the last drop of my ink.

SGAN. May I . . .

PAN. (*As before*). Yes, I shall defend this proposition *pugnis et calcibus*, *unguibus et rostro.*[12]

---

[10] The literal translation is: "You err the whole extent of Heaven, the whole length of the road;" something like the familiar "You are as wrong as you can be."

[11] Pancrace makes here a scholastic joke. In Molière's time logic used a great many syllogisms, which were called by barbarous names, such as, *Barbara*, *Celerant*, *Darii*, *Ferio*, &c., but the doctor invents a syllogism in *Balordo*, because *balourd* is the French for a "noodle."

[12] With fists and feet, with nails and beak.

SGAN. Mr. Aristotle, may I ask what has put you in such a rage?

PAN. The best possible reason.

SGAN. But what?

PAN. An ignoramus dared to maintain an erroneous proposition, a frightful, terrible, execrable, proposition.

SGAN. May I ask what it is?

PAN. Ah, Mr. Sganarelle, everything nowadays is subverted, and the world has fallen into general corruption. A horrible license reigns everywhere; and the magistrates, who are appointed to maintain order in the state, ought to die of shame, to suffer a scandal so intolerable as this which I shall reveal to you.[13]

SGAN. What is it then?

PAN. Is it not a horrible thing, a thing crying for the vengeance of Heaven, to allow any one to say in public "the form of a hat?"

SGAN. How?

PAN. I maintain that we ought to say "the figure of a hat," and not "the form;" for as much as there is this difference between the form and the figure, that the form is the external disposition of animate bodies, and the figure is the external disposition of inanimate bodies; and since the hat is an inanimate body, we ought to say, "the figure of a hat," and not "the form." (*Turning again to the side by which he entered*). Yes, ignoramus that you are, that is the manner in which you ought to express yourself, and these are Aristotle's own terms in his chapter on *Qualities*.

SGAN. (*Aside*). I thought we were all undone. (*To Pancrace*). Master Doctor, think no more of this. I . .

PAN. I am in such a rage, that I do not know what I am doing.

SGAN. Leave the form and hat in peace. I have something to tell you. I . . .

PAN. Impertinent fellow! [14]

---

[13] This is a hit at the University of Paris, who prosecuted those who differed in opinion from it, and invoked the arms of the magistrates to punish those who were opposed to it. See Introductory Notice page 472.

[14] The original has *impertinent fieffé*, a relic of the feudal times, when a noble who possessed a fief was called *un noble fieffé*, or one who pos-

SGAN. Pray, be quiet. I . . .

PAN. Ignoramus!

SGAN. Good Heavens! I . . .

PAN. To dare to maintain such a proposition!

SGAN. He is wrong. I . . .

PAN. A proposition condemned by Aristotle.

SGAN. It is true. I . . .

PAN. In so many words!

SGAN. You are right. (*Going round to the side by which Pancrace entered*). Yes, you are a fool, an impudent fellow, to pretend to argue with a Doctor who can read and write. Now, that is done with. I beg you to listen to me. I am come to consult you on an affair which perplexes me. I intend to take a wife, to keep me company at home. The lady is handsome and well made; she charms me greatly, and is delighted to marry me; her father has given her to me; but I am rather afraid of, you know what—the disgrace for which no one pities a man; I wish much to beg of you, as a philosopher, to give me your opinion. Eh? What is your advice in the matter?

PAN. Rather than admit that we ought to say "the form of a hat," I would admit that *datur vacuum in rerum natura*,[15] and that I am a mere ass.

SGAN. (*Aside*). Plague take the man. (*To Pancrace*). Why, Master Doctor, do hear one for a moment. I have been talking to you for an hour, and you do not reply to what is said to you.

PAN. I ask your pardon. A just wrath engrosses my mind.

SGAN. Well, let it pass; and be at pains to listen to me.

PAN. I will. What do you wish to say to me?

SGAN. I wish to speak to you of something.

PAN. And what tongue would you use with me?

SGAN. What tongue?

PAN. Ay.

SGAN. Zounds! the tongue I have in my mouth. I do not think I shall go and borrow my neighbour's.

---

sessed all advantages—namely, title and property; hence *un impertinent fieffé* is a fellow who possesses all the qualifications of impertinence.

15 Literally, "A vacuum exists in the things of nature." The peripatetic school denied the existence of a vacuum.

PAN. I ask you, what idiom, what language?

SGAN. Oh! that is another thing.

PAN. Do you wish to speak to me in Italian?

SGAN. No.

PAN. Spanish?

SGAN. No.

PAN. German?

SGAN. No.

PAN. English?

SGAN. No.

PAN. Latin?

SGAN. No.

PAN. Greek?

SGAN. No.

PAN. Hebrew?

SGAN. No.

PAN. Syriac?

SGAN. No.

PAN. Turkish?

SGAN. No.

PAN. Arabic?

SGAN. No, no! French, French, French![16]

PAN. Ah, French!

SGAN. Quite so.

PAN. Then go to the other side; for this ear is set apart for the learned and foreign languages, and the other is for the vulgar and mother tongue.

SGAN. (*Aside*). One must employ many ceremonies with this sort of people.

PAN. What do you desire?

SGAN. To consult you in a little difficulty.

PAN. Ah! a difficulty in philosophy, no doubt.

SGAN. Pardon me. I . . .

PAN. You would know perhaps if substance and accident be synonymous terms, or equivocal in respect of entity?

SGAN. Not at all. I . . .

---

16 In the ninth chapter of the second book of Rabelais' *Pantagruel*, "How Pantagruel found Panurge," whom he loved all his life time, the first addresses the latter also in a dozen different languages, before speaking to him.

PAN. If logic be an art or a science?

SGAN. It is not that. I . . .

PAN. If its object be the three operations of the mind, or the third only?

SGAN. No. I . . .

PAN. If there be ten categories, or only one?

SGAN. Not so. I . . .

PAN. If the conclusion be of the essence of a syllogism?

SGAN. No-o! I . . .

PAN. If the essence of good be placed in appetibility or incongruity?

SGAN. No. I . . .

PAN. If good be reciprocal with finality?

SGAN. Oh, no! I . . .

PAN. Whether finality can affect us by its real, or by its intentional being?

SGAN. No, no, no, no, no! By all the devils, no!

PAN. Unfold then your thought; for I cannot divine it.

SGAN. That is just what I wish to do; but you must listen to me. The business I have to mention to you is that I have a mind to marry a girl who is young and handsome. I love her very much, and I have asked her of her father; but I fear . . .

PAN. (*Not listening to Sganarelle*). Speech has been given to man to express his thoughts;[17] and just as thoughts are the representations of things, so our words are the representations of our thoughts. (*Sganarelle impatiently stops the Doctor's mouth with his hand; but the latter continues to speak as soon as Sganarelle withdraws his hand. This is repeated several times*). But these representations differ from other representations, inasmuch as these other representations are distinguished everywhere by their originals, whilst speech includes its original in itself; being nothing but thought explained by an external sign; whence it follows that they who think well are also they who speak the best. Explain to me then your thoughts by words, which are the most intelligible of all signs.

[17] A formula employed by several of Molière's successors. The reverse has also been maintained :—" Speech was given to man to disguise his thoughts."

SGAN. (*Pushing the Doctor into his house, and pulling the door to prevent his coming out*). Plague take the man!

PAN. (*Within*). Yes, speech is *animi index et speculum*, that is, the interpreter of the heart, the image of the soul. (*He gets up to the window and continues*). It is a mirror which plainly reproduces for us the innermost secrets of our individualisms. Since, then, you have the faculty of reasoning, and also of speaking, why do you not make use of speech in order to make me understand your thoughts?

SGAN. That is just what I wish to do; but you will not listen to me.

PAN. I listen to you; speak.

SGAN. I say then, Doctor, that . . .

PAN. But above all, be brief.

SGAN. I will.

PAN. Avoid prolixity.

SGAN. Oh! Sir . . .

PAN. Contract your discourse into a laconic apophthegm.

SGAN. I . . .

PAN. No diffuseness nor circumlocution. (*Sganarelle, in his vexation at being unable to speak, picks up stones to throw at the Doctor's head*). Eh, what? Are you flying into a passion instead of explaining yourself? Go along, you are more impertinent than the fellow who would have it that one ought to say "the form of a hat;" and I will prove to you upon all occasions, by clear and convincing reasons, and by arguments in *Barbara*, that you are not, and never will be, aught but an animal, and that I am, and ever shall be, Doctor Pancrace, *in utroque jure*.

SGAN. What an eternal gabbler!

PAN. (*Coming down*). A man of letters, a man of learning.

SGAN. What, more?

PAN. A man of sufficiency, a man of capacity. (*Going away*). A man supreme in all the sciences, natural, moral, and political. (*Returning*). A learned, most learned man, *per omnes modos et casus*. (*Going away*). A man who possesses, in the superlative degree, a knowledge of fables, mythologies, and histories—(*returning*)—grammar, poetry, rhetoric, dialectics, and sophistry—(*going away*)

—mathematics, arithmetic, optics, oneirocritics, physics and metaphysics—(*returning*) — cosmometry, geometry, architecture, the speculory and speculatory arts—(*going away*)—medicine, astronomy, astrology, physiognomy, metoposcopy, cheiromancy, geomancy, etc.[18]

SCENE VII.—SGANARELLE, *alone.*

The devil take these scholars, who will never listen to people! I was rightly informed that his master, Aristotle, was nothing but a talker. I must go and find the other one. Perhaps he may be more composed and reasonable. Soho, there!

SCENE VIII.—MARPHURIUS, SGANARELLE.

MAR. What do you want with me, Mr. Sganarelle?

SGAN. Doctor, I have need of your advice in a little matter of business, and that is why I have come to you. (*Aside*). Ah! this is all right. This gentleman lets people speak.

MAR. Mr. Sganarelle, pray change this mode of speaking. Our philosophy enjoins us not to enunciate a positive proposition, but to speak of everything dubiously, and always to suspend our judgment. For this reason, you should not say, I am come, but it seems that I am come.

SGAN. Seems?

MAR. Yes.

SGAN. Upon my word! no doubt it seems, because it is so.

MAR. That does not follow: it might seem, and yet not be true.

SGAN. How? Is it not true that I am come?

MAR. That is questionable; and we must doubt everything.

---

18 Instead of *metaphysics* the original has again *mathematics*, which appears an error. *Oneirocritics* is the interpretation of dreams; *the speculory art* showed in a mirror the image of absent persons; *the speculatory art* interpreted the future through observing thunder, lightning, and meteors; *metoposcopy* was the art of predicting what would happen by studying the countenance; *cheiromancy* is divination by looking at the lines in the hand; *geomancy*, by observing the lines, or crevices and undulations of the ground.

SGAN. What! I am not here? and you are not speaking to me?

MAR. It appears to me that you are there, and it seems that I am speaking to you; but it is not certain that it is so.

SGAN. Eh! what the deuce! You are joking. Here I am, and there you are, plainly enough; and there is no "seems" in all that. Let us dispense with these quirks and quibbles, I beg, and talk of my business. I am come to tell you that I wish to marry.

MAR. I know nothing of this.

SGAN. I tell it you.

MAR. It may be so.

SGAN. The girl whom I intend to marry is very young and very lovely.

MAR. It is not impossible.

SGAN. Shall I do well or ill to marry her?

MAR. The one or the other.

SGAN. (*Aside*). Oh, dear! here is another tune. I ask you, if I shall do well to marry the girl I speak of?

MAR. As it may chance.

SGAN. Shall I do ill?

MAR. Just as it happens.

SGAN. Pray, answer me properly.

MAR. That is my intention.

SGAN. I have a great liking for the girl.

MAR. That may be.

SGAN. The father has given his consent.

MAR. He may have done so.

SGAN. But if I marry her, I fear to be made a cuckold.

MAR. The thing is feasible.

SGAN. What do you think of it?

MAR. There is no impossibility in it.

SGAN. But what would you do, if you were in my place?

MAR. I do not know.

SGAN. What do you advise me to do?

MAR. Whatever you please.

SGAN. I shall go mad!

MAR. I wash my hands of it.

SGAN. Devil take the dreamer!

MAR. As it may be.[19]

SGAN. (*Aside*). Plague take the rascal! I'll make you change your tune, mad hang-dog of a philosopher! (*Beats him.*)

MAR. Oh, oh, oh!

SGAN. There is something for your nonsense! And now I am satisfied!

MAR. How! What insolence is this! To outrage me in this manner! To have the audacity to beat a philosopher like me!

SGAN. Pray, correct this manner of speaking. We are to doubt everything; and you ought not to say that I have beaten you, but that it seems I have beaten you.

MAR. Ugh! I shall go and complain to a magistrate of this beating.

SGAN. I wash my hands of it.

MAR. I have the marks on my body.

SGAN. It may be so.

MAR. You know it was you who did it.

SGAN. It is not impossible.

MAR. I will get a summons against you.

SGAN. I know nothing about it.

MAR. And you will be convicted.

SGAN. As it may be.

MAR. Leave me alone for that.

SCENE IX.—SGANARELLE, *alone.*

What now? One cannot get a word from that beastly man, and I am as wise at the end as at the beginning. What shall I do in this uncertainty as to the consequences of getting married? Never was a man more perplexed than I. Ah! here come the gipsies: they shall tell me my fortune.

SCENE X.—TWO GIPSIES, SGANARELLE.

The two Gipsies come in, with tabors, singing and dancing.

SGAN. They are very merry. I say, you good women, can you tell me my fortune?

---

19 This scene is an imitation of the thirty-sixth chapter of the third book of Rabelais' *Pantagruel*, where Panurge asks Trouillogan's advice if he should marry.

20 The original has *commissaire de quartier*. See *The School for Husbands*.

1 GIP. Ay, my good sir, both of us here will tell it you.

2 GIP. Just give us your hand, and cross ours with a small bit of silver,[21] and we shall tell you something that shall be of service to you.

SGAN. Here: there are both my hands, with what you ask in them.

1 GIP. You have a good phiz, master—a good phiz.

2 GIP. Ay, a good phiz; the phiz of a man that will be something one of these days.

1 GIP. You will be married before long, good master, you will be married before long.

2 GIP. You will wed a pretty wife, a pretty wife.

1 GIP. Ay, a wife that will be courted and loved by every one.

2 GIP. A wife that will make you many friends, good master, many friends.

1 GIP. A wife that will bring plenty to your house.

2 GIP. A wife that will gain you great repute.

1 GIP. You will be esteemed for her sake, good master; you will be esteemed for her sake.

SGAN. That is well. But just tell me, is there fear of my being cuckold?

2 GIP. Cuckold!

SGAN. Ay!

1 GIP. Cuckold!

SGAN. Ay; is there fear of my being cuckolded? (*The Gipsies sing and dance*). What the devil! that is no answer. Come here. I ask you whether I shall be a cuckold.

2 GIP. A cuckold! You?

SGAN. Ay, shall I be a cuckold?

1 GIP. You a cuckold!

SGAN. Yes; shall I, or not?

(*The Gipsies go off, singing and dancing.*

SCENE XI.—SGANARELLE, *alone.*

Plague take the baggages for leaving me in this uncer-

---

[21] The original has *avec la croix dedans,* literally, with a cross in it; because formerly some coins had on one side a cross; hence also the French for playing pitch and toss, *jouer à croix ou pile*, and the expression, *loger le diable dans sa bourse*, literally, "to lodge the devil in one's purse," because there was no cross to drive him away.

tainty! I must really know the upshot of my marriage; so I shall go and find that great magician of whom everybody is talking, and who, by his marvelous art, enables us to see all that we wish. Upon my word! I believe I have only to go to the magician, and he will show me all that I ask of him.

SCENE XII.—DORIMÈNE, LYCASTE, SGANARELLE (*out of sight, at the back of the stage*).

LYC. What! lovely Dorimène, do you speak seriously?

DOR. Most seriously.

LYC. You really mean to marry?

DOR. Really.

LYC. And your wedding is to be this evening?

DOR. This evening.

LYC. And you can forget, cruel maid, the love I feel for you, and the kind words you have spoken to me?

DOR. I? By no means. I shall always think the same of you; and this marriage need not trouble you. I am not marrying the man for love; it is only his wealth that makes me resolve to accept him. I have no fortune; no more have you; and you know that, without fortune, it goes hard with us in the world. At whatever cost, therefore, we must try to get it. I have jumped at this opportunity of making myself comfortable; I have done it in the hope of being soon delivered from the old fool that I am marrying. He will shortly die; he has not more than six months to live. I guarantee that he is dead in the time I say; I shall not long have to pray Heaven for the happy state of widowhood. (*Seeing Sganarelle*). Ah, we were talking of you, and saying much in your praise too.

LYC. Is that the gentleman . . .

DOR. Yes, that is the gentleman who is going to marry me.

LYC. Allow me, sir, to congratulate you on your marriage, and at the same time to offer you my most humble services. Let me tell you that the lady, whom you are marrying, possesses great merits; as for you, Miss Dorimène, I congratulate you also on the happy choice you have made. You could not have found a better, and this gentleman has all the appearance of making a very good husband. Yes, sir, I should be delighted to strike up a friendship with you, and to arrange a slight interchange of visits and entertainments.

DOR. You are doing us too much honour. But come, time presses, and we shall have plenty of opportunities to converse together.

SCENE XIII.—SGANARELLE, *alone*.

There, now I am fairly disgusted with my match; I think I shall not do amiss to go and get out of my engagement. It has cost me a little money; but I had better even lose that than run the risk of something worse. I shall try if I cannot be clever enough to get out of this scrape. Within there! (*He knocks at Alcantor's door*.

SCENE XIV.—ALCANTOR, SGANARELLE.

AL. Ah, son-in-law, you are welcome.

SGAN. Sir, my duty to you.

AL. You come to conclude the marriage?

SGAN. Excuse me.

AL. I promise you that I am as impatient as yourself.

SGAN. I come here for another purpose.

AL. I have given the necessary orders for the entertainment.

SGAN. That is not what I am come about.

AL. The violins are engaged, the feast is bespoke, and my daughter is ready dressed to receive you.

SGAN. It is not that which has brought me.

AL. In short, you are about to have your wish; and nothing can delay your happiness.

SGAN. Good Lord, there is something else to think of.

AL. Come, son-in-law, will you walk in?

SGAN. I have just a word to say to you.

AL. Oh goodness, let us have no ceremony! Enter quickly, if you please.

SGAN. No, I tell you. I wish to speak to you first.

AL. You have something to say to me?

SGAN. Yes.

AL. What is it, then?

SGAN. Mr. Alcantor, it is true I asked your daughter in marriage, and you granted my request; but I find that I am rather old; I think that I am by no means a proper match for her.

AL. Pardon me. My daughter likes you as you are; and I am sure that she will live very happily with you.

SGAN. Nay. I am given to strange whims at times, and she would have too much to endure from my ill humour.

AL. My daughter is of a very mild and obliging disposition; you shall see that she will accommodate herself entirely to you.

SGAN. I have some bodily infirmities which might disgust her.

AL. That is nothing. A virtuous woman is never disgusted with her husband.

SGAN. Must I then speak plainly? I do not advise you to give her to me.

AL. Surely you are jesting? I would rather die than break my word.

SGAN. Oh dear, I absolve you from it, and I . . .

AL. By no means. I have promised her to you, and you shall have her, in spite of all who are running after her.

SGAN. (*Aside*). The devil I shall!

AL. Look here. I have a special respect and friendship for you; and I would refuse my daughter to a Prince, to give her to you.

SGAN. Mr. Alcantor, I am obliged for the honour you do me, but I declare to you that I will not marry.

AL. Not marry, you say?

SGAN. Yes, not marry.

AL. And why?

SGAN. Why? Because I feel I am not fit for marriage; and because I wish to be like my father, and all my ancestors, who never would marry.

AL. Hark ye. Every one to his liking; I am not the man to force anyone. You gave me your word that you would marry my daughter, and everything is prepared for the wedding; but since you wish to withdraw, I shall go and see what can be done in the matter; you shall hear from me presently.

SCENE XV.—SGANARELLE, *alone.*

Now he is more reasonable than I expected. I thought I should have much more trouble in getting off. Upon my word, when I think of it, I have done very prudently in withdrawing from this business. I was going to take a step of which I should perhaps have repented at leisure. But here comes the son, to bring me my answer.

SCENE XVI.—ALCIDAS, SGANARELLE.

ALCID. (*In a mild and complaisant tone*). Sir, your most obedient servant.

SGAN Sir, I am entirely yours.

ALCID. My father has told me, sir, that you came to withdraw your promise to marry my sister.

SGAN. Yes, sir. It is with regret; but . . .

ALCID. Oh! sir, there is no harm in that.

SGAN. I am extremely sorry, I assure you, and I could wish . . .

ALCID. That is nothing, I tell you (*Offers Sganarelle two swords*). Sir, have the goodness to choose one of these swords.

SGAN. One of these swords?

ALCID. Yes, if you please.

SGAN. For what?

ALCID. Sir, as you refuse to marry my sister, after giving your word, I think you will not take amiss the little compliment I have paid you.

SGAN. How?

ALCID. Other people would make more noise, and get into a rage with you; but we are the sort of people to take things quietly; and I have come to tell you very politely that we must, by your favour, cut each other's throats.

SGAN. That is a sorry compliment.

ALCID. Come, sir, I beg you will make your choice.

SGAN. I am your very humble servant, but I have no throat worth cutting. (*Aside*). Here is a scurvy style of speech!

ALCID. Sir, by your leave, it must be so.

SGAN. My dear sir, a truce, I beg, to this compliment.

ALCID. Let us be quick about it, sir. I have a little business on hand.

SGAN. I have no mind for this, I tell you.

ALCID. You will not fight?

SGAN. I will not, upon my soul.

ALCID. You mean it?

SGAN. I mean it.

ALCID. (*Giving him a few blows with his cane*). At least, sir, you cannot complain; you see that I do things by rule. You break your word with us, I wish to fight you, you refuse to fight, I cane you,—all that is according to form; and you are too much of a gentleman to find fault with my mode of acting.

SGAN. *Aside*). Here is a devil of a fellow!

ALCID. (*Again offering the swords*). Come, sir, do things like a gentleman, before I pull your ears.

SGAN. What! are you determined?

ALCID. Sir, I force no one; but you must either fight or marry my sister.

SGAN. Sir, I assure you, I cannot do either.

ALCID. Really?

SGAN. Really.

ALCID. By your leave then . . . (*Beats him again.*

SGAN. Oh, oh, oh!

ALCID. Sir, I infinitely regret to be obliged to treat you thus; but if you please I shall not stop until you have promised to marry my sister. (*Raises his cane.*

SGAN. Well then, I will marry, I will marry!

ALCID. My dear Sir, I am delighted that you have returned to your senses, and that things can go smoothly. For I swear that I esteem you more than any one in the world; and I should have been grieved if you had compelled me to maltreat you. I shall call my father, and let him know that everything is settled.

(*Goes and knocks at Alcantor's door.*

SCENE XVII.—ALCANTOR, DORIMÈNE, ALCIDAS, SGANARELLE.

ALCID. Father, this gentleman is now pleased to listen

to reason. He has determined to do things with a good grace, and you can give my sister to him.

ALCAN. Sir, here is her hand; you have only to give her yours. Heaven be praised! I have got rid of her; it is for you henceforth to take charge of her character. Let us make merry, and celebrate this happy marriage.

END OF VOL. I.

www.ingramcontent.com/pod-product-compliance
Lightning Source LLC
LaVergne TN
LVHW021231110826
845150LV00002B/307

* 9 7 8 1 4 2 5 5 6 2 9 8 4 *